Pragmatism and Justice

| Pragmatism and Justice

Edited by SUSAN DIELEMAN,
DAVID RONDEL,
AND CHRISTOPHER VOPARIL

OXFORD
UNIVERSITY PRESS

OXFORD
UNIVERSITY PRESS

Oxford University Press is a department of the University of Oxford. It furthers
the University's objective of excellence in research, scholarship, and education
by publishing worldwide. Oxford is a registered trade mark of Oxford University
Press in the UK and certain other countries.

Published in the United States of America by Oxford University Press
198 Madison Avenue, New York, NY 10016, United States of America.

Library of Congress Cataloging-in-Publication Data
Names: Dieleman, Susan, editor. | Rondel, David, 1978– editor. |
Voparil, Christopher J., 1969– editor.
Title: Pragmatism and justice / edited by Susan Dieleman, David Rondel,
and Christopher Voparil.
Description: New York, NY : Oxford University Press, 2017. | Includes
bibliographical references and index.
Identifiers: LCCN 2016028625 | ISBN 9780190459246 (pbk. : alk. paper) |
ISBN 9780190459239 (cloth : alk. paper) | ISBN 9780190459260 (online course) |
ISBN 9780190459253 (pdf)
Subjects: LCSH: Pragmatism. | Justice (Philosophy)
Classification: LCC B832 .P564 2017 | DDC 172/.2—dc23
LC record available at https://lccn.loc.gov/2016028625

CONTENTS

PERMISSIONS

ABBREVIATIONS

Citations of Charles Sanders Peirce's writings are to the eight-volume *Collected Papers* (Belknap Press of Harvard University Press, 1931–1958). Parenthetical citations follow the standard formula, according to which (CP 1:123) denotes paragraph 123 of volume 1 of Peirce's *Collected Papers*.

Citations of John Dewey's writings are to the thirty-seven-volume *The Collected Works of John Dewey* (Southern Illinois University Press, 1969–1991). The *Collected Works* is organized into three chronological periods, *The Early Works, The Middle Works*, and *The Later Works*. Parenthetical citations follow the standard formula, according to which (EW 4:30) denotes page 30 of volume 4 of *The Early Works* and (MW 6:100) designates page 100 of volume 6 of *The Middle Works*.

Citations of William James's writings are to the 19-volume *The Works of William James* (Harvard University Press, 1975–1988). Parenthetical citations follow the standard formula, according to which (WWJ 1:44) denotes page 44 of volume 1 of *The Works of William James*.

CONTRIBUTORS

Patricia Hill Collins is Distinguished University Professor of Sociology at the University of Maryland, College Park. She is the author of nine books, among them *Black Feminist Thought: Knowledge, Consciousness, and the Politics of Empowerment* (1990, 2000); *Black Sexual Politics: African Americans, Gender, and the New Racism* (2004); *On Intellectual Activism* (2013), and *Intersectionality* (2016). Professor Collins has lectured widely in the United States and internationally, and served in many capacities in professional and community organizations. In 2008, she became the one hundredth President of the American Sociological Association.

Susan Dieleman is Assistant Professor of Philosophy (with term) at the University of Saskatchewan in Saskatoon, Canada. Her research takes a pragmatist-feminist approach to issues that arise at the intersection of political philosophy and epistemology. Her work has been published in *Hypatia: A Journal of Feminist Philosophy, Social Epistemology: A Journal of Knowledge, Culture, and Policy, Social Philosophy Today, The Pluralist,* and elsewhere. She is currently working on a monograph that borrows resources from feminist and pragmatist philosophies to show how ethical and epistemic success are more likely when deliberative democratic spaces are guided by norms of epistemic justice.

Matthew Festenstein is Professor in the Department of Politics at the University of York. He has researched and published widely in political theory and the history of political thought. His work has particularly focused on the character and significance of pragmatism for political theory and the politics of cultural diversity. His books include *Pragmatism and Political Theory* (University of Chicago Press, 1997), *Negotiating*

Diversity: Culture, Deliberation, Trust (Polity Press, 2005), and, as co-editor, *Richard Rorty: Critical Dialogues* (Polity Press, 2001), *Political Ideologies* (Oxford University Press, 2005), and *Radicalism in English Political Thought, 1550–1850: Tradition or Fabrication?* (Cambridge University Press, 2007).

Nancy Fraser is Loeb Professor of Philosophy and Politics at the New School for Social Research and holder of the "Global Justice" Chair at the Collège d'études mondiales in Paris. Her most recent books are *Domination et anticipation: pour un renouveau de la critique*, with Luc Boltanski (2014), *Transnationalizing the Public Sphere: Nancy Fraser Debates Her Critics* (2014), and *Fortunes of Feminism: From State-Managed Capitalism to Neoliberal Crisis* (2013). Other works include *Redistribution or Recognition?* (2004, with Axel Honneth), *Adding Insult to Injury* (2008), *Scales of Justice* (2009), *Justice Interruptus* (1997), and *Unruly Practices* (1989).

V. Denise James is Associate Professor of Philosophy at the University of Dayton, where she facilitates the Diversity Across the Curriculum faculty workshop. She writes and researches about the politics of geography, identity, and social justice. She has published essays about the intersections of classical American pragmatism and black feminism, street violence against young women and girls, radical social justice theory, and the philosophical significance of the seminal black feminist thinker Anna J. Cooper. She is at work on a book about the banality of the dying city and geopolitical racism.

Colin Koopman is Associate Professor in the Department of Philosophy at the University of Oregon. His research is focused on the critical traditions of pragmatism and genealogy and their applicability to current issues in politics, ethics, and culture. His publications include *Pragmatism as Transition* (Columbia University Press, 2009), *Genealogy as Critique* (Indiana University Press, 2013), and articles in *Critical Inquiry, Constellations, Contemporary Pragmatism, Transactions of the Charles S. Peirce Society*, and elsewhere. He is working on a book on the politics of data.

Peter T. Manicas (1934–2015) was Professor of Philosophy at University of Hawai'i at Manoa, where he was Director of the Interdisciplinary Studies program (1988–2011), and Emeritus Professor at Queens College, CUNY. His research interests include the history and philosophy of the social sciences, American pragmatism, Marxism, and political and social theory. Among his many books are *The Death of the State* (1974), *A History and*

Philosophy of the Social Sciences (1987), *War and Democracy* (1989), *A Realist Philosophy of Science* (2006), and *Rescuing Dewey: Essays in Pragmatic Naturalism* (2008).

José Medina received his Ph.D. from Northwestern University and is Professor of Philosophy at Vanderbilt University. Drawing on American and European critical theorists and philosophers of language, he has published primarily in social epistemology, speech act theory, feminist theory, queer theory, and critical philosophy of race. His articles in these areas have appeared in journals such as *Inquiry, Metaphilosophy, Philosophical Studies*, and *Social Epistemology*. His books include *Speaking from Elsewhere* (SUNY Press, 2006), and *The Epistemology of Resistance* (Oxford University Press, 2012), which received the 2012 North-American Society for Social Philosophy Book Award.

Cheryl Misak is Professor in the Department of Philosophy at the University of Toronto. Her research interests include pragmatism, history of analytic philosophy, philosophy of medicine, ethics, and political philosophy. She is the author of many books, including *Truth and the End of Inquiry* (Oxford University Press, 1990), *Truth, Politics, Morality* (Routledge, 2000), and *The American Pragmatists* (Oxford University Press, 2013).

Gregory Fernando Pappas is Professor at Texas A&M University. He is the author of numerous articles on the philosophy of William James and John Dewey. Pappas is the author of *Pragmatism in the Americas*, a work on the philosophical connections between American pragmatism and Latin American philosophy. He is also the author of *John Dewey's Ethics: Democracy as Experience*, the first comprehensive interpretation of Dewey's ethics. Pappas has been a Fulbright scholar and the recipient of a Ford Foundation Postdoctoral Fellowship, the William James and the Latin American Thought prizes by the American Philosophical Association, and the Mellow Prize by the Society for the Advancement of American Philosophy.

Hilary Putnam (1926–2016) was Cogan University Professor Emeritus at Harvard University. His research areas include philosophy of language, philosophy of mathematics, philosophy of science, and American pragmatism. His most recent books include *Philosophy in an Age of Science* (2012), *Jewish Philosophy as a Guide to Life* (2008), *Ethics without Ontology* (2004), *The Threefold Cord* (1999), *Pragmatism: An Open Question* (1995), and *Words and Life* (1995).

Ruth Anna Putnam is Professor Emerita of Philosophy at Wellesley College. She has written extensively on ethics, political philosophy, and pragmatism. Her writings include *The Cambridge Companion to William James* (1997) and many influential essays.

David Rondel is Assistant Professor in the Department of Philosophy at the University of Nevada, Reno. His main research areas are political philosophy, ethics, and American pragmatism. He has published widely in these areas. His essays have appeared, among other places, in the *Canadian Journal of Philosophy*, the *Journal of Philosophical Research*, the *Journal of Speculative Philosophy, Dialogue, Contemporary Pragmatism*, and *Socialist Studies*. He is also coeditor of a volume of professor Kai Nielsen's political-philosophical essays, published by the University of Calgary Press in 2012.

Richard Rorty (1931–2007) was a prolific philosopher and public intellectual who, throughout his illustrious career, taught at Princeton, the University of Virginia, and, until his death, Stanford University. His many works include *Philosophy and the Mirror of Nature* (1979), *Consequences of Pragmatism* (1982), *Contingency, Irony, and Solidarity* (1989), *Achieving Our Country: Leftist Thought in Twentieth-Century America* (1998), *Philosophy and Social Hope* (1999), and four volumes of philosophical papers.

Shannon Sullivan is Chair of Philosophy and Professor of Philosophy and Health Psychology at University of North Carolina, Charlotte. She is the author of four books, most recently *Good White People: The Problem with Middle-Class White Anti-racism* (2014) and *The Physiology of Sexist and Racist Oppression* (2015). *Good White People* was named a 2014 *Choice* Outstanding Academic Title and a *Ms.* magazine Must-Read Feminist Book of 2014. She also is coeditor of four books, including *Race and Epistemologies of Ignorance* (2007) and *Feminist Interpretations of William James* (2015).

Robert B. Talisse is W. Alton Jones Professor of Philosophy and Chair of the Philosophy Department at Vanderbilt University. He specializes in contemporary political philosophy and pragmatism. He has written many books, including *A Pragmatist Philosophy of Democracy* (Routledge, 2007), *Democracy and Moral Conflict* (Cambridge University Press, 2009), and *Pluralism and Liberal Politics* (Routledge, 2012). He is also the editor (with Scott F. Aikin) of *The Pragmatism Reader* (Princeton University Press, 2011).

Paul C. Taylor teaches philosophy and African American studies at Pennsylvania State University, where he also serves as the Associate Dean of undergraduate studies. His books include *Race: A Philosophical Introduction* (2003) and *Black Is Beautiful: A Philosophy of Black Aesthetics* (2016), and he was one of the founding editors of the journal *Critical Philosophy of Race*.

Christopher Voparil is on the Graduate Faculty of Union Institute & University, where he teaches philosophy and political theory. He is author of *Richard Rorty: Politics and Vision* (2006) and articles in, among others, *Contemporary Pragmatism, Journal of Speculative Philosophy, Philosophy and Social Criticism*, and *Transactions of the Charles S. Peirce Society*. With Richard J. Bernstein he is coeditor of *The Rorty Reader* (2010). He has been a Fulbright scholar, served as Secretary of the Society for the Advancement of American Philosophy, and is founding President of the Richard Rorty Society.

Introduction

Perspectives on Pragmatism and Justice

SUSAN DIELEMAN, DAVID RONDEL,
AND CHRISTOPHER VOPARIL

Any observed form or object is but a challenge. The case is not
otherwise with ideals of justice or peace or human brotherhood, or
equality, or order. They too are not things self-enclosed to be known
by introspection, as objects were once supposed to be known by
rational insight. Like thunderbolts and tubercular disease and the
rainbow they can be known only by extensive and minute observation
of consequences incurred in action.

—JOHN DEWEY, *Human Nature and Conduct*

THE CHARGE THAT THE tradition of American pragmatism has had relatively little to contribute to philosophical discussions of justice is point-
less to dispute. There are no distinctively pragmatist theories of justice,
if by "theory of justice" one has in mind the sort of thing that Locke,
Kant, Rawls, or Nozick offered their readers. A theory of justice in this
conventional sense typically endorses a set of principles that attempts an
elucidation of the concept and content of justice, along with a set of claims
about the institutions, practices, and behaviors that best realize these principles. One looks in vain for a theory of justice in this conventional sense
in the writings of virtually all major pragmatist thinkers—both classical
and "neo." Even in the work of John Dewey, easily the most politically
engaged of the classical pragmatists, there is nothing even approaching a
well worked out theory of this kind. The word "justice" appears noticeably
infrequently in Dewey's voluminous writings.

It is certainly true that pragmatists have expended considerable energy developing rich accounts of democracy and have contributed incisively to a range of important political-philosophical debates. Yet, as Robert Talisse points out in his contribution to this volume, the democratic ideal that pragmatists have formulated may "ring hollow" unless it is "supplemented by an accompanying vision of the fundamental social and material entitlements of democratic citizens. This latter task calls for theorizing justice."

Why have pragmatists had so little to say about this age-old philosophical topic? What best explains this apparent oversight? And to the extent that the tradition of American pragmatism has anything to contribute to thinking more clear-headedly about justice and injustice, what might such a contribution look like?

In this introduction we attempt to shed light on pragmatism's conspicuous silence about justice, and to briefly outline some of the ideas and commitments that together gesture toward a broadly pragmatist orientation toward these questions. Our claim is certainly not that there is unanimity among pragmatists about how justice is best understood, pursued, or theorized; indeed, some of these disagreements will become apparent in the chapters ahead. What we offer in this introduction rather is a stylized and tentative sketch of some central pragmatist commitments, along with reflections about how they suggest a pragmatist—or pragmatist-*ish* or pragmatist-*friendly*— approach to questions of justice and injustice.[1] For, while there may be no conventionally philosophical theories of justice in the pragmatist canon, the writings of many pragmatists demonstrate an obvious sensitivity and responsiveness to injustice. Many pragmatists were and are moved by a deep sense of justice—by an awareness of the suffering of people, of the need to build just institutions, and to search for a tolerant and nondiscriminatory culture that regards all people with equal concern and respect.

Dewey famously sought to reconstruct philosophy so that it ceases to be "a device for dealing with the problems of philosophers and becomes a method, cultivated by philosophers, for dealing with the problems of men" (MW 10:46). He worked on behalf of the women's movement and was a cofounder of the National Association for the Advancement of Colored

---

[1] We readily acknowledge that pragmatism can mean many things, and that there are deep disagreements about how it is best understood, and about the comparative merits and demerits of various brands of pragmatist thought. "Pragmatism," says the most noteworthy pragmatist of the second half of the twentieth century, is "a vague, ambiguous, and overworked word" (Rorty 1982, 160). We use the phrases *pragmatist-ish* and *pragmatist-friendly* to gesture at a set of ideas that undoubtedly reside in the pragmatist solar system, while remaining largely noncommittal about some of these interpragmatist disagreements.

People (Seigfried 2002). For all of his idiosyncratic Emersonian preoccupations, William James intervened publicly on multiple occasions to protest the domination and moral insensitivity toward others endemic to America's imperial projects around the turn of the nineteenth century and its lynching practices at home, after diagnosing such "blindness" in himself (Cotkin 1990). Jane Addams's lifetime of tireless reform efforts on behalf of the least advantaged and progressive social activism for peace, public health, and the protection of women would seem of a piece with her social philosophy and social ethics (Knight 2005). More recently, Cornel West has been a persistent critic not only of American imperialism but its racist legacies, drawing on the tradition of pragmatism, filtered through the traditions and experiences of African American life, to voice a public prophecy of protest against subjugation and injustice (Mendieta 2007). Even Richard Rorty attuned his later philosophical reflections to victims of ethnic cleansing and excluded and oppressed groups, and claimed that to "intervene in cultural politics" should be philosophers' primary assignment (Voparil 2011). Yet are these public interventions expressions of philosophical commitments or merely contingent facts of solely biographical import?

The most obvious explanation for pragmatism's apparent failure to theorize justice has to do with the fact that, as William James famously asserted, "Pragmatism is a method only" that "does not stand for any special results" (WWJ 1:31). On one interpretation of this claim, pragmatism concerns itself with procedures for deciding what to do and what to believe; it does not concern itself, by and large, with what such procedures might substantively yield. That is, pragmatism does not tell us what to believe or what to do. At most, it provides us with methods for deciding these questions. On this view, because pragmatism does not deliver conclusions, endorse ends, or insist on specific outcomes, it is neutral between various substantive moral and political claims. As Eric MacGilvray glosses this thought:

> Pragmatism was only ever meant to provide a theory of meaning and justification, and not a substantive theory of the good. It is this theory of meaning and justification that the founding pragmatists (and their critics) were talking about *when they were talking about pragmatism*, and so we must be careful to define pragmatism in these terms rather than to associate it with the moral and ethical commitments of any particular time, place, or thinker. (MacGilvray 2004, 11)[2]

---

[2] See also Rorty 1999; Posner 1990; Fish 1998 for additional defenses of pragmatism's supposed "neutrality."

Many have persuasively challenged the claim that pragmatism lacks moral and political valence, but the details of that dispute need not detain us here.[3] It will be enough to note that if the general gist of the "neutralist" reading of pragmatism is on the mark, that may go a long way to explaining why pragmatists have had relatively little to say about justice.

Whatever readers are inclined to think about the "neutrality" issue, we argue that the pragmatist silence about justice can be accounted for, at least partially, in terms of three related and mutually reinforcing ideas to which virtually all pragmatists are committed. In no particular order, these are

(1) A prioritization of concrete problems and real-world injustices ahead of abstract precepts
(2) A distrust of a priori theorizing, along with a corresponding fallibilism and methodological experimentalism
(3) A deep and persistent pluralism, both in respect to what justice is and requires, and in respect to how real-world injustices are best recognized and remedied

To see how these three large clusters of ideas inform a broadly pragmatist approach to justice and injustice, consider a distinction drawn recently by Amartya Sen (ironically, someone who has never self-identified with the pragmatist tradition). In his magisterial work *The Idea of Justice*, Sen distinguishes between two kinds of theoretical approaches to justice, both of which, he claims, have many eminent proponents in the history of moral and political philosophy. The first is a group of theories that Sen consolidates under the banner "transcendental institutionalism." Such theories are "transcendental" in that they aim "to offer resolutions of questions about the nature of perfect justice" (Sen 2009, ix); they tend to focus on the pure concept of justice—the unchanging and essential nature of "the just"— rather than on relative comparisons of justice and injustice. And they are "institutionalist" in that they concentrate on getting the institutions right, as it were, while neglecting (or ignoring altogether) questions that arise about the actual societies that would ultimately emerge from any given set of institutional arrangements. Sen cites Hobbes, Locke, Rousseau, Kant, and Rawls as paradigmatic examples of this kind of approach.

"Transcendental" accounts of justice stand in contrast to what Sen calls "comparative" accounts. Comparative accounts abjure the search for

---

[3] See, for instance, Anderson 2006; Hilary Putnam (this volume); and Misak and Talisse 2014.

perfect justice, focusing instead on locating criteria for some alternative state of affairs being "less unjust" than another. Adam Smith, Condorcet, Wollstonecraft, Bentham, Marx, and John Stuart Mill are cited as exemplars. While Sen does not mention the names of any pragmatist philosophers in his discussion, we believe that pragmatists are far more likely to be "comparativists" than "transcendentalists." Like comparativists, pragmatists will be skeptical about the usefulness of trying to specify—absent some particular project, context, or specific complaint—what ideally just institutions would be like. They are likely to regard such attempts as emblematic of what Dewey criticized as "philosophy's search for the immutable" (LW 4:21), as yet further examples of philosophy's ambition for "finality and foreverness" (LW 2:357). Comparativists and pragmatists will agree that perfect and consummate justice—like perfect and consummate truth—is chimerical. Just as many of the beliefs we take to be true may turn out to be false, many of the laws, institutions, and behaviors we take to be just may turn out to contain hidden, previously undetected, injustices. In both cases, a healthy commitment to fallibilism ensures that such possibilities can never be finally ruled out.

From a pragmatist view, there are obvious advantages to conceiving of justice in "comparative" rather than "transcendental" terms. First, a comparative approach helps us make sense of real-world struggles for justice in a way that transcendental approaches simply cannot. "What moves us," Sen writes in his book's preface, "is not the realization that the world falls short of being completely just . . . but that there are clearly remediable injustices around us which we want to eliminate" (2009, vii). This focus on "clearly remediable injustices" chimes with pragmatism's basic appreciation for concrete problems. Unlike the famous rationalists, for whom philosophy begins with disinterested contemplation, and unlike the famous empiricists, for whom it begins with passively receiving sensory stimuli, pragmatists believe that thinking and inquiry are fundamentally occasioned by problems. Problems spur us into action. They unsettle previously settled experience, disrupting the normal flow of things. When genuine problems arise, it is no longer possible for us to carry on as usual. While the language of "problems" is characteristically Deweyan—he preferred the clunky phrase "problematic situation"—the same basic idea underlies virtually all pragmatist thought.

The pragmatist prioritization of "problems" goes hand in hand with an approach for which real-world struggles carried out in the name of justice, as opposed to abstract and idealized principles, will be given priority. Pragmatists need not insist that abstract (idealized) philosophizing about justice is useless or always beside the point. Minimally, perhaps, it can do no harm. Maximally, it can be useful to the extent that it moves people to see the present setup as one alternative among many, thus inspiring them to dream up new options (Rorty 2006, 58).[4] Nevertheless, the kind of approach favored by pragmatists affords a certain priority to questions about how injustice is actually experienced in the real world, and to questions about the specific problems (political, moral, cultural, economic) to which this gives rise. Comparativists and pragmatists will agree that questions about the concepts and content of justice cannot be satisfactorily answered from the philosopher's armchair, in isolation from some context, complaint, or problem. They agree that in the real world, demands for justice always reveal themselves as demands made by specific people, at specific times and places, and always for something specific. There has never been a political movement that mobilized without an agenda or a set of demands—in the name of nothing but transcendental "justice itself." As Dewey well summed up the point, "Men have constructed a strange dream-world when they have supposed that without a fixed ideal of remote good to inspire them, they have no enticement to get relief from present troubles, no desires for liberation from what oppresses and for clearing-up what confuses present action" (MW 14:195).

Because pragmatists tend not to be involved in the search for "perfect justice"—because justice is not, they think, the sort of thing one "gets right" once and for all—they tend also not to be perturbed by the fact that judgments of justice and injustice suffer from a certain degree of vagueness and indeterminacy. Unlike conventional theories of justice, which aim to establish a set of principles from which all claims about justice can be understood to follow, pragmatists adopt the different (more modest) goal of trying to find better ways of meeting this or that complaint, solving this or that problem, overcoming this or that injustice. This is not a plea for simplifying or dumbing-down theoretical reflection about justice. Nor is it a plea to focus on the "practical" in place of the "theoretical." On the contrary, as C. I. Lewis writes, "Pragmatism could be characterized as the doctrine that ... there can be ultimately no valid distinction of theoretical and practical, so there can be no final

---

[4] Iris Young writes, "Appeals to principles of justice have a more pragmatic function in political interaction than many theorists of justice attribute to them. Where practical judgments are the result at which discussants aim, appeals to principles of justice are steps in arguments about what should be done" (2000, 29).

separation of questions of truth ... from questions of the justifiable ends of action" (Lewis 1970, 108). The aspiration rather is that theoretical reflection on justice and real-world struggles against injustice become correlated, integrated, aligned. The aspiration is born of the conviction that a philosophical theory of justice, no matter how intellectually alluring or elegant, must be modified or discarded if it cannot intelligently speak to the problems that men and women find themselves having to contend with.

The pragmatist emphasis on concrete "problems" thus also goes hand in hand with a methodological experimentalism. Different problems can be dealt with in a variety of ways, some better and more intelligent than others. Solutions, in turn, are potentially as diverse and numerous as the problems they seek to address. No one can say in advance how a particular problem will best be resolved. Discovering that requires conducting experiments, and even then such knowledge is always tentative and revisable. Put differently, if we construe our fallibility in terms of the idea that improved habits and beliefs are always possible and desirable, then it becomes reasonable to view our theorizing about justice not as the search for absolute truth or unmovable certainty, but as a generic name for problem solving: as shorthand for the activity, as Dewey put it, of generating hypotheses "to be used and tested in projects of reform" (MW 12:189). As Richard Rorty captures the thought, "Pragmatists are entirely at home with the idea that political theory should view itself as suggestions for future action emerging out of recent historical experience, rather than attempting to legitimate the outcome of that experience by reference to something ahistorical" (1999, 272).

One of Sen's central arguments is that there is no such thing as *the* one best approach to justice, one ideal form of reasoning, one privileged perspective, one procedure or rubric with which to make all decisions about justice. He emphasizes throughout his book "the need to accept the plurality of reasons that may be sensibly accommodated in an exercise of evaluation," sensibly noting that "The fact that a person can reason his or her way into rejecting slavery ... does not indicate that the same person must be able to decide with certainty whether a 40 per cent top rate of income tax would be better than—or more just than—a top rate of 39 per cent" (2009, 394–396). Again, this pluralist outlook is one with which pragmatists are likely to be sympathetic. Pragmatists will agree that wisdom is to be potentially found in all corners. No one has a monopoly on insight; there are a variety of different ways of fruitfully proceeding. Here it is helpful to remember William James's characterization of the pragmatist methodological temperament from the *Pragmatism* lectures:

> She [pragmatism] is willing ... to follow either logic or the senses and to count the humblest and most personal experiences. ... Her only test of probable truth is what works best in the way of leading us, what fits every part of life best and combines with the collectivity of experience's demands, nothing being omitted ... [Y]ou see already how democratic she is. Her manners are as various and flexible, her resources as rich and endless, and her conclusions as friendly as those of mother nature. (WWJ 1:44)

As we will see more clearly in the chapters ahead, pragmatism's approach to questions of justice and injustice will be likewise open-minded, eclectic, and "completely genial."

It is sometimes easier to specify what one is against in theorizing justice and injustice than it is to articulate an affirmative theory. This may well be true of pragmatist approaches to the subject, which have tended to express skepticism about "ideal theory"—of trying to discern principles of justice that are timeless, universal, and insensitive to context—and a similar reluctance to offer a theory of the state, its justification, and the conditions under which its exercise of coercion is legitimate. We believe that some of the issues briefly explored above help make sense of the silence from pragmatists about justice, and to gesture at the contours of a pragmatist orientation to these issues. The real and difficult work of grappling with these questions, however, takes place in the chapters ahead.

Despite the fact, noted above, that the tradition of American pragmatism has had relatively little to contribute to philosophical discussions of justice, there have been in recent years occasional reflections on how pragmatists might contribute to philosophical debates about what justice is, how it can be achieved, and by and for whom. Part I, "The Pragmatist Turn to Justice," brings some of these early reflections together with new essays that consider what a pragmatist approach to questions of justice and injustice might look like.

The volume begins with Richard Rorty's 1997 essay "Justice as a Larger Loyalty." Rorty there asks,

> Would it be a good idea to treat "justice" as the name for loyalty to a certain very large group, the name for our largest current loyalty, rather than the name of something distinct from loyalty? Could we replace the notion

of "justice" with that of loyalty to that group—for example, one's fellow-citizens, or the human species, or all living things? Would anything be lost by this replacement?

Rorty answers this final question in the negative. *Pace* Kantian thinkers like Jürgen Habermas, who insists that reason provides us with "universal and unconditional moral obligations" that we think of as obligations of justice, while loyalty is nothing more than our "affectional relations," Rorty argues that justice is just the name we give to loyalty expanded to the widest possible community. In other words, by rejecting the dichotomy between reason and sentiment, Rorty thereby rejects the dichotomy between justice and loyalty. He suggests, with theorists like Annette Baier and Michael Walzer, that our relationships with and obligations to our fellow humans begin "thickly" and become "thin" as they expand to incorporate increasing numbers of people who are different from ourselves. Conceiving of justice as a larger loyalty would provide us with a better vocabulary for engaging with distant others in the global context.

In "Abnormal Justice" Nancy Fraser takes up Rorty's distinction between normal and abnormal discourse (an adaptation of Thomas Kuhn's famous distinction between normal and revolutionary science) to characterize different sorts of justice claims. The one sort takes place under conditions of *normal* justice; these involve the "what" of justice, that is, the "substance with which it is concerned." The other sort takes place under conditions of *abnormal* justice, where, absent the recognizable structure and shared "grammar" of normal discourse, not only the "what" but the "who" or "how" of justice is up for grabs. Fraser's contribution exhibits a pragmatist orientation insofar as it represents a move from ideal theory to nonideal theory, where that move is motivated by the need to attend to the actual practices of our responses to and attempts to grapple with the injustices and abnormalities of the contemporary scene.

In chapter 3 of the volume, "Pragmatism's Contribution to Nonideal Theorizing: Fraser, Addams, and Rorty," Christopher Voparil uncovers and builds upon the pragmatist themes in Fraser's nonideal theorizing, including her embrace of fallibilism and her recognition of the need to actively foster habits and practices. These intimate the potential for Fraser's project to be advanced "beyond the conceptual." However, Voparil suggests that, if this potential is to be realized, Fraser's efforts to "democratize the process of frame setting" need to be supplemented by an explanation of how such democratization might occur. Voparil finds these added resources in the work of Jane Addams and Richard Rorty, both of whom "understood that the ethical and epistemic virtues of open-mindedness and responsiveness must be fostered on the part of the privileged." Specifically, Addams's attention to the *social* dimension of justice and Rorty's emphasis on cultural politics provide tools for cultivating "social sensibilities and the virtues of open-mindedness and listening that promote responsiveness to injustice."

In "Empirical Approaches to Problems of Injustice: Elizabeth Anderson and the Pragmatists," Gregory Pappas also explores the ideal-nonideal theory debate, via Anderson's *The Imperative of Integration* (2010). Though Pappas applauds Anderson's "characterization of the pragmatist approach," he worries that it does not fully capture its inherently radical nature. Drawing primarily on Dewey's "more 'unorthodox' and more demanding" method of inquiry, Pappas suggests that there are two specific features of the pragmatist approach that Anderson overlooks: the starting point of inquiry, which refers to "the concrete problems of injustice as they are experienced in the midst of social life," and the "initial experiential material" that exists prior to diagnosis. Had Anderson made fuller use of pragmatism's methodological commitments and practices, Pappas thinks, she would have been able to avoid criticisms regarding, for example, her lack of "experiential basis for the knowledge that she has produced."

In "Ideal and Actual in Dewey's Political Theory," Matthew Festenstein revisits recent arguments that position Dewey as an exemplar of nonideal normative theorizing, including by Anderson, Medina, and Pappas. Calling attention to the "bold appeal to ideals" that Dewey makes at key points, Festenstein distinguishes between two distinct views of ideals that exist in Dewey's work: a critical view of ideals severed from the means necessary for their achievement and an affirmation of the positive role ideals play in the context of practical inquiry and political thinking. Festenstein introduces much-needed clarity to the varied and often conflicting ways that the line between ideal and nonideal theory has been drawn by discerning three distinct claims of nonideal theorists: the inappropriateness of idealization, the methodological priority of injustice, and the commitment to making local improvements rather than achieving perfect justice. While he finds support for all three in Dewey's work, he also argues that genuine ideals play an important role for Dewey. As hypotheses constructed in response to problematic situations, ideals are not dispensable but "a feature of a reflective response to a problem," without which the possibilities they open would remain undiscovered. Festenstein charts a novel middle course that is critical of projects of ideal theory that rely on Dewey's conception of deliberative inquiry, while at the same time recovering Dewey's positive account of ideals as projected possibilities.

Some of the concerns that prompt Voparil's move beyond both ideal theory and nonideal theory, as well Pappas's more radically empirical approach to nonideal theorizing about justice, can be spotted already in Ruth Anna Putnam's 1990 essay "Justice in Context." For example, Putnam argues that "ideal theory and nonideal practice constitute each other and for a pragmatist this is not paradoxical." Indeed, on Putnam's view, James's "cries of the wounded" must be complemented by a "standard of justice" if we are to see something as an injustice, as a wrong that ought to be righted, rather than as mere expression of pain or resentment. Putnam argues that, conceived in this way, pragmatism can be defended against two common charges: that it is inherently conservative and merely seeking to defend the status quo, and that it deprives us of a secure sense of justice.

Part I concludes with Susan Dieleman's "Realism, Pragmatism, and Critical Social Epistemology," a reflection on the connections between pragmatism and the project of critical social epistemology, which examines "those epistemic practices that create and maintain injustices, and explores ways of reforming epistemic practices so as to achieve greater justice." Dieleman focuses on the tendency among critical social epistemologists, like Charles Mills and Linda Martín Alcoff, to defend realist "appeals to a way the world really is—to an antecedent and determinate reality that has been hidden behind an ignorance produced by and for political purposes." Dieleman asserts, contra these thinkers, that Rorty's rejection of realism (or rather, of the realism-antirealism distinction) does not undermine possibilities of resisting oppression and injustice, but makes room for them instead. Using the examples of feminist and trans social movements that resist the epistemic injustices that give rise to those very movements, Dieleman concludes that "a pragmatist account of (epistemic) justice, and especially one of a distinctly Rortyan variety that takes contingency seriously, pairs well with critical social epistemology."

One of the greatest challenges to liberal, ideal theories of justice has been the indictment of its deep, unacknowledged gendered and racialized hierarchies that privilege white males at the expense of women and people of color.[5] Seen from the margins, the apparent neutrality and universality of liberal conceptions are "predicated on the white experience" rather than informed by the experience of racial and gender injustice (Mills 2008, 1385). In the face of this bias, Charles Mills has argued that "Making racial sociopolitical oppression methodologically central would put us on

---

[5] See Pateman 1988; Mills 1997; Pateman and Mills 2007.

very different theoretical terrain from the start" (2008, 1387). The essays that comprise Part II, "Resisting Oppression and Injustice," take up the challenge of making oppression and injustice methodologically central. They see in pragmatism some of the resources required to resist and respond to forms of injustice that affect different social groups unequally, and they share an interest in strengthening the weaknesses of pragmatism or responding to apparent lacunae.

Patricia Hill Collins's "Social Inequality, Power, and Politics: Intersectionality in Dialogue with American Pragmatism" argues that pragmatist conceptual tools are valuable for understanding community and conceptualizing forward-looking social movements in the pursuit of social justice. However, the value of these contributions needs to be complemented by an awareness of what has been marginalized by and has therefore helped to shape pragmatist thought through its absence, namely, attention to "social inequality, power, and politics." This awareness can be provided, Collins thinks, and pragmatism pushed to a more self-reflective mode, by combining pragmatism with intersectionality, a "newly recognized field of study within the academy whose purpose has been to analyze social inequality, power, and politics." Collins highlights four themes on which intersectionality and pragmatism could fruitfully engage: the nature of collective identities, the epistemological implications of social locatedness, the importance of relational processes, and the relations between knowledges and communities. "In all," Collins suggests, "in both discourses, using the pragmatist construct of community and infusing it with intersectionality's ideas about social inequality, power, and politics might animate new avenues of investigation."

Like Collins, V. Denise James sees both strengths and weaknesses in pragmatism. In "Pragmatism and Radical Social Justice: Dewey, Du Bois, and Davis," James seeks to retrieve the radical potential of Dewey's thought, which she thinks problematically prioritizes freedom over justice. However, its radical potential can be actualized by bringing Dewey's thought into conversation with that of W. E. B. Du Bois, which provides a "black radical corrective . . . that is compatible with Dewey's pragmatism even as it enlarges and enriches it." Bringing the thought of these two classical pragmatists together reveals, James contends, that "if we are to think through radical justice, we must reject the common philosophical distinctions made between freedom and justice. The resulting messy, complex attempt to define social justice is thoroughly pragmatic and radical." James shows that the picture of social justice that results from bringing Dewey and Du Bois together can be fruitfully evaluated using the lens of Angela

Davis's work, which is a valuable source of "radical, pragmatic habits of justice" that can replace habits of oppression.

James's contribution shares with others in Part II a desire to find hope for radical change within pragmatism. Another way to understand this project of making oppression and injustice methodologically central is as an attempt to meet what Leonard Harris has called "the insurrectionist challenge": "whether there exist features of pragmatism that require, as necessary conditions to be a pragmatist, support for participation in insurrection" (2002, 201). In "Contesting Injustice: Why Pragmatist Political Thought Needs Du Bois," Colin Koopman sets for himself the task of imagining a pragmatism that could "motivate critique of entrenched orders of inequality, unfreedom, domination, and oppression." He argues that a *contestatory* pragmatism, understood as an orientation that has resources for, and can motivate, contestation, gets us at least some of the way to meeting the insurrectionist challenge. However, Koopman worries that pragmatists have for too long centered Dewey in the pragmatist pantheon, and particularly in contemporary efforts to develop pragmatist political theory. We would be better off, he suggests, to look elsewhere for resources for this contestatory pragmatism: to William James's reminder that pragmatism can be "articulated in a key that is about as far from the pitches of utilitarian efficiency and romanticizing idealization as one can get," and W. E. B. Du Bois's pragmatist vision of contestation constituted simultaneously by strife and by hopefulness.

Like Koopman, José Medina is interested in the potential of pragmatism to meet the insurrectionist challenge. In "Pragmatism, Racial Injustice, and Epistemic Insurrection: Toward an Insurrectionist Pragmatism," he defends an insurrectionist pragmatism that is capable of radical transformation in the face of tragic racial injustices. He suggests that, despite common charges, pragmatism is neither "naively optimistic nor reducible to a gradualist reformism." Nevertheless, if pragmatism is going to be capable of motivating radical changes to situations of domination and oppression, it will have to give up its focus on "predictability and controllability." It can do this, Medina thinks, by recentering its focus on "embodied, lived experience," which provides "an important shared commitment in pragmatism and insurrectionism: the *egalitarian* commitment to facilitate the human flourishing of all subjects and groups."

In "An Aesthetics of Resistance: Deweyan Experimentalism and Epistemic Injustice," Paul C. Taylor offers a "friendly amendment" to Medina's project as presented in *The Epistemology of Resistance*. Specifically, he urges Medina to consider the *aesthetic* dimension of epistemic injustice, "as a domain for the reformation and retraining of our identities and sensibilities." Drawing on Dewey's *Art as Experience*, Taylor thinks that a rich, phenomenological account of aesthetic practice is important for developing the moral imagination and thereby an aesthetic of resistance. Rather than trying to expand epistemology to account for the ethical and political in the way that Medina does, Taylor recommends what he calls a "historicist phenomenology" instead, since it "immediately builds in the affective, emotive, and social considerations that Medina takes such pains to highlight."

In the final chapter of Part II, "Setting Aside Hope: A Pragmatist Approach to Racial Justice," Shannon Sullivan offers us a harsh reminder of the toll that fighting injustice, and seemingly intractable racial injustice in particular, can take. This reminder is presented against the backdrop of Cornel West's emphasis on hope as important for resistance to injustice. Sullivan worries that this emphasis is misplaced, as the empirical evidence suggests that hope wears down its bearers: hope, she suggests, "does not tend to help African Americans cope well with the insidious effects of white racism, and it even can contribute to a decline in black people's psychological and physiological health." And so Sullivan turns to the work of Derrick Bell and Calvin Warren instead, as sources of "alternative strategies for addressing antiblack racism." She recommends "setting aside hope" of achieving racial justice to focus on small, everyday forms of resistance, as a pragmatically better strategy for black communities in the United States.

Part III of the volume, "Pragmatism, Liberalism, and Democracy," revisits the works of the classical pragmatists to consider what, if anything, they can contribute to efforts by contemporary pragmatists to theorize justice and injustice. Hilary Putnam's "Reconsidering Deweyan Democracy" offers a justification of democracy grounded in Dewey's theory of inquiry. Democracy is often defended on ethical grounds, but Putnam's argument is that it can be defended on cognitive or epistemic grounds as well. Putnam explains and defends the Deweyan thesis that "democracy is a precondition for the full application of intelligence to solving social problems." On this view, the epistemic quality of inquiry is established in large part by the extent to which the inquiring community is inclusive or exclusive, democratic or elitist. Inquiry is best when it is democratic (when it weighs all interests and respect all voices). To be properly "scientific" on this view is thus to be democratic. While Putnam is less impressed with the power of Deweyan pragmatism to satisfactorily answer questions of individual ethics, he commends Dewey's as the best approach to adopt for the resolution of collective and social problems. The advantages of Dewey's approach, Putnam concludes, are its methodological experimentalism and its commitment to the (Peircean) idea of a community of free inquirers.

In the volume's earliest essay, "John Dewey and the Problem of Justice," Peter T. Manicas addresses head on Dewey's "lack of discussion of the theory and problems of justice," especially given that it cannot be explained "by a failure to *see* problems, nor by an unwillingness to deal with them at the theoretical or practical level." We can account for this relative inattention, Manicas thinks, by the fact that Dewey took the liberal conception of justice to be too narrow. In seeking to enlarge this conception of justice, partly by attending to the virtues of love and sympathy, Dewey displaced the problem of justice as a substantive theoretical problem and replaced it with a working program or orientation that emphasized problems connected more directly to method and to practice. And because "the problem of justice ... cannot be 'solved' by 'experts' or by philosophers [but only by] people in the everyday world in their doings and sufferings," Manicas thinks that Dewey's social philosophy seems both thin and obvious; hence a failure to engage substantively with the concept or a theory of justice.

Like Manicas, Robert B. Talisse, in "Pragmatism, Democracy, and the Need for a Theory of Justice," begins by investigating Dewey's "atypical silence" on the topic of justice. This is a silence that is manifest, Talisse thinks, in his neglect of the issues of "marginalization, exclusion, discrimination, and disadvantage," which are not merely *bad*, but *wrong*, and therefore constitute a society that "is not merely *in need of improvement*, but also *illegitimate*." Particularly because Dewey, and other pragmatist political theorists who take their cue from his thought, are "epistemic participationists," he and they have a special obligation to consider the ways in which individuals' ability to engage in those activities that are constitutive of democracy might be impacted. Talisse's recommendation, therefore, is that pragmatists "build camp" among the democratic egalitarians, who agree that "the *point* or *aim* of justice is to establish and maintain conditions under which citizens are able to interact as democratic equals," even if this means revisiting those key pragmatist commitments, such as the view that "democracy is a way of life," that are likely to act as roadblocks in the development of a pragmatist approach to justice.

In "A Pragmatist Account of Legitimacy and Authority: Holmes, Ramsey, and the Moral Force of Law," Cheryl Misak similarly emphasizes the epistemic dimensions of democracy, legitimacy, and justice. The epistemic response to the question of legitimacy and authority—"Why is that law authoritative for me?" or "How does this law make a normative demand on me?"—suggests there is value in "taking the perspectives and experiences of others seriously, given that we want to reach the right, or warranted, decision." Misak traces this argument back to the work of Oliver Wendell Holmes, to see "how the pragmatist epistemic argument was first carved out."Holmes, Misak suggests, offered a definition of "well-settled belief" as a belief that will "stand up to experience and standards," which meets up with questions of legitimacy and justice: a citizen might "object to a law because it goes against [her] moral code, but [she] should nonetheless regard it as binding on [her] or legitimate, because it was made by the best possible process, a process that is also moral."

The volume concludes with "William James on Justice and the Sacredness of Individuality," David Rondel's exploration of how "democratic individuality" shows up in James's ongoing efforts to consider "how things look differently when considered from diverse vantage points." Our inner lives and unique perspectives give rise to an "imperative of tolerance," Rondel suggests, which in turn prompts two questions that bring the issue of justice into view: a perceptual question, about "perceiving sympathetically the lived experience of injustice," and an ethical one, about "responding appropriately to injustice by interrogating our own habits, biases, and blindnesses." For James these questions prompt obligations that he defends through an epistemic argument that resembles Talisse's epistemic participationism, according to which we have an obligation "to weigh all ideals and consider all points of view," and through a metaphysical argument, which Rondel refers to as James's "cosmic" egalitarianism, according to which "each inner ocean has the same incommensurable value." Rondel suggests that we see the "personal" register of James's thinking about justice as complementing—not competing with—"more institutionally and culturally focused approaches."

Works Cited

Anderson, Elizabeth. 2006. "The Epistemology of Democracy." *Episteme* 3: 8–22.
———. 2010. *The Imperative of Integration*. Princeton, NJ: Princeton University Press.
Cotkin, George. 1990. *William James: Public Philosopher*. Baltimore: Johns Hopkins University Press.
Fish, Stanley. 1998. "Truth and Toilets: Pragmatism and the Practices of Life." In *The Revival of Pragmatism: New Essays on Social Thought, Law, and Culture*, edited by Morris Dickstein, 418–433. Durham, NC: Duke University Press.
Harris, Leonard. 2002. "Insurrectionist Ethics: Advocacy, Moral Psychology, and Pragmatism." In *Ethical Issues for a New Millennium,* edited by J. Howie, 192–210. Carbondale: Southern Illinois University Press.

Knight, Louise W. 2005. *Citizen: Jane Addams and the Struggle for Democracy.* Chicago: University of Chicago Press.

Lewis, C. I. 1970. *Collected Papers.* Palo Alto, CA: Stanford University Press.

MacGilvray, Eric. 2004. *Reconstructing Public Reason.* Cambridge: Harvard University Press.

Mendieta, Eduardo. 2007. "Translating Democracy or Democratic Acts of Translation: On Cornel West's *Democracy Matters.*" *Contemporary Pragmatism* 4(1): 25–37.

Mills, Charles W. 1997. *The Racial Contract.* Ithaca, NY: Cornell University Press.

———. 2008. "Racial Liberalism." *PMLA* 123(5): 1380–1397.

Misak, Cheryl, and Robert Talisse. 2014. "Pragmatist Epistemology and Democratic Theory: A Reply to Eric MacGilvray." *Journal of Political Philosophy* 22: 366–376.

Pateman, Carole. 1988. *The Sexual Contract.* Stanford, CA: Stanford University Press.

Pateman, Carole, and Charles W. Mills. 2007. *The Contract and Domination.* Malden, MA: Polity Press.

Posner, Richard. 1990. *The Problems of Jurisprudence.* Cambridge: Harvard University Press.

Rorty, Richard. 1982. *Consequences of Pragmatism.* Minneapolis: University of Minnesota Press.

———. 1999. *Philosophy and Social Hope.* London: Penguin.

———. 2006. "An Interview with Richard Rorty." *Gnosis* 8: 54–59.

Seigfried, Charlene Haddock, ed. 2002. *Feminist Interpretations of John Dewey.* University Park: Pennsylvania State University Press.

Sen, Amartya. 2009. *The Idea of Justice.* Cambridge: Harvard University Press.

Voparil, Christopher J. 2011. "Rortyan Cultural Politics and the Problem of Speaking for Others." *Contemporary Pragmatism* 8(1): 115–131.

Young, Iris. 2000. *Inclusion and Democracy.* Oxford: Oxford University Press.

PART I | The Pragmatist Turn to Justice

CHAPTER 1 | Justice as a Larger Loyalty

RICHARD RORTY

ALL OF US WOULD expect help if, pursued by the police, we asked our family to hide us. Most of us would extend such help even when we know our child or our parent to be guilty of a sordid crime. Many of us would be willing to perjure ourselves in order to supply such a child or parent with a false alibi. But if an innocent person is wrongly convicted as a result of our perjury, most of us will be torn by a conflict between loyalty and justice.

Such a conflict will be felt, however, only to the extent to which we can identify with the innocent person whom we have harmed. If the person is a neighbor, the conflict will probably be intense. If a stranger, especially one of a different race, class, or nation, it may be considerably weaker. There has to be *some* sense in which he or she is "one of us," before we start to be tormented by the question of whether or not we did the right thing when we committed perjury. So it may be equally appropriate to describe us as torn between conflicting loyalties—loyalty to our family and to a group large enough to include the victim of our perjury—rather than between loyalty and justice.

Our loyalty to such larger groups will, however, weaken, or even vanish altogether, when things get really tough. Then people whom we once thought of as like ourselves will be excluded. Sharing food with impoverished people down the street is natural and right in normal times, but perhaps not in a famine, when doing so amounts to disloyalty to one's family. The tougher things get, the more ties of loyalty to those near at hand tighten, and the more those to everyone else slacken.

Consider another example of expanding and contracting loyalties: our attitude toward other species. Most of us today are at least half—convinced that the vegetarians have a point, and that animals do have some sort of rights. But suppose that the cows, or the kangaroos, turn out to be carriers of a newly mutated virus, which, though harmless to them, is invariably fatal to humans. I suspect that we would then shrug off accusations of "speciesism" and participate in the necessary massacre. The idea of justice between species will suddenly become irrelevant, because things have gotten very tough indeed, and our loyalty to our own species must come first. Loyalty to a larger community—that of all living creatures on our home planet—would, under such circumstances, quickly fade away.

As a final example, consider the tough situation created by the accelerating export of jobs from the First World to the Third. There is likely to be a continuing decline in the average real income of most American families. Much of this decline can plausibly be attributed to the fact that you can hire a factory worker in Thailand for a tenth of what you would have to pay a worker in Ohio. It has become the conventional wisdom of the rich that American and European labor is overpriced on the world market. When American business people are told that they are being disloyal to the United States by leaving whole cities in our Rust Belt without work or hope, they sometimes reply that they place justice over loyalty.[1] They argue that the needs of humanity as a whole take moral precedence over those of their fellow-citizens and override national loyalties. Justice requires that they act as citizens of the world.

Consider now the plausible hypothesis that democratic institutions and freedoms are viable only when supported by an economic affluence that is achievable regionally but impossible globally. If this hypothesis is correct, democracy and freedom in the First World will not be able to survive a thoroughgoing globalization of the labor market. So the rich democracies face a choice between perpetuating their own democratic institutions and traditions and dealing justly with the Third World. Doing justice to the Third World would require exporting capital and jobs until everything is leveled out—until an honest day's work, in a ditch or at a computer, earns no higher a wage in Cincinnati or Paris than in a small town in Botswana. But then, it can plausibly be argued, there will be no money to support free public libraries, competing newspapers and networks, widely available

---

[1] Donald Fites, the CEO of the Caterpillar tractor company, explained his company's policy of relocation abroad by saying that "as a human being, I think what is going on is positive. I don't think it is realistic for 250 million Americans to control so much of the world's GNP" (quoted in Luttwak 1993, 184).

liberal arts education, and all the other institutions that are necessary to produce enlightened public opinion, and thus to keep governments more or less democratic.

What, on this hypothesis, is the right thing for the rich democracies to do? Be loyal to themselves and each other? Keep free societies going for a third of mankind at expense of the remaining two-thirds? Or sacrifice the blessings of political liberty for the sake of egalitarian economic justice?

These questions parallel those confronted by the parents of a large family after a nuclear holocaust. Do they share the food supply they have stored in the basement with their neighbors, even though the stores will then only last a day or two? Or do they fend those neighbors off with guns? Both moral dilemmas bring up the same question: Should we contract the circle for the sake of loyalty, or expand it for the sake of justice?

I have no idea of the right answer to these questions, neither about the right thing for these parents to do, nor about the right thing for the First World to do. I have posed them simply to bring a more abstract, and merely philosophical, question into focus. That question is: Should we describe such moral dilemmas as conflicts between loyalty and justice, or rather, as I have suggested, between loyalties to smaller groups and loyalties to larger groups?

This amounts to asking: Would it be a good idea to treat "justice" as the name for loyalty to a certain very large group, the name for our largest current loyalty, rather than the name of something distinct from loyalty? Could we replace the notion of "justice" with that of loyalty to that group—for example, one's fellow-citizens, or the human species, or all living things? Would anything be lost by this replacement?

Moral philosophers who remain loyal to Kant are likely to think that a *lot* would be lost. Kantians typically insist that justice springs from reason, and loyalty from sentiment. Only reason, they say, can impose universal and unconditional moral obligations, and our obligation to be just is of this sort. It is on another level from the sort of affectional relations that create loyalty. Jürgen Habermas is the most prominent contemporary philosopher to insist on this Kantian way of looking at things: the thinker least willing to blur either the line between reason and sentiment, or the line between universal validity and historical consensus. But contemporary philosophers who depart from Kant, either in the direction of Hume (like Annette Baier) or in the direction of Hegel (like Charles Taylor) or in that of Aristotle (like Alasdair MacIntyre), are not so sure.

Michael Walzer is at the other extreme from Habermas. He is wary of terms like "reason" and "universal moral obligation." The heart of his new book, *Thick and Thin*, is the claim that we should reject the intuition that Kant took as central: the intuition that "men and women everywhere begin with some common idea or principle or set of ideas and principles, which they then work up in many different ways." Walzer thinks that this picture of morality "starting thin" and "thickening with age" should be inverted. He says that, "Morality is thick from the beginning, culturally integrated, fully resonant, and it reveals itself thinly only on special occasions, when moral language is turned to special purposes" (Walzer 1994, 4). Walzer's inversion suggests, though it does not entail, the neo-Humean picture of morality sketched by Annette Baier in her book *Moral Prejudices*. On Baier's account, morality starts out not as an obligation but as a relation of reciprocal trust among a closely knit group, such as a family or clan. To behave morally is to do what comes naturally in your dealings with your parents and children or your fellow clan-members. It amounts to respecting the trust they place in you. Obligation, as opposed to trust, enters the picture only when your loyalty to a smaller group conflicts with your loyalty to a larger group.[2]

When, for example, the families confederate into tribes, or the tribes into nations, you may feel obliged to do what does not come naturally: to leave your parents in the lurch by going off to fight in the wars, or to rule against your own village in your capacity as a federal administrator or judge. What Kant would describe as the resulting conflict between moral obligation and sentiment, or between reason and sentiment, is, on a non-Kantian account of the matter, a conflict between one set of loyalties and another set of loyalties. The idea of a *universal* moral obligation to respect human dignity gets replaced by the idea of loyalty to a very large group—the human species. The idea that moral obligation extends beyond that species to an even larger group becomes the idea of loyalty to all those who, like yourself, can experience pain—even the cows and the kangaroos—or perhaps even to all living things, even the trees.

This non-Kantian view of morality can be rephrased as the claim that one's moral identity is determined by the group or groups with which one identifies—the group or groups to which one cannot be disloyal and still like oneself. Moral dilemmas are not, in this view, the result of a conflict

---

[2] Baier's picture is quite close to that sketched by Wilfrid Sellars and Robert Brandom in their quasi-Hegelian accounts of moral progress as the expansion of the circle of beings who count as "us."

between reason and sentiment but between alternative selves, alternative self-descriptions, alternative ways of giving a meaning to one's life. Non-Kantians do not think that we have a central, true self by virtue of our membership in the human species—a self that responds to the call of reason. They can, instead, agree with Daniel Dennett that a self is a center of narrative gravity. In nontraditional societies, most people have several such narratives at their disposal, and thus several different moral identities. It is this plurality of identities that accounts for the number and variety of moral dilemmas, moral philosophers, and psychological novels in such societies.

Walzer's contrast between thick and thin morality is, among other things, a contrast between the detailed and concrete stories you can tell about yourself as a member of a smaller group and the relatively abstract and sketchy story you can tell about yourself as a citizen of the world. You know more about your family than about your village, more about your village than about your nation, more about your nation than about humanity as a whole, more about being human than about simply being a living creature. You are in a better position to decide what differences between individuals are morally relevant when dealing with those whom you can describe thickly, and in a worse position when dealing with those whom you can only describe thinly. This is why, as groups get larger, law has to replace custom, and abstract principles have to replace phronesis. So Kantians are wrong to see phronesis as a thickening up of thin abstract principles. Plato and Kant were misled by the fact that abstract principles are designed to trump parochial loyalties into thinking that the principles are somehow prior to the loyalties—that the thin is somehow prior to the thick.

Walzer's thick-thin distinction can be aligned with Rawls's contrast between a shared *concept* of justice and various conflicting *conceptions* of justice. Rawls sets out that contrast as follows:

> the concept of justice, applied to an institution, means, say, that the institution makes no arbitrary distinctions between persons in assigning basic rights and duties, and that its rules establish a proper balance between competing claims.... [A] conception includes, besides this, principles and criteria for deciding which distinctions are arbitrary and when a balance between competing claims is proper. People can agree on the meaning of justice and still be at odds, since they affirm different principles and standards for deciding these matters. (Rawls 1993a, 14n)

Phrased in Rawls's terms, Walzer's point is that thick "fully resonant" *conceptions* of justice, complete with distinctions between the people who matter most and the people who matter less, come first. The thin concept, and its maxim "do not make arbitrary distinctions between moral subjects," is articulated only on special occasions. On those occasions, the thin concept can often be turned against any of the thick conceptions from which it emerged, in the form of critical questions about whether it may not be merely arbitrary to think that certain people matter more than others.

Neither Rawls nor Walzer think, however, that unpacking the thin concept of justice will, by itself, resolve such critical questions by supplying a criterion of arbitrariness. They do not think that we can do what Kant hoped to do—derive solutions to moral dilemmas from the analysis of moral concepts. To put the point in the terminology I am suggesting: we cannot resolve conflicting loyalties by turning away from them all toward something categorically distinct from loyalty—the universal moral obligation to act justly. So we have to drop the Kantian idea that the moral law starts off pure but is always in danger of being contaminated by irrational feelings that introduce arbitrary discriminations among persons. We have to substitute the Hegelian-Marxist idea that the so-called moral law is, at best, a handy abbreviation for a concrete web of social practices. This means dropping Habermas's claim that his "discourse ethics" articulates a transcendental presupposition of the use of language, and accepting his critics' claim that it articulates only the customs of contemporary liberal societies.[3]

Now I want to raise the question of whether to describe the various moral dilemmas with which I began as conflicts between loyalty and justice, or rather as conflicting loyalties to particular groups, in a more concrete form. Consider the question of whether the demands for reform made on the rest of the world by Western liberal societies are made in the name of something not merely Western—something like morality, or humanity, or rationality—or are simply expressions of loyalty to local, Western, conceptions of justice. Habermas would say that they are the former. I would say that they are the latter, but are none the worse for that. I think it is better not to say that the liberal West is better informed about rationality

---

[3] This sort of debate runs through a lot of contemporary philosophy. Compare, for example, Walzer's contrast between starting thin and starting thick with that between the Platonic-Chomskian notion that we start with meanings and descend to use, and the Wittgensteinian-Davidsonian notion that we start with use and then skim off meaning as needed for lexicographical or philosophical purposes.

and justice, and instead to say that, in making demands on nonliberal societies, it is simply being true to itself.

In a recent paper called "The Law of Peoples," Rawls discusses the question of whether the conception of justice he has developed in his books is something peculiarly Western and liberal or rather something universal. He would like to be able to claim universality. He says that it is important to avoid "historicism," and believes that he can do this if he can show that the conception of justice suited to a liberal society can be extended beyond such societies through formulating what he calls "the law of peoples" (Rawls 1993b, 44).[4] He outlines, in that paper, an extension of the constructivist procedure proposed in his *A Theory of Justice*—an extension which, by continuing to separate the right from the good, lets us encompass liberal and nonliberal societies under the same law.

As Rawls develops this constructivist proposal, however, it emerges that this law applies only to *reasonable* peoples, in a quite specific sense of the term "reasonable." The conditions that nonliberal societies must honor in order to be "accepted by liberal societies as members in good standing of a society of peoples" (Rawls 1993b, 81) include the following: "its system of law must be guided by a common good conception of justice . . . that takes impartially into account what it sees not unreasonably as the fundamental interests of all members of society" (61).

Rawls takes the fulfillment of that condition to rule out violation of basic human rights. These rights include "at least certain minimum rights to means of subsistence and security (the right to life), to liberty (freedom from slavery, serfdom, and forced occupations) and (personal) property, as well as to formal equality as expressed by the rules of natural justice (for example, that similar cases be treated similarly)" (Rawls 1993b, 62). When Rawls spells out what he means by saying that the admissible nonliberal societies must not have unreasonable philosophical or religious doctrines, he glosses "unreasonable" by saying that these societies must "admit a measure of liberty of conscience and freedom of thought, even if these freedoms are not in general equal for all members of society." Rawls' notion of what is reasonable, in short, confines membership of the society of peoples to societies whose institutions encompass most of the hard-won achievements of the West in the two centuries since the Enlightenment.

---

[4] I am not sure why Rawls thinks historicism is undesirable, and there are passages, both early and recent, in which he seems to throw in his lot with the historicists. (See the passage quoted in note 5 below from his recent "Reply to Habermas.") Some years ago I argued for the plausibility of an historicist interpretation of the metaphilosophy of Rawls's *A Theory of Justice* in my "The Priority of Democracy to Philosophy" (see Rorty 1991).

It seems to me that Rawls cannot both reject historicism and invoke this notion of reasonableness. For the effect of that invocation is to build most of the West's recent decisions about which distinctions between persons are arbitrary into the conception of justice that is implicit in the law of peoples. The differences between different *conceptions* of justice, remember, are differences between what features of people are seen as relevant to the adjudication of their competing claims. There is obviously enough wriggle room in phrases like "similar cases should be treated similarly" to allow for arguments that believers and infidels, men and women, blacks and whites, gays and straights should be treated as relevantly *dis*similar. So there is room to argue that discrimination on the basis of such differences is *not* arbitrary. If we are going to exclude from the society of peoples societies in which infidel homosexuals are not permitted to engage in certain occupations, those societies can quite reasonably say that we are, in excluding them, appealing not to something universal, but to very recent developments in Europe and America.

I agree with Habermas when he says, "What Rawls in fact prejudges with the concept of an 'overlapping consensus' is the distinction between modern and premodern forms of consciousness, between 'reasonable' and 'dogmatic' world interpretations" (Habermas 1993, 95). But I disagree with Habermas, as I think Walzer also would, when he goes on to say that Rawls can defend the primacy of the right over the good with the concept of an overlapping consensus only if it is true that postmetaphysical worldviews that have become reflexive under modern conditions are epistemically superior to dogmatically fixed, fundamentalistic worldviews— indeed, only if such a distinction can be made with absolute clarity (95).

Habermas's point is that Rawls needs an argument from transculturally valid premises for the superiority of the liberal West. Without such an argument, he says, "the disqualification of 'unreasonable' doctrines that cannot be brought into harmony with the proposed 'political' concept of justice is inadmissible" (95).[5]

---

[5] Habermas is here commenting on Rawls's use of "reasonable" in writings earlier than "The Law of Peoples," since the latter appeared subsequent to Habermas's book. When I wrote the present paper, the exchange between Rawls and Habermas published in the *Journal of Philosophy* (see Rawls 1995) had not yet appeared. This exchange rarely touches on the question of historicism versus universalism. But one passage in which this question emerges explicitly is to be found on p. 179 of Rawls's "Reply to Habermas": "Justice as fairness is substantive . . . in the sense that it springs from and belongs to the tradition of liberal thought and the larger community of political culture of democratic societies. It fails then to be properly formal and truly universal, and thus to be part of the quasi-transcendental presuppositions (as Habermas sometimes says) established by the theory of communicative action."

Such passages make clear why Habermas and Walzer are at opposite poles. Walzer is taking for granted that there can be no such thing as a non-question -begging demonstration of the epistemic superiority of the Western idea of reasonableness. There is, for Walzer, no tribunal of trans-cultural reason before which to try the question of superiority. Walzer is presupposing what Habermas calls "a strong contextualism for which there is no single 'rationality.'" On this conception, Habermas continues, "in-dividual 'rationalities' are correlated with different cultures, worldviews, traditions, or forms of life. Each of them is viewed as internally interwoven with a particular understanding of the world" (95).

I think that Rawls's constructivist approach to the law of peoples can work if he adopts what Habermas calls a "strong contextualism." Doing so would mean giving up the attempt to escape historicism, as well as the attempt to supply a universalistic argument for the West's most recent views about which differences between persons are arbitrary. The strength of Walzer's *Thick and Thin* seems to me to be its explicitness about the need to do this. The weakness of Rawls's account of what he is doing lies in an ambiguity between two senses of universalism. When Rawls says that "a constructivist liberal doctrine is universal in its reach, once it is extended to . . . a law of peoples" (Rawls 1993b, 46), he is not saying that it is universal in its validity. Universal reach is a notion that sits well with constructivism, but universal validity is not. It is the latter that Habermas requires. That is why Habermas thinks that we need really heavy philo-sophical weaponry, modeled on Kant's—why he insists that only transcen-dental presuppositions of any possible communicative practice will do the job.[6] To be faithful to his own constructivism, I think, Rawls has to agree with Walzer that this job does not need to be done.

Rawls and Habermas often invoke, and Walzer almost never invokes, the notion of "reason." In Habermas, this notion is always bound up with that of context-free validity. In Rawls, things are more complicated. Rawls distinguishes the reasonable from the rational, using the latter to mean simply the sort of means-end rationality that is employed in engineering, or in working out a Hobbesian modus vivendi. But he often invokes a third notion, that of "practical reason," as when he says that the authority of a constructivist liberal doctrine "rests on the principles and conceptions of

---

[6] My own view is that we do not need, either in epistemology or in moral philosophy, the notion of universal validity. I argue for this in "Sind Aussagen Universelle Geltungsansprüche?" (see Rorty 2000). Habermas and Apel find my view paradoxical and likely to produce performative self-contradiction.

practical reason" (Rawls 1993b, 46). Rawls's use of this Kantian term may make it sound as if he agreed with Kant and Habermas that there is a universally distributed human faculty called practical reason (existing prior to, and working quite independently of, the recent history of the West), a faculty that tells us what counts as an arbitrary distinction between persons and what does not. Such a faculty would do the job Habermas thinks needs doing: detecting transcultural moral validity.

But this cannot, I think, be what Rawls intends. For he also says that his own constructivism differs from all philosophical views that appeal to a source of authority, and in which "the universality of the doctrine is the direct consequence of its source of authority" (Rawls 1993b, 45). As examples of sources of authority, he cites "(human) reason, or an independent realm of moral values, or some other proposed basis of universal validity" (45). So I think we have to construe his phrase "the principles and conceptions of practical reason" as referring to *whatever* principles and conceptions are in fact arrived at in the course of creating a community.

Rawls emphasizes that creating a community is not the same thing as working out a modus vivendi—a task which requires only means-end rationality, not practical reason. A principle or conception belongs to practical reason, in Rawls's sense, if it emerged in the course of people starting thick and getting thin, thereby developing an overlapping consensus and setting up a more inclusive moral community. It would not so belong if it had emerged under the threat of force. Practical reason for Rawls is, so to speak, a matter of procedure rather than of substance—of how we agree on what to do rather than of what we agree on.

This definition of practical reason suggests that there may be only a verbal difference between Rawls's and Habermas's positions. For Habermas's own attempt to substitute "communicative reason" for "subject-centered reason" is itself a move toward substituting "how" for "what." The first sort of reason is a source of truth, truth somehow coeval with the human mind. The second sort of reason is not a source of anything, but simply the activity of justifying claims by offering arguments rather than threats. Like Rawls, Habermas focuses on the difference between persuasion and force, rather than, as Plato and Kant did, on the difference between two parts of the human person—the good rational part and the dubious passionate or sensual part. Both would like to de-emphasize the notion of the *authority* of reason—the idea of reason as a faculty which issues decrees—and substitute the notion of rationality as what is present whenever people communicate, whenever they try to justify their claims to one another, rather than threatening each other.

The similarities between Rawls and Habermas seem even greater in the light of Rawls's endorsement of Thomas Scanlon's answer to the "fundamental question why anyone should care about morality at all," namely that "we have a basic desire to be able to justify our actions to others on grounds that they could not reasonably reject—reasonably, that is, given the desire to find principles that others similarly motivated could not reasonably reject" (Rawls 1993a, 49n). This suggests that the two philosophers might agree on the following claim: The only notion of rationality we need, at least in moral and social philosophy, is that of a situation in which people do not say "your own current interests dictate that you agree to our proposal," but rather "your own central beliefs, the ones which are central to your own moral identity, suggest that you should agree to our proposal."

This notion of rationality can be delimited using Walzer's terminology by saying that rationality is found wherever people envisage the possibility of getting from different thicks to the same thin. To appeal to interests rather than beliefs is to urge a modus vivendi. Such an appeal is exemplified by the speech of the Athenian ambassadors to the unfortunate Melians, as reported by Thucydides. To appeal to your enduring beliefs as well as to your current interests is to suggest that what gives you your *present* moral identity—your thick and resonant complex of beliefs—may make it possible for you to develop a new, supplementary, moral identity.[7] It is to suggest that what makes you loyal to a smaller group may give you reason to cooperate in constructing a larger group, a group to which you may in time become equally loyal or perhaps even more loyal. The difference between the absence and the presence of rationality, on this account, is the difference between a threat and an offer—the offer of a new moral identity and thus a new and larger loyalty, a loyalty to a group formed by an unforced agreement between smaller groups.

In the hope of minimizing the contrast between Habermas and Rawls still further, and of rapprochement between both and Walzer, I want to suggest a way of thinking of rationality that might help to resolve the problem I posed earlier: the problem of whether justice and loyalty are different sorts of things, or whether the demands of justice are simply the demands of a larger loyalty. I said that question seemed to boil down to the question of whether justice and loyalty had different sources—reason and sentiment, respectively. If the latter distinction disappears, the former one

---

[7] Walzer thinks it is a good idea for people to have lots of different moral identities. "[T]hick, divided selves are the characteristic products of, and in turn require, a thick, differentiated, and pluralistic society" (1994, 101).

will not seem particularly useful. But if by rationality we mean simply the sort of activity that Walzer thinks of as a thinning out process—the sort that, with luck, achieves the formulation and utilization of an overlapping consensus—then the idea that justice has a different source than loyalty no longer seems plausible.[8]

For, on this account of rationality, being rational and acquiring a larger loyalty are two descriptions of the same activity. This is because *any* unforced agreement between individuals and groups about what to do creates a form of community, and will, with luck, be the initial stage in expanding the circles of those whom each party to the agreement had previously taken to be "people like ourselves." The opposition between rational argument and fellow feeling thus begins to dissolve. For fellow feeling may, and often does, arise from the realization that the people whom one thought one might have to go to war with, use force on, are, in Rawls' sense, "reasonable." They are, it turns out, enough like us to see the point of compromising differences in order to live in peace, and of abiding by the agreement that has been hammered out. They are, to some degree at least, trustworthy.

From this point of view, Habermas's distinction between a strategic use of language and a genuinely communicative use of language begins to look like a difference between positions on a spectrum—a spectrum of degrees of trust. Baier's suggestion that we take trust rather than obligation to be our fundamental moral concept would thus produce a blurring of the line between rhetorical manipulation and genuine validity-seeking argument—a line that I think Habermas draws too sharply. If we cease to think of reason as a source of authority, and think of it simply as the process of reaching agreement by persuasion, then the standard Platonic and Kantian dichotomy of reason and feeling begins to fade away. That dichotomy can be replaced by a continuum of degrees of overlap of beliefs and desires.[9] When people whose beliefs and desires do not overlap very

---

[8] Note that in Rawls's semitechnical sense an overlapping consensus is not the result of discovering that various comprehensive views already share common doctrines, but rather something that might never have emerged had the proponents of these views not started trying to cooperate.

[9] Davidson has, I think, demonstrated that any two beings that use language to communicate with one another necessarily share an enormous number of beliefs and desires. He has thereby shown the incoherence of the idea that people can live in separate worlds created by differences in culture or status or fortune. There is always an immense overlap—an immense reserve army of common beliefs and desires to be drawn on at need. But this immense overlap does not, of course, prevent accusations of craziness or diabolical wickedness. For only a tiny amount of nonoverlap about certain particularly touchy subjects (the border between two territories, the name of the One True God) may lead to such accusations, and eventually to violence.

much disagree, they tend to think of each other as crazy or, more politely, as irrational. When there is considerable overlap, on the other hand, they may agree to differ and regard each other as the sort of people one can live with—and eventually, perhaps, the sort one can be friends with, intermarry with, and so on.[10]

To advise people to be rational is, on the view I am offering, simply to suggest that somewhere among their shared beliefs and desires there may be enough resources to permit agreement on how to coexist without violence. To conclude that someone is irredeemably *irr*ational is not to realize that she is not making proper use of her God-given faculties. It is rather to realize that she does not seem to share enough relevant beliefs and desires with us to make possible fruitful conversation about the issue in dispute. So, we reluctantly conclude, we have to give up on the attempt to get her to enlarge her moral identity, and settle for working out a modus vivendi— one which may involve the threat, or even the use, of force.

A stronger, more Kantian, notion of rationality would be invoked if one said that being rational guarantees a peaceful resolution of conflicts—that if people are willing to reason together long enough, what Habermas calls "the force of the better argument" will lead them to concur.[11] This stronger notion strikes me as pretty useless. I see no point in saying that it is more rational to prefer one's neighbors to one's family in the event of a nuclear holocaust, or more rational to prefer leveling off incomes around the world to preserving the institutions of liberal Western societies. To use the word "rational" to commend one's chosen solution to such dilemmas, or to use the term "yielding to the force of the better argument" to characterize one's way of making up one's mind, is to pay oneself an empty compliment.

More generally, the idea of "the better argument" makes sense only if one can identify a natural, transcultural relation of relevance, which connects propositions with one another so as to form something like Descartes's "natural order of reasons." Without such a natural order, one can only evaluate arguments by their efficacy in producing agreement among particular persons or groups. But the required notion of natural, intrinsic relevance—relevance dictated not by the needs of any given community but by human reason as such—seems no more plausible or useful than that of a God whose Will can be appealed to in order to resolve

---

[10] I owe this line of thought about how to reconcile Habermas and Baier to Mary Rorty.
[11] This notion of "the better argument" is central to Habermas's and Apel's understanding of rationality. I criticize it in the article cited above in note 6.

conflicts between communities. It is, I think, merely a secularized version of that earlier notion.

Non-Western societies in the past were rightly skeptical of Western conquerors who explained that they were invading in obedience to divine commands. More recently, they have been skeptical of Westerners who suggest that they should adopt Western ways in order to become more rational. (This suggestion has been abbreviated by Ian Hacking as "Me rational, you Jane.") On the account of rationality I am recommending, both forms of skepticism are equally justified. But this is not to deny that these societies *should* adopt recent Western ways by, for example, abandoning slavery, practicing religious toleration, educating women, permitting mixed marriages, tolerating homosexuality and conscientious objection to war, and so on. As a loyal Westerner, I think they should indeed do all these things. I agree with Rawls about what it takes to count as reasonable, and about what kind of societies we Westerners should accept as members of a global moral community.

But I think that the rhetoric we Westerners use in trying to get everyone to be more like us would be improved if we were more frankly ethnocentric, and less professedly universalist. It would be better to say: Here is what we in the West look like as a result of ceasing to hold slaves, beginning to educate women, separating church and state, and so on. Here is what happened after we started treating certain distinctions between people as arbitrary rather than fraught with moral significance. If you would try treating them that way, you might like the results. Saying that sort of thing seems preferable to saying: Look at how much better we are at knowing what differences between persons are arbitrary and which not—how much more *rational* we are.

If we Westerners could get rid of the notion of universal moral obligations created by membership in the species, and substitute the idea of building a community of trust between ourselves and others, we might be in a better position to persuade non-Westerners of the advantages of joining in that community. We might be better able to construct the sort of global moral community that Rawls describes in "The Law of Peoples." In making this suggestion, I am urging, as I have on earlier occasions, that we need to peel apart Enlightenment liberalism from Enlightenment rationalism.

I think that discarding the residual rationalism that we inherit from the Enlightenment is advisable for many reasons. Some of these are theoretical and of interest only to philosophy professors, such as the apparent incompatibility of the correspondence theory of truth with a naturalistic account of the origin of human minds.[12] Others are more practical. One practical reason is that getting rid of rationalistic rhetoric would permit the West to approach the non-West in the role of someone with an instructive story to tell, rather than in the role of someone purporting to be making better use of a universal human capacity.

Works Cited

Habermas, Jürgen. 1993. *Justification and Application: Remarks on Discourse Ethics*. Cambridge: MIT Press.

Luttwak, Edward. 1993. *The Endangered American Dream*. New York: Simon & Schuster.

Rawls, John. 1993a. *Political Liberalism*. New York: Columbia University Press.

———. 1993b. "The Law of Peoples." In *On Human Rights: The Oxford Amnesty Lectures*, edited by Stephen Shute and Susan Hurley, 41–82. New York: Basic Books.

———. 1995. "Reply to Habermas." *Journal of Philosophy* 92(3): 132–180.

Rorty, Richard. 1991. *Objectivity, Relativism and Truth: Philosophical Papers*, Vol. 1. Cambridge: Cambridge University Press.

———. 1994. "Does Academic Freedom Have Philosophical Presuppositions?" *Academe* 80(6): 52–63.

———. 2000. "Universality and Truth." In *Rorty and His Critics*, edited by Robert B. Brandom, 1–30. Malden, MA: Blackwell Publishers. An earlier, abridged version appeared as "Sind Aussagen Universelle Geltungsansprüche?" *Deutsche Zeitschrift für Philosophie* 42(6) (1994): 975–988.

Searle, John. 1992. "Rationality and Realism: What Difference Does It Make?" *Daedalus* 122(4): 55–84.

Walzer, Michael. 1994. *Think and Thin: Moral Argument at Home and Abroad*. Notre Dame, IN: Notre Dame University Press.

---

[12] For a claim that such a theory of truth is essential to "the Western Rationalist Tradition," see Searle 1992. See also my reply to Searle (Rorty 1994b, 52–63). I argue there that we should be better off without the notion of "getting something right," and that writers such as Dewey and Davidson have shown us how to keep the benefits of Western rationalism without the philosophical hang-ups caused by the attempt to explicate this notion.

CHAPTER 2 | Abnormal Justice

NANCY FRASER

IN SOME CONTEXTS, PUBLIC debates about justice assume the guise of normal discourse.[1] However fiercely they disagree about what exactly justice requires in a given case, the contestants share some underlying presuppositions about what an intelligible justice claim looks like. These include ontological assumptions about the kind(s) of actors who are entitled to make such claims (usually individuals) and about the kind of agency from which they should seek redress (typically a territorial state). Also included are assumptions about scope, which fix the circle of interlocutors to whom claims for justice should be addressed (usually the citizenry of a bounded political community) and which delimit the universe of those whose interests and concerns deserve consideration (ditto). Finally, the disputants share social-theoretical assumptions about the space in which questions of justice can intelligibly arise (often the economic space of distribution) and about the social cleavages that can harbor injustices (typically class and ethnicity). In such contexts, where those who argue about justice share a set of underlying assumptions, their contests assume a relatively regular, recognizable shape. Constituted through a set of organizing principles

---

[1] In memory of Richard Rorty, an inspiration in more ways than one.

This essay was begun during my fellowship year at the Wissenschaftskolleg zu Berlin, whose support 1gratefully acknowledge. Discussions there and at other venues where I presented this work greatly helped me refine its argument. For especially insightful responses, I am indebted to Horst Bredekamp, Vincent Descombes, Rainer Forst, Robert Goodin, Kimberly Hutchings, Will Kymlicka, Maria Pia Lara, Jane Mansbridge, Faviola Rivera-Castro, Gabriel Rockhill, Nancy Rosenblum, Philippe van Parijs, Ann Laura Stoler, Eli Zaretsky, W. J. T. Mitchell, and the *Critical Inquiry* editorial collective.

and manifesting a discernible grammar, such conflicts take the form of "normal justice."[2]

Of course, it is doubtful that justice discourse is ever fully normal in the sense just described. There may well be no real-world context in which public debates about justice remain wholly within the bounds set by a given set of constitutive assumptions. And we may never encounter a case in which every participant shares every assumption. Whenever a situation approaching normality does appear, moreover, one may well suspect that it rests on the suppression or marginalization of those who dissent from the reigning consensus.

Nevertheless, and notwithstanding these caveats, we may still speak of normal justice in a meaningful sense. By analogy with Thomas Kuhn's (1996) understanding of normal science, justice discourse is normal just as long as public dissent from and disobedience to its constitutive assumptions remains contained. As long as deviations remain private or appear as anomalies, as long as they do not cumulate and destructure the discourse, the field of public-sphere conflicts over justice retains a recognizable, hence a "normal," shape.

By this standard, the present context is one of "abnormal justice."[3] Even as public debates about justice proliferate, they increasingly lack the structured character of normal discourse. Today's disputants often lack any shared understanding of what the authors of justice claims should look like, as some countenance groups and communities, while others admit only individuals. Likewise, those who argue about justice today often share no view of the agency of redress, as some envision new transnational or cosmopolitan institutions, while others restrict their appeals to territorial states. Often, too, the disputants hold divergent views of the proper circle of interlocutors, as some address their claims to international public opinion, while others would confine discussion within bounded polities. In addition, present-day contestants often disagree about who is entitled to consideration in matters of justice, as some accord standing to all human

---

[2] One aspect of my debt to Richard Rorty will be obvious here: my appropriation of his distinction between normal and abnormal discourse. What may be less evident is the larger inspiration he provided. By his example, Rorty emboldened an entire generation of American philosophers to refuse the intimidation of professional analytic philosophy, which had seemed so overwhelming and crippling in graduate school. It was from *Philosophy and the Mirror of Nature* that I gleaned the courage to chart my own path in philosophy, to write in my own voice about what I consider truly important. I cannot thank him enough for that.

[3] If one were to be strictly faithful to Kuhn, one would speak here of "revolutionary justice." But, given that expression's associations, I prefer to take my cue from Rorty and speak instead of "abnormal justice." Rorty distinguishes normal from abnormal discourse in Rorty 1979 and 1989.

beings, while others restrict concern to their fellow citizens. Then, too, they frequently disagree about the conceptual space within which claims for justice can arise, as some admit only (economic) claims for redistribution, while others would admit (cultural) claims for recognition and (political) claims for representation. Finally, today's disputants often disagree as to which social cleavages can harbor injustices, as some admit only nationality and class, while others accept gender and sexuality.

The result is that current debates about justice have a freewheeling character. Absent the ordering force of shared presuppositions, they lack the structured shape of normal discourse. This is patently true for informal contests over justice in civil society, where it has always been possible in principle to problematize *doxa*—witness the affair of the Danish cartoons, which is better grasped as a species of abnormal discourse about justice than as a dash of civilizations, on the one hand, or as an exercise in liberal public reason, on the other. But abnormality also swirls around institutionalized arenas of argument, such as courts and arbitration bodies, whose principal raison d'être is to normalize justice; witness the dispute among the justices of the US Supreme Court in a recent death penalty case over whether it is proper to cite opinions of foreign courts. As such contests over basic premises proliferate, deviation becomes less the exception than the rule. Far from appearing in the guise of anomalies within a relatively stable field of argument, abnormality invades the central precincts of justice discourse. No sooner do first-order disputes arise than they become overlaid with metadisputes over constitutive assumptions concerning who counts and what is at stake. Not only substantive questions, but also the grammar of justice itself, are up for grabs.

This situation is by no means unprecedented. Even the most cursory reflection suggests some historical parallels. One prior era of abnormal justice in Europe is the period leading up to the Treaty of Westphalia, when the feudal political imaginary was unraveling, but the system of territorial states had not yet been consolidated.[4] Another is the period following World War I, when nascent internationalisms collided with resurgent nationalisms amidst the ruins of three major empires.[5] In those cases, absent a secure and settled hegemony, competing paradigms clashed, and efforts to normalize justice did not succeed. Such cases are scarcely exceptional. It is likely, in fact, that normal justice is historically abnormal, while abnormal justice represents the historical norm.

---

[4] See Ruggie 1993.
[5] See Arendt 1973.

Nevertheless, today's abnormalities are historically specific, reflecting recent developments, including the breakup of the Cold War order, contested US hegemony, the rise of neoliberalism, and the new salience of globalization. Under these conditions, established paradigms tend to unsettle, and claims for justice easily become unmoored from, preexisting islands of normalcy. This is the case for each of three major families of justice claims: claims for socioeconomic redistribution, claims for legal or cultural recognition, and claims for political representation. Thus, in the wake of transnationalized production, globalized finance, and neoliberal trade and investment regimes, redistribution claims increasingly trespass the bounds of state-centered grammars and arenas of argument. Likewise, given transnational migration and global media flows, the claims for recognition of once-distant others acquire a new proximity, destabilizing horizons of cultural value that were previously taken for granted. Finally, in an era of contested superpower hegemony, global governance, and transnational politics, claims for representation increasingly break the previous frame of the modern territorial state. In this situation of denormalization, justice claims immediately run up against counterclaims whose underlying assumptions they do not share. Whether the issue is redistribution, recognition, or representation, current disputes evince a heteroglossia of justice discourse, which lacks any semblance of normality.

In this situation, our familiar theories of justice offer little guidance. Formulated for contexts of normal justice, they focus largely on first-order questions. What constitutes a just distribution of wealth and resources? What counts as reciprocal recognition or equal respect? What constitutes fair terms of political representation and equal voice? Premised upon a shared grammar, these theories do not tell us how to proceed when we encounter conflicting assumptions concerning moral standing, social cleavage, and agency of redress. Thus, they fail to provide the conceptual resources for dealing with problems of abnormal justice, so characteristic of the present era.

What sort of theory of justice could provide guidance in this situation? What type of theorizing could handle cases in which first-order disputes about justice are overlaid with metadisputes about what counts as an intelligible first-order claim? In this chapter, I shall suggest a way of approaching questions of (in)justice in abnormal times. What I have to say divides into three parts. First, I shall identify three nodes of abnormality in contemporary disputes about justice. Then, I shall formulate three corresponding conceptual strategies for clarifying these abnormalities. Finally,

I shall consider some implications for the theory and practice of struggles against injustice in abnormal times.

Nodes of Abnormality in a Globalizing World

I begin by sketching a recent dispute over social justice. Claiming to promote justice for workers at home and abroad, labor unions in developed countries seek to block imports whose production conditions do not meet domestic environmental, health, and safety standards. Organizations representing workers in the developing world object that, in imposing standards they cannot possibly meet at the present time, this seemingly progressive approach is actually a species of unjust protectionism. Debated in both domestic and transnational public spheres, the first position finds support among those who advocate the pursuit of justice through democratic politics at the level of the territorial state, while the second is championed both by proponents of global justice and by free marketeers. Meanwhile, corporations and states dispute related issues in international legal arenas. For example, a North American Free Trade Agreement arbitration panel hears arguments from a US-based multinational, which contends that Canada's relatively stringent environmental and labor laws constitute an illegal restraint on trade. The US representative on the three-judge panel finds for the corporation, on free-trade grounds. The Canadian representative finds against, invoking the self-government rights of the Canadian citizenry. The Mexican representative casts the deciding vote; finding for the corporation, and thus siding with the United States, he invokes poor nations' right to development. At the same time, however, the legitimacy of these proceedings is disputed. In transnational civil society, demonstrators protest against NAFTA, the World Trade Organization, and other governance structures of the global economy. Pronouncing these structures unjust and undemocratic, activists meeting at the World Social Forum debate the contours of an alternative globalization from below.

This is an example of abnormal justice. Traversing multiple discursive arenas—some formal, some informal, some mainstream, some subaltern—the locus of argument shifts with dizzying speed. And far from going without saying, the topography of debate is itself an object of dispute. Offshore contestants strive to pierce the bounds of domestic debates, even as nationalists and country-level democrats seek to territorialize them. Meanwhile, states and corporations work to contain disputes within regional juridical institutions, even as transnational social movements strain to widen them.

Thus, the very shape of controversy, uncontested in normal discourse, is here a focus of explicit struggle. Even as they dispute substantive issues, then, the contestants also rehearse deep disagreements about who is entitled to address claims to whom concerning what; about where and how such claims should be vetted; and about who is obliged to redress them, if and when they are vindicated.

The abnormalities are not wholly random, however, as they constellate around three principal nodes. The first node reflects the absence of a shared view of the "what" of justice. At issue here is the matter of justice, the substance with which it is concerned. Given that justice is a comparative relation, what is it that justice compares? What social-ontological presuppositions distinguish well-formed from ill-formed claims? Such matters go without saying in normal justice—as, for example, when all parties conceive justice in distributive terms, as concerned with the allocation of divisible goods, which are typically economic in nature. In abnormal contexts, by contrast, the "what" of justice is in dispute. Here we encounter claims that do not share a common ontology. Where one party perceives distributive injustice, another sees status hierarchy, and still another political domination. Thus, even those who agree that the status quo is unjust disagree as to how to describe it.

Divergent assumptions concerning the "what" suffuse the example just sketched. There, offshore workers' economic claims, aimed at dismantling protectionist barriers, which maintain distributive injustice, collide with a territorial citizenry's political claims, aimed at repulsing neoliberal encroachments, which imperil the democratic sovereignty of a bounded polity. The effect is a bewildering lack of consensus, even among professed democrats and egalitarians, as to how to understand the injustice, let alone how to redress it. The very "what" of justice is up for grabs.

A second node of abnormality reflects the lack of a shared understanding of the "who" of justice. At issue here is the scope of justice, the frame within which it applies. Who counts as a subject of justice in a given matter? Whose interests and needs deserve consideration? Who belongs to the circle of those entitled to equal concern? Such matters go without saying in normal justice—as, for example, when all parties frame their disputes as matters internal to territorial states, thereby equating the "who" of justice with the citizenry of a bounded polity. In abnormal justice, by contrast, the "who" is up for grabs. Here we encounter conflicting framings of justice disputes. Where one party frames the question in terms of a domestic, territorial "who," others posit "whos" that are regional, transnational, or global.

Divergent assumptions about these matters, too, pervade the example just sketched, which encompasses conflicting frames. There, some of the disputants evaluate Canadian labor regulations in terms of their domestic effects, while others consider the effects on the larger North American region, and still others look further afield to the interests of workers in the developing world or of global humanity. The result is a lack of consensus as to who counts. Not just the "what" of justice but also the "who" is in dispute.

The third node of abnormality reflects the lack of a shared understanding of the "how" of justice. Here the issue is in essence procedural. *How*, in a given case, should one determine the pertinent grammar for reflecting on justice? By which criteria or decision procedure should one resolve disputes about the "what" and the "who"? In normal justice, such questions do not arise by definition, as the "what" and the "who" are not in dispute. In abnormal contexts, by contrast, with both those parameters up for grabs, disagreements about the "how" are bound to erupt. Here we encounter conflicting scenarios for resolving disputes. Where one party invokes the authority of an interstate treaty, others appeal to the United Nations, the balance of power, or the institutionalized procedures of a cosmopolitan democracy that remains to be invented.

Uncertainty about the "how" suffuses the example just sketched. There, states and corporations look to NAFTA for resolution, while antineoliberalism activists look to transnational popular struggle aimed at influencing global public opinion. Whereas the former appeal to a treaty-based regional arena of dispute resolution, the latter appeal to a "World Social Forum" that lacks institutionalized authority to make and enforce binding decisions. Here, then, there is no agreement as to how disputes about the grammar of justice should be resolved. Not just the "what" and the "who," but also the "how" of justice is up for grabs.

Together, these three nodes of abnormality reflect the destabilization of the previous hegemonic grammar. Today's uncertainty about the "what" reflects the decentering of that grammar's definition of the substance of justice. What has been problematized here is the view that identifies justice exclusively with fair economic distribution. That understanding organized the lion's share of argument in the decades following World War II. Subtending the otherwise disparate political cultures of First World social democracy, Second World communism, and Third World developmentalism, the distributive interpretation of the "what" tended to marginalize noneconomic wrongs. Casting maldistribution as the quintessential injustice, it obscured injustices of misrecognition, rooted in hierarchies of status, as well as injustices of misrepresentation, rooted in the political constitution of society.

Analogously, today's uncertainty about the "who" reflects the destabilization of the previous grammar's frame. In this case, what has been problematized is the Westphalian view that the modem territorial state is the sole unit within which justice applies. That view framed most justice discourse in the postwar era. In conjunction with the distributive conception, it organized otherwise disparate political cultures throughout the world, notwithstanding lip service to human rights, proletarian internationalism, and Third World solidarity.[6] Effectively territorializing justice, the Westphalian frame equated the scope of concern with the citizenry of a bounded political community. The effect was to drastically limit, if not wholly to exclude, binding obligations of justice that cut across borders. Constructing a set of territorially bounded domestic "whos," discrete and arrayed side by side, this frame obscured transborder injustices.

Finally, today's uncertainty concerning the "how" reflects the new salience of a previously unspoken feature of the postwar grammar. What has become visible, and therefore contestable, is a hidden hegemonic assumption. As long as the lion's share of justice discourse was governed by Westphalian-distributivist assumptions, there was little overtly perceived need for institutions and procedures for resolving disputes about the "what" and the "who." On those occasions when such a need was perceived, it was assumed that powerful states and private elites would resolve those disputes, in intergovernmental organizations or smoke-filled back rooms. The effect was to discourage open democratic contestation of the "what" and the "who."

Today, however, none of these three normalizing assumptions goes without saying. The hegemony of the distributive "what" has been challenged from at least two sides: first, by diverse practitioners of the politics of recognition, ranging from multiculturalists who seek to accommodate differences to ethnonationalists who seek to eliminate them; and, second, by diverse practitioners of the politics of representation, ranging from

---

[6] Some readers have suggested that colonized people never accepted the legitimacy of the Westphalian frame, hence that this frame was never truly normalized. In my view, however, the great majority of anticolonialists in the post–World War II era sought to achieve independent Westphalian states of their own. In contrast, only a small minority consistently championed justice within a global frame—for reasons that are entirely understandable. My claim, then, is that, far from contesting the Westphalian frame per se, anti-imperialist forces generally sought rather to realize it in a genuinely universal, evenhanded way. Thanks to Ann Laura Stoler for forcefully raising this issue, although she will not be satisfied with my answer.

feminists campaigning for gender quotas on electoral lists to national minorities demanding power-sharing arrangements. As a result, there are now in play at least three rival conceptions of the "what" of justice: redistribution, recognition, and representation.

Meanwhile, the hegemony of the Westphalian "who" has been challenged from at least three directions: first, by localists and communalists, who seek to locate the scope of concern in subnational units; second, by regionalists and transnationalists, who propose to identify the "who" of justice with larger, though not fully universal, units, such as Europe or Islam; and, third, by globalists and cosmopolitans, who propose to accord equal consideration to all human beings. Consequently, there are now in play at least four rival views of the "who" of justice: Westphalian, local-communalist, transnational-regional, and global-cosmopolitan.

Finally, the silent sway of the hegemonic "how" has been challenged by a general rise in democratic expectations, as mobilized movements of all these kinds demand a say about the "what" and the "who." Contesting hegemonic institutions and frames, such movements have effectively challenged the prerogative of states and elites to determine the grammar of justice. Inciting broad debates about the "what" and the "who," they have put in play, alongside the hegemonic presumption, populist and democratic views of the "how" of justice.

The appearance of rival views of the "what," the "who," and the "how" poses a major problem for anyone who cares about injustice today. Somehow, we must work through these metadisputes without losing sight of pressing problems of first-order justice. But, with all three parameters in play simultaneously, we have no firm ground on which to stand. Abnormality confronts us at every turn.

Strategies for Theorizing Justice in Abnormal Times

What sort of theory of justice could provide guidance in this situation? To find a convincing answer, one must start with a balanced view of the matter at hand. The key, I think, is to appreciate both the positive and negative sides of abnormal justice. The positive side is an expansion of the field of contestation, hence the chance to challenge injustices that the previous grammar elided. For example, the decentering of the distributive "what" renders visible, and criticizable, noneconomic harms of misrecognition and misrepresentation. Likewise, the denormalization of the Westphalian "who" makes conceivable a hitherto obscure type of metainjustice, call it misframing, in which first-order questions of justice are unjustly framed—as when the national framing of distributive issues forecloses the claims of the global poor. If we assume, as I think we should, that misrecognition, misrepresentation, and misframing belong in principle in the catalog of genuine injustices, then the destabilization of a grammar that obscured them must rank as a positive development. Here, then, is the good side of abnormal justice: expanded possibilities for contesting injustice.

But abnormal justice also has a negative side. The problem is that expanded contestation cannot by itself overcome injustice. Overcoming injustice requires at least two additional conditions: first, a relatively stable framework in which claims can be equitably vetted and, second, institutionalized agencies and means of redress. Both these conditions are absent in abnormal justice. How can demands be fairly evaluated and injustices be legitimately rectified in contexts in which the "what," the "who," and the "how" are in dispute? Here then is the negative side of abnormal justice: amidst expanded contestation, reduced means for corroborating and redressing injustice.

Those who would theorize justice in abnormal times must keep both sides of this equation in view. What sort of theorizing could simultaneously valorize expanded contestation and strengthen diminished capacities of adjudication and redress? Without pretending to present a full answer, I propose to hunt for clues by reexamining the three nodes of abnormality just described. Considered in turn, each can tell us something important about how to think about justice in abnormal times.

The "What" of Justice: Participatory Parity in Three Dimensions

Consider, first, the problem of the "what." Here, the question is: what sort of approach can validate contestation of reductive distributivism while also clarifying prospects for resolving disputes that encompass rival understandings of the matter of justice? The short answer is an approach that combines a multidimensional social ontology with normative monism. Let me explain.

In order to validate expanded contestation, a theory of justice must hold out the prospect of a fair hearing for disputants' claims. If it is to avoid foreclosing demands in advance, the theory must be able to entertain claims that presuppose nonstandard views of the "what" of justice. Erring on the side of inclusiveness, then, it should begin by assuming that injustice comes in more than one form and that no single view of the "what" can capture them all. Rejecting social-ontological monism, it should conceive justice as encompassing multiple dimensions, each of which is associated with an analytically distinct genre of injustice and revealed through a conceptually distinct type of social struggle.

Consider three possibilities I have already alluded to. As seen, first, from the standpoint of labor struggles, justice comprises an economic dimension, rooted in political economy, whose associated injustice is *maldistribution* or class inequality. As seen, in contrast, from the perspective of struggles over multiculturalism, justice encompasses a cultural dimension, rooted in the status order, whose corresponding injustice is *misrecognition* or status hierarchy. As seen, finally, through the lens of democratization struggles, justice includes a political dimension, rooted in the political constitution of society, whose associated injustice is *misrepresentation* or political voicelessness.

Here, then, are three different views of the "what" of justice. Insofar as each of them corresponds to a bona fide form of injustice that cannot be reduced to the others, none can be legitimately excluded from contemporary theorizing. Thus, ontological monism with respect to injustice is deeply misguided.[7] Contra those who insist on a single monistic account of the "what," justice is better viewed as a multidimensional concept that encompasses the three dimensions of *redistribution, recognition*, and *representation*.[8] Such a conception is especially useful in abnormal times. Only by assuming at the outset that claims in all three dimensions are in principle intelligible can one provide a fair hearing to all claimants in disputes that harbor multiple views of the "what."

But why only three? The examples just given suggest that, rather than being given all at once, the dimensions of justice are disclosed historically, through the medium of social struggle. On this view, social movements disclose new dimensions of justice when they succeed in establishing as plausible claims that transgress the established grammar of normal justice, which will appear retrospectively to have obscured the disadvantage their members suffer. But, in the moment before a novel understanding of the "what" becomes broadly intelligible, the irruption of transgressive claims sparks abnormal discourse.[9] At such times, it remains unclear whether a new dimension of justice is being disclosed. It follows that any attempt

---

[7] Two examples, from opposite ends of the philosophical spectrum, are Dworkin (1981) and Honneth (2003). Dworkin maintains that all injustices reduce in the end to resource maldistribution, while Honneth holds that all are at bottom variants of misrecognition. For critiques of Dworkin and Honneth, see Anderson 1999 and Fraser 2003b, respectively.

[8] For a fuller elaboration and defense of this view, see Fraser 2003a.

[9] For an account of second-wave feminism along these lines, see Rorty 1991.

to theorize justice in these conditions must allow for that possibility. Whoever dogmatically forecloses the prospect declares his or her thinking inadequate to the times.

What follows for a theory of justice for abnormal times? At the outset, one should practice hermeneutical charity with respect to claimants' non-standard views of the "what," according them the presumption of intelligibility and potential validity. At the same time, the theory should test such views by considering whether they do in fact render visible genuine forms of injustice that the previous grammar foreclosed and, if so, whether these newly disclosed forms are rooted in hitherto overlooked dimensions of social ordering. In today's context, this means accepting as well-formed and intelligible in principle claims premised on at least three distinct views of the "what" of justice: redistribution, recognition, and representation. Provisionally embracing a three-dimensional view of justice, centered on economy, culture, and politics, the theory should nevertheless remain open to the disclosure of further dimensions through social struggle.

By itself, however, a multidimensional social ontology is not a solution. As soon as we admit multiple genres of injustice, we need a way to bring them under a common measure. Thus, we need a normative principle that overarches them all. Absent such a commensurating principle, we have no way to evaluate claims across different dimensions, hence no way to process disputes that encompass multiple views of the "what."

What might such a principle look like? My proposal is to submit claims in all three dimensions to the overarching normative principle of *parity of participation*. According to this principle, justice requires social arrangements that permit all to participate as peers in social life.[10] On the view of justice as participatory parity, overcoming injustice means dismantling institutionalized obstacles that prevent some people from participating on a par with others, as full partners in social interaction. As the forgoing discussion suggests, such obstacles can be of at least three types. First, people can be impeded from full participation by economic structures that deny them the resources they need in order to interact with others as peers; in that case they suffer from distributive injustice or maldistribution. Second, people can be prevented from interacting on terms of parity by institutionalized hierarchies of cultural value that deny them the requisite standing; in that case they suffer from status inequality or misrecognition.[11] Third,

---

[10] I have elaborated and defended this principle in Fraser 2003a.
[11] This *status model* of recognition represents an alternative to the standard *identity model*. For a critique of the latter and a defense of the former, see Fraser 2000.

people can be impeded from full participation by decision rules that deny them equal voice in public deliberations and democratic decision-making; in that case they suffer from political injustice or misrepresentation.[12]

Here, then, is an account in which three different types of injustice lead to a common result: in each case, some social actors are prevented from participating on a par with others in social interaction. Thus, all three injustices violate a single principle, the principle of participatory parity. That principle overarches the three dimensions and serves to make them commensurable.

The exact details of this account are less important than its overall conceptual structure. What is paramount here is that this view of the "what" of justice combines a multidimensional social ontology with normative monism. As a result, it reckons with both sides of abnormal justice, the negative as well as the positive. Thanks to its ontological multidimensionality, it validates contestation of normalizing distributivism. Stipulating that misrecognition and misrepresentation are genuine injustices in principle, it provides a fair hearing for claims that transgress the previous grammar. At the same time, thanks to its normative monism, this approach brings the three genres of injustice under a common measure. Submitting claims for redistribution, recognition, and representation to the overarching principle of participatory parity, it creates a single discursive space that can accommodate them all. Thus, this approach offers the prospect of evaluating claims under conditions of abnormal discourse, where multiple views of the "what" of justice are in play.

And yet a major question remains. Parity of participation *among whom*? *Who* exactly is entitled to participate on a par *with whom* in *which* social interactions? Unless we can find a suitable way of addressing the "who" of justice, this approach to the "what" will not be of any use.

The "Who" of Justice: Misframing and Subjection

I turn, accordingly, to the second node of abnormal justice, concerning the "who." For this issue, too, the pressing need is to reckon with both the positive and negative sides of abnormal justice. What sort of theorizing can valorize contestation of the Westphalian frame while also clarifying disputes that encompass conflicting views about who counts? The short

---

[12] In the first case, the problem arises from the economic structure of society, which corresponds to the economic dimension of justice. In the second case, the problem is the status order, which corresponds to the cultural dimension. In the third case, the problem is the constitution of the political system, which corresponds to the political dimension of justice.

answer is theorizing that is simultaneously reflexive and determinative. Let me explain.

In order to valorize expanded contestation, reflection on abnormal justice must be open to claims that first-order questions of justice have been wrongly framed. To ensure that such claims receive a fair hearing, one should assume at the outset that injustices of misframing could exist in principle. Thus, the theorizing of abnormal justice must be reflexive. In order to apply the principle of participatory parity to first-order questions of distribution, recognition, and representation, one must be able to jump to the next level, where the frame itself is in dispute. Only by becoming reflexive can one grasp the question of the "who" as a question of justice.

How can one generate the reflexivity needed in abnormal justice? The strategy I propose draws on a distinctive conception of the political dimension. So far, I have considered this dimension in the usual way, as concerned exclusively with injustices of *ordinary-political misrepresentation*. These are political injustices that arise within a political community whose boundaries and membership are widely assumed to be settled. Thus, ordinary-political misrepresentation occurs when a polity's rules for decision-making deny some who are counted in principle as members the chance to participate fully, as peers. Recently, such injustices have given rise to demands for changes in the mode of ordinary-political representation—ranging from demands for gender quotas on electoral lists, multicultural rights, indigenous self-government, and provincial autonomy, on the one hand, to demands for campaign finance reform, redistricting, proportional representation, and cumulative voting, on the other.

Important as such matters are, they make up only half the story. In addition to ordinary-political injustice, which arises *within* the frame of a bounded polity, we can also conceptualize another level, call it *metapolitical injustice*, which arises as a result of the division of political space into bounded polities. This second level comprehends injustices of *misframing*. Such injustices occur when a polity's boundaries are drawn in such a way as to wrongly deny some people the chance to participate at all in its authorized contests over justice. In such cases, those who are constituted as nonmembers are wrongly excluded from the universe of those entitled to consideration within the polity in matters of distribution, recognition, and ordinary-political representation. The injustice remains, moreover, even when those excluded from one polity are included as subjects of justice in another—as long as the effect of the political division is to put some relevant aspects of justice beyond their reach. An example is the way in which the international system of supposedly equal sovereign states gerrymanders political space at the expense of the global poor.

Although the term itself isn't used, the notion of misframing implicitly informs the claims of many "alternative globalization" activists associated with the World Social Forum. In their eyes, the Westphalian frame is unjust, as it partitions political space in ways that block many who are poor and despised from challenging the forces that oppress them. Channeling their claims into the domestic political spaces of relatively powerless, if not wholly failed, states, this frame insulates offshore powers from critique and control. Among those shielded from the reach of justice are more powerful predator states and transnational private powers, including foreign investors and creditors, international currency speculators, and transnational corporations. Also protected are the governance structures of the global economy, which set exploitative terms of interaction and then exempt them from democratic control. Finally, the Westphalian frame is self-insulating, as the architecture of the interstate system excludes transnational democratic decision-making on issues of justice.

Such, at any rate, are the claims of some World Social Forum activists. Their concerns pertain to our second level of justice, the metapolitical level, which encompasses wrongs of misframing. Oriented to the possibility that first-order framings of justice may themselves be unjust, this level grasps the question of the frame *as* a question of justice. As a result, it provides the reflexivity needed to parse disputes about the "who" in abnormal justice.

By itself, however, reflexivity is not a solution. As soon as we accept that injustices of misframing can exist in principle, we require some means of deciding when and where they exist in reality. Thus, a theory of justice for abnormal times requires a determinative normative principle for evaluating frames. Absent such a determinative principle, we have no way to assess the alternatives, hence no way to clarify disputes that encompass conflicting understandings of the "who."

What might a determinative principle for evaluating frames look like? Currently, there are three major candidates on offer. Proponents of the *membership principle* propose to resolve disputes concerning the "who" by appealing to criteria of political belonging. For them, accordingly, what turns a collection of individuals into fellow subjects of justice is shared citizenship or shared nationality.[13] Because this approach delimits frames on

---

[13] For the citizenship variant of the membership principle, see Rawls 1999; Kymlicka 2001; and Nagel 2005. For the nationality variant, see Miller 1995, esp. chap. 3.

the basis of political membership, it has the advantage of being grounded in existing institutional reality and/or in widely held collective identifications. Yet that strength is also its weakness. In practice, the membership principle serves all too easily to ratify the exclusionary nationalisms of the privileged and powerful—hence to shield established frames from critical scrutiny.

No wonder, then, that some philosophers and activists look instead to the *principle of humanism*. Seeking a more inclusive standard, they propose to resolve disputes concerning the "who" by appealing to criteria of personhood. For them, accordingly, what turns a collection of individuals into fellow subjects of justice is common possession of distinguishing features of humanity, such as autonomy, rationality, language use, capacity to form and pursue an idea of the good, or vulnerability to moral injury. Because this approach delimits frames on the basis of personhood, it provides a critical check on exclusionary nationalism. Yet its lofty abstraction is also its weakness. Cavalierly oblivious to actual or historical social relations, it accords standing indiscriminately to everyone in respect to everything. Adopting the one-size-fits-all frame of global humanity, it forecloses the possibility that different issues require different frames or scales of justice.

Understandably, then, yet another group of philosophers and activists rejects both the exclusionary nationalism of membership and the abstract globalism of humanism. Aiming to conceptualize transnational justice, proponents of the *all-affected principle* propose to resolve disputes about the "who" by appealing to social relations of interdependence. For them, accordingly, what makes a group of people fellow subjects of justice is their objective coimbrication in a web of causal relationships. This approach has the merit of providing a critical check on self-serving notions of membership, while also taking cognizance of social relations. Yet by conceiving relations objectivistically, in terms of causality, it effectively relegates the choice of the "who" to mainstream social science. In addition, the all-affected principle falls prey to the reductio ad absurdum of the butterfly effect, which holds that everyone is affected by everything. Unable to identify *morally relevant* social relations, it has trouble resisting the one-size-fits-all globalism it sought to avoid. Thus, it too fails to supply a defensible standard for determining the "who" in abnormal times.

Given the respective deficiencies of membership, humanism, and affectedness, what sort of determinative principle can help us evaluate rival frames in abnormal justice? I propose to submit allegations of misframing to what I shall call the *all-subjected principle*. According to this principle, all those who are subject to a given governance structure have moral standing as subjects of justice in relation to it. On this view, what turns a collection of people into fellow subjects of justice is neither shared citizenship or nationality, nor common possession of abstract personhood, nor the sheer fact of causal interdependence, but rather their joint subjection to a structure of governance, which sets the ground rules that govern their interaction. For any such governance structure, the all-subjected principle matches the scope of moral concern to that of subjection.[14]

Of course, everything depends on how we interpret the phrase "subjection to a structure of governance." I understand this expression broadly, as encompassing relations to powers of various types. Not restricted to states, governance structures also comprise nonstate agencies that generate enforceable rules that structure important swaths of social interaction. The most obvious examples are the agencies that set the ground rules of the global economy, such as the World Trade Organization and the International Monetary Fund. But many other examples could also be cited, including transnational agencies governing environmental regulation, atomic and nuclear power, policing, security, health, intellectual property, and the administration of civil and criminal law. Insofar as such agencies regulate the interaction of large transnational populations, they can be said to subject the latter, even though the rule-makers are not accountable to those whom they govern. Given this broad understanding of governance structures, the term *subjection* should be understood broadly as well. Not restricted to formal citizenship or even to the broader condition of falling within the jurisdiction of a state, this notion also encompasses the further condition of being subject to the coercive power of nonstate and transstate forms of governmentality.

Understood in this way, the all-subjected principle affords a critical standard for assessing the justice of frames. An issue is justly framed if and only if everyone subjected to the governance structure(s) that regulate the relevant swath(s) of social interaction is accorded equal consideration. To deserve such consideration, moreover, one need not already be an officially accredited member of the structure in question; one need only be subjected to it. Thus, sub-Saharan Africans who have been involuntarily disconnected from the global economy as a result of the rules imposed by its governance structures count as subjects of justice in relation to it, even if they are not officially recognized as participating in it.[15]

---

[14] The expression "all-subjected principle" is my own, but the idea can be found in Cohen and Sabel 2006 and Forst 2006.
[15] See Ferguson 1999.

The all-subjected principle remedies the major defects of the previous principles. Unlike membership, it pierces the self-serving shield of exclusionary nationalism so as to contemplate injustices of misframing. Unlike humanism, it overcomes abstract, all-embracing globalism by taking notice of social relationships. Unlike affectedness, it avoids the indiscriminateness of the butterfly effect by identifying the morally relevant type of social relation, namely, joint subjection to a governance structure. Far from substituting a single global "who" for the Westphalian "who," the all-subjected principle militates against any one-size-fits-all framing of justice. In today's world, all of us are subject to a plurality of different governance structures, some local, some national, some regional, and some global. The need, accordingly, is to delimit a variety of different frames for different issues. Able to mark out a plurality of "whos" for different purposes, the all-subjected principle tells us when and where to apply which frame—and, thus, who is entitled to parity of participation with whom in a given case.

For this proposal too, however, the details are less important than the overall conceptual structure. What is crucial here is that this approach combines the reflexive questioning of justice frames with a determinative evaluative principle. In this way, it pays heed to both sides of abnormal justice, the negative as well as the positive. Thanks to its reflexivity, the concept of misframing validates contestation of the Westphalian frame. Because it is pitched to the metalevel, this concept permits us to entertain the possibility that first-order questions of justice have been unjustly framed. At the same time, thanks to its determinative character, this approach offers a way of assessing the justice of various "whos." By submitting proposed frames to the all-subjected principle, it enables us to weigh their relative merits. Thus, this approach holds considerable promise for clarifying disputes about the "who" in abnormal times.

And yet another major question remains. *How* exactly ought we to implement the all-subjected principle? By way of what procedures and processes can that principle be applied to resolve disputes about who counts in abnormal times? Unless we can find a suitable way of addressing the "how" of justice, this approach to the "who" will not be of any use.

The "How" of Justice: Institutionalizing Metademocracy

This brings me, finally, to the problem of the "how." For this issue, too, the trick is to reckon with both the positive and negative sides of abnormal justice. What sort of justice theorizing can valorize expanded contestation while also clarifying disputes in which there is no shared understanding of the "how" of justice? The short answer is theorizing that is at once dialogical and institutional. Let me explain.

In order to valorize expanded contestation, a theory of justice for abnormal times must abjure two approaches that have already surfaced in the previous considerations. First, it must suspend the hegemonic presumption that powerful states and private elites should determine the grammar of justice. As we saw, this view went without saying in normal justice, when disputes about the "who" were sufficiently rare and restricted to be settled in smoke-filled back rooms. Today, however, as social movements contest the Westphalian frame, they are challenging such prerogatives by the mere fact of treating the question of the frame as a proper subject of broad public debate. Asserting their right to a say in determining the "who," they are simultaneously problematizing the hegemonic "how." Above and beyond their other demands, then, these movements are effectively demanding something more: the creation of new, nonhegemonic procedures for handling disputes about the framing of justice in abnormal times. This demand too deserves a fair hearing. In order to avoid foreclosing it in advance, a theory of justice for times such as these must entertain nonstandard views of the "how."

Second, a theory of justice for abnormal times must reject what I shall call the scientistic presumption. Supposed by some proponents of the all-affected principle, this understanding of the "how" of justice holds that decisions about the frame should be determined by normal social science, which is presumed to possess uncontroversial facts concerning who is affected by what and thus who deserves consideration in respect of which issues. In abnormal justice, however, disputes about the frame are not reducible to simple questions of empirical fact, as the historical interpretations, social theories, and normative assumptions that necessarily underlie factual claims are themselves in dispute.[16] Under conditions of *in*justice, moreover, what passes for social "science" in the mainstream may well reflect the perspectives, and entrench the blind spots, of the privileged. In these conditions, to adopt the scientistic presumption is to risk foreclosing the claims of the disadvantaged. Thus, a theory committed to expanded contestation must reject this presumption. Without denying the relevance of social knowledge, it must refuse any suggestion that disputes about the "who" be settled by "justice technocrats."

---

[16] See Fraser 2007.

What other possibilities remain? Despite the differences between them, the hegemonic presumption and the scientistic presumption share a common premise. Both propose to settle framing disputes monologically, by appeal to an authority (in one case power, in the other science) that is not accountable to the discursive give-and-take of political debate. A theory of justice for abnormal times must reject this monological premise. To validate contestation, it must treat framing disputes *dialogically*, as political conflicts whose legitimate resolution requires unconstrained, inclusive public discussion. Rejecting appeals to authority, abnormal justice theorizing must envision a dialogical process for applying the all-subjected principle to disputes about the "who."

Thus, a theory of justice for abnormal times must be dialogical. By itself, however, dialogue is not a solution. As soon as we accept that conflicts concerning the frame must be handled discursively, we need to envision a way in which public debates concerning the "who" could eventuate in binding resolutions. Absent an account of the relation between contestation and legitimate decision-making, we have no way to implement the all-subjected principle, hence no way to process disputes in abnormal justice.

How should one conceive this relation? One approach, call it populism, would situate the nexus of contest and decision in civil society. Thus, this approach would assign the task of applying the all-subjected principle to social movements or discursive arenas like the World Social Forum. Although it appears to fulfill the dialogism requirement, populism is nevertheless unsatisfactory for at least two reasons. First, even the best civil-society formations are neither sufficiently representative nor sufficiently democratic to legitimate their proposals to reframe justice. Second, these formations lack the capacity to convert their proposals into binding political decisions. Put differently, although they can introduce novel claims into public debate, by themselves civil-society actors can neither *warrant claims* nor *make binding decisions*.

These limitations suggest the need for a second track of the dialogical process, a formal institutional track. This second track should stand in a dynamic, interactive relation to the first track. Conceived as one pole of a two-way communicative process, the formal institutional track must be responsive to the civil-society track. But it should differ from the latter in two respects. First, the institutional track requires fair procedures and a representative structure to ensure the democratic legitimacy of its deliberations. Second, the representatives, while accountable via publicity and elections, must have the capacity to make binding decisions about the "who" that reflect their communicatively generated judgment as to who is in fact subjected to a given structure of governance.

The upshot is that abnormal justice requires the invention of new global democratic institutions where disputes about framing can be aired and re-solved. Assuming that such disputes will not go away anytime soon and may not be susceptible to any definitive, final resolution, the approach I propose views them as an enduring feature of political life in a global-izing world. Thus, it advocates new institutions for staging and provision-ally resolving such disputes democratically, in permanent dialogue with transnational civil society.

Certainly, much more needs to be said about the design and workings of such arrangements. But in this case, too, the details are less important than the overall conceptual structure of the proposal. What is paramount here is that this view of the "how" of justice combines dialogical and in-stitutional features. As a result, it pays heed to both sides of abnormal jus-tice, the negative as well as the positive. Thanks to its dialogism, it validates contestation of previously taken-for-granted parameters of justice. Rejecting monologism, it seeks a fair hearing for claims that hegemonism and scientism foreclose. At the same time, thanks to its two-track character, it overcomes the decisional and legitimacy deficits of populism. Submitting metaclaims for the reframing of justice to a process of two-way communica-tion between civil society and new global representative institutions, it envi-sions procedures for implementing the all-subjected principle in contexts of disagreement about the "who." Thus, this approach holds out the prospect of provisionally resolving conflicts over framing in abnormal justice.

But that is not all. By providing a means to sort out metaproblems, this proposal clears a path to the pressing first-order problems with which we began. Coming to terms with injustices of misframing, it simultaneously opens the way to tackling injustices of maldistribution, misrecognition, and misrepresentation. Thus, this approach enables us to envision political scenarios for overcoming or reducing injustice in abnormal times.

It is with the aim of fostering that end that I have devised the argu-ment of this section. I have argued here that a theory of justice suited to conditions of abnormal discourse should combine three features. First, such a theory should encompass an account of the "what" of justice that is multidimensional in social ontology and normatively monist—for ex-ample, an account that submits claims for redistribution, recognition, and ordinary-political representation to the principle of participatory parity. Second, such a theory should encompass a view of the "who" that is simul-taneously reflexive and determinative—for example, a view that submits claims against injustices of misframing to the all-subjected principle. Finally, a theory of justice for abnormal times should encompass a view of the "how" that is simultaneously dialogical and institutional—for example, a view that envisions new global representative institutions where metapolitical claims can be submitted to deliberative-democratic decision procedures.

More important than these specifics, however, is the general problem I have outlined here. Under conditions of abnormal justice, previously taken-for-granted assumptions about the "what," the "who," and the "how" no longer go without saying. Thus, these assumptions must themselves be subject to critical discussion and reevaluation. In such discussions, the trick is to avoid two things. On the one hand, one must resist the reactionary and ultimately futile temptation to cling to assumptions that are no longer appropriate to our globalizing world, such as reductive distributivism and passé Westphalianism. On the other hand, one should avoid celebrating abnormality for its own sake, as if contestation were itself liberation. In this section, I have tried to model an alternative stance, which acknowledges abnormal justice as the horizon within which all struggles against injustice must currently proceed. Only by appreciating both the perils and prospects of this condition can we hope to reduce the vast injustices that pervade our world.

A New Normal or Reflexive Justice? Concluding Conceptual and Political Reflections

Before closing, I want to consider some of the larger conceptual and political implications of my overall argument. To this point, my discussion has encompassed two heterogeneous parts, one diagnostic, the other reconstructive. In the first, diagnostic, section, I characterized the present as an era of abnormal justice, in which the basic parameters of political contestation are up for grabs. Identifying three distinct nodes of abnormality, I mapped the contours of a (Westphalian-distributivist) discursive formation in the throes of denormalization. In the second, reconstructive, section, I proposed three corresponding strategies for reflecting on justice in abnormal times. Noting that our familiar theories of justice presuppose conditions of normal discourse, I sought to develop alternative models of theorizing better suited to contexts in which there is no agreement as to the "what," the "who," and the "how" of justice. Given the heterogeneity of these two parts of my argument, a question arises as to the relation between them. What conceptual logic and political aspiration links my *Zeitdiagnose* of the present conjuncture with my attempts at theoretical reconstruction?[17]

Two possibilities suggest themselves. On one reading, the negative features of abnormal justice are sufficiently disabling of struggles against injustice to warrant efforts at renormalization. This view stresses the impossibility of emancipatory change in the absence of a relatively stable framework for vetting and redressing claims. Given that premise, the goal should be to reconstruct such a framework for the current conjuncture. The result, were things to go well, would be a new paradigm of normal discourse about justice, premised on new interpretations of the "what," the "who," and the "how" more appropriate to a globalizing world. On this reading, therefore, my specific proposals would be aimed at constructing such a paradigm. The point of the overall exercise would be to develop a new normal.

Certainly, one could do a lot worse than devising a new normal able to reframe justice conflicts in forms suited to a globalizing world. Yet there are reasons to doubt that such an approach could be fully adequate to the present situation. For one thing, renormalization risks prematurely closing down new avenues of contestation before they have had a fair shot at establishing their plausibility. For another, it risks instating a new, restrictive predefinition of what counts as an intelligible claim for justice, thereby entrenching new exclusions. Finally, the proposal to establish a new normal risks enshrining a fixed set of justice assumptions at a historical juncture when the circumstances of justice are in flux and demand flexibility. For all these reasons, it is worth considering another reading of the overall argument presented here.

The second reading I have in mind envisions an outcome that unsettles the distinction between normal and abnormal justice. Underlining the respective shortcomings of each of those genres of discourse, this reading seeks an alternative model that avoids their defects while incorporating the best features of each. Unlike abnormal discourse, the desired model would have sufficient structuring capacities to stage today's justice struggles as *arguments*, in which the parties *confront* one another, compelling the attention and *judgment* of those looking on. Unlike normal discourse, however, the hoped-for model would have sufficient self-problematizing capacities to entertain novel claims about the "what," the "who," and the "how."

---

[17] Thanks to the many interlocutors who raised this question, especially Nancy Rosenblum, whose characteristically forceful and crisp formulation made the issue impossible to evade.

Combining features of normal and abnormal discourse, the result would be a grammar of justice that incorporates an orientation to closure, needed for political argument, but that treats every closure as *provisional*—subject to question, possible suspension, and thus to reopening. Cultivating responsiveness to emergent exclusions, such a model would feature concepts, such as *misframing*, that invite reflexive self-problematization with the aim of disclosing injustices that were previously occluded. On this reading, the point of the overall exercise would be neither to revel in abnormality nor to rush to instate a new normal. The point, rather, would be to develop a third genre of discourse that we might call *reflexive justice.*

The idea of reflexive justice is well suited to the present context of abnormal discourse. In this context, disputes about the "what," the "who," and the "how" are unlikely to be settled soon. Thus, it makes sense to regard these three nodes of abnormality as persistent features of justice discourse for the foreseeable future. On the other hand, given the magnitude of first-order injustice in today's world, the worst conceivable response would be to treat ongoing metadisputes as a license for paralysis. Thus, it is imperative not to allow discursive abnormalities to defer or dissipate efforts to remedy injustice. The expression *reflexive justice* expresses that dual commitment, signaling a genre of theorizing that works at two levels at once: entertaining urgent claims on behalf of the disadvantaged while also parsing the metadisagreements that are interlaced with them. Because these two levels are inextricably entangled in abnormal times, reflexive justice theorizing cannot ignore either one of them. Working at their intersection and tacking back and forth between them, such theorizing mobilizes the corrective capacities of each to mitigate the defects of the other. In this way, it scrambles the distinction between normal and abnormal discourse.[18]

For these reasons, I prefer to understand the telos of my overall argument not as a new normal but as a species of reflexive justice. That reading has two additional implications that are worth considering. The

---

[18] My current interest in scrambling the distinction between normal and abnormal discourse is prefigured in my earlier exchanges with Rorty. In a 1988 essay, I noted Rorty's tendency to align abnormal discourse with "private irony" and normal discourse with "public solidarity," and I proposed that radical social criticism upset those dichotomies insofar as it was both abnormal and solidaristic; see Fraser 1988. Later, in his 1991 Tanner lecture, Rorty (1991) provocatively transgressed his original alignment by reading radical second-wave feminism as both abnormal and publicly relevant. In my response (Fraser 1991), I applauded that move, even as I faulted Rorty's account for individualizing and aestheticizing the process of linguistic innovation in feminism, hence for neglecting the latter's collective, democratic character. That argument now appears, in retrospect, to presage my present proposal to unsettle the distinction between normal and abnormal discourse.

first concerns the well-known opposition in political philosophy between discourse-ethical approaches, on the one hand, and agonistic approaches, on the other. Rightly or wrongly, the first are sometimes portrayed as objectionably normalizing, while the second are often seen as irresponsibly reveling in abnormality. Without pretending to assess the merits of these charges and countercharges, I propose that the idea of reflexive justice scrambles this opposition as well. Like agonistic models, reflexive justice valorizes the moment of opening, which breaches the exclusions of normal justice, embracing claimants the latter has silenced and disclosing injustices the latter has occluded—all of which it holds essential for contesting injustice. Like discourse ethics, however, reflexive justice also valorizes the moment of closure, which enables political argument, collective decision-making, and public action—all of which it deems indispensable for remedying injustice. Seeking to accommodate both moments, the moment of opening and the moment of closure, reflexive justice views the standard opposition between agonism and discourse ethics as a false antithesis. Refusing to absolutize either model and thus to exclude the insights of the other, it draws on elements of each to fashion a new genre of theorizing for abnormal times.

The second implication concerns the relation between the problematic of abnormal justice and that of hegemony. As is well known, hegemony theory conceptualizes a second, discursive, face of power alongside that of brute repression. This second face includes the capacity to construct a "common sense" for a diverse array of constituencies, whom the hegemon thereby inducts into a shared political universe. Within that universe, each constituency can recognize itself as a political subject and formulate its interests and goals in a way that is intelligible to others. Seen this way, hegemony includes the capacity to define the legitimate universe of political disagreement while simultaneously constituting the latter's exterior as a region of unintelligibility. The point can also be put like this: by instituting a structuring set of background assumptions, which itself largely goes without saying, hegemony predetermines what will count as a plausible claim for a claim for justice—and what will not.

Understood this way, hegemony theory has clear affinities with the problematic elaborated here. In its terms, episodes of normal justice would correspond to periods of relatively secure, uncontested hegemony in which extracommonsensical claims remain dispersed, failing to coalesce into a counterhegemonic bloc. In contrast, episodes of abnormality would correlate with periods of overt struggles for hegemony in which counterhegemonic formations achieve sufficient cohesion to problematize what had previously passed for common sense. Affinities aside, however, the hegemony problematic suggests a different historical account of today's abnormalities. Through its lens, the latter are traceable less to the subject-less process of globalization than to the decline of US hegemony since the collapse of the USSR in 1989. Insofar as US hegemony was based on the Cold War, the demise of that geopolitical order presented a challenge to the (Westphalian-distributivist) grammar of justice that defined "the free world." Having failed to articulate a plausible post–Cold War common sense centered on the "war on terror," the United States has so far proved unable to perpetuate its hegemony. The result is a glaring discrepancy between the two faces of power; US military supremacy is not matched by any comparable capacity to constitute a shared common sense that could normalize conflicts over justice. No wonder, then, that justice discourse is undergoing denormalization and that disputes about the "what," the "who," and the "how" are proliferating.

Compelling as this story is, it is not in fact a rival to the one I have developed here. On the contrary, the hegemony perspective complements the problematic of abnormal/normal discourse. Whereas the former views justice discourse historically and strategically, aiming to understand shifts in power, the latter interrogates it philosophically and normatively, aiming to disclose present possibilities for emancipatory change. Thus, far from being mutually incompatible, these two perspectives enrich one another. Like hegemony theory, the abnormal/normal framework acknowledges the historicity and power-laden character of justice discourse. What it adds, however, is an insistence that the grammar of justice be reconstituted so as to enable the subaltern to speak in *authoritative terms*. In this way, the perspective developed here supplies a crucial ingredient of critical theorizing, which hegemony theory taken alone does not provide: the elusive but inspiring vision of a discourse of justice that could reveal contemporary injustices for the moral outrages they surely are. It supplies, in Richard Rorty's terms, the otherwise missing ingredient of "social hope."

Works Cited

Anderson, Elizabeth S. 1999. "What Is the Point of Equality?" *Ethics* 109(2): 287–337.

Arendt, Hannah. 1973. *The Origins of Totalitarianism.* New York: Harcourt Brace Jovanovich.

Cohen, Joshua, and Charles Sabel. 2006. "Extra Rempublicam Nulla Justitia?" *Philosophy and Public Affairs* 34(2): 147–175.

Dworkin, Ronald. 1981. "What Is Equality? Part 2: Equality of Resources." *Philosophy and Public Affairs* 10(4): 283–345.

Ferguson, James. 1999. "Global Disconnect: Abjection and the Aftermath of Modernism." In *Expectations of Modernity: Myths and Meanings of Urban Life on the Zambian Copperbelt*, edited by James Ferguson, 234–254. Berkeley: University of California Press.

Forst, Rainer. 2006. "Justice, Morality, and Power in the Global Context." In *Real World Justice: Grounds, Principles, Human Rights, and Social Institutions*, edited by Andreas Follesdal and Thomas W. Pogge, 27–36. Dordrecht: Springer.

Fraser, Nancy. 1988. "Solidarity or Singularity? Richard Rorty between Romanticism and Technocracy." *Praxis International* 8(3): 257–272.

———. 1991. "From Irony to Prophecy to Politics: A Response to Richard Rorty." *Michigan Quarterly Review* 30(2): 259–266.

———. 2000. "Rethinking Recognition." *New Left Review* 3(May–June): 107–120.

———. 2003a. "Social Justice in the Age of Identity Politics." In *Redistribution or Recognition? A Political-Philosophical Exchange*, edited by Nancy Fraser and Axel Honneth and translated by Joel Golb, James Ingram, and Christiane Wilke, 7–109. London: Verso.

———. 2003b. "Distorted beyond All Recognition: A Rejoinder to Axel Honneth." In *Redistribution or Recognition? A Political-Philosophical Exchange*, edited by Nancy Fraser and Axel Honneth, translated by Joel Golb, James Ingram, and Christiane Wilke, 198–236. London: Verso.

———. 2007. "Democratic Justice in a Globalizing Age: Thematizing the Problem of the Frame." In *Varieties of World-Making: Beyond Globalization*, edited by Nathalie Karagiannis and Peter Wagner, 193–215. Liverpool: Liverpool University Press.

Honneth, Axel. 2003. "Redistribution as Recognition: A Response to Nancy Fraser." In *Redistribution or Recognition? A Political-Philosophical Exchange*, edited by Nancy Fraser and Axel Honneth and translated by Joel Golb, James Ingram, and Christiane Wilke, 110–197. London: Verso.

Kuhn, Thomas S. 1996. *The Structure of Scientific Revolutions*. Chicago: University of Chicago Press.

Kymlicka, Will. 2001. "Territorial Boundaries: A Liberal Egalitarian Perspective." In *Boundaries and Justice: Diverse Ethical Perspectives*, edited by David Miller and Sohail H. Hashmi, 249–275. Princeton, NJ: Princeton University Press.

Miller, David. 1995. *On Nationality*. Oxford: Oxford University Press.

Nagel, Thomas. 2005. "The Problem of Global Justice." *Philosophy and Public Affairs* 33(2): 113–147.

Rawls, John. 1999. *The Law of Peoples*. Cambridge: Harvard University Press.

Rorty, Richard. 1979. *Philosophy and the Mirror of Nature*. Princeton, NJ: Princeton University Press.

———. 1989. *Contingency, Irony, and Solidarity*. New York: Cambridge University Press.

———. 1991. "Feminism and Pragmatism." *Michigan Quarterly Review* 30(2): 231–258.

Ruggie, John Gerard. 1993. "Territoriality and Beyond: Problematizing Modernity in International Relations." *International Organization* 47(1): 139–174.

CHAPTER 3 | Pragmatism's Contribution
to Nonideal Theorizing

Fraser, Addams, and Rorty

CHRISTOPHER VOPARIL

IN A SERIES OF essays over the last decade, including "Abnormal Justice"
(this volume), Nancy Fraser has advanced the discourse of justice via a
novel paradigm of "post-Westphalian democratic justice," which addresses
injustices generated by globalization, multinational capitalism, and transnational migration, to which familiar liberal theories of justice have
proved inadequate. Attending to each of what she calls the "three families
of justice claims"—claims for socioeconomic redistribution, for legal or
cultural recognition, and for political representation—this work highlights
the shortcomings of monological theories of social justice that focus solely
on first-order questions of substance—the "what" of justice—as defined
and answered by privileged theorists. Inspired by Richard Rorty's reading of Thomas Kuhn's distinction between normal and revolutionary discourse, Fraser's key insight is that under conditions of "abnormal justice"
it is the frame or grammar of justice itself that excluded voices who seek a
hearing contest, not merely the "what" or content of justice.

Fraser's approach to normative theorizing is in the vein of recent work
by Elizabeth Anderson (2009), José Medina (2013), Charles Mills (2011),
Shannon Sullivan (2014), and others working under the sign of nonideal
theory, who, like Fraser, draw inspiration from the pragmatic tradition in
various ways. A hallmark of Fraser's work has long been grounding normativity historically rather than in ideal theory (Allen 2012, 826).[1] If we follow

---

[1] See, for example, Fraser 1990.

Mills in identifying the mark of the nonideal as "locating issues of normative theory, moral and political, in the actual non-ideal world in which we live," with particular attention to "constraining circumstances" (2011, 428–429), Fraser falls squarely in this camp. In this chapter, I frame her shift from normal to abnormal justice as a move to the nonideal that brings historical oppression and asymmetrical relations between human beings into the theory and practice of justice. Using the unlikely pairing of Jane Addams and Richard Rorty, I then argue that a pragmatic turn advances the nonideal project of justice in two important ways: first, by conceiving the normative theorizing of justice as a transformative or melioristic project rather than a purely conceptual, representationalist one; and second, by socializing justice, in Addams's distinct sense, so that enlarging the sphere of justice becomes an ethical and sociopolitical, not merely epistemic, effort that demands active cultivation of sympathetic knowledge and affective ties with others. My concern is less to affirm the nonideal over the ideal than to encourage a move beyond both ideal and nonideal theorizing alike to a pragmatist "working program" of ameliorating injustice.[2]

To be sure, Fraser does not explicitly take up the banner of nonideal theory. The historical grounding of her normative theorizing, her attention to constraining circumstances, and her understanding that reigning theories of justice "do not tell us how to proceed when we encounter conflicting assumptions concerning moral standing, social cleavage, and agency of redress" (2008, 396) nevertheless orient her well outside the purview of the ideal. Yet at the same time, her chief concern is that we as theorists have adequate "conceptual resources" and "conceptual strategies for clarifying" problems of abnormal justice: "What sort of theory of justice could provide guidance in this situation? What type of theorizing could handle cases in which first-order disputes about justice are overlaid with metadisputes about what counts as an intelligible first-order claim?" (397). While these are certainly compelling questions, my worry is that Fraser's prioritizing of conceptual clarity risks granting temporal priority to theorizing (abnormal) justice at the expense of addressing pressing current injustices.[3]

That pragmatism and nonideal theory share a common orientation away from the ideal and toward social reality and experience as lived is not a novel claim. This orientation is deeply endemic to the classical pragmatists, and is exemplified in the productive use made

---

[2] The phrase "working program" is Dewey and Tufts's. See Manicas (this volume).
[3] For a good account of the difference between logical and temporal priority, see Hendrix 2013.

of pragmatism by such recent thinkers as noted above.[4] Yet the ways that a pragmatic turn can alleviate particular shortcomings of nonideal theorizing and further advance the redress of injustice have not been spelled out in detail. Pragmatism pushes ideal and nonideal theorizing alike out of the space of the conceptual and into the social. As we shall see, for Addams and Rorty this means not simply altering the starting point of theorizing, as with nonideal theory, but moving beyond theoretical diagnoses to the active pursuit of more social experience and the forging of democratic social relations. This is important to the extent that Fraser's project, at bottom, seeks to reclaim social knowledge as essential to determining the "who" and "how" of justice, thereby displacing the authority of states, elites, and normal social science to fix the "grammar" of justice. What Addams and Rorty understood is that, absent the cultivation of affective ties of sympathetic understanding, the mere presence of social knowledge will fail to ameliorate existing hierarchies and entrenched privilege.

After outlining Fraser's key contributions in the first section, in the second I underscore what I call the pragmatic moments in her account, which I argue can be developed to alleviate several limitations, including the limits of appeals to democratic dialogue as a way to overcome entrenched power and social privilege, and of admitting previously excluded voices without fostering habits of listening. Drawing on both Addams and Rorty, the third section argues that enlarging the sphere of justice to make it more responsive to excluded groups requires moving beyond the conceptual to the cultivation of responsive ethical and epistemic virtues as correctives for insensitivities on the part of the privileged.

From Abnormal to Reflexive Justice

Capturing in a brief space the subtlety, conceptual clarity, and insight of Fraser's ongoing effort to rethink the nature of justice and injustice in an increasingly globalized world is not possible. Over the course of nearly two decades, she has developed a multidimensional, reflexive, critical-democratic approach to theorizing justice informed by both key theoretical critiques of previous conceptions and challenges sparked by social movements and the changing global environment. At the center of Fraser's recent work is the important recognition that "the Keynesian-Westphalian

---

[4] Anderson has called Dewey "the deepest advocate of nonideal theory" (2009, 138).

frame," with its largely unquestioned assumptions about territorial states and national publics as the proper contexts for the making and redress of justice claims, has, at best, proven inadequate in the face of injustices that have accompanied globalization and, at worst, become itself "a powerful instrument of injustice, which gerrymanders political space at the expense of the poor and despised" (2005, 78). Fraser elucidates how this frame gives a distinctive shape to arguments about social justice, focusing them on the "what" or substance of justice—what should count as a just ordering of society—leaving the "who" of justice, assumed to be the national citizenry, unquestioned and outside debate. Globalization along economic, technological, and cultural lines; the growth of supranational and international organizations; and transnational threats, like climate change, terrorism, and HIV-AIDS, all have destabilized the existing structure of claims-making. As a result, Fraser observes, the "grammar of argument" has been altered so that disputes involve not only the "what" but the "who" of justice—"*who* should count as a member and *which* is the relevant community" (2005, 71–80).

Among Fraser's many contributions are the conceptual categories she offers for getting a handle on the complexity of these changes. The shift from the "what" to the "who" of justice can be understood as a move from "first-order questions of substance" to "second-order, meta-level questions" that pertain to the proper frame for considering first-order questions: "*Who* counts as a subject of justice in a given matter? Whose interests and needs deserve consideration? Who belongs in the circle of those entitled to equal concern?" (2005, 72; 2008, 398–399). Attending to problems of the frame, in turn, prompts a third species of question about the "how" of justice—procedural considerations that ask, "by which criteria or decision procedure should one resolve disputes about the 'what' and the 'who'?" (2008, 399).

These fundamental shifts amount to a recognition of the "political" as a dimension of justice itself—that is, of its character as continually contested and contestable. Fully embracing this political dimension, Fraser's is thus a theory of "post-Westphalian democratic justice"—"democratic" as opposed to "social" justice, to distinguish the former's inclusive, "dialogical" approach, which locates disputes over the metaissue of the frame within democratic publics, from the latter's exclusive, "monological" appeal to experts and elites (2005, 78, 86). The strategy Fraser offers for thinking about these problems of the frame entails a three-dimensional theory of justice that incorporates the political dimension of representation, as well as the economic dimension of distribution and the cultural dimension of recognition. Three distinct nodes of injustice emerge: maldistribution of economic and social goods, misrecognition arising from entrenched cultural hierarchies, and injustices of misrepresentation or misframing where either political borders or the boundaries of a moral community exclude individuals or groups via the way questions of justice are framed.

Fraser subsequently labels the state of affairs that results from recognition of this condition of continual contestation "abnormal justice," taking a cue from Rorty's twist on Kuhn's categories. Unlike conditions of normal justice, where challenges to the dominant frame's presuppositions are minimal and contained, abnormal justice obtains when a "heteroglossia of justice discourse" (2008, 396) is present and, as a result, competing claims and counterclaims admit of no commensurating principle that adequately addresses the what, who, and how of justice from the perspectives of all involved.

Fraser's conception of abnormal justice rests on three key insights that characterize a nonideal approach to thinking about justice. The first is her move to democratize the process of frame setting by making it a matter of democratic dialogue rather than monological theory. The second is her insight that arguments about justice have a "double character" that involves both epistemic and political dimensions. Epistemically, arguments entail knowledge claims that cannot be adjudicated via public reason, since under conditions of abnormal justice, there is no consensus about what counts as a good reason that would settle the exchange of reasons and counterreasons. Politically, the hierarchies of power that permeate disputes between claimants who are differently positioned, both socially and geographically, mean that "the disputants do not participate on terms of parity in arguments about the frame" (2009, 41–42). The implication is that disputes about metaissues of justice, like that of the frame, cannot be settled simply by appealing to criteria or decision rules, since injustices of misframing challenge these very provisions. This leads to her third insight: that these shifts can be understood as an effort to reclaim social knowledge "from the experts and to resituate it within a wide-ranging democratic debate about the 'who' " (2009, 42–43). Importantly, her "critical-democratic" orientation calls attention to the limitations of what she calls, following Kuhn, "the normal-social-science approach," which holds that the task of adjudicating competing claims can be entrusted to a positivistically conceived social science. By appealing to objective relations of social interdependence as a way to determine the relevant subjects of justice, such an approach "effectively relegates the choice of the 'who' to mainstream social scientists," thereby removing it from the sphere of politics and contestation (2009, 37–38; 2008, 411).[5]

From the Nonideal to the Pragmatic

As we have seen, a primary contribution is the conceptual clarity Fraser brings to the project of theorizing justice under abnormal conditions. From the outset, her chief concern is addressing the inability of "our familiar theories of justice" to provide the "conceptual resources" for dealing with problems of abnormal justice (2008, 396–397). To be sure, the "new genre of theorizing for abnormal times" in which her diagnosis culminates—"reflexive justice theorizing"—is an attractive model that meets these conceptual needs, working at two levels simultaneously: "entertaining urgent claims on behalf of the disadvantage while also parsing the metadisagreements that are interlaced with them" (2008, 419).

Without minimizing the significance of these insights, I would like to call attention to the pragmatic moments in Fraser's account, where she intimates the need for something more than a new genre of *theorizing*, for it is here that the pragmatist tradition provides change- and action-oriented resources that advance Fraser's project beyond the conceptual. One of these moments is the embrace of fallibilism in reflexive justice theorizing's striving for "a grammar of justice that incorporates an orientation to closure, needed for political argument, but that treats every closure as *provisional*—subject to question, possible suspension, and thus to reopening" (2008, 419). Another of these moments is the move outside the conceptual to habits and practices that must be actively fostered: the virtue of "hermeneutical charity" that should accord unfamiliar claims "the presumption of intelligibility and potential validity" (2008, 404); the value of "self-problematizing capacities" among those with power and privilege that would permit these novel claims to be entertained (2008, 418); and the need for "cultivating responsiveness" to these excluded and neglected voices (2008, 419).

Developing these pragmatic inclinations also remedies several limitations of Fraser's approach. One limitation concerns Fraser's appeal

---

[5] This effort to reclaim social knowledge and critical view of normal social science for its tendency to buttress existing frames and grammars puts Fraser's account potentially at odds with the work of Anderson (2010).

to democratic dialogue as a mechanism that, by its very nature, will provide "legitimate resolution" of conflicting claims. Here the remedy for settling disputes previously adjudicated by monological theory and normal social science is creating a space where "unconstrained, inclusive public discussion" and "fair public contestation" will carry the day (2008, 414; 2009, 42). While a salutary move, as far as it goes, the turn to dialogical spaces smooths over rather than addresses the (unequal and hierarchical) social relations that obtain among participants in democratic discourse. Fraser is aware of this issue, citing it as one of her approach's "conceptual challenges" and underscoring the need to promote "social arrangements that are sufficiently just to permit all to participate as peers in democratic discussion and decision-making" (2009, 45). Yet she writes off this objection as an unavoidable problem all democracies face and suggests that attaining "good-enough deliberation" is sufficient (2009, 45). As a result, asymmetrical power relations that threaten democratic dialogue do not receive sufficient attention in the proposed solutions, which merely call for "new, nonhegemonic procedures for handling disputes" (2008, 414).

While I applaud Fraser's "expansion of the field of contestation, hence the chance to challenge injustice that the previous grammar elided" (2008, 402), because her account stays within the realm of strategies for *theorizing* justice, precisely how and by what means previously excluded voices will enter this expanded field and contribute to this process is relatively undeveloped. Fraser is not unaware of this issue either. She understands how "the dimensions of justice are disclosed historically, through the medium of struggle," and notes the need for "any attempt to theorize justice" to remain open to the prospect of "a new dimension of justice being disclosed" (2008, 404). Nevertheless, how the "inspiring vision of a discourse of justice" she offers, with its "insistence that the grammar of justice be reconstituted so as to enable the subaltern to speak *in authoritative terms*," is to be realized and put into practice is as yet unclear (2008, 422).

Lastly, while Fraser is admirably aware of the insensitivities of privileged participants in the dialogue and how they can become entrenched (e.g., 2008, 414), there is little attention to means of rectifying these obstacles to justice, beyond her call for "self-problematizing capacities." That such insensitivities will be overcome via inclusive public discussion and dialogue seems to be taken on faith. By contrast, Addams places the need for the ideals of the privileged to undergo revision at the center of her experiential and relational approach, and offers mechanisms and practices for doing so, as does Rorty.

Justice as Forging Democratic Relations through Sympathetic Knowledge

In the remainder of this chapter, I suggest how Fraser's pragmatic moments can be developed via Addams and Rorty. Fraser's effort to democratize justice and reclaim social knowledge by creating a dialogical space where dominant perspectives are challenged can be seen, to borrow a term from Addams, as a project of "socializing" justice.[6] By her own lights, Fraser's work on justice is motivated by the task of reconstructing our concepts of justice "in the light of a post-positivistic understanding of social knowledge" (2009, 42). Her insight here is that under conditions of abnormal justice, any attempt at neutral arbitration—e.g., via normal social science—will do violence to the "evaluative and interpretive commitments" of those who contest the existing frame (2009, 42). As a result, Fraser seeks to democratize justice, creating a space where these commitments can be subjected to democratic debate. While this democratizing move is welcome, absent the active cultivation of democratic social relations that generate sympathetic knowledge, subjecting the interests and interpretive commitments of the excluded to democratic debate is insufficient. Addams and Rorty understood that the ethical and epistemic virtues of open-mindedness and responsiveness must be actively fostered on the part of the privileged.[7]

For Addams and Rorty, remedying injustice requires creating a democratic moral community attainable only through sympathetic knowledge and mutual understanding. As Charlene Haddock Seigfried has explained, "Sympathetically understanding multiple perspectives . . . is a requirement for intelligible insight into any realm of reality" (2001, 19).[8] In Addams's moral vision, epistemic and ethical communities merge to form democratic ones. In Maurice Hamington's words, for Addams "empathy, understanding, and action on behalf of one another are essential for democracy to be effective" (2004, 217–218). The chapters of *Democracy and Social Ethics* recount richly contextualized examples of the "various types and groups" whose social experiences have generated what Jean Bethke Elshtain has called the "ethics of realizable action made possible by sympathetic knowledge" that Addams's view of democracy requires (2002, 72). For Addams,

---

[6] On this notion, see Seigfried 1999 and Sarvasy 2010.

[7] It is here that both Addams and Rorty are relevant to Anderson's (2010) and Medina's (2013) work on epistemic integration and interaction.

[8] As Seigfried notes, "Knowledge, for Addams, aimed at bettering the community and was most usefully acquired through social sympathy" (2001, 18).

like Rorty, sympathetic understanding is a key component of taking into account "the needs and interests of more and more diverse human beings" (Rorty 1999, 82). Rorty dubbed this "sentimental education"—a Humean cultivation of sentiment to create felt identifications with others by seeing "the similarities between ourselves and people very unlike us as outweighing the differences" (1998a, 181). What Rorty's account demands is "as rich and full a knowledge of other people as possible—in particular, knowledge of their own descriptions of their actions and of themselves" (2010, 393). Addams's concern for "the sympathetic understanding that enlarges the sphere of justice," as Seigfried nicely captures it, is reflected in Rorty's effort to promote "justice as a larger loyalty" (see Rorty 2007).

The centrality of social experience for Addams enables us to see that democratizing our approach to the frame setting of justice entails more than opening up our theories to contestation and creating formal, legitimized spaces of dialogue; it requires promoting a "wider and more thorough human experience" (2002, 7). Attaining a social perspective on ethics is not merely a matter of broadening our theoretical categories for Addams; on the contrary, social perspective can only come about "from contact with social experience"—that is, "by mixing on the thronged and common road where all must turn out for one another, and at least see the size of one another's burdens" (2002, 7). Such "diversified human experience and resultant sympathy" is for Addams nothing less than "the foundation and guarantee of Democracy" (7).

What makes Addams's attention to the social so crucial is the foregrounding of our embeddedness in social relations it makes possible, including those relations characterized by inequities of power and privilege. In itself, enabling the marginalized to speak raises but does not yet rectify these inequalities. As several recent commentators have noted, Addams had a nuanced understanding of what today we would call intersectionality, which enabled her to make a concern for disparities of power central to her project of creating democratic experience.[9] Not unlike recent critiques of colorblindness by Anderson (2010) and Mills (2008), she perceived that any purportedly neutral means for reconciling conflicting claims was likely to perpetuate the privilege of those with power (Fischer 2011, 489). For Addams, the project of giving democracy social expression involves "transition into a new type of democratic relation" via sympathetic understanding (2002, 118). A key insight here is how intersectionality is not

---

[9] See, for example, Hamington 2009 and Sarvasy 2010.

just about those of privilege sympathetically entering the standpoints of the marginalized; it also offers a basis for persons of privilege to thematize and self-reflectively encounter their own privilege. Thus, for Addams, democratic experience requires forging relations that are reciprocal, like her own interactions with immigrants and others at Hull House, in that they allow the less fortunate to speak and compel the privileged to rethink their own ideals in light of these experiences.[10]

Similarly, Rorty gave significant attention to those whose views fall outside the bounds of our moral communities and to the need to expand the range of people we regard as "possible conversation partners" (1991, 203). Unlike Addams, Rorty understood this intersubjective element in terms of discourse, epistemic agreement, even shared moral identity, though not experience. Nevertheless, his project of "extend[ing] the reference of 'us' as far as we can" has similar aims (1991, 23). Also cognizant of those with whom we are unwilling to forge democratic relations, he took up the plight of victims of ethnic cleansing and marginalized and oppressed groups.[11] For Rorty, to be part of a society is to be taken as a possible conversational partner by those who shape that society's self-image. He understood the need for empathy and affect in what Medina calls "the epistemology of social recognition" (2013, 315), exemplified in Rorty's now familiar account of moral progress as "the expansion of the circle of beings who count as 'us' " (2007, 45 n. 3). In keeping with Addams's view of social experience as a "corrective" for the insensitivities of the privileged, Rorty instructs, "We should stay on the lookout for marginalized people—people whom we still instinctively think of as 'they' rather than 'us' " so that we can enlarge both our individual and cultural self-descriptions to make them as inclusive as possible (1989, 196; 2007, 124). Absent the sympathetic understanding and responsiveness both Addams and Rorty sought to cultivate, these insensitivities will be perpetuated rather than remedied by appeals to democratic dialogue.

The value of Rorty's perspective, like Addams's, is its appreciation of the "double character" of arguments, addressing both epistemic and political dimensions. Two insights in particular stand out in Rorty's account that expand Fraser's pragmatic inclinations. The first centers on his notion of philosophy as cultural politics, which he describes as aiming to subvert the idea inherent in Enlightenment rationalism that "persistent argument will lead all inquirers to the same set of beliefs" (2007, 92).

---

[10] See Hamington 2004, 221; and Seigfried 1999, 225.
[11] See "Human Rights, Rationality, and Sentimentality" in 1998a; and 1998b.

Rorty's "cultural politics" can be understood as a catch-all phrase for conversation that takes place in the absence of agreed-upon criteria to govern argument—precisely what Fraser calls the condition of abnormal justice. The issue of how to generate "fruitful conversation" in the face of philosophical disagreement was a preoccupation of Rorty's from his earliest published work.[12] In his later writings, he simply transfers this idea from the philosophical to the political realm. Rorty understood that in abnormal conditions, even theoretical interventions are themselves "moves in the game of cultural politics" (2007, 8), and that we must shift from antecedent commensurating principles to the active cultivation of sympathetic understanding and practice of virtues, like listening, to bridge conflicting claims.[13]

On the epistemic side, Rorty's second insight resides in his critique of approaches, like Kant's, that assume "all the logical space necessary for moral deliberation is now available—that all important truths about right and wrong can not only be stated but be made plausible, in language already at hand" (1998a, 203). In the context of appeals to justice, he foregrounds the issue to which Fraser also is attentive, of "a voice saying something never heard before" (1998b, 202). Unless the logical space necessary for moral deliberation is expanded, these claims will fail to register in the dominant discourse, even if victims of oppression are able to give voice to their suffering by entering the dialogue.[14] As I noted above, while Fraser is aware of the problem, her suggestion that theorists simply not foreclose this possibility so as to remain conceptually open is not yet a remedy. Rorty's insight is that this logical space can only be expanded by "nonlogical" means, or what he calls "unwarranted assertions"—novel metaphors, redescriptions, creative misuses of language, and voices saying something never heard before. Because logical means of argumentation and persuasion rely on appeals to antecedently shared criteria to function, they are incapable of expanding the frame. In their embrace of narrative and their efforts to broaden our capacities of imagination, both Rorty and

---

[12] Possible responses to the lack of antecedently shared criteria to settle philosophical disputes were a key preoccupation of Rorty's, beginning with his first published essays of the early 1960s. See Voparil and Bernstein 2010, 11–19.

[13] See Voparil 2014.

[14] Although I don't have space to develop this here, in going beyond simply opening us up to the meanings and experiences of others, to grasp how our own epistemological assumptions and orientations can be responsible for their suffering, Rorty offers insights into what recent scholars have called epistemic injustice. See Fricker 2009; Medina 2013; and Dieleman (this volume). Rorty had a keen awareness of what Medina calls the "cognitive-affective functioning" that sustains oppressive normative structures.

Addams appreciate that we must foster awareness of and responsiveness to these voices, beyond expanding our conceptual repertoire.[15]

The last area where I want to highlight their pragmatist contribution is in understanding normativity amid conflicting and contested claims. As Fraser explains, "a theory of justice for abnormal times requires a determinative normative principle for evaluating frames. Absent such a determinative principle, we have no way to assess the alternatives, hence no way to clarify disputes that encompass conflicting understandings of the 'who' " (2008, 410). In order to provide such a commensurating normative principle, while ensuring that previously unseen demands are not foreclosed in advance, Fraser counsels the combination of "a multidimensional social ontology with normative monism" (405). Because widely accepted standards for adjudicating claims are not available under abnormal conditions, she argues that any commensurating principle must be procedural rather than substantive. She proposes the principle of "parity of participation" as covering the three dimensions of justice and making them commensurable (405–406).

Fraser's solution to the problem of abnormal normativity is logically sound. The issue I want to raise concerns its ability to meet the political and not just the conceptual demands of justice. Anderson has explained that the normativity of ideals is transformed rather than jettisoned under nonideal theorizing: "In nonideal theory, ideals embody imagined solutions to identified problems in a society. They function as *hypotheses*, to be tested in experience" (2010, 6). The question is whether a proceduralist solution meets the higher demands of justice sought by Anderson: "our aim is not merely to correct the distributive consequences of unjust social relations, but to eliminate unjust and unequal group relations" (22). In the vocabulary I have employed here, this is a demand for forging democratic relations.

Rorty's response to the problem of normativity under abnormal justice suggests an alternative, more transformative approach capable of meeting Anderson's goal.[16] Instead of appealing to a commensurating principle to settle conflicting claims, Rorty's understanding of normativity locates norms and standards within social practices and the web of communal relations in which we find ourselves. His conception comprises two important

---

[15] As Addams asserts, "We have learned as common knowledge that much of the insensibility and hardness of the world is due to lack of imagination which prevents a realization of the experiences of other people" (2002, 8). Rorty discusses this in many places; see in particular 1999 and 2010.

[16] The claims in this paragraph are developed more fully in Voparil 2014.

shifts that direct us toward our implicit ties to others that undergird normativity. One is his embrace of an alternative, noncriterial conception of rationality understood as "responsibility to larger and more diverse communities of human beings" (2003, 46). If rationality is understood in terms of our relations with others, then to be rational is "to be willing to pick up the jargon of the interlocutor rather than translating it into one's own" (1979, 318). The second is the renewed role accorded "politico-moral" or "social" virtues (1997, 176; 2000, 62).[17] Curiosity—"the urge to expand one's horizons of inquiry"—and other "social virtues," like conversability, decency, respect for others, and toleration, are for Rorty what generates interest in "talking to foreigners, infidels, and anybody else who claims to know something you do not know, to have some ideas that you do not have" (2000, 17). Absent the assumption of commensuration, knowledge becomes more like "getting acquainted with a person than like following a demonstration" (1979, 319). And "getting into conversation with strangers" is for Rorty a matter of acquiring a "new virtue or skill" (319). The goal is "to broaden the size of the audience [we] take to be competent, to increase the size of the relevant community of justification" (2000, 9). Not only is this project relevant to democratic politics, he suggests, "it pretty much *is* democratic politics" (9).

I have argued for the relevance of the pragmatic insights of Addams and Rorty to Fraser's central question, "What sort of theorizing could simultaneously valorize expanded contestation and strengthen diminished capacities of adjudication and redress?" (2008, 403). Fraser's conception of reflexive justice is pregnant with pragmatic possibilities that take rectification of injustice beyond theory to a working program. The insights offered by Addams and Rorty extend Fraser's important turn to reflexive justice by recognizing that democratizing the process of frame setting needs more than opening a conceptual and political space for democratic dialogue. It requires forging new democratic social relations that generate democratic experience and expand our sympathetic and imaginative capacities of responsiveness, particularly across disparities of power and privilege. Nonideal theory's attention to the actual exclusion of marginalized groups and carving out space within privileged discourses is not enough; we need to get outside abstract dialogical models to build democratic relations through actively seeking out experiences with excluded others so that our normative ideals themselves undergo revision in the process. As Addams

---

[17] For an original reading of Rorty as advancing a virtue liberalism, see Curtis 2015.

well knew, it starts with accepting that these others have something to teach us: "no one so poignantly realizes the failures in social structure as the man at the bottom, who has been most directly in contact with those failures and has suffered the most" (1981, 137).

In ways that both anticipate and advance work on the leading edge of nonideal theorizing about justice, Addams and Rorty took abnormal conditions as their starting point, and recognized the barriers to parity of participation and the need to address the problem of insensitivity, through active cultivation of social sensibilities and the virtues of open-mindedness and listening that promote responsiveness to injustice. They also push us to take seriously the idea that, as privileged philosophers and social theorists, there are moments in the struggle for social justice when we simply must get out of the way.[18]

Works Cited

Addams, Jane. 1981. *Twenty Years at Hull-House*. New York: Signet Classic.

——. 2002. *Democracy and Social Ethics*. Urbana: University of Illinois Press.

Allen, Amy. 2012. "The Public Sphere: Ideology and/or Ideal?" *Political Theory* 40(6): 822–829.

Anderson Elizabeth. 2009. "Toward a Non-Ideal, Relational Methodology for Political Philosophy: Comments on Schwartzmann's *Challenging Liberalism*." *Hypatia* 24(4): 130–145.

——. 2010. *The Imperative of Integration*. Princeton, NJ: Princeton University Press.

Curtis, William M. 2015. *Defending Rorty: Pragmatism and Liberal Virtue*. New York: Cambridge University Press.

Elshtain, Jean Bethke. 2002. *Jane Addams and the Dream of American Democracy*. New York: Basic Books.

Fischer, Marilyn. 2011. "Interpretation's Contrapuntal Pathways: Addams and the Averbuch Affair." *Transactions of the Charles S. Peirce Society* 47(4): 482–506.

Fraser, Nancy. 1990. "Rethinking the Public Sphere: A Contribution to the Critique of Actually Existing Democracy." *Social Text* 25/26: 56–80.

——. 1991. "From Irony to Prophecy to Politics: A Response to Richard Rorty." *Michigan Quarterly Review* 30(2): 259–266.

——. 2005. "Reframing Justice in a Globalizing World." *New Left Review* 36(November–December): 69–88.

——. 2008. "Abnormal Justice." *Critical Inquiry* 34(Spring): 393–422.

——. 2009. "Two Dogmas of Egalitarianism." In *Scales of Justice: Reimagining Political Space in a Globalizing World*, 30–47. New York: Columbia University Press.

---

[18] Fraser praised Rorty (1998b) for de-emphasizing the role of male philosophers, suggesting they should be "the junior partner" in the proposed alliance with feminism (1991, 260). For an extended engagement with Rorty's thinking in this essay, see Voparil 2011.

Fricker, Miranda. 2009. *Epistemic Injustice: Power and the Ethics of Knowing.* New York: Oxford University Press.

Hamington, Maurice. 2004. "Addams's Radical Democracy: Moving beyond Rights." *Journal of Speculative Philosophy* 18(3): 216–223.

———. 2009. "Feminist Prophetic Pragmatism." *Journal of Speculative Philosophy* 23(2): 83–91.

Hendrix, Burke A. 2013. "Where Should We Expect Social Change in Non-ideal Theory?" *Political Theory* 41(1): 116–143.

Medina, José. 2013. *The Epistemology of Resistance: Gender and Racial Oppression, Epistemic Injustice, and Resistant Imaginations.* New York: Oxford University Press.

Mills, Charles W. 2008. "Racial Liberalism." *PMLA* 123(5): 1380–1397.

———. 2011. "Vice's Vicious Virtues: The Supererogatory as Obligatory." *South African Journal of Philosophy* 30(4): 428–439.

Rorty, Richard. 1979. *Philosophy and the Mirror of Nature.* Princeton, NJ: Princeton University Press.

———. 1989. *Contingency, Irony, and Solidarity.* New York: Cambridge University Press.

———. 1991. *Objectivity, Relativism, and Truth: Philosophical Papers,* Vol. 1. New York: Cambridge University Press.

———. 1997. "What Do You Do When They Call You a Relativist?" *Philosophy and Phenomenological Research* 57(1): 173–177.

———. 1998a. *Truth and Progress: Philosophical Papers,* Vol. 3. New York: Cambridge University Press.

———. 1998b. "Feminism and Pragmatism." In *Truth and Progress: Philosophical Papers,* Vol. 3, 202–227. New York: Cambridge University Press.

———. 1999. "Ethics Without Principles." In *Philosophy and Social Hope,* 72–90. New York: Penguin.

———. 2000. *Rorty and His Critics.* Edited by Robert B. Brandom. Malden, MA: Blackwell.

———. 2003. "Some American Uses of Hegel." In *Das Interesse des Denkens: Hegel aus heutiger Sicht,* edited by Wolfgang Welsch and Klaus Vieweg, 33–46. Munich: Wilhelm Fink Verlag.

———. 2007. *Philosophy as Cultural Politics: Philosophical Papers,* Vol. 4. New York: Cambridge University Press.

———. 2010. "Redemption from Egotism: James and Proust as Spiritual Exercises." In *The Rorty Reader,* edited by Christopher J. Voparil and Richard J. Bernstein, 389–406. Malden, MA: Wiley-Blackwell.

Sarvasy, Wendy. 2010. "Engendering Democracy by Socializing It: Jane Addams's Contribution to Feminist Political Theorizing." In *Feminist Interpretations of Jane Addams,* edited by Maurice Hamington, 292–310. University Park: Penn State University Press.

Seigfried, Charlene Haddock. 1999. "Socializing Democracy: Jane Addams and John Dewey." *Philosophy of the Social Sciences* 29(2): 207–230.

———. 2001. "Pragmatist Metaphysics? Why Terminology Matters." *Transactions of the Charles S. Peirce Society* 37(1): 13–21.

Sullivan, Shannon. 2014. "The Hearts and Guts of White People." *Journal of Religious Ethics* 42(4): 591–611.

Voparil, Christopher J. 2011. "Rortyan Cultural Politics and the Problem of Speaking for Others." *Contemporary Pragmatism* 8(1): 115–131.

———. 2014. "Taking Other Human Beings Seriously: Rorty's Ethics of Choice and Responsibility." *Contemporary Pragmatism* 11(1): 83–102.

Voparil, Christopher J., and Richard J. Bernstein, eds. 2010. *The Rorty Reader*. Malden, MA: Wiley-Blackwell.

CHAPTER 4 | Empirical Approaches to Problems of Injustice

Elizabeth Anderson and the Pragmatists

GREGORY FERNANDO PAPPAS

ELIZABETH ANDERSON's *The Imperative of Integration* (2010) has been considered one of the most important recent developments in a pragmatist approach to a social problem. Anderson sees her book as an instantiation of a nonideal pragmatist approach to political philosophy, one that challenges the way mainstream analytic political philosophy is typically done. Indeed, in its subject matter and its methodology, *The Imperative of Integration* stands out when compared to the predominant ways that scholars work today in post-Rawlsian sociopolitical philosophy. In blending social science research, moral philosophy, and political theory, Anderson's approach is reminiscent of John Dewey.

However, Anderson's brief characterization of the pragmatist approach leaves out its more radical aspects, raising some interesting challenges to philosophers today claiming to practice an "empirical" nonideal approach to actual injustices. I will claim that, while Anderson's characterization of the pragmatist approach is on target, it is incomplete and sometimes narrow in regard to: (*a*) the starting point of inquiry; and (*b*) the experiential resources that pragmatism considers important. My criticism of Anderson is offered in the spirit of reformulating and strengthening the pragmatist approach to injustice in a way that can answer some of the objections that already have been raised against Anderson, and, more importantly, in a way that offers a more promising approach to inquiry into present and future injustices.

Anderson places pragmatism in the nonideal camp of the contemporary ideal versus nonideal debate.[1] In contrast to mainstream ideal approaches that start with a theory or theoretical abstraction about what justice is, pragmatism starts "from a diagnosis of injustices in our actual world, rather than from a picture of an ideal world" (Anderson 2010, 3). In regard to experiential resources, Anderson stresses how pragmatism relies on and seeks the empirical diagnoses provided by the social sciences via studies and analysis of the structural causes of the concrete problems of injustice. Let us consider why Anderson's characterization of the pragmatist approach does not fully capture how radical the pragmatists' "empirical" approach to injustice is. Doing so will help us determine what the more radical approach that pragmatism in fact recommends has to contribute today to nonideal approaches to injustice.

Pragmatism: Problematic Situations of Injustice as Starting Point

Anderson's claim is that the pragmatists' "method is unorthodox" because it starts "from a diagnosis of injustices in the actual world" (2010, 3). However, under Dewey's formulation, the pragmatist methodology is more "unorthodox" and more demanding than Anderson thinks it is, because beginning with a diagnosis is already to start with a theoretical account and not with the concrete problems of injustice as they are experienced in the midst of social life. Let us examine the methodological reasons why Dewey thinks designation should precede diagnosis in an empirical philosophy.

In *Experience and Nature*, Dewey names the empirical way of doing philosophy the "denotative method" (LW 1:371). What Dewey means by "denotation" is simply the phase of an empirical inquiry where we are concerned with designating, as free from theoretical presuppositions as possible, the concrete problem (subject matter) for which we can provide different and even competing descriptions and theories. Once we designate the subject matter, we then engage in the inquiry itself, including diagnosis, possibly even constructing theories and developing concepts. Of course, that is not the end of the inquiry. We must then take the results of that inquiry "as a path pointing and leading back to something in primary experience" (LW 1:17). This looping back is essential, and it never ends

---

[1] On the history of this debate, see Stemplowska and Swift 2012.

as long as there are new experiences that may require a revision of our theories.

Injustices are events suffered by concrete people at particular times and in particular situations. We should start by pointing out and describing these problematic experiences, instead of starting with a theoretical account or diagnosis of them. Dewey is concerned with the consequences of not following the methodological advice to distinguish designation from diagnosis. Definitions, theoretical criteria, and diagnosis can be useful; they have their proper place and function once inquiry is on its way. But if stressed too much at the start of inquiry, they can lead us to overlook aspects of concrete problems that escape our theoretical lenses. We must attempt to designate the subject matter *pretheoretically*, i.e., to "point" in a certain direction, even if it's with only a vague or crude description of the problem. This is a difficult task for philosophers because we are often too prone to interpret the particular problem in a way that confirms our most cherished theories of injustice. One must be careful to designate the subject matter in such a way as to not slant the question in favor of one's theory or theoretical preconceptions. A philosopher must make an honest effort to designate the injustices based on what is experienced as such, because a concrete social problem (e.g., injustice) is independent of and neutral with respect to the different possible competing diagnoses or theories about its causes. Moreover, without this effort, there is no way to test or adjudicate between competing accounts.

That designation precedes diagnosis is true of any inquiry that claims to be empirical. To start with the diagnosis is to start with something other than the problem. The problem is pretheory or preinquiry not in any mysterious sense, but simply in the sense that it is first suffered by someone in a particular context. Otherwise, efforts to diagnose the causes of the problem lack an object and the inquiry cannot even be initiated. In his *Logic*, Dewey lays out the pattern of all empirical inquiries. All inquiries start with what he calls an "indeterminate situation," prior even to a "problematic situation" (LW 12). Here is a sketch of the process:

Indeterminate situation → Problematic situation → Diagnosis: What is the problem? What is the solution? (operations of analysis, ideas, observations, clarification, formulating and testing hypothesis, reasoning, etc.) → Final judgment (resolution: determinate situation).

To make more clear or vivid the difference between Anderson and Dewey on the starting point, we can use the example of medical practice. The doctor's starting point is the experience of a particular illness of a particular patient, i.e., concrete and unique embodied patients experiencing a disruption or problematic change in their lives (LW 6:6). The problem becomes an object of knowledge once the doctor engages in certain interactions with the patient, analysis, and testing, which lead to a diagnosis. For Dewey, "diagnosis" occurs when the doctor is engaged in operations of experimental observation in which she is already narrowing the field of relevant evidence, concerned with the correlation between the nature of the problem and possible solutions.

Dewey uses the example of the doctor to emphasize the radical contextualism and particularism of his view. The good doctor never forgets that this patient and "this ill is just the specific ill that it is. It never is an exact duplicate of anything else" (MW 12:176). Similarly, the empirical philosopher in her inquiry about an injustice brings forth general knowledge or expertise to an inquiry into the causes of an injustice. She relies on sociology and history, as well as knowledge of all forms of injustice, but it is all in the service of inquiry about the singularity of each injustice suffered in a situation. Just as with the doctor, empirical inquirers about injustice must return to the concrete problem for testing, and should never forget that their conceptual abstractions and general knowledge are just means to ameliorate what is particular, context-bound, and unique.

The correction or refinement that I am making to Anderson's characterization of the pragmatists' approach has methodological and practical consequences for how we approach an injustice. The distinction between the *diagnosis* of the problem and the *designation* of the problem (the illness, the injustice) is an important functional distinction that must be kept in inquiry because it keeps us alert to the provisional and hypothetical aspect of any diagnosis. To rectify or improve any diagnosis we must return to the concrete problem; as with the patient, this may require attending as much as possible to the uniqueness of the problem. This is in the same spirit as Anderson's preference for an empirical inquiry that tries to "capture all of the expressive harms" in situations of injustice (2010, 6). But this requires that we begin with and return to concrete experiences of injustice rather than beginning with a diagnosis of the causes of injustice provided by studies in the social sciences. For instance, a diagnosis of causes that are due to systematic, structural features of society or the world disregards aspects of the concrete experiences of injustice that are not systematic and structural.

Making the designation of problematic situations of injustice our explicit methodological starting point functions as a directive to inquirers to locate the problem before venturing into descriptions, diagnosis, analysis, clarifications, hypothesis, and reasoning about the problem. These operations are instrumental to its amelioration and must ultimately return to and be tested against the problem that sparked the inquiry. This directive makes inquirers more attentive to the complex ways in which such differences as race, culture, class, or gender intersect in a problem of injustice. Sensitivity to complexity and difference in matters of injustice is not easy; it is a very demanding methodological prescription because it means that no matter how confident we may feel about applying solutions designed to ameliorate systematic evil, our cures should try to address as much as possible the unique circumstances of each injustice.

This directive is not opposed to inquiry into how big categories (race, capitalism, colonialism, modernity) produce and perpetuate injustices. However, such abstract and general inquiries are ultimately just tools to illuminate particular injustices, just as knowledge of research about diseases of entire populations can assist a doctor. The directive keeps us honest, fallible, and aware of our limitations as intellectuals because it implies that there is always a gap between our best diagnoses and theories of injustice, and the concrete problems of injustice. We cannot assume that our theories or our ways of gathering evidence have captured all there is in concrete problematic contexts. This is relevant to the second qualification that I want to make to Anderson's characterization of pragmatism as a nonideal: the breadth of experiential resources.

Pragmatism: A Broad View of the Experiential Resources for Inquiry

Given its starting point, pragmatism has a broad view of the initial experiential material to be analyzed by inquiry. Contrary to what Anderson seems to suggest, there is no good reason for a pragmatist approach to injustice to limit its experiential resources to the empirical research and material provided by scientific studies. In fact, without the use of other resources, we risk not capturing those aspects of injustices that may not be amenable to scientific types of inquiry. Starting inquiry with the features of events or injustices that are already known or as they are diagnosed or accounted for by a scientific investigation (such as the social sciences) is valuable, but prior to these theoretical lenses there is the problem experienced (sometimes suffered) by concrete human beings in their robust and raw character. We cannot ignore the crudities of life just because they are crude.

In making a diagnosis, we are already reflectively removed from the problem and have been selective in disregarding those features that seem irrelevant to our inquiries. For pragmatism, admitting the selectivity of theoretical lenses in all inquiries does not undermine the notion that some inquiries are better than others (more on this later). But it does imply that what scientific research reveals about a concrete problem is partial and may need to be supplemented by other approaches and experiential resources.

In *The Imperative of Integration,* Anderson reaches her conclusions based on empirical academic research, including social science findings in economics, sociology, and psychology. These findings are important since they seek causal regularities behind the problems, but they need to be complemented with other ways of capturing the complexity and uniqueness of the concrete problems of injustice. For instance, Anderson's diagnosis would have benefited from more concrete interactions with the marginalized of whom she wrote, just as a doctor can enhance her diagnosis via interaction with her patient. Jane Addams used this method of first-order empiricism to inform her work (1902). She thought that one must interact and converse with others to understand, as closely as possible, their experiences of social inequality, discrimination, and oppression. Addams did not confine herself to academia; she put herself into the world. Importantly, experience was her data—interactions unmitigated by statistical compilations, theoretical interpretations, and the like. Sometimes a doctor needs to engage, be participant, and take a sympathetic interest in the condition of the patient to gather new evidence. To understand persons, communities, and even social structures requires that we experience them as historically evolving in a particular context.

I am not claiming that Anderson's conclusions are invalidated by her distance from the raw data of experience, or her lack of interaction with the experiences of those who directly suffer injustice; they may be perfectly sound. The point I want to make is a more general one about how pragmatists should try to approach problems of injustice. Both empirical research and first-order experiences can be utilized together in an effort to identify the problems that persist in society and to develop solutions to these problems.

The idea of enmeshing oneself in the circumstances of others, and thereby gaining a broad and rich perspective, received uptake in sociology (e.g., Robert Park) under the influence of John Dewey and George Herbert Mead in Chicago in the first part of the twentieth century. This is what today is known as the qualitative and ethnographic approach to sociology. However, it would be a mistake to identify the pragmatist approach as one that negates the importance of other techniques such as the ones stressed in quantitative research; they too have their proper place and function. Recently, there has been a new generation of sociologists that has rectified this narrow conception of the pragmatist approach. In fact, pragmatism is now considered the philosophical basis of mixed-methods research (MMR).[2]

However, in regard to methodologies and experiential resources, pragmatism has an even more inclusive view than does MMR. Quantitative and qualitative methods are sociological and as such are only interested in the sort of data that interest sociology: facts about human beings as social animals or members of groups. Therefore, in the study of concrete injustices, they will be selective in ways different than other sciences like psychology. There are as many different ways to capture and understand experiences of injustice as there are types of inquiry. This pluralism is a strength of pragmatism, one that sets an inclusive framework that supports interdisciplinary and cooperative research about problems of injustices. What the philosopher provides is the critical perspective needed to help inquirers from different disciplines avoid reductionism and other common mistakes by reminding them of their particular biases.

However, the pragmatist approach is even more radically open with regard to the evidence it can draw on in its designation and diagnosis of problems of injustice. It isn't restricted to the evidence of any particular academic discipline; neither is it restricted to the evidence that is gathered and validated via the academic disciplines, full stop. Among the experiential resources that pragmatism can draw on are also autobiographical texts, narratives, and stories that the Eurocentric paradigm of knowledge and science often discard as irrelevant, as fiction, or art. For example, Gloria Anzaldúa's *Borderlands / La Frontera* (1987) is a first-person autobiographical account of multiple forms of oppression suffered by Mexican Americans growing up in the border. Without the stories of different oppressed groups, academics would lack the resources needed to begin to

---

[2] See Morgan 2014.

understand the complex experiences of oppression as they are lived and the structural constraints as they are experienced in everyday lives.

By explicitly holding a broader sense of the "empirical," Anderson's view could have avoided some of the objections that have been raised since the publication of her book. More than one commentator has raised questions about whether a privileged, white scholar like Anderson is too removed or out of touch with the Black community's experience to be able to offer a reliable inquiry about their experiences of injustice. Paul Taylor, for example, writes, "Anderson endorses the Deweyan thought that social and political philosophy needs to be grounded in an empirically adequate understanding of the problems we face. But Dewey never tired of explaining that empirical adequacy had to do with experience in all of its existential and phenomenological depth" (2013, 201). And V. Denise James has argued, "my deepest concern [about Anderson] is rooted in another of classical Deweyan pragmatism's central claims that our work should attend to and get not only data from, but also be interpreted through, lived experience" (2013, 1). These are concerns about Anderson's experiential basis for the knowledge that she has produced.

To be sure, the view that just because an inquirer is a member of a privileged group (e.g., a white intellectual) she could not possibly produce reliable knowledge about the injustices suffered by the oppressed is an extreme and implausible view. But one could, and sometimes should, raise the question of whether an investigator's position in her society may have in some way limited the experiential resources of her inquiry into an injustice. In the case of someone like Anderson, one can ask, beyond relying on the best social sciences, whether she considered other experience-based resources that may have had an impact on the scientific research. One could ask, of course, the same questions about Black scholars who for some other reason, such as being academic intellectuals, may be too far removed from the same experiential resources. In the case of Anderson, what became a red flag for her critics was the simple fact that she did not realize that the term "integration" has many negative connotations in Blacks' lived experience.[3]

Anderson's personal distance from the problem of injustice in the lives of Blacks may not invalidate her conclusions, but it raises the question of whether she missed experiential data obtainable via other means, such as a cross-racial dialogue about the very causes of the problem. There is

---

[3] This is an objection raised by Taylor (2013) and James (2013).

in Anderson's work an oversight; that is, she does not acknowledge other sources for inquiry. She may reply that the only sources of knowledge she needs are the causal mechanisms reproducing undemocratic and unjust race relations as they have been revealed by studies in the social sciences. But even these studies are limited if they are too far removed from and not sensitive enough to the particular experiences, daily struggles, and circumstances of particular communities and situations in the United States.

Pragmatism's Methodological Warnings to Contemporary Nonideal "Empirical" Approaches

The pragmatist approach to problems of injustice can be distinguished by its starting point and its broad view of empirical inquiry. There is in this view a demanding commitment to be sensitive to the uniqueness and complexity of the problematic contexts that trigger inquiry. However, does pragmatism provide more specific lessons or directives that can be useful for today's nonideal theorists in their efforts to provide a better alternative to traditional ideal theories in addressing problems of injustice?

First, pragmatism issues the warning to contemporary nonideal theories not to take for granted that their approach is "empirical" simply because they are critical of ideal theories or because they have the intention to be empirical. Theories and categories, no matter how empirically grounded they may seem by virtue of the fact that they are grounded in history or science, can function as "blinders" in our efforts to capture and resolve concrete injustices. Second, while Dewey provided no infallible method by which one can guarantee success in the empirical method he proposes, he would suggest that nonideal theorists learn from other philosophers' mistakes. In this respect, Dewey's occasional efforts to summarize the general and systematic kinds of mistakes nonempirical philosophers tend to make can prove helpful. Specifically, he identifies a series of methodological fallacies that nonideal theorists would do well to avoid.

Dewey formulated different ways in which philosophers have made the same basic mistake, which is the tendency to begin with reflective products or theoretical abstractions, as if there is no prior nontheoretical problematic context. Hence, Dewey concludes that "the most pervasive fallacy of philosophic thinking goes back to neglect of context" (LW 6:5). I will sort out how the different versions of this fallacy have made their way into sociopolitical philosophy, in particular, in philosophical inquiry about injustice. While these fallacies are more common or even to be expected from ideal theories, it is worth demonstrating that nonideal ones are not immune from them either.

The Fallacy of Unlimited Universalization

When philosophers ignore the fact that judgments arise out of limiting conditions set by the contextual situation of particular inquiries, they tend to elevate the conclusions of their inquiries to the point of giving them unlimited application. Philosophers are prone to this fallacy because they are the ones who are usually trying to formulate theories about truth, good, justice, or the absolute, writ large. In many instances of this fallacy, "It is easy and too usual to convert abstraction from *specific* context into abstraction from all context whatsoever" (LW 6:16).

Dewey was aware of how abstract conceptions such as justice, freedom, and democracy have been used by intellectuals and politicians to ignore or divert attention from the concrete social problems in need of our intelligence. However, he was also aware of how the categories of nonideal theories, while seemly empirical, may have the same effect. In fact, one could argue that these categories are more pernicious since they foster the illusion of empirical grounding in solving problems. Rationalist philosophers are not the only ones liable to forget the instrumental and context-bound character of their abstract conceptions.

Political philosophy inspired by sociology often focuses on broad universal-general abstractions (categories) such as the state, individuals, groups, society, capitalism, racism, white supremacy, oppression, structural racism, and the people, even though in the end there are only particular and unique instances of all of these categories in a situation at a particular time and place. To be sure, abstractions, generalities, and universal concepts have a legitimate function in inquiry. They are "tools" to be employed and tested in clarifying concrete social problems. The danger is when intellectuals (especially philosophers) tend to forget both the proper function of these tools and the details of concrete particular contexts. When this happens, they impose their theoretical abstractions upon particulars and oversimplify their empirical complexity. But the concrete troubles or evils that provoke our philosophical inquiries are situation specific and often far more complex than our intellectual analysis may suggest. The failure to recognize this specificity and complexity is an oversight with serious consequences, especially reductionistic, oversimplified, and one-sided solutions to serious social problems. This oversight also tends to generate among academics theoretical problems that are based on false oppositions among their abstract conceptions, which are barriers to continuing inquiry. In this regard, Dewey mentions debates about individualism and collectivism, but today, examples include debates about whether race, class, or gender is the key cause of an injustice.

Anderson seems to be aware of the same danger with abstract conceptions when she replies to the charge that she disregards capitalism and white hegemony in her analysis of racial injustice in the United States. She replies that these concepts are "too lumpy to do the practical work non-ideal theory needs" (Anderson 2013, 4). She would not mind "white hegemony" if all it means is "the entire interlocking and mutually reinforcing set of mechanisms that reproduce systematic black oppression today" (2010, 16). But the concept is one that covers in broad strokes a lot of history across time and place when nonideal theory should be more meticulous and focused on more specific problems of the here and now. She claims that nonideal theory "demands splitting, not lumping" and should be committed to being "meticulous and precise in differentiating the variety and interaction of discrete causal mechanisms underlying the problem at hand" (2013, 4). This resonates with Dewey's metaphilosophical standpoint, but given Dewey's starting point (his radical particularism and contextualism), he would wonder if Anderson's view is immune to the same danger of "lumpiness" that worries her about others' analysis of racial injustice.

Anderson argues in *The Imperative of Integration* that, even though the United States may have legally abolished segregation, de facto segregation is worse; it is the cause of racial injustice. Her solution is that we must integrate in all areas of social life. From Dewey's perspective, Anderson should recognize that her use of "segregation" and "integration" may be as susceptible to the same dangers as "white supremacy" or "capitalism"; they are all abstract concepts that, while useful, may sometimes cover over or lump together too much. Even if one can theoretically discriminate the same general structural cause across cases of racial injustice, there is no single cause called "segregation." Segregation is experienced differently in a variety of complex and unique injustice events. Without this qualification, one runs the risk of lumping all cases together under one name and even disregarding other causes that may be operative in an inextricable way in a problematic situation. Even the specific mechanism of segregation that Anderson identifies varies depending on what other contextual conditions are present in different areas of the United States.

In inquiry, simplicity or lumping in the diagnosis by means of an abstract concept usually results in an answer or solution that has the same, simplistic character. In Anderson's case, the solution is integration. To be fair, Anderson does provide plenty of differentiation in the variety of multiple strategies needed to undertake the problem. But nonideal theorists must be careful not to forget that behind a single conceptual handle there is a plurality of means depending on the particular problem. The temptation to seek and want a single cure under a single name has to be one of the most common temptations in any inquiry about injustice, and nonideal theorists are not immune from this.

The Analytic and Selective Fallacies

When inquirers forget their intellectual dissections, they commit the analytic fallacy. When they forget that evidence of their intellectual dissections indicates that they have been selective from the original subject matter, it is called the fallacy of selective interest. The analytic and selective fallacies are for Dewey two facets of the same general tendency to neglect context, and they are counterproductive in ameliorating concrete problems. Let us consider how they can undermine inquiries about injustice.

Anderson claims that "Non-ideal theory demands splitting, not lumping" (2013, 4). She is, of course, correct. However, the analytic fallacy represents a way of splitting that is undesirable from a pragmatist point of view. Analysis is that process where we discriminate some particulars or elements within a context. Of course, what hangs those particulars together, i.e., what gives them their connection and continuity, is the context itself. Philosophers commit the analytic fallacy when "the distinctions or elements that are discriminated are treated as if they were final and self-sufficient" (LW 6:7).

Philosophers, as a result of their analyses (e.g., as a result of adopting historical accounts and scientific studies), have provided a diagnosis of a particular injustice. For instance, Anderson has shown that inquiry can result in a meticulous and precise differentiation of "the variety and interaction of discrete causal mechanisms underlying the problem" of racial injustice (2013, 4). This is as it should be. However, the danger comes when inquirers neglect or forget the concrete, integral contexts from which things were dissected in the first place. They may then invent artificial, intellectual problems that center on how the variety of causal mechanisms discriminated (analyzed) can be brought together or unified, or, what is more likely, engage in endless debates about which among the plurality of diagnoses is the correct or "real" one. However, these causal mechanisms (after inquiry has formulated them) are not antecedent to the concrete problem, nor can the problem be reduced to their intellectual analysis.

Nonideal theorists must also guard against committing the related fallacy of selectivity. Different types of inquiry will discriminate different causal mechanisms underlying the same problem because each is selective in some way. Pluralism of diagnoses about the same problem of injustice is not problematic unless, by failing to recognize selectivity (i.e., ignoring context), we postulate some ontologically or epistemologically privileged access or approximation to some antecedent "reality" of the problem. When we forget or overlook the unavoidable selectivity of even our best theoretical tools, we run the risk of becoming complacent in the belief that our accounts exhaust all of the causes in the case, or we may proclaim it as the "real" cause and anything else as illusory.

Anderson is correct in that ideal theories tend to overlook or ignore concrete injustices like racism. This is a function of their starting point, which is unreasonably, and some may argue, suspiciously, selective. But even the best nonideal "empirical" views will be selective as well, for, as Dewey says, "there is selectivity (and rejection) found in every operation of thought" (LW 6:14). Pragmatism, however, does not think that admitting or embracing selectivity means that all selectivity is equally good or equally distortive (i.e., biased or partial) with respect to an antecedent reality. Standpoints and perspectives are not things that stand against a uniform and antecedent reality of a problem of injustice. While selectivity is unavoidable, there are usually contextual grounds, depending on the nature of the problem, for distinguishing better from worse selections in a situation without the need to presuppose an Archimedean standpoint or privileged epistemic access by some group or person.

For pragmatism, all selectivity or bias in inquiry has both a positive and a negative aspect. The positive is that it makes available for inquirers aspects of a concrete problem that someone without that particular bias would not have experienced or appreciated. The negative is that no matter how productive our bias is, one may have left out something from the concrete problem that has not been disclosed by our tools of analysis. In other words, the particular forms of selectivity that we bring to an inquiry account both for our limitations and for our particular power-capacity to inquire and ameliorate the problem. The particular selectivity that we bring to an inquiry into a problem of injustice can have different sources. We would do well to distinguish two broad categories of selectivity or bias: theoretical ones (of the type of inquiry) and pretheoretical (of the investigator).

Even the best of the sciences are limited by the purposes, methods, and selectivity particular to them. Yet this also accounts for their advantages over other types of inquiry (e.g., their capacity to control and predict). There can be a plurality of scientific approaches to the causes of an injustice. For instance, each of the social sciences will be selective in a different way in its approach—which includes the starting point and the analysis—to a concrete social problem (e.g., an injustice). This does not mean that all scientific approaches are equally good or that we should resign ourselves to a plurality of sometimes conflicting scientific accounts of the causes of our social problems. Pragmatism derives some positive methodological prescriptions from acknowledging the limitations of each type of inquiry and the resulting pluralism. One important prescription is that we should try to turn our selectivity or bias into part of a larger scheme or collective effort to approach a problem from as many angles or types of inquiry as needed and possible. It is because we have become aware of certain types of selectivity and the limitations associated with them that we have been able to introduce new forms of inquiry that respond to our sense that things are being left out of our understanding of the concrete problem.

Pragmatism argues that, in principle, there are ways of combining the plurality of specialized approaches to a problem. Social scientists could point to ventures in which the resources of different social sciences (with different levels of analysis) are being combined to focus on specific problems. We should then ask: when it comes to problems of injustice, has there been a similar cooperative inquiry between the different variety of academic disciplines and the plurality of theoretical traditions about social injustices? Have we taken advantage of this pluralism in order to ameliorate the concrete problems of injustice in our society?

The variety of "nonideal theories" of injustice today resembles specializations in medicine; they all wish to "cure" the injustice via empirical means, but there are different "injustice specialists" depending on the type of injustice (class, race, gender, etc.) and preferred theoretical explanations. In principle, this is good news, since each of these theories has perfected and makes possible capturing certain aspects of injustices that are historically and empirically grounded and not obvious to the uninformed observer. However, are they spending too much of their time criticizing each other, and therefore forgetting about the integrity of the particular injustice?

The methodological prescription of pragmatism is to try to put our theoretical prejudices aside and to try to designate how the problem is experienced at a pretheoretical level. Importantly, this does not presuppose some antecedent "pure" or "neutral" standpoint from which an investigator can totally divest herself of her conceptual and cultural "baggage" and see the problems of injustice "as they are." Race, class, gender, culture, and character are among the factors that make one more or less sensitive to particular injustices or make different people from different groups experience the same problems differently. For pragmatism, these personal or group sources of selectivity should not be ignored; they are experiential resources for inquiry about injustice even while being biases.

Pragmatism can make sense of the idea that some groups that are "closer" to the problem of injustice are to be taken very seriously without succumbing to the notion that, a priori, some group has epistemic privilege in accessing the truth of an injustice. Nor is the method prescribed committed a priori to a pluralism of irreconcilable or incommensurable experiences of a problem. Prior to experiencing a particular problem, there is no way of determining the extent to which there is agreement or disagreement or even shared experiences of a problem. However, the method does presuppose or hope for change, as well as improvement in how a problem of injustice is captured and conceived as more inquirers, new standpoints, new criticisms, and new evidence are found. This method is predicated on the hope of transcending our biases as communal inquiry about injustice proceeds, not on transcending all biases in order to achieve objectivity as an Archimedean standpoint. The method postulates an extratheoretical check for our theories and denies the necessity of everyone being trapped in his or her ideologies or theories, but it does not assume freedom from our historical circumstances.

The pragmatists' prescription for a more communal, pluralistic, and inclusive inquiry when faced with problems of injustice is based on the hope, shared by both Dewey and Addams, that criticism from others would make individuals become more aware of their own sources of bias about concrete injustices. The remedy for our unavoidably partial, one-sided biases and limitations when experiencing a problem of injustice is to try to engage as much as possible in inclusive and empathetic intercommunication with others via a plurality of means such as history, literature, art, and dialogue.

The hope for a more inclusive and "sympathetic intercommunication" in Dewey and Addams is tied to the importance they placed on certain democratic habits such as "empathy" to help ameliorate our biases in the face of problems of injustice. For them, impartiality has been over-rated in the history of ethical and political theory. Impartiality can be a virtue but only in some contexts—and there is no such thing as absolute impartiality; strict objectivity or impartiality is a myth. Since there are always partialities, the only reasonable question is: which partiality is best? There are better and worse "biases" relative to their capacity to disclose the scope and depth of the situation. As Dewey held, "A stand-point which is nowhere in particular is an absurdity. But one may have an affection for a standpoint which gives a rich and ordered landscape rather than for one from which things are seen confusedly and mea-gerly" (LW 6:15).

Works Cited

Addams, Jane. 1902. *Democracy and Social Ethics.* Accessed May 5, 2014. http://www.gutenberg.org/files/15487/15487-h/15487-h.htm#page_001.

Anderson, Elizabeth. 2013. "Reply to My Critics." *Symposia on Gender, Race and Philosophy* 9(2): 4.

———. 2010. *The Imperative of Integration.* Princeton, NJ: Princeton University Press.

Anzaldúa, Gloria E. 1987. *Borderlands / La Frontera: The New Mesitza.* San Francisco, CA: Aunt Lute Books.

Dewey, John. 1969–1991. *The Collected Works of John Dewey,* edited by Jo Ann Boydston. 37 vols. Carbondale: Southern Illinois University Press. (See List of Abbreviations.)

James, V. Denise. 2013. "The Burdens of Integration." *Symposia on Gender, Race and Philosophy* 9(2):1–4.

Morgan, David. 2014. "Pragmatism as a Paradigm of Social Research." *Qualitative Inquiry* 20(8): 1045–1053.

Stemplowska, Zofia, and Adam Swift. 2012. "Ideal and Nonideal Theory." In *The Oxford Handbook of Political Philosophy,* edited by David Estlund, 373–389. New York: Oxford University Press.

Taylor, Paul C. 2013. "Whose Integration? What's Imperative?" *Symposia on Gender, Race and Philosophy* 9(2): 201–205.

CHAPTER 5 | Ideal and Actual in Dewey's
Political Theory

MATTHEW FESTENSTEIN

IN CURRENT DEBATES AMONG theorists of justice, one key area of contention is between so-called ideal and nonideal theorists. It is a central claim
of the tradition of thinking about justice set in motion by John Rawls, for
example, that we need a view of an ideal conception of society in order
to appraise existing, nonideal circumstances. For Rawls, ideal theory
provides "the only basis for the systematic grasp" of nonideal problems
(1999a, 8). Any "[n]on-ideal theory presupposes that ideal theory is already on hand" (Rawls 1999b, 89–90).[1] An important strand in contemporary political theory challenges this kind of approach, on a number of
grounds.[2] For proponents of nonideal theory, ideal theory is viewed as
masking injustice, cognitively blinkered, and ideological.[3]

In this chapter, I want to consider the claims of nonideal theory not
primarily in themselves but rather in how they relate to and fuel a particular approach to pragmatism, and, in particular, to Dewey's work. Authors
such as Elizabeth Anderson, José Medina, and Gregory Pappas invoke
Dewey as a source and inspiration for this nonideal approach, "a perfect
exemplar," as Medina puts it, of "nonideal normative theorizing of social
practices" (Medina 2012, 8).[4] Here I want to argue that there are certainly

---

[1] See also Simmons 2010.
[2] Of course, Rawls's own conception of this relationship has also famously been challenged on the
grounds that it is too concessive to nonideal feasibility and practical possibility. See Cohen 2008.
[3] See Anderson 2011; Knight and Johnson 2011, Pappas 2016; and Bagg 2016. See also Miller
2008; Mills 2005; Sen 2009. For some critical discussion and response, see Hamlin and
Stemplowska 2012; Simmons 2010; Stemplowska and Swift 2012; Valentini 2009.
[4] See also Medearis 2015; and, from the standpoint of critical theory, Honneth 2014. See
Festenstein 2001.

resources for a nonideal conception of justice, ethics, and political theory in Dewey's pragmatism; given his focus on contingency, problem-solving, quotidian dilemmas, and the overall worldly forward-looking tenor of his thought, this should be unsurprising—even if his terminological eccentricity and theoretical framework need careful navigation.

At the same time, Dewey's ethical and political thought is distinguished by a bold appeal to ideals at key points. Famously, for example, in a passage in *The Public and Its Problems* that I will come back to, he claims that democracy is an "ideal in the only intelligible sense of ideal: namely, the tendency and movement of some thing carried to its final limit, viewed as completed, perfected" (LW 2:328). Now we could view this as merely inspirational rhetoric or the expression of the utopian social hope identified by Richard Rorty in his well-known interpretation of Dewey. Or we could see this as an unresolved tension in Dewey's thought, between his pragmatist conception of inquiry and the role of ideals in political thought.

However, my argument here is different. The elements of Dewey's philosophy that support the nonideal approach are embedded within his account of inquiry and agency. The latter also contains a specific positive conception of the role of ideals in inquiry, which allow us to understand his treatment of political ideals. So we need to distinguish two views of the ideal in Dewey's pragmatist work. In the traditional form that he rejects, the ideal involves the setting up of ends or goals abstracted from the means for their achievement, which he thinks presupposes an incoherent account of practical deliberation and rests on an ideologically distorted conception of value. In its other form, within his account of practical inquiry, we can view ideals as having certain roles in our practical lives and in political thinking.

I will begin (in the first section) by outlining the key claims made by nonideal theorists against the project of ideal theory, before (in the second section) offering an account of what Dewey can offer the nonideal theorist. This includes not only a critical approach to the project of ideal theory built on Dewey's conception of deliberative inquiry, but also a specific picture of the function of ideals within this conception. I will then (in the third section) explore how this makes sense of some of the distinctive features of Dewey's picture of political ideals, taking the opportunity to discuss some alternative recent interpretations.

The Claims of Nonideal Theory

While the distinction between ideal and nonideal theory is now frequently invoked, there is little agreement on precisely how to draw the line between these two approaches. For our purposes here, we can see nonideal theorists as pressing three claims: the inappropriateness of idealization, the methodological priority of injustice, and the commitment to making local improvements rather than achieving perfect justice.[5]

Ideal theories advance principles and ideals for a perfectly just society and then seek to use these as standards by which normatively to assess actual social arrangements. Nonideal theorists object that the resulting models detach the standards of justice arrived at from the motivational and cognitive capacities of actual people, rendering them irrelevant to actual practical deliberation and decision-making (Farrelly 2007; Miller 2008). Idealization also runs the risk of making invisible harms and injustices that only appear in the nonideal world. For example, Elizabeth Anderson argues that the color-blindness of ideal theory renders invisible certain forms of racial stigmatization and expressive harm that are only visible as a wrong or harm outside the ideal model: the "principled color-blindness of ideal theory is epistemologically disabling: it makes us blind to the existence of race-based injustice" (Anderson 2011, 6, 45–53). To this, nonideal theorists add the objection that idealization tends to be ideological. They offer debunking explanations of the content of ideal models as having their genesis in, or as supporting, specific class or group interests, experience, and perspectives. As Mills puts it, for example, the idealizing assumption that everyone relates to one another in an autonomous way reflects the interests and experience of "middle-to-upper-class white males—who are hugely over-represented in the professional philosophical population" (Mills 2005, 172).

Second, nonideal theorists stress the methodological priority of injustice, of starting from a diagnosis of injustice in the actual world rather than with an idealized conception of a perfectly just world (Anderson 2011, 6; Shklar 1992; Fricker 2007). What should drive theorizing about justice is the attempt to identify and understand the contours of existing injustices in the first instance. We do not need a normatively prior, agreed-upon conception of ideal justice in order to embark on this project, and making injustice the methodological priority helps us be more sensitive to the diversity of actual forms of injustice. As Sen says, "We can have a

---

[5] See Hamlin and Stemplowska 2012 and Valentini 2012, who offer variant typologies. As they point out, there are other, overlapping issues, notably of full versus partial compliance, and idealization versus abstraction, which have also been significant in the literature and which are not fully captured here. There is an overlapping but distinct space of arguments carved out by so-called realists in political theory, which I have discussed in Festenstein 2016. See also Bagg 2016; Koopman 2016.

strong sense of injustice on many different grounds, and yet not agree on one particular ground as being *the* dominant reason for the diagnosis of injustice" (Sen 2009, 2). We do not need a single conception of justice in order to identify injustice.

Finally, nonideal theorists have "a commitment to *meliorism*, to making things better without being shackled to any particular picture of 'the best'" (Medina 2012, 12; Anderson 2011; Sen 2009). For this perspective, we can arrive at knowledge of a better state of affairs—an improvement on the status quo—without claiming to, or aspiring to, knowledge of an ideal state of affairs. It is not only that (as in the first line of criticism) aspiration to an ideal model can distort our sense of what is ethically valuable; it is also the case that we do not need an ideal model to act as a standard for local criticism and improvement.

Dewey on Ideals and Potentialities

Turning to Dewey's ethical theory, we can find resources to support the rejection of idealization, the methodological priority of injustice, and meliorism in practical inquiry. With respect to the first of these, it is a persistent theme in his writings that in seeking "a measure for the worth of any given mode of social life" we "cannot set up, out of our heads, something we regard as an ideal society" (MW 9:88). Underpinning the rejection is his specific theory of practical judgment and inquiry.[6] For Dewey, in engaging evaluatively with the goals or ends of actions we cannot avoid identifying the means available to achieve these goals or ends: the "object finally valued as an end to be reached is determined in its concrete makeup by appraisal of existing conditions as means" (LW 13:213). We can try to *contemplate* ends without any sense of the means to achieve them, or we can try to stop thinking about our goals altogether, but we cannot coherently evaluate how we act or orient our agency in the world, in the absence of this kind of appraisal. Detaching a conception of the goals or standards that orient action from the evaluation of the means that we employ to achieve these goals distorts how we should understand our own agency.

In this context, then, we can see the critique of ideals in texts such as *The Quest for Certainty* as specifically targeting a view of ideals as

---

[6] This is not the place for a detailed account of Dewey's accounts of practical judgment, valuation, and inquiry. For a fuller account of the view underlying this, see Festenstein 1997, 34–46; Festenstein 2008. Helpful guides include Bernstein 1971; Tiles 1988; Pappas 2008; Welchman 2010; Fesmire 2015.

setting up fixed ends or standards which are detached from the continuum of practical inquiry. That is, the target is the defective tradition of thinking about agency in which this conception of ideals is embedded. This tradition dooms them to spectral irrelevance:

> The very meaning of the word "ideals" is significant of the divorce which has obtained between means and ends. "Ideals" are thought to be remote and inaccessible of attainment; they are too high and fine to be sullied by realization. They serve vaguely to arouse "aspiration" but they do not evoke and direct strivings for embodiment in actual existence. They hover in an indefinite way over the actual scene; they are expiring ghosts of a once significant kingdom of divine reality whose rule penetrated to every detail of life. (LW 4:222–223)[7]

Further, focusing on ideals in this sense is cognitively disabling, taking attention away from "problems of men" and the needs of the present situation.

Dewey's diagnosis of the ideological content of ideals rests on his view of the inherently practical and socially engaged character of philosophy, which he views as entangled in social interests and conflicts. In keeping with this view, Dewey supports the idea that there are ideological sources and effects in this form of idealization. Famously, the divorce of means from ends, and associated distinctions between instrumental and intrinsic forms of value, spring from a social division between a leisured and a laboring class and serve to reinforce that division by making it appear part of the conceptual or natural fabric of the world.[8] As a mode of practical deliberation, Dewey believes (as he says in a review of Lippmann's *An Inquiry into the Principles of the Good Society*) that "[e]very system of social thought which sets up ends without reference to the means by which they are to be brought about tends in effect to support the *status quo*, no matter how good the intentions of those who paint the picture" (LW 11:489). Without a concrete conception of how to effect transformation, ideals generate only resignation, violence, and despair.

Second, while Dewey does not subscribe to the language of the priority of injustice, his conception of practical deliberation sees it as an activity rooted in problems, triggered by the breakdown of established habits and "a condition of tension between a person and environing conditions"

---

[7] See also LW 1:295–296.
[8] See MW 14:160, 185–158; LW 4:225; LW 14:235; MW 12:275.

(LW 13:231). The starting point for ethical inquiry, like other forms of inquiry, is the recognition of a problem, and it consists in the search for ways of rendering problematic situations "determinate" and resolving them.[9] Situations that present no obstacles or disruptions do not prompt inquiry and we are driven into critical reflection of means and ends only when our preexisting unreflective habits fail in some way. It is important also to note that ethical theories are interpreted as tools to aid in this deliberative process, rather than as themselves setting the agenda for inquiry. In the second edition of *Ethics*, for example, Dewey and J. H. Tufts offer an interpretation of teleology, deontology, and virtue ethics as providing contrasting methodological orientations for identifying, describing, and addressing problems: such theories "are treated not as incompatible rival systems which must be accepted or rejected *en bloc*, but as more or less adequate methods of surveying the problem of conduct" (LW 7:6).

Third, we can find in Dewey's account of inquiry the nonideal theorist's focus on local or situational improvement rather than on achieving perfect justice. We can make sense of improvement and progress without matching it against a fixed standard of perfection:

> The process of growth, of improvement and progress, rather than the static outcome and result, becomes the significant thing. Not health as an end fixed once and for all, but the needed improvement in health—a continual process—is the end and good. The end is no longer a terminus or limit to be reached. It is the active process of transforming the existent situation. (MW 12:181)

An agent's practical judgments aim to "unify" or "integrate" the problematic situation that she confronts. "Here is the factor which cuts short the process of foreseeing and weighing ends-in-view in their function as means," writes Dewey: "sufficient unto the day is the evil thereof and sufficient also is the *good* of that which does away with the existing evil" (LW 13:232).

However, while Dewey shares these three commitments with the nonideal theorist, he also seeks to make space for ideals within his positive account of deliberation. It is worth noting that Dewey's sense of the practical and ideological entanglement of philosophy extends to a diagnosis of realist *skepticism* about ideals as such, which accompanies his account of ideal theory as ideology.[10] He views the rejection of ideals as itself an

---

[9] See Festenstein 2001, 2007.
[10] See Farr 1999.

understandable response to the struggles of idealism and realpolitik, but emphasizes that the response should instead be the recognition of "the impotency and harmfulness of any and every ideal that is proclaimed wholesale and in the abstract, that is, as something apart from the detailed concrete existences whose moving possibilities it embodies" (MW 12:154). In this context, he explains ideals as hypotheses within his conception of inquiry, as a component in the response we construct to a problematic situation.[11] He writes in *Experience and Nature*:

> Water that slakes thirst, or a conclusion that solves a problem have ideal character as long as thirst or a problem persists in a way which qualifies the result. But water that is not a satisfaction of need has no more ideal quality than water running through pipes into a reservoir; a solution ceases to be a solution and becomes a bare incident of existence when its antecedent generating conditions of doubt, ambiguity and search are lost from its context. While the precarious nature of existence is indeed the source of all trouble, it is also an indispensable condition of ideality. (LW 1:58)

Here the ideality of water derives from its constituting the solution to a problem, that of thirst. In a deliberative context, ideality requires precariousness, the antecedent conditions of doubt, ambiguity, and the search for a resolution. In this sense, ideality is not dispensable but a feature of a reflective response to a problem: we construct ideals that make sense in the light of the problems we confront, as part of the process of practical inquiry. Ideals lack an ideal quality without a problem within an existing state of affairs, the presence of doubt, or unmet needs.

The ideal quality of, say, water to the thirsty seems rather different from theorizing with ideals. However, this thought—that this ideal quality emerges from the precarious, troubled character of the situation requiring deliberation—is a bridge to the thought that idealization plays a role in this conception of inquiry. In contrast to the view of ideals as irrelevant ghosts, in this strand of his thinking Dewey views ideals as developed from immanent possibilities of concrete social life:

> There are values, goods, actually realized upon a natural basis—the goods of human association, of art and knowledge. The idealizing imagination seizes upon the most precious things found in climacteric moments of

---

[11] This is a part of the accounts offered by Anderson (2011) and Medina (2012) but not by Pappas (2016), to whose approach I will turn shortly; see also the account in MacGilvray 2004.

experience and projects them. We need no external criterion and guarantee of their goodness. They are had, they exist as good, and out of them we frame our ideal ends. (LW 8:33)

Ideals "express possibilities" but "they are genuine ideals only in so far as they are possibilities of what is now moving." If not "related to actualities, they are pictures in a dream" (LW 5:112).[12]

Genuine ideals, in this sense, have the right relationship to our practical deliberation because they are not severed from the means necessary to achieve them: "We cannot set up, out of our heads, something we regard as an ideal society. We must base our conception upon societies which actually exist, in order to have any assurance that our ideal is a practicable one" (MW 9:88). But, he goes on, an ideal cannot uncritically reflect traits of the existing society. Since any actual society contains a variety of values and tendencies, including conflicting ones, merely pointing to the social embeddedness of ideals does not tell us which values in a pluralistic environment we should cherish and act on, or how to address conflicts among those values: "the problem is to extract the desirable traits of forms of community life which actually exist, and employ them to criticize undesirable features and suggest improvement" (MW 9:88–89). In projecting ideals, we expose possibilities that would otherwise not be discovered. In the discussion of definitions in *Logic*, Dewey writes:

> Like ideals, [definitions] are not intended to be themselves realized but are meant to direct our course to realization of potentialities in existent conditions—potentialities which would escape our notice if not for the guidance which an ideal, or a definition, provides. . . . To sanctify the ideal and to disparage the actual because it never copies the ideal, are two connected ways of missing the point of the *function* of the ideal and actual. A vision is not a scene but it can enable us to construct scenes which would not exist without it. To suppose that a vision is worthless unless it can be directly determined to be a scene is for those who take the idea seriously, the high road to pessimism, and for others the road to fantasy. To ignore or depreciate the ideal because it cannot be literally translated into existence is to acquiesce not only to things "as they are"—as is sometimes said—but also to things "as they are not" because all things that are have potentialities. (LW 12:303)

---

[12] See also MW 12:151.

In this sense, idealization suggests possibilities, providing a way in which agents as inquirers can relate to their surroundings, that disclose new potentialities of action and resources that they otherwise would not possess for the construction of ends-in-view. We can judge idealizations in terms of the fruitfulness in helping us to generate more specific "scenes," or analyses of problematic situations. The vision only *enables* us to construct the scene: it is necessary but does not do this for us. The task of construction, and success or failure within it, is still up to the agents involved. It is a misunderstanding to think that the connection to "potentialities" forms an aspiration to guarantee that the goals that we construct are coherent or achievable.[13] Whether something is a potential is a matter of experiment and interaction by situated inquirers, not of theory or the a priori projection of an inherent telos (LW 12:386). Rather, the point is that projects that are either disconnected from potentialities or view potentialities in a way disconnected from actuality can't succeed—or, at least, they can't succeed in achieving their aims, even if they have immense effects.

Understanding Dewey's Political Ideals

The positive account of ideal theorizing in Dewey gives us a grip on some of the more well-known statements about ideals in his political philosophy. Consider the claim in *The Public and Its Problems* that "democracy is not an alternative to other principles of associated life" but is rather "the idea of community life itself":

> It is an ideal in the only intelligible sense of ideal: namely, the tendency and movement of some thing carried to its final limit, viewed as completed, perfected. Since things do not attain such fulfillment but are in actuality distracted and interfered with, democracy in this sense is not a fact and never will be. But neither in this sense is there or has there ever been anything which is a community in its full measure, a community unalloyed by alien elements. The idea or ideal of a community presents, however, actual phases of associated life as they are freed from restrictive and disturbing elements, and are contemplated as having attained their limit of development. (LW 2:328)[14]

---

13 See Markell 2007, 119.
14 In his lecture notes on political philosophy from the same year Dewey delivered what became *The Public and Its Problems* at Kenyon College, he writes: "An ideal is a tendency viewed as

Ideals here are explicitly conceptualized as unachievable, and as representing a form of completion that cannot be fulfilled. What makes the democratic ideal the ideal of community life itself is its "concrete" reconciliation of ideals that otherwise come into conflict, namely, fraternity, liberty, and equality.

Dewey does not claim that actually existing democracies (or societies that purport to be democracies) in fact reconcile these values; nor indeed does he claim that they can. Rather, the claim is that this is what the ideal *projects*. In the second edition of *Ethics*, Dewey and Tufts describe the democratic ideal as "an endeavor to unite two ideas which have historically often worked antagonistically: liberation of individuals on one hand and promotion of a common good on the other" (LW 7:349). Crucially, the democratic ideal poses, but does not solve, "the great problem" of these historically antagonistic ideas.

One interpretation, offered by Richard Bernstein, proposes that we view this as "not an impossible 'utopian' ideal—or even a regulative principle in the Kantian sense that can never, in principle, be realized. Rather it is an end-in-view that can guide our actions *here and now*" (Bernstein 2010, 295). However, textually this does not fit well with Dewey's own emphasis, since he indeed claims that democracy "in this sense is not a fact and never will be" (LW 2:328). More importantly, the interpretation pushes us back to the question of how an ideal in this sense is meant to guide our actions in the here and now. Instead, then, interpreters have tended to converge on the thought that the democratic ideal here should be understood as a regulative ideal, one which can guide critical assessment of practices but should not be thought of as achievable in practice.[15] The question, then, is how such an ideal should be understood—what it means to be a regulative ideal in this sense in the Deweyan account of practical deliberation. One response is to interpret Dewey as proposing that actual citizens should act *as if* the ideal conditions in fact hold. Jason Stanley, for example, argues the following about this passage:

Dewey even has a particular suggestion about how these ideals ought to regulate the behavior of an actual society struggling with "the ills of democracy." When confronted with the daily reminders of the nonrealistic features inherent

---

carried to its limit. It is a limiting conception of empirically observance tendency though not itself observable" (Dewey 1926).

[15] See, for example, MacGilvray 2004, 143; Knight and Johnson 2011, 34; Rogers 2008, 139–140.

in the ideals of democracy, we should nevertheless adhere to the ideals, which means trusting our fellow deliberators and abiding by the outcome of the deliberative process. (Stanley 2015, 174)

If this is Dewey's suggestion, it seems problematic, on his own terms. Prompting actual political agents to behave as if the posited ideal conditions hold returns us to some of the criticisms of idealization already discussed, since it seems to detach the standards that people are meant to adhere to from their actual motivations and capacities, as well as closing off the nonideal perspective from which some existing wrongs can be perceived (Stanley 2015, 196). However, it is difficult to find textual support for the claim that this is in fact Dewey's suggestion for the authority of a regulative ideal, which seems in conflict with his insistence on the reciprocity of means and ends.

A different version of this idea is to think of ideals as regulative assumptions of inquiry—" 'guiding' or 'leading' principles of inquiry" which are "operationally *a priori*" in inquiry (LW 12:19–21).[16] These are principles, such as rules of inference, which experience teaches us we should take for granted in the course of inquiry. Now this certainly is an idea that plays a significant role in Dewey's account of inquiry, and seems to be a more promising approach as it anchors the ideal to practice in a way that chimes with Dewey's wider claim about the relation of the two. There is a well-known line of argument to the effect that certain democratic commitments are indeed regulative assumptions, in this sense, of a commitment to inquiry. As Cheryl Misak, who has done the most to develop and promote this approach, puts it, if "we are to have any hope of success in reaching beliefs that stand up to all experience, we must take the experiences of others seriously. The best way of taking them seriously is some form of democratic representation and collective decision-making" (Misak 2013, 138).[17] However effective this line of thought is as a pragmatist argument for some core democratic commitments, this interpretation does not seem to capture what is distinctive about Dewey's claims on behalf of the ideal in this passage. We may accept the idea that inquiry requires taking the experience of all others seriously, and that this grounds a certain sense in which we should treat each individual as an equal participant. But Dewey's claims on behalf of the democratic ideal are rather different. It is a "clear consciousness of a communal life" in which "the realization of the [shared]

---

[16] See also LW 12:108, 325–326. Dewey cites Peirce here. See Misak 2013, 50–52, 138.
[17] See Putnam 1992; Misak 2000; Westbrook 2005; Festenstein 2004, 2007; Talisse 2007. To be clear, I am not suggesting that this interpretation of Deweyan ideals is Misak's.

good is such as to effect an energetic desire and effort to sustain it in being just because it is a good shared by all" (LW 2:328), and tied, as we have seen, to interdependent values of liberty, equality, and fraternity.

The Deweyan alternative is to see the ideal functioning here in the way he sets out in *Logic*, as a heuristic formed in nonideal circumstances which suggests possibilities for action and for how our values may relate to one another. Ideals set out "visions," understood as possibilities to be experimentally tested and explored, but they do not specify the ends-in-view that we work to. We are not committed to the ideal as a condition of searching for beliefs that we can rely on (the regulative assumptions view), nor to acting as if the ideal holds in actuality, nor to the idea that we should view the ideal as a goal to be achieved. Rather, ideals "direct our course to realization of potentialities in existent conditions—potentialities which would escape our notice if not for the guidance which an ideal ... provides" (LW 12:303). Ideal theorizing becomes part of the process of inquiry, from this perspective. So Dewey's articulation of the democratic ideal suggests how we should think about the relationship among the values of liberty, equality, and fraternity, and what it would mean to instantiate them. Alternatively, developing an idealized conception of justice on the basis of a particular account of rationality and of social primary goods can form part of inquiry.

Rejecting outright the function of this kind of idealization in inquiry closes down a way of thinking about alternative social possibilities and of generating fresh ways of identifying, analyzing, and resolving problems. However, they do not themselves offer resolutions. What these idealizations contain in Dewey's ethics is a recognition of conflict among values.[18] The *Ethics* formulation of the democratic ideal makes explicit something implicit in the earlier text. Ideals can themselves be constitutive of a problematic or indeterminate situation—one that is, to recall, "disturbed, troubled, ambiguous, confused, full of conflicting tendencies, obscure, etc" (LW 12:109). Modern political ideals do not in themselves resolve problems, in the sense of removing troubles and providing an unambiguous blueprint for action. To describe the content of the democratic ideal, as Dewey does, as projecting the reconciliation of different values does not deny the potentiality for conflict between different conceptions of the good, nor that we need to find ways of resolving or living with such conflicts that do not involve their reconciliation. Rather, in proposing ways of

---

[18] There is a broader context of pluralism to consider here. See, for example, Festenstein 2008; Welchman 2010.

resolving conflict, political ideals set problems for actual agents; at least, they do for those sensitive to those ideals. The project of *The Public and Its Problems* is then "the search for the Great Community," sketching how the material interdependence and complexity of the "Great Society" can be controlled through the arts of public communication and the revival of local forms of community. The patterns of interdependence that form a Great Society are in place, Dewey argues, but do not constitute the Great Community, with a shared sense of belonging and capacities for shared understandings and effective public action. In Dewey's work on freedom, individualism, and liberalism, the stress falls on what he takes to be an in-adequate specification of ideals of liberty and the individual in "negative" terms. If negative liberty ever delivered freedom, he thinks, it certainly cannot do so in the conditions of modern industrial society.

Certain nonideal criticisms of idealization fall away for this account. Dewey's view does not suggest that idealization is either a necessary or a sufficient condition for arriving at a well-grounded practical judgment about what to do. It is not imposing cognitive blinkers or insisting on un-realistic moral assumptions since this is not a standpoint that it takes to be *required* for social criticism. Rather, this is a standpoint or activity that we can adopt in the course of problem-solving, and the value of idealiza-tion lies in its capacity to suggest practical judgments that we can act on in "actuality," which help us to identify and resolve real problems. Dewey counters the fear that idealization is an inherently ideological mode of inquiry with the thought that it opens up new possibilities, and reminds us of how socially established habits of thinking and acting can appear to be unquestionably natural. Idealization does move us away from taking injustice as methodologically prior, but in Dewey's conception it is, like any theorizing, a functional moment embedded within a wider view of inquiry as driven by concrete problems. Finally, ideals do not directly act as blueprints or standards of judgment of existing society, on this account. Rather, they suggest pathways for change: clarifying and following those paths, and judging the ideals in the light of this, form tasks for actual, nonideal agents.

The interpretation offered here suggests an alternative to the strongly particularist account of Dewey as nonideal theorist offered by Gregory Pappas in his important discussion (Pappas 2016). For Pappas, a pragma-tist should be critical of approaches to justice that start with a theoretical abstraction about what justice is, with the assumption of a noncontextual ahistorical universal point of view, and with a particular political ideol-ogy or agenda. While pragmatism should avoid what he calls "atomistic particularism," which overlooks the continuities between different cases (for example, of racism), it needs to adopt a problem-centered and contextual approach to injustice, employing inquiry to address the lived experience of concrete agents: "Injustices are events suffered by concrete people at a particular time and in a situation. We need to start by pointing out and describing these problematic experiences instead of starting with a theoretical account or diagnosis of them" (Pappas 2016, 70). He distinguishes pragmatism from views (such as those of Mills and of Anderson) that make use of social theoretical generalizations to form the basis of these diagnoses.

From an interpretative standpoint, I think this account diverges in two key ways from the commitments to be found in Dewey. First, Pappas's account overdraws a distinction between problem-driven and theory-driven inquiry. For Dewey, as he puts it in *Logic*, the facts of inquiry are not "just there." We need a *"generalization* in the form of a *hypothesis"* to order the material "as facts" (LW 12:491). Generalization is ineliminable if we are going to inquire into a problem we have identified, and our past inquiries inform our current ones. Of course, in any particular case inquirers may fall into the trap of defining a problem so that it fits their favored method (for example) or of failing to see a link between two particular problems that is important. But this kind of mistake is identified case by case: it is not true that applying a theory is inherently cognitively flawed. Second, as I've emphasized, Dewey makes space for "ideality" and idealization in his account of inquiry. It is important for Dewey that we do not focus merely on problems in front of us, as we happen to conceive them, but "[m]an is under just as much obligation to develop his most advanced standards and ideals as to use conscientiously those which he already possesses" (MW 12:180).

Conclusions

Dewey's experimental view does not respect the self-denying ordinance of nonideal theory.[19] Instead, what Dewey calls ideality and idealization are accommodated as functions in his wider conception of inquiry, and this account allows us to understand the particular treatment of ideals in his political writings. He develops this conception explicitly to support a

---

[19] Any more than it should respect the self-denying ordinance of Rawlsian political liberalism. See Festenstein 2010.

wider problem-focused and situated conception of ethics and inquiry, and in order to avoid various moral and epistemic defects that he identifies with idealized thinking that is detached from practical deliberation. This suggests one way in which we can think of idealizing political theory from within an account of ethics and practical judgment that is overall supportive of the perspective and project of the nonideal theorist. Of course, this is in keeping with Dewey's broader reinterpretation of dualisms in functional terms. In engaging with Dewey's view of idealization in this way, I have not of course discussed whether or not his particular conception of a democratic ideal is plausible, only the terms in which he offers it to us, and its significance for breaking down barriers in current thinking about justice.

Works Cited

Anderson, Elizabeth. 2011. *The Imperative of Integration*. Princeton, NJ: Princeton University Press.

Bagg, Samuel. 2016. "Between Critical and Normative Theory: Predictive Political Theory and Deweyan Realism." *Political Research Quarterly*. doi:10.1177/1065912916634898.

Bernstein, Richard J. 1971. *Praxis and Action*. Philadelphia: University of Pennsylvania Press.

———. 2010. "Dewey's Vision of Radical Democracy." In *The Cambridge Companion to John Dewey*, edited by Molly Cochran, 288–308. Cambridge: Cambridge University Press.

Cohen, G. A. 2008. *Rescuing Justice and Equality*. Cambridge: Harvard University Press.

Dewey, John. 1969–1991. *The Collected Words of John Dewey*, edited by Jo Ann Boydston. 37 vols. Carbondale: Southern Illinois University Press. (See List of Abbreviations.)

———. 1926. Political Philosophy. Lecture Notes. Dewey Papers, Special Collections, Morris Library, Southern Illinois University, Box 65/1.

Farr, James. 1999. "John Dewey and American Social Science." *American Journal of Political Science* 43(2): 520–541.

Farrelly, Colin. 2007. "Justice in Ideal Theory: A Refutation." *Political Studies* 55(4): 844–864.

Fesmire, Stephen. 2015. *Dewey*. New York: Routledge.

Festenstein, Matthew. 1997. *Pragmatism and Political Theory*. Cambridge: Polity Press.

———. 2001. "Inquiry as Critique: On the Legacy of Deweyan Pragmatism for Political Theory." *Political Studies* 49(4): 730–748.

———. 2004. "Deliberative Democracy and Two Models of Pragmatism." *European Journal of Social Theory* 7(3): 291–306.

———. 2007. "Inquiry and Democracy in Contemporary Pragmatism." In *Pragmatism and European Social Theory*, edited by Patrick Baert and Bryan S. Turner, 115–136. Cambridge: Bardwell Press.

————. 2008. "John Dewey: Inquiry, Ethics and Democracy." In *The Oxford Handbook of American Philosophy*, edited by Cheryl Misak, 87–109. Oxford: Oxford University Press.

————. 2010. "Pragmatism, Inquiry and Political Liberalism." *Contemporary Political Theory* 9: 25–44.

————. 2016. Pragmatism, Realism and Moralism. *Political Studies Review* 14(1): 39–49.

Fricker, Miranda. 2007. *Epistemic Injustice*. Oxford: Oxford University Press.

Hamlin, Alan, and Zofia Stemplowska. 2012. "Theory, Ideal Theory, and the Theory of Ideals." *Political Studies Review* 10(1): 48–62.

Honneth, Axel. 2014. *Freedom's Right: The Social Foundations of Democratic Life*. Translated by Joseph Ganahl. Cambridge: Polity Press.

Knight, Jack, and James Johnson. 2011. *The Priority of Democracy: The Political Consequences of Pragmatism*. Princeton, NJ: Princeton University Press.

Koopman, Colin. 2016. "Unruly Pluralism and Inclusive Tolerance: The Normative Contribution of Jamesian Pragmatism to Non-ideal Theory." *Political Studies Review* 14(1): 27–38.

MacGilvray, Eric. 2004. *Reconstructing Public Reason*. Cambridge: Harvard University Press.

Markell, Patchen. 2007. "The Potential and the Actual: Mead, Honneth and the 'I.'" In *Recognition and Power: Axel Honneth and the Tradition of Critical Social Theory*, edited by Bert Van Den Brink and David Owen, 100–132. Cambridge: Cambridge University Press.

Medearis, John. 2015. *Why Democracy Is Oppositional*. Cambridge: Harvard University Press.

Medina, José. 2012. *The Epistemology of Resistance: Gender and Racial Oppression, Epistemic Injustice, and the Social Imagination*. Oxford: Oxford University Press.

Miller, David. 2008. "Political Philosophy for Earthlings." In *Political Theory: Methods and Approaches,* edited by David Leopold and Marc Stears, 29–48. Oxford: Oxford University Press.

Mills, Charles. 2005. "Ideal Theory and Ideology." *Hypatia* 20(3): 165–184.

Misak, Cheryl. 2000. *Truth, Politics, Morality: Pragmatism and Deliberation*. New York: Routledge.

————. 2013. *The American Pragmatists*. Oxford: Oxford University Press.

Pappas, Gregory F. 2008. *John Dewey's Ethics: Democracy as Experience*. Bloomington: Indiana University Press.

————. 2016. "Pragmatists and Injustice." *Pluralist* 11(1): 58–77.

Putnam, Hilary. 1992. *Renewing Philosophy*. Cambridge: Harvard University Press.

Rawls, John. 1999a. *A Theory of Justice*. 2nd ed. Cambridge: Harvard University Press.

————. 1999b. *The Law of Peoples*. Cambridge: Harvard University Press.

Rogers, Melvin. 2008. *The Undiscovered Dewey: Religion, Morality and the Ethos of Democratic Politics*. New York: Columbia University Press.

Sen, Amartya. 2009. *The Idea of Justice*. London: Allen Lane.

Shklar, Judith. 1992. *The Faces of Injustice*. New Haven: Yale University Press.

Simmons, A. John. 2010. "Ideal and Nonideal Theory." *Philosophy and Public Affairs* 38(1): 5–35.

Stanley, Jason. 2015 *How Propaganda Works*. Princeton, NJ: Princeton University Press.

Stemplowska, Zofia, and Adam Swift. 2012. "Ideal and Nonideal Theory." In *The Oxford Handbook of Political Philosophy*, edited by David Estlund, 373–389. Oxford: Oxford University Press.

Talisse, Robert B. 2007. *A Pragmatist Philosophy of Democracy*. New York: Routledge.

Tiles, J. E. 1988. *Dewey*. London: Routledge.

Valentini, Laura. 2012. "Ideal vs. Nonideal Theory: A Conceptual Map." *Philosophy Compass* 7(9): 654–664.

Welchman, Jennifer. 2010. "Dewey's Moral Philosophy." In *The Cambridge Companion to Dewey*, edited by Molly Cochran, 166–186. Cambridge: Cambridge University Press.

Westbrook, Robert B. 2005. *Democratic Hope: Pragmatism and the Politics of Truth*. Ithaca, NY: Cornell University Press.

CHAPTER 6 | Justice in Context

RUTH ANNA PUTNAM

WE PRAGMATISTS BELIEVE THAT inquiry begins in an indeterminate situation. I take it that the inquiry to which this conference[1] is devoted begins as follows: We find ourselves in a situation in which society has disappointed the hopes and legitimate expectations of the poor and the powerless (women and minorities, children, and those who are ill) in spite of legislation and Supreme Court decisions that promised to meet those hopes and expectations. Currently, it is unclear whether this situation will improve or deteriorate; the situation is truly indeterminate. How it will develop depends on what someone will do. What, then, is to be done, and who will do it?

Once we ask what is to be done to improve the life prospects of the disadvantaged in our midst, we have formulated a problem. But we may have arrived at that formulation of the problem by two distinct routes. We may have appealed to a standard of justice to which the situation fails to conform, or we may have responded to what James called "the cries of the wounded" (WWJ 6:158). We may have approached the indeterminate situation in a "structured" or in a "contextual" manner. I am inclined to think that if the disadvantaged did not press their claims upon us in some way, if it were possible for us neither to see nor to hear them, we would not realize that their situation violates the standards of justice that we profess. I also think that lacking such a standard, or embracing a different standard, we would not formulate the problem as I just did. Instead we might inquire how to keep the disadvantaged out of sight and out of earshot.

---

[1] The conference to which Putnam refers is the Symposium on the Renaissance of Pragmatism in American Legal Thought held on February 23–24, 1990 at the University of Southern California Law Center, the proceedings of which are published in *Southern California Law Review* 63(6).

I have assumed here that "we" are, at any rate, not poor, not uneducated, and not entirely powerless. But even the poor and the powerless must hear the cries of others who are similarly oppressed if they are to consider joint action as a possible solution to their problem, i.e., if they are to see their problem as a political problem. And even the poor and the powerless must have some sense that what is done to them is an injustice rather than merely painful, lest they accept the claims of the rich and the powerful that the poor and the powerless are poor and powerless because they are inadequate.

What has just been described is the first step in Dewey's famous pattern of inquiry, transforming an indeterminate situation into a problem.[2] The next step in that pattern is the formulation of a problem solution. In our case, a problem solution would be what Dewey calls elsewhere an end-in-view, the claim that a certain change in the situation would be a change for the better. A universal health insurance plan comes to mind as an example. Such an end-in-view will then guide what steps are to be taken: For example, studying various types of national health insurance in other countries, determining where opposition to such a plan is centered and how it might best be overcome, deciding how to organize support for the plan, and acting in accordance with the results of the investigation.

It is important to note that if our problem had been purely scientific (for instance, how to explain earthquakes) the process would have been the same. The suggested problem solution would then have been called a hypothesis rather than an end-in-view, but it too would have guided subsequent inquiry and action (experimentation). Moreover, although a hypothesis, once it has been well established, will be treated differently and will play different roles in subsequent inquiries, no scientific theory is ever immune from revision if later experience calls for it. Similarly, the ends-in-view, once they have been realized, remain open to re-evaluation; they are, says James, experiments "to be judged, not *a priori*, but by actually finding, after the fact of their making, how much more outcry or how much appeasement comes about" (WWJ 6:157).

This application of Dewey's pattern of inquiry to our common situation as citizens prompts several reflections appropriate to our situation as participants in a symposium on pragmatism and the law. My reflections are relevant, in particular, to the papers by Minow and Spelman, Radin, and Wells.

---

[2] See Dewey's *Logic: The Theory of Inquiry* (LW 12).

I

My first point is that an indeterminate situation does not alone determine whether a problem is to be seen as a private or a political problem. Indeed, the same problem can and must often be seen as both; the distinction between the private and the political is orthogonal to the distinction between approaching the problem "situationally" and approaching it "structurally." In the first section, we saw that the formulation of our problem as the political problem of improving the life prospects of the poor required that it be approached both situationally and structurally. We had to be sufficiently aware of the details of the lives of our fellow citizens to see that their situation was grim. We had to subsume those details under the rubric "injustice" (perhaps in the sense of a violation of Rawls's difference principle) in order to formulate the problem in terms of an improvement in their life prospects (Rawls 1971, 83).

On the other hand, neither approach by itself, nor indeed in combination, guarantees that a problem will be seen as political. When Gilligan posed the Heinz problem—the problem of the man who cannot afford the medication that his wife needs—both those children who responded by subsuming the problem under the rubric "right to life dominates right to property" and those who considered the circumstances in greater detail treated the problem as a private problem (Gilligan 1982, chap. 2). None of them achieved a perspective from which Heinz's problem could be seen as the kind of problem that demands a change in public policy for its solution. Thus, those who claimed that the right to life dominates the right to property failed to notice that the sort of public health policy that gives rise to Heinz's problem belies the principle to which they appealed. And those who approached the problem in a caring way failed to care for the thousands of others in similar predicaments.

Here it seems worth pointing out that seeing a problem as a public problem, seeing that it shares features with a reasonably large number of other problems, is more general than seeing it as a political problem; the political, I want to claim, is only one sphere of the public. Consider the case of the window of a Bangladeshi laborer:

> My husband died two nights ago. You must have heard. His body was hot
> with fever and I bathed his forehead with a wet cloth, but it was no use. All
> we had in the house was 25 *poisha*, so I couldn't buy anything good for him
> to eat. He died with nothing in his stomach. I didn't have the money to buy

wood to cremate him, or even to wrap him in a new cloth. (Hartman and Boyce 1983, 175)

Surely this woman has a private problem, a problem that requires immediate attention and cannot wait for a public solution. But her sympathetic neighbors who supply the wood for the cremation leave the structural problem or problems untouched. Seeing her problem as public entails seeing what features it shares with other problems. Any two things or cases have features in common—the trick is to find those common features that are fruitful for further development. The case of the dead Bangladeshi is seen as a case of an inadequate rice harvest by some and as a case of unjust land distribution by others. Is there a right way to see it? Pragmatists may well say that both ways are right, as is the private way that prompted the gifts of wood. Looking at the case politically does not preclude looking at it botanically; advocating land reform does not preclude research to develop better rice. Moreover, one cannot recognize these public or political aspects of the problem without looking at details. One needs to know, for example, that the people in question eat rice rather than wheat; the research on wheat done some time ago that produced the green revolution in India is irrelevant to the problem of the Bangladeshi.

Nevertheless, attention to context in the sense of detail is feared to lead to fragmentation, to privatizing all problems because too much attention will be paid to the details that distinguish one case from another. Prompted by this fear, some feminists deny the distinction between the private and public sphere. They argue that the latter dichotomy has been used to keep women in their place, their place being the private one of *Kinder, Küche, Kirche* (children, kitchen, church). Such feminists appeal to pragmatists to join them in that rejection, nothing that pragmatists have rejected many other dichotomies. But here it is important to note that there are different ways in which one may reject a dichotomy. We cannot reject the biological dichotomy between men and women. We can only say that it is irrelevant in most contexts and, in particular, that it does not match the public-private distinction.

In contrast, Dewey rejected the means-ends dichotomy by pointing out that the same state of affairs, the end-in-view, has three functions: (*a*) it enables one to formulate a plan of action, thus serving as a means to planning; (*b*) it is one's goal and when accomplished marks the end of that phase of one's life; and (*c*) once realized, it becomes a means or an obstacle to further ends. In other words, whether we see a state of affairs as means or as end depends on the context. Similarly, while some problems and some activities are strictly private, having to do with intimate relations between two human beings, most serious problems are both private and public.

Indeed, as feminists, we deal with the political problem of the legality of abortions by pointing out that the problems to which abortion may be the answer are private problems. In other words, we point out that government regulation or prohibition of abortions violates a (political) right to privacy. We add to this argument the further observation that there are other related public problems (prenatal and postnatal care, housing, and adequate nutrition) that must also be solved if women are to be truly free to make the private choice to have or not have children. In this case, at least (and I suspect in others as well), denying the existence of a private sphere would be as self-defeating as an extreme contextualism that views every situation as unique.

Pragmatism here occupies a middle ground. We cannot avoid all abstraction, all generalization, but neither can we manage only with large generalities. Zoology deals with phyla as well as species, and many intermediate levels of generality; the right level of generality is a function of the problem that confronts us. Often the appropriate and most useful categories are discovered by trial and error. Early in the nineteenth century, abolitionism made the personhood of the slaves apparent to many whites, but that point was made in conjunction with an appeal to the rights of "men" (persons) in general. Without that second premise, nothing would have followed from acknowledging the personhood of people of African descent. The same sort of argumentation was repeated in the civil rights movement in the middle of this century. Feminism, both in the nineteenth century and in our century, came a little later; having learned that color is irrelevant to personhood, we came to learn that gender, sexual orientation, and religious persuasion are equally irrelevant. However, neither women, nor blacks, nor any other groups have a monopoly on being oppressed; rather, there are times when these groups have common goals to be achieved in concert and times when they pursue disparate aims. One cannot know a priori when cooperation will be fruitful. Pragmatists reiterate that looking at context is a means, not an end in itself. How much context we need to consider is itself a practical issue that depends on context.

II

I have made the point that mere attention to detail and differences is not enough to solve problems. Even insisting on the perspective of the oppressed and on introducing the categories of domination and oppression, of power and exploitation, into our discourse is not enough. Politics requires common ideals, a common conception of justice. That conception, in turn, seems to require an impartial perspective. The Enlightenment and liberalism offer such a perspective and the assurance that the complaints of the poor and the powerless are not merely expressions of resentment, but constitute legitimate claims that even the rich and the powerful, were they but reasonable, would have to acknowledge. Pragmatism, it is claimed, calls that assurance into question. This charge is supported either by a misreading of pragmatism—the claim that pragmatists subscribe to a coherence theory of truth and goodness—or by reference to the pragmatists' acknowledgment that we can only begin where we are, from whatever point of view we happen to occupy. I will now address both of these points.

Although Kant and other authors of the Enlightenment did not distinguish between facts and values (lawyers seem to say "facts and opinions") in the manner of positivists and ethical relativists, they did distinguish contingent knowledge based on and refutable by experience from the necessarily true deliverances of Reason (with a capital "R"). The latter included fundamental moral conceptions. Pragmatists deny the fact/value distinction; values, for them, are neither beyond challenge nor unsupportable. They fare, in the pragmatists' web of beliefs, neither better nor worse than any other beliefs.[3] It is, however, not this fallibilism that concerns Radin; rather, she suggests that pragmatism subscribes to a coherence theory of truth and that this theory, in turn, traps it in a conservative attitude (Radin 1990). Whatever values are part of pragmatism's web of beliefs would then be useless to those who want to change the world. Given the well-known radicalism of Dewey and the less known similar leanings of James, one suspects that something has gone wrong.

Near the end of his life, William James collected all his writings on truth and published them in *The Meaning of Truth* (WWJ 2). In the preface to that volume, he expressed his frustration at the widespread failure to understand the pragmatist theory of truth. He wrote, "The pivotal part of my book named *Pragmatism* is its account of the relation called 'truth' which

---

[3] See, for example, Putnam 1987.

may obtain between an idea (opinion, belief, statement, or what not) and its object. It means their 'agreement,' as falsity means their disagreement, with 'reality' " (WWJ 2:3). This, of course, is merely a verbal definition; the theory of truth will be James's account of that relation of agreement. Still, it is important to note that while our ideas are part of reality, there is more to reality than our ideas.

It might be suggested that the "more" (to our reality) merely consists in more ideas, that we must interpret Peirce's "reality is only the object of the final opinion to which sufficient investigation would lead" (CP 2:693) or James's "there can be no final truth in ethics any more than in physics until the last man has had his experience and said his say" (WWJ 6:141) as meaning simply that any particular belief of any particular person or group agrees with reality if and only if it coheres with the beliefs that constitute the final opinion. But this suggestion fails to capture James's intentions for several reasons. First, the object of the final opinion cannot just be the final opinion; thus, while a true belief will indeed cohere with the final opinion, it will cohere because it agrees with the final opinion's object. Second, even if one rejects Peirce's view as too metaphysical for later pragmatism, the "more" does not simply consist in more ideas. James speaks sometimes of experiences and sometimes of facts; he writes, for example, "facts come independently and determine our beliefs provisionally. But these beliefs make us act, and as fast as they do so, they bring into sight or into existence new facts which re-determine the beliefs accordingly" (WWJ 1:108).

Thus, pragmatists do not subscribe to a coherence theory of truth; nor do they believe that human beings engage only in conversation. Pragmatists reject the Cartesian idea that human beings are passive spectators of the world. If humans were passive spectators standing outside the world, attempting to mirror it, then indeed we could only have a coherence view of truth. We would thus be imprisoned in the circle of our ideas, and nothing in reality would hinge on the kind of coherence we invented. The world is not changed if it is mirrored in a distorting mirror, and the mirror cannot know or care that it distorts. (If so, "bad coherence" could only mean incoherence.) But we are not mirrors of nature; we are part of nature. What Radin calls "bad coherence" is not merely incoherence (though it is that too if only the context be drawn widely enough); "bad coherence" issues in actions that cause pain, where both the actions and the pain they cause lie outside the circle of beliefs that prompt the actions (Radin 1990, 1710). The first and fundamental great achievement of the pragmatists as philosophers was to see that we human beings are agents in the world, that beliefs are what we act on, that we interact with the world, and that true beliefs are those that do not lead to unpleasant surprises. How then is it possible for highly intelligent people to claim that pragmatists subscribe to a coherence theory of truth?

I suspect the source of the difficulty is this: On the old Cartesian picture, the inquiring mind strives to reflect reality as it is, so to speak, "untouched by human hands." The pragmatist tells us that we cannot have that. "The trail of the human serpent thus is over everything" (WWJ 1:37). Anything we know, indeed, any thought we entertain and any experience we have, is already subsumed under some set of categories or other. The sense data of the philosophers, wrote Dewey, are the result of philosophical abstraction, less immediate than the midsized objects of everyday life.[4] That common-sense world, says James, is the conceptual framework that human beings have evolved and have found to be useful over the millennia (WWJ 1:81–94). To be sure, within that framework it is not a question of coherence whether there is a grapefruit in my refrigerator. Nor is it a question of coherence, in the framework of the relevant social sciences, whether, on average, women are paid less for equal work, or whether black men have a shorter life expectancy than white men. Nevertheless, some may think that the conceptual framework and the beliefs together simply form a coherent version and that we are free to adopt any coherent version. This is what I have just denied; some versions will simply clash with experience when we try to act on them. Even Goodman distinguishes between right and wrong versions.[5]

Nevertheless, we are conservatives; confronted by experience with a fact that does not fit into our world picture, we try all sorts of denial strategies. On a personal level, we employ various forms of self-deception; on the public level, we may not collect the data, or the data may be collected but explained away or redescribed. We resist, in particular, experiences that require a change in our conceptual system. Even in the physical sciences, conservatism works in just this way; major paradigm shifts are rare enough to make headlines in the daily newspapers, just as do major interpretive shifts by the Supreme Court. This conservatism, this desire to hold onto old ways of thinking—precisely what pragmatism is not in spite of the fact that James called it "a new name for some old ways of thinking"[6]—imposes an unequal burden on those who are powerless. It

---

[4] See Dewey's *The Existence of the World as a Logical Problem* (MW 8).

[5] The term is Nelson Goodman's. See Goodman 1978, 124.

[6] This was his subtitle for *Pragmatism* (WWJ 1). But, as James well knew, that old way was not the way of mainstream philosophy. Indeed, in *Pragmatism,* he attacks again and again, in the name of those for whom the world is not a good place, the warm and fuzzy rationalist idealism that leaves the victims of injustice out in the cold. To be sure, he offers pragmatism as a third

makes them invisible, as anything for which we have no label tends to be invisible or, at any rate, not memorable. Since pragmatists contend that we can begin only where we are, the objector worries that we pragmatists are ultimately fated to remain where we are, to support the status quo.

For pragmatists, there is no fundamental epistemological distinction between science and politics. The objection just considered, when applied to scientists, would read as follows: Since scientists can only begin where they are, at the level of knowledge and understanding reached by their predecessors, using the instruments and theories invented by them, they can make no progress. But, of course, they do. They make progress because they look at new problems, and in the process of solving those new problems, they find themselves obliged to invent new instruments, new theories, and sometimes whole new ways of looking at their subject.

What enables the pragmatist as judge, legislator, or plain citizen to make progress and to change her or his conceptions of justice, of oppression, of legitimate power, etc. is the fact that the world changes for the better as well as for the worse. The situations described by Radin, situations in which we find ourselves in a double bind, are the result of just such changes (Radin 1990, 1699–1704). New reproductive techniques make it possible to think of "renting a womb," but the resulting double bind shows that that is the wrong way to think about this situation. Rather, we should recognize that three human beings, all vulnerable in different ways, are involved.

Affirmative action programs respond to the systematic rejection of women and minorities without consideration of their qualifications. But the focus on qualifications enabled those who oppose these programs— programs that force employers and admissions officers to consider applicants of color and women—to invent the double bind that concerns Radin. It is indeed oppression that gives rise to a double bind, not by causing women and minorities to be less qualified, but by causing society to believe the myth that they are less qualified. What counts as a qualification is itself, in part, a political matter.

I raise these points not as criticisms of Radin's analysis, but because these examples illustrate the ways in which new developments are used by pragmatists to re-examine old concepts and old beliefs. As Radin rightly

---

option, neither rationalism nor a cold materialist empiricism that leaves the individual's spiritual needs unmet. But in *Pragmatism*, it is the former rather than the latter that he seeks to replace, emphasizing the fact that the possibility for greater justice exists but that its realization depends on what we do.

states, ideal theory and nonideal practice constitute each other and for a pragmatist this is not paradoxical (Radin 1990, 1701). For a pragmatist, normative theories function in the same manner as do descriptive or explanatory theories. They guide actions, and they are confirmed or disconfirmed, corroborated or discorroborated, by the outcome of those actions.

III

If pragmatism has been successfully defended against the charge of conservatism, it may now be said that pragmatism deprives us of a secure conception of justice that can guide our conduct (more correctly, that pragmatism challenges our sense that our conception of justice is secure). We pragmatists respond to this charge by saying that our conception of justice is as secure as it needs to be and as revisable as well. How far our society falls short of the ideal of justice depends on what we do, not on whether we think of that ideal as laid up eternally in some Platonic heaven or as embodying the best that human intelligence can devise in response to the demands of human beings. Even if justice were laid up in some Platonic heaven, we pragmatists would be in the same position in which we find ourselves now; we would have to use our intelligence and our sensitivity to the cries of the wounded to solve our problems. Democracy, we pragmatists believe, makes it possible to apply human intelligence to the problem of finding the best conception of justice and to coming as close as possible to realizing it. Of course, we pragmatists recognize that our children will find our conception of justice woefully inadequate.

Minow and Spelman (1990) develop perspective as a sense of context. The demand to see things in context may be an exhortation to change perspective. If the various forms of feminism that compete for our attention are taken to offer alternative feminist perspectives, some may fear that women will find no common ground on which to stand and from which to challenge the dominant perspective. That worry is justified by historical experience. Too often the rich and the powerful prevail because they stand united against a fragmented opposition. Yet history has also shown that people can lay aside what divides them and unite around a single issue to considerable effect. In any case, pragmatism is not to blame for a lack of common ground. In fact, by making us all aware of alternative perspectives, pragmatists have aided the search for a common ground. Knowledge of obstacles is not itself an obstacle unless it leads to defeatism; for pragmatists it serves as a spur to seek a way to overcome those obstacles.

The concern raised by the pragmatists' "unstable" conception of justice may be directed not at us as citizens but at our conception of a judge's role. Judges, as Wells (1990) points out, begin as spectators, but as spectators who are not confined to one angle of vision. They hear a story from many witnesses and can request additional reports before they decide. During this stage, they are indeed impartial spectators. At the end of the trial, judges become agents. They interact with others—not only with those involved in the case, but with untold unknown others whose cases will be decided in accordance with this case. Here judges may have to be aware of their own circumstances, aware that they have made for themselves stories out of the witnesses' stories, and that their stories are colored by their past and by the values to which they are committed. It cannot be otherwise; it is this way whether the judges are "situationalists" or "formalists."

It may be objected that formalist judges come to the case armed with a set of preexisting rules. Nevertheless, formalist judges must decide which rules are applicable to the case and what following the rules means; these are not things that can be specified by further rules on pain of an infinite regress. Rather, this is what the judges' prior training equips them to do. Here the pragmatist warns that, especially in hard cases, the judges' character and past experience cooperate with their training to bring about the manner in which they follow the rules.

The "situated" judges, on the other hand, are said to approach the case without any preconceived ideas, without any "theory." But that too is an illusion. No judge comes to a case without a vision trained in legal categories and without deeply internalized values (the trail of the human serpent is indeed over everything). Without these, judges would not know which details of the case, which features of the context, are relevant and how much weight they should bear. "Situated" judges' intuition is shaped by their prior training, their character, and the totality of their past experience. What "situationalist" and "formalist" judges share is precisely that they were trained in the same legal system and that their understanding of the contexts of the cases before them is inevitably theory-laden—shaped, that is, by the categories they learned and by the theory implicit in those categories. They differ in the way they see themselves and in how they determine what to do at the next step (particularly in hard cases).

John Dewey quotes Justice Holmes as saying "the whole outline of the law is the resultant of a conflict at every point between logic and good sense—the one striving to work fiction out to consistent results, the other restraining and at last overcoming that effort when the results become too manifestly unjust" (MW 15:68). The formalist judge, let us say, represents logic, while the situationalist judge represents good sense. The latter agrees with Justice Holmes that

> [t]he actual life of the law has not been logic: it has been experience. The felt necessities of the times, the prevalent moral and political theories, intuitions of public policy, avowed or unconscious, even the prejudices which judges share with their fellow-men, have a good deal more to do than the syllogism in determining the rules by which men should be governed. (MW 15:69)

Dewey, however, points out that Holmes here uses "logic" in a narrow "syllogistic" sense and goes on to advocate his own sense of "experimental logic" (MW 15:69). There is more to this than a desire for an honorific name, though we pragmatists can do with a little honor now and then. Rather, to speak of experimental logic is to show that we rely not on insupportable and uncriticizable intuitions, but on a method, a procedure. Dewey describes it in a nutshell as follows:

> [T]hinking actually sets out from a more or less confused situation, which is vague and ambiguous with respect to the conclusion it indicates, and … the formation of both major premises and minor [of principles and of descriptions of the case to show that it falls under the principles] proceeds tentatively and correlatively in the course of analysis of this situation and of prior rules. (MW 15:72)

This is, of course, precisely the method that I illustrated at the outset of these remarks.

Legal theorists, as distinct from sitting judges (of course, these may be the same person at different times), tell conflicting stories. Some tell the formalist story, while others tell variants of the pragmatist story. How is this possible? Dewey suggests that legal theorists look at different phases in the judicial process as the characteristic phase: the pragmatist looks at the "finding judgment" phase, while the formalist looks at the "writing of opinions" phase when the decision must be justified to the community. Although judging is not politics in the sense of the arbitrary exercise of power, judging is politics in the sense of requiring the community's consent for its legitimacy. Thus, in writing an opinion, the judge seeks language that will seem to reflect a rigorous deductive logic and will "give an illusion of certitude" as well as ensure "the maximum possible of stability and regularity of expectation" (MW 15:73).

But here, according to Dewey, we confuse practical certainty, the sort of stability human beings need to plan their lives and to foresee the legal consequences of their actions, with theoretical certainty, the desire for absolutely immutable laws. The latter desire, he continues, is actually an attempt to evade the responsibility of developing rules of law that will secure a reasonable amount of stability for one's community (MW 15:73–74).

So, context and prior rules cooperate to generate new rules and new contexts constrained by certain desiderate of stability. And here lies the rub; I shall quote Dewey one last time:

> Failure to recognize that general rules and principles are working hypotheses, needing to be constantly tested by the way in which they work out in application to concrete situations, explains the otherwise paradoxical fact that the slogans of the liberalism of one period often become the bulwarks of reaction in a subsequent era. (MW 15:75–76)

Similarly, failure to recognize that appeal to context is a working hypothesis needing constant testing in practice explains both the anxiety that pragmatism tends to produce in its opponents and the tendency of radical critics of liberalism to give up the gains of the last revolution before they have won the next one.

I will end by elaborating on the mapmaking analogy of Wells (1990, 1740–1742). The mapmaker, like the judge, has been trained. The mapmaker recognizes certain features of a landscape as relevant and has means to represent them on a map. Which features are deemed relevant depends on the kind of map one wants to produce. Judges, too, recognize certain features of a case as relevant; they also have some choice in how they want to see a case. When we use a map, we know, for the most part, where we are; the map enables us to continue. Many cases that come before a judge are of a familiar, routine kind, and the legal system provides the map that leads the case to a successful conclusion, whatever that may be.

But one may be lost or have reason to distrust the map. This may happen, for example, when one is hiking in the mountains. Streams have changed their course, ponds appear where there were none at the time when the map was made, and ponds shown on the map have turned into meadows. Some trails have eroded and other trails have been established, but the mountains are just where they always were. Finally, an earlier mapmaker may simply have made a mistake. Experienced hikers and mapmakers recognize the telltale signs of old stream beds, ponds, and trails. The old map is not useless, although some of its features need to be redrawn. Just so, a judge's training enables the judge to deal with new contexts—for instance, defendants and child witnesses in child abuse cases. It may seem, at times, as if pragmatism, by insisting on what Dewey calls an "experimental logic," questions the relevance of the judge's training. That is not so; the mapmaking analogy shows yet again that attention to context and knowledge of rules need to go hand in hand, and that only training and experience enable one to achieve the proper balance.

Works Cited

Dewey, John. 1969–1991. *The Collected Words of John Dewey*, edited by Jo Ann Boydston. 37 vols. Carbondale: Southern Illinois University Press. (See List of Abbreviations.)

Gilligan, Carol. 1982. *In a Different Voice: Psychological Theory and Women's Development*. Cambridge: Harvard University Press.

Goodman, Nelson. 1978. *Ways of Worldmaking*. Indianapolis: Hackett.

Hartman, Betsy, and James K. Boyce. 1983. *A Quiet Violence: View from a Bangladesh Village*. London: Zed Books.

James, William. 1975–1988. *The Works of William James*, edited by Frederick H. Burkhardt, Fredson Bowers, and Ignas K. Skrupskelis. 19 vols. Cambridge: Harvard University Press. (See List of Abbreviations.)

Minow, Martha, and Elizabeth V. Spelman. 1990. "In Context." *Southern California Law Review* 63(6): 1597–1652.

Putnam, Ruth Anna. 1987. "Weaving Seamless Webs." *Philosophy* 62(240): 207–220.

Peirce, Charles S. 1931–1958. *Collected Papers of Charles Sanders Peirce*, edited by Charles Hartshorne and Paul Weiss (vols. 1–6), Arthur Burks (vols. 7 and 8). Cambridge, MA: Belknap Press of Harvard University Press. (See List of Abbreviations.)

Radin, Margaret Jane. 1990. "The Pragmatist and the Feminist." *Southern California Law Review* 63(6): 1699–1726.

Rawls, John. 1971. *A Theory of Justice*. Cambridge: Belknap Press of Harvard University Press.

Wells, Catharine. 1990. "Situated Decisionmaking." *Southern California Law Review* 63(6): 1727–1746.

CHAPTER 7 | Realism, Pragmatism, and Critical
Social Epistemology

SUSAN DIELEMAN

IN GENERAL, SOCIAL EPISTEMOLOGISTS are interested in the social dimensions of our knowledge practices—how knowledge is gained through
testimony; when we should trust others as reliable sources of testimony;
whether collective entities can be said to possess knowledge; what counts
as expertise and why experts disagree; and so on. Social epistemology becomes *critical* when it is guided by the goal of achieving justice, however it
is conceived. Critical social epistemology (CSE), therefore, looks at those
epistemic practices that create and maintain injustices, and explores ways
of reforming epistemic practices so as to achieve greater justice.[1] For many
critical social epistemologists, a commitment to realism seems to be a key
feature of their project. This realist bent among critical social epistemologists sits uneasily with—if not in outright contradiction to—the suggestion I have made elsewhere that we would be well served by thinking of
Richard Rorty as an ally to critical social epistemology.[2] In this chapter,
I aim to defend my suggestion that pragmatism—and Rorty's version of
pragmatism in particular—has valuable resources for critical social epistemology projects, despite, or perhaps even because of, the (neo)pragmatist
tendency to reject robust forms of realism.

I begin my defense of a pragmatist critical social epistemology by providing an overview of the realist bent among critical social epistemologists.
In the section that follows, I bring Rorty into the conversation to show why

---

[1] Those who practice social epistemology in this critical vein include Miranda Fricker, Linda
Martín Alcoff, Charles Mills, and José Medina.
[2] See Dieleman 2012.

this apparent commitment to realism is overblown and unnecessary. I then look to feminist and trans movements to demonstrate how efforts to resist and overcome epistemic injustices can be and have been accomplished in the absence of realist commitments. By turning to real-world examples of efforts to correct epistemic injustices, I aim to show that a critical social epistemology informed by pragmatism works just as well—if not better— to accomplish the ethicopolitical and theoretical goals critical social epistemologists have set for themselves.

The Realist Bent in Critical Social Epistemology

Recent work by critical social epistemologists, including work on epistemic injustice and on epistemologies of ignorance, has revealed a commitment to realism, whether that commitment is implicit or explicitly endorsed. One influential text where that commitment is both presumed and defended is Charles Mills's *The Racial Contract* (1997), which is taken as the jumping-off point for recent work in epistemologies of ignorance. The specific point that epistemologists of ignorance have taken as their inspiration is the following passage:

> on matters related to race, the Racial Contract prescribes for its signatories an inverted epistemology, an epistemology of ignorance, a particular pattern of localized and global cognitive dysfunctions (which are psychologically and socially functional), producing the ironic outcome that whites will in general be unable to understand the world they themselves have made. (Mills 1997, 18)

Mills's realist leanings are made apparent when he insists that, under the Racial Contract, "official sanctioned reality is divergent from actual reality" (18). In other words, the social contract is a fiction that was created and is maintained by whites to present a version of or narrative about reality that is at odds with, because it covers over, actual reality. The constructed reality hides the actual reality of the racial (and racist) relations that make the social contract seem like a legitimate explanation of political affairs. One of Mills's goals in *The Racial Contract,* therefore, is to show the social contract for what it is, encouraging us to see the fiction, but also the reality of the Racial Contract that it covers over.

In the course of this project, Mills makes a point of distancing himself from postmodernism, which he claims to sympathize with politically, but which he also sees as "an epistemological and theoretical dead end, itself symptomatic rather than diagnostic of the problems of the globe as we enter the new millennium" (Mills 1997, 129). Implicit in Mills's theoretical distancing from postmodernism and his invocation of the idea of an "inverted epistemology" is the assumption that there is a way the world really is, and that racialized power asymmetries introduce a barrier that makes it difficult, if not impossible, for those who wield power to pull aside the curtain to see the truth that is hidden behind it; whites have come to believe in the Wizard just as much do the denizens of Oz. Epistemological investigations into the phenomenon of ignorance involve pointing to and pulling aside the curtain to reveal the reality behind the appearances.

Realism is integral to Mills's epistemological project insofar as it helps to make sense of the idea that it is possible to see the world "wrongly," as well as the correlative idea that it is possible to see the world "rightly." And it is the *critical* element of critical social epistemology that lends a sense of urgency to this defense of realism. Indeed, it is what motivates Linda Martín Alcoff to maintain a realist perspective in her own version of critical social epistemology; the epistemological backdrop of social progress is, she argues, a realist epistemology. This point comes out most clearly in her rejection of Richard Rorty's (supposed) antirealism. Alcoff worries that antirealism pulls the rug out from under social justice movements. She uses the example of sexual violence (and feminist efforts to identify and name it as such) to illustrate why antirealism is ill-suited to critical projects aimed at greater social justice. She writes,

> to characterize the sort of progress that is made by feminism here [in the case of sexual violence] we might go one of two ways: we might say that an improved representational narrative would at least include both [the rapist's and the victim's] points of view, both sets of experiences, and thus be a more adequate representation of the event itself because it is more inclusive, or we might say that the rapist's point of view is probably riddled by self-delusion, ideological mystification, and self-justifying maneuvers that obscure perception. But either way we go, *the feminist account provides an improved adequacy and accuracy of representation.* (Alcoff 2010, 149; emphasis added)

In short, Alcoff thinks that critical projects need a set of tools that makes it possible to say that one description of a state of affairs is better than another description of that same state of affairs, and "better" here is used not in the pragmatist sense that someone like Rorty might endorse, but in an avowedly representational sense.

Alcoff's concern with Rorty's (supposed) antirealism is that, with *Philosophy and the Mirror of Nature,* he threw out the baby of realism with the bathwater of representationalism; he ignored the fact, she contends, that "many epistemologists and philosophers of science were busily constructing versions of realism without attributions of a thing-in-itself, or undescribed noumenal realms, and even without correspondence claims. These versions of realism were not motivated by or committed to any desire to mirror nature" (Alcoff 2010, 137). I disagree with Alcoff's claim that Rorty *ignored* such efforts—indeed, his lengthy engagements with those thinkers Alcoff identifies, like Hilary Putnam and Michael Williams, seem to contradict this claim—but it certainly is the case that he wasn't *convinced* by those efforts. Either way, Alcoff maintains that Rorty's unwillingness to even countenance a non-Philosophical version of realism—that is, a version of realism that doesn't "keep philosophers tethered to the useless problematic of the appearance/reality distinction and, related to this, the binaries of reason/cause and fact/value" (Alcoff 2010, 137)—was premature and misguided.

In sum, many critical social epistemologists have endorsed a realism that they think makes social progress possible. The literature on ignorance in particular appeals to a way the world really is—to an antecedent and determinate reality that has been hidden behind an ignorance produced by and for political purposes. In Alcoff's words, the sort of ignorance critical social epistemologists are interested in—"structural ignorance"—exists when the dominant group in a society is "actively pursuing or supporting a distorted or otherwise *inaccurate* account" (Alcoff 2007, 48; emphasis added). It's important, however, not to overstate or impart too strong a position to these critical social epistemologists, many of whom seek to develop a framework that has room for more and less accurate representations of reality, but also that recognizes that (social) reality is partly constituted by our words and deeds. In other words, thinkers like Mills, Alcoff, Fricker, and others do not aim to simply reinscribe a naive representationalist account of knowledge and knowledge practices. Alcoff, for example, in her evaluation of Miranda Fricker's *Epistemic Injustice,* wants to claim that "changes in the terms by which we bring experiences under a description can affect the actual things themselves—especially insofar as these are experiences—that are referred to by the terms" (Alcoff 2010, 136). She continues, suggesting that "hermeneutic democracy might yield new *worlds,* and not merely new *words*" (136; emphasis added).

Efforts to articulate this middle ground prompt Matthew Congdon to search for an epistemological framework that can undergird those critical social epistemology projects that want to hold accuracy of representation and the transformative effects of naming in a single vision. In Congdon's words, he is searching for "a single view [that] can simultaneously accommodate the transformative nature of articulation *and* a realist sensitivity to something we can neither master nor will away through articulation" (Congdon 2015, 82). Congdon turns to the Sellarsian concept of the space of reasons to find a framework that is able to meet this challenge; ultimately, the framework that he defends is John McDowell's "non-traditional empiricist" conception of the space of reasons over Robert Brandom's "social rationalist" conception. This is because he thinks the former is able to make sense of these seemingly contradictory positions, while the latter simply abandons the "realist sensitivity" critical social epistemologists are looking for: "Whereas for social rationalism our socially established epistemic practices exhaustively determine the layout of the space of reasons, for non-traditional empiricism, these inherited schemes are rationally vulnerable to experiential episodes capable of warping the topography of intelligibility" (Congdon 2015, 85).[3]

Though Congdon never mentions Rorty in his essay, his worries about the social rationalist conception of the space of reasons could easily be read as worries about the positions defended by Rorty. This likely comes as no surprise to those familiar with Rorty's work, as he explicitly sides with Brandom over McDowell for precisely the reasons that are at issue here. Take, for example, the following passage from Congdon's "Epistemic Injustice in the Space of Reasons": "That the layout of the space of reasons evolves alongside our efforts to articulate it in no way contradicts the realist claim that there exist objective reasons that are not simply the constructions of subjective spontaneity" (Congdon 2015, 82). Consider, moreover, his charge that it would be a "non sequitur" to move from the claim that "the space of reasons is transformed by our very efforts to articulate it" to the claim that "our commitment to realism ought to be jettisoned" (82). Of course, this is the very move that Rorty is accused of making, especially because he sides with Brandom over McDowell. Specifically, in

---

[3] Congdon provides a detailed overview of his reasons for choosing McDowell that I do not have the space to rehearse here. But in short, he sees promise in the McDowellian idea that who counts as a knower is responsive not just to social or political power (i.e., who says who gets to be a knower) but to empirical facts of the matter too, namely, the physical cues that tell us someone is a knower. Thus, "the languages and traditions by which we are inducted into the space of reasons are socially and historically developed yet empirically revisable" (Congdon 2015, 86).

two 1996 lectures, published later in the 1998 volume *Truth and Progress,* Rorty contrasts Brandom's *Making It Explicit* with John McDowell's *Mind and World.* The pivotal difference between these authors, according to Rorty, comes down to the notion of "human answerability to the world" (Rorty 1998, 143). While Brandom, like Sellars and Davidson, discards this notion, McDowell wants to retain it. Rorty, of course, sides with the former thinkers. This allegiance is motivated by his worry that getting things right about how the world is simply leads back to the scheme-content distinction and the Myth of the Given (Rorty 1998, 150–151).

My impression is that Congdon attributes too strong a position to critical social epistemologists like Mills, Alcoff, and especially Fricker. Though each abjures postmodernism and the relativism they worry accompanies it, this *negative claim* is not equivalent to the *positive claim* of a "robust form of realism" that then needs to be squared with their "articulationist" or "conceptualist" leanings, via, for example, a McDowellian reading of the space of reasons. So, whereas Congdon takes the position that we're not justified in moving from the belief that the space of reasons is transformed through our efforts to the belief that we ought to jettison our commitment to realism, I want to suggest that, even if we recognize that there are features of the world that stand in a causal relationship to humans, this does not give us reason to adopt a version of realism any more robust than this admission requires. We certainly don't need to go as far as Congdon thinks many critical social epistemologists, like Mills and Alcoff, have gone. Instead, we would be wise to follow Rorty here. Charles Taylor is right to note that Rorty tends to repudiate labels like "antirealist" and "relativist" and "subjectivist" because he thinks that "we should get away from a number of philosophical dichotomies that have supposedly outlived their usefulness" (Taylor 2003, 158). Yet at the same time, Rorty admits to being willing to take on the title of "realist," at least if we understand the term to signify nothing more than a person who grants that "human practices and languages are conditioned by determinate features of the world" (Rorty 2001, 130). However, if we push "realism" to "representationalism," we have gone too far: "there are lots of descriptions of the world, some more useful and some less, but none that match the way the world independently is. The latter notion is one for which I can find no good use" (Rorty 2001, 131).

This is a point pressed by Harvey Cormier in his 2007 paper "Ever Not Quite," in which he challenges, on pragmatist grounds, the viability of a project along the lines of an epistemology of ignorance such as that which Mills, Alcoff, and other critical thinkers advocate. He worries that recent efforts to develop this project rely too much on the traditional, but trivial, distinction between appearance and reality. He writes, "Getting things wrong, being ignorant, is not a matter of betraying logical, material, or racial reality; getting things wrong on the way to getting things right is just what we do as we try to make things better, we makers and remakers of ourselves and the world" (Cormier 2007, 74). I think Cormier goes too far in his challenge—that producing ignorance is itself a substantive epistemic practice is a point he seems unwilling to accept—but we can read him as offering us a powerful reminder: if we are going to talk of "ignorance" as something more than just a "lack of knowledge," then we must talk of ignorance as more than just glimpsing beyond the appearances to reality.

Of course, this reminder is motivated not by the worry that such a reality is beyond our reach as some sort of inaccessible noumenal realm. That is, the hesitance that Cormier, Rorty, and I express (or would express) when it comes to epistemologies of ignorance is not premised on the idea that it is impossible to pull back the curtain to reveal the Wizard. Rather, it is to suggest that the Oz metaphor, though powerful, is misguided. To rely on the Oz metaphor would be to run afoul of the accusation (leveled by McDowell and others against Rorty) of linguistic idealism. Rorty's neo-pragmatist denial of realism is not premised on an impenetrable appearance behind which lurks a reality that we are, as fallible and located knowers, unable to glimpse—this would be to maintain the appearance-reality distinction that he explicitly abjures early in building his neopragmatist position. Instead, it is to deny that there is any test that we can use to figure out whether what we've glimpsed this time is *really* reality, or just another appearance. As Rorty puts it,

> On an antirepresentationalist view, it is one thing to say that a prehensile thumb, or an ability to use the word 'atom' as physicists do is useful for coping with the environment. It is another thing to attempt to explain this utility by reference to representationalist notions, such as the notion that the reality referred to by 'quark' was 'determinate' before the word 'quark' came along. ... Antirepresentationalists ... see no way of formulating an *independent* test of accuracy of representation—of reference or correspondence to an 'antecedently determinate' reality—no test distinct from the success which is supposedly explained by this accuracy. (Rorty 1991, 5–6)

In the context of something like white ignorance, then—contra Alcoff and Mills—it would be a mistake to think that one vocabulary would better represent the "reality" of race relations as they are or as they should be in, say, the United States. There is the vocabulary that we choose, given our priorities and its usefulness in helping us achieve our priorities; once that vocabulary is chosen, then the world appears to us and influences us in particular ways. By changing the vocabulary, new and different aspects of reality become salient, conditioning our language and practices.

So, Rorty is a realist in the sense that the world shapes human practices and languages; indeed, he is a realist up to that point at which we abandon pragmatism for representationalism. If we justify our choice of language by pointing to that language's usefulness in helping us cope with the world, given the ends that we have, then we are still on the right side of the ledger. If we decide instead to justify our choice of language by pointing to its representational adequacy, then we are in the red. In what follows, I hope to show that this is realist *enough* to make sense of resistance to injustices, and specifically to epistemic injustices. In other words, I will, in the spirit of pragmatism, turn to real-world cases of epistemic injustice to show that resistance to such injustices need not invoke or assume a realism any more robust than this.

Learning from Resistance

When pragmatists say that theory ought to start from experience, what we generally mean is that armchair theorizing that is ignorant of or inattentive to the real-world problems to which it is meant to be applied is at best irrelevant (or, if relevant, only luckily so), and at worst harmful. This will especially be the case when that theorizing involves questions of justice. A theory of justice that fails to consider or address the particular features that shape any given injustice is bound to be inadequate. And so a pragmatist methodology requires turning attention to real-world *injustices* in order to develop a satisfactory and productive account of *justice*. Elsewhere, I have suggested that Rorty's engagement with the writings of feminist scholars like Catharine MacKinnon and Marilyn Frye, and his written dialogue with feminist thinkers like Nancy Fraser, made his work more explicitly political.[4] Here, I want to suggest that, through this engagement with feminist theorists and activists, Rorty developed a pragmatist set of tools for thinking about justice more generally, and that these tools are helpful in thinking through and learning from the successes of trans social movements. What I wish to highlight as relevant in relation to the

---

[4] See Dieleman 2011.

preceding discussion is that these tools do not depend upon the commitment to realism that many critical social epistemologists claim their work requires. Thus, a pragmatist account of social progress—and by extension, of justice—provides us with a nonrealist framework in which to theorize and practice critical social epistemology.

Activist histories, including those involving sex and gender as identity categories, which are my focus here, can be recounted using various lenses. One such lens is an epistemic lens; it involves looking at the changing terms, concepts, and categories that have been developed with the goal of better understanding and expressing—but also of manipulating and controlling—individuals' desires and experiences, self-understandings, and social positionings. This epistemic lens sheds light on the extent to which the psycho-medical community has, since the middle of the twentieth century, exerted significant control over the epistemic terrain that gives shape to, determines the possibilities for, and controls the medical technologies available to, trans people—up to and including the designations of being "disordered" or "crazy."[5] These designations exist partly because one has to match up with the psycho-medical definitions and criteria of gender dysphoria as it is presented in the Diagnostic and Statistical Manual (DSM-V) in order to receive access to surgery (or insurance coverage that makes surgery accessible). Thus, trans people who seek medico-technological interventions are, *by definition*, disordered. As a result, as Susan Stryker points out, the testimony of the trans person is easily dismissed—indeed, even appropriately dismissible—owing to the narrow epistemic terrain that labels them as quite literally disordered or diseased or crazy: "the sounds that come out of my mouth can be summarily dismissed as the confused ranting of a diseased mind" (Stryker 2006, 249).[6]

There can be, it seems to me, no clearer case of what Fricker has in mind when she explains the concept of epistemic injustice, which refers to the experience of being wronged as a knower.[7] On Fricker's account, there

---

[5] According to theorists Sandy Stone and Judith Butler, one result of the psycho-medical control of this epistemic terrain was that trans people took on a gender-essentialist position specifically to gain access to medico-technological interventions. Consider that there are, as Butler points out, "dramaturges of transsexuality who will help you make the case for no fee" (Butler 2006, 191), or that trans people who sought surgery read the very same books as the researchers who were to decide their fate. That way, they were able to satisfactorily match up with the criteria required to obtain surgery (Stone 2006, 228).

[6] The DSM-IV used the diagnosis "Gender Identity Disorder," while the DSM-V, released in 2013, uses the "less-stigmatizing" diagnosis "Gender Dysphoria." This change in diagnostic terminology was intended to "avoid stigma and ensure clinical care for individuals who see and feel themselves to be a different gender than their assigned gender" (APA 2013).

[7] See Taylor and Medina, this volume, for additional background regarding the concept of epistemic injustice.

are two forms of epistemic injustice. The first is *testimonial*; this occurs when negative identity stereotypes are used by a hearer, consciously or otherwise, to deflate a speaker's credibility. For example, a speaker experiences a testimonial injustice when her testimony is taken to be less believable than it otherwise might be, owing to that individual's identity and the negative stereotypes that are associated with it by the hearer. This form of injustice is transactional, which means that it is a wrong that occurs in testimonial exchanges between speakers and hearers. A second form of epistemic injustice is *hermeneutical*; this form of injustice exists when there are insufficient conceptual or hermeneutical resources available for individuals to access in order to understand and/or explain their experiences. For example, individuals who inhabit a less powerful station in society will have had less opportunity to develop the hermeneutical resources that structure and explain that society. And so, it is likely that they will suffer from a lack of resources that reflect their own experiences. This form of injustice is structural, which means that it is a wrong diffused throughout society, rather than perpetrated by individuals.[8]

It is important to keep in mind Fricker's claim that the wrong of epistemic injustice is basic or primary. That is, epistemic injustices (and testimonial injustices in particular) are not merely epistemic; they are injustices because they degrade or undermine the humanity of the speaker. They do this by questioning the very possibility that the speaker could be a knower, which is a feature understood to be essential for membership in the category "human being." As Fricker puts it,

> The capacity to give knowledge to others is one side of that many-sided capacity so significant in human beings: namely, the capacity for reason. . . . No wonder, then, that being insulted, undermined, or otherwise wronged in one's capacity as a giver of knowledge is something that can cut deep. No wonder too that in contexts of oppression the powerful will be sure to undermine the powerless in just that capacity, for it provides a direct route to undermining them in their very humanity. (Fricker 2007, 44)[9]

In other words, epistemic injustices contribute to, and perhaps are even constitutive of, dehumanization and oppression. Thus, resisting and

---

[8] See Dotson 2014; Anderson 2012; and Mason 2011 for helpful overviews of these forms of injustice, as well as critiques of the extent to which they are actually discrete.
[9] This brings to mind Rorty's assertion that there are "three main ways in which we paradigmatic humans distinguish ourselves from borderline cases" (Rorty 1989, 168). These are by distinguishing ourselves from those who are (1) animal-like (2) childlike, (3) nonmale.

eliminating epistemic injustices is, at root, a struggle against dehumanization and oppression; such struggles are simultaneously struggles for justice more broadly conceived.

An epistemic terrain in which trans people are disordered by definition is one that is inclined toward injustices of the epistemic variety at the very least, but more likely toward dehumanization and oppression. In order to overcome the predicament that this form of epistemic injustice creates, where everything the speaker says is already, by default, "the confused ranting of a diseased mind," trans activists have had to lay claim to a credibility traditionally denied them. The key to claiming credibility seems to be, in this case, eliminating the presumption of confusion and disorder by constructing identity categories that legitimate rather than undermine the credibility and competence of those who identify as trans. This means that it is by combating *hermeneutical injustices* that the testimonial injustice might be remedied. This strategy is captured by Riki Anne Wilchins, who writes,

> In order to grasp our bodies, to think of them as well as to understand the cultural gaze that fixes upon them, we must construct what our bodies can be said to mean and to look like. We rely upon other members of our speech community to do this, since it is in the meanings reflected back at us through culture that we find *truth*. Almost everything about bodies is discovered through comparison from the collection of meanings stored in a common language. (Wilchins 2006, 551)[10]

This strategy seems to have worked in feminist contexts; consider Cressida Heyes's suggestion that feminist efforts to weaken "the grip of oppressive sex and gender dimorphisms in Western cultures, with their concomitant devaluing of the lesser terms *female* and *feminine* . . . has opened up new possibilities for individuals, but it is also, over time, *generating a whole new field of meaning within which some identities may eventually*

---

[10] The struggle to overcome injustices sometimes leads to the reclamation of previously derogatory terminology. For example, Stone argues that trans people and their allies should not try to find space within or among available resources, but should rather aim for deconstruction. She writes, "To attempt to occupy a place as speaking subject within the traditional gender frame is to become complicit in the discourse which one wishes to deconstruct. Rather, we can seize upon the textual violence inscribed in the transsexual body and turn it into a reconstructive force" (Stone 2006, 230). She suggests that if society wants to label trans people "monsters," then those labels should be adopted and exploited by trans people themselves. The cognitive dissonance that results would serve to undermine the oppressive force of the psycho-medical, essentialist discourse.

cease to exist while others are being created" (Heyes 2003, 1094; emphasis added).[11] It is this strategy that Rorty latches onto in his engagement with feminist theorists and activists, that prompts him to develop a theory of social progress that makes room for achieving justice by creating new worlds through language.

What trans social movements demonstrate is that one particularly successful method of resistance to the sorts of epistemic injustices (and testimonial injustices in particular) I've identified involves redescriptions and redefinitions of the concept of gender itself.[12] Thanks to the efforts of trans theorists and activists, the threefold distinction that has generally been accepted by feminists in the academy, and to some extent in popular culture, is slowly being undermined. According to this distinction, (1) *sex* refers to biological characteristics, (2) *gender* to the behaviors thought by some to *reflect* the biological categories and by others to be social constructions *imposed* upon those categories, and (3) *sexuality* to romantic and/or erotic attractions. With the efforts of trans theorists and activists to reshape the collection of hermeneutical resources available, and thereby resist and respond to the testimonial injustices they face, this tripartite distinction between sex-gender-sexuality has come to be replaced by a more nuanced picture, such as that represented by the "genderbread person" (Killermann 2015). This new picture generally retains the categories of sex, gender, and sexuality, but complicates the picture to include additional categories such as gender identity and gender presentation.

Though social movements that resist the particular forms of epistemic injustice that trans people face are ongoing projects, they provide a valuable example of what social progress can look like. Moreover, keeping in mind that epistemic injustices are basic or fundamental injustices that can and do amount to dehumanization and oppression, such movements provide a fruitful starting point for considering what a productive account of justice might look like. The case as I've outlined it suggests that one of the ways to resist epistemic injustices, and therefore injustice more broadly conceived, is to lay claim to a credibility that is otherwise denied

---

[11] I borrow Heyes's hesitancies, but also many of her motivations, to write about trans issues as a cis-woman (Heyes 2003, 1096–1098). See also Shotwell 2011, who notes, "It is too easy to mine trans stories, in particular, to back up academic points; I am leery of participating in the ongoing hip academic concern with trans issues, narratives, and (sometimes) actual people" (128). I am conscious of these difficulties, but also think there are unique generative sites for building theory out of trans activism that those interested in justice would do well not to ignore.

[12] Whether gender is problematically emphasized, at the expense of other axes of oppression that intersect with gender (such as race or ability), is a debate I do not explore here. See Shotwell and Sangrey 2009 for a brief discussion of these issues.

to members of the group in question. In at least some cases, this task of claiming credibility can be achieved, at least in part, by developing and promoting new hermeneutical resources. As in the case outlined above, developing the new concepts of gender identity and gender presentation, and by extension redefining gender itself, creates a hermeneutical and testimonial climate, or epistemic terrain, in which trans people are no longer seen as "disordered" or "crazy" and thereby lacking credibility.

The feature of this account that I want to draw attention to is how new hermeneutical resources function in combating epistemic injustice: they serve to replace hermeneutical resources that have been found wanting, or to give voice to experiences for which no hermeneutical resources existed or were thought to be necessary. Such an account requires coming to terms with the idea that hermeneutical resources are the sort of thing that can be developed and promoted and defined and redefined. In other words, an important background feature of this account is the fact that concepts—even concepts like identity categories, which are often established by the science of the day and are dearly and firmly held—must be open to revision. This means that the concepts that we have used and currently use and, indeed, will use in the future, are historically contingent. An account of justice that has room for this fact—the fact of historical contingency—will help make sense of struggles for (epistemic) justice.

This is why a pragmatist account of (epistemic) justice, and especially one of a distinctly Rortyan variety that takes contingency seriously, pairs well with critical social epistemology. The successes of feminist and trans movements are premised on the idea that the concepts that we use to describe our world are not fixed or immutable, are not more or less accurate representations. Unless we think of concepts like gender as fundamentally redefinable, then epistemic justice for trans people (at least as it has been conceived and pursued so far) will be a long way off. Indeed, it is this very contingency that Rorty argues feminists must embrace in their struggles for justice: "Only if somebody has a dream, and a voice to describe that dream, does what looked like nature begin to look like culture, what looked like fate begin to look like a moral abomination" (Rorty 1998, 203). Notably, Rorty continues, "For until then only the language of the oppressor is available, and most oppressors have had the wit to teach the oppressed a language in which the oppressed will sound crazy—*even to themselves*—if they described themselves *as* oppressed" (203). The pragmatist feminist, Rorty argues, "will see herself as helping to create women rather than attempting to describe them more accurately" (Rorty 1989, 212). Rorty's appeal to feminists can help us think through trans people's resistances to epistemic injustice, where new hermeneutical resources and new identity categories are created in the struggle for greater justice.

Let's return briefly to Alcoff's example of sexual violence: she suggests that feminist interventions provide not just alternative, but better, more accurate representations of women's experiences. But would she also want to suggest that many feminist interventions were now mistaken, specifically, the theoretical sex-gender distinction that served as the basis for feminist thinking for so long and which has caused so much trouble for trans people? If she's willing to admit that they were poor representations, is she committed to the claim that we are now in possession of still better representations of the state of affairs? If yes, is she thereby committed not only to some form of realism, but to some overarching narrative of progress as well, where good descriptions come to be replaced by better descriptions, until we asymptotically achieve perfect descriptions? Even if Alcoff would be unwilling to take these further steps, finding the stopping point before them is simply too difficult. Rorty is right, I contend, to suggest it's better to find an altogether different project—one that evaluates descriptions for their usefulness in achieving the ends of justice rather than their representational accuracy. So it seems that there is good reason to jettison the commitment to realism, and that doing so is compatible with the critical social epistemologist's project. Looking to the historical and ongoing efforts of feminist and trans theorists and activists to resist the epistemic injustices they face shows this to be the case.

Works Cited

Alcoff, Linda Martín. 2007. "Epistemologies of Ignorance: Three Types." In *Race and Epistemologies of Ignorance*, edited by Shannon Sullivan and Nancy Tuana, 39–58. Albany: State University of New York Press.

———. 2010. "Rorty's Antirepresentationalism in the Context of Sexual Violence." In *Feminist Interpretations of Richard Rorty,* edited by Marianne Janack, 131–154. University Park: The Pennsylvania University Press.

American Psychiatric Association (APA). 2013. "Gender Dysphoria." Accessed November 25, 2015. http://www.dsm5.org/documents/gender%20dysphoria%20 fact%20sheet.pdf

Anderson, Elizabeth. 2012. "Epistemic Justice as a Virtue of Social Institutions." *Social Epistemology* 26(2): 163–173.

Butler, Judith. 2006. "Doing Justice to Someone: Sex Reassignment and Allegories of Transsexuality." In *The Transgender Studies Reader,* edited by Susan Stryker and Stephen Whittle, 183–193. New York: Routledge.

Congdon, Matthew. 2015. "Epistemic Injustice in the Space of Reasons." *Episteme* 12(1): 75–93.

Cormier, Harvey. 2007. "Ever Not Quite: Unfinished Theories, Unfinished Societies, and Pragmatism." In *Race and Epistemologies of Ignorance,* edited by Shannon Sullivan and Nancy Tuana, 59–76. Albany: State University of New York Press.

Dieleman, Susan. 2011. "The Roots of Rorty's Philosophy: Catharine A. MacKinnon." *Pragmatism Today: The Journal of the Central-European Pragmatist Forum* 2(1): 123–132.

———. 2012. "Solving the problem of Epistemic Exclusion: A Pragmatist Feminist Approach." In *Contemporary Feminist Pragmatism,* edited by Maurice Hamington and Celia Bardwell-Jones, 90–112. New York: Routledge.

Dotson, Kristie. 2014. "Conceptualizing Epistemic Oppression." *Social Epistemology: A Journal of Knowledge, Culture, and Policy* 28(2): 115–138.

Fricker, Miranda. 2007. *Epistemic Injustice: Power and the Ethics of Knowing.* Oxford: Oxford University Press.

Heyes, Cressida. 2003. "Feminist Solidarity after Queer Theory: The Case of Transgender." *Signs: Journal of Women in Culture and Society* 28(4): 1093–1120.

Killermann, Sam. 2015. "The Genderbread Person." *It's Pronounced Metrosexual.* Accessed August 31, 2015. http://itspronouncedmetrosexual.com/2015/03/the-gender bread-person-v3/

Mason, Rebecca. 2011. "Two Kinds of Unknowing." *Hypatia* 26(2): 294–307.

Mills, Charles W. 1997. *The Racial Contract.* Ithaca: Cornell University Press.

Rorty, Richard. 1989. *Contingency, Irony, and Solidarity.* Cambridge: Cambridge University Press.

———. 1991. *Objectivity, Relativism, and Truth: Philosophical Papers.* Cambridge: Cambridge University Press, Vol 1.

———. 1998. *Truth and Progress: Philosophical Papers*, Vol 3. Cambridge: Cambridge University Press.

———. 2001. "Response to Kate Soper." In *Richard Rorty: Critical Dialogues*, edited by Matthew Festenstein and Simon Thompson, 130–133. Malden, MA: Polity.

Shotwell, Alexis. 2011. *Knowing Otherwise: Race, Gender, and Implicit Understanding.* University Park: Pennsylvania State University Press.

Shotwell, Alexis and Trevor Sangrey. 2009. "Resisting Definition: Gendering through Interaction and Relational Selfhood." *Hypatia* 24(3): 56–76.

Stone, Sandy. 2006. "The *Empire* Strikes Back: A Posttranssexual Manifesto." In *The Transgender Studies Reader*, edited by Susan Stryker and Stephen Whittle, 221–235. New York: Routledge.

Stryker, Susan. 2006. "My Words to Victor Frankenstein above the Village of Chamounix: Performing Transgender Rage." In *The Transgender Studies Reader*, edited by Susan Stryker and Stephen Whittle, 244–256. New York: Routledge.

Taylor, Charles. 2003. "Rorty and Philosophy." In *Richard Rorty*, edited by Charles Guignon and David R. Hiley, 158–180. Cambridge: Cambridge University Press.

Wilchins, Riki Anne. 2006. "What Does It Cost to Tell the Truth?" In *The Transgender Studies Reader*, edited by Susan Stryker and Stephen Whittle, 547–551. New York: Routledge.

PART II | Resisting Oppression and Injustice

CHAPTER 8 | Social Inequality, Power, and Politics

Intersectionality in Dialogue with American Pragmatism

PATRICIA HILL COLLINS

Freedom is indivisible or it is nothing at all besides sloganeering
and temporary, short-sighted, and short-lived advancement for a few.
Freedom is indivisible, and either we are working for freedom or
you are working for the sake of your self-interests and I am working
for mine.

—JUNE JORDAN, "A New Politics of Sexuality"

JUNE JORDAN (1992) HAD her eye set on an understanding of freedom that
challenged social inequality as being neither natural, normal, nor inevitable. Instead, she believed that power relations of racism, class exploitation, sexism, and heterosexism were socially constructed outcomes of
human agency and, as such, were amenable to change. For Jordan, the path
toward a re-envisioned world where "freedom is indivisible" reflected aspirational political projects of the civil rights and Black Power movements,
feminism, the antiwar movement, and the movement for gay and lesbian
liberation. These social justice projects required a messy politics of taking
the risks that enabled their participants to dream big dreams.

I often wonder what June Jordan would make of conceptions of social
inequality, power, and politics within contemporary social theories.
Heady terms such as *freedom* that were so central to the emancipatory
projects of Jordan's times seem relegated to the dustbin of ideas from
the mid-twentieth century. In their place, we encounter understandings
of the here and now as curiously "post" or "after" major developments.
Postmodernism, poststructuralism, postcolonialism, and postraciality all

suggest that we inhabit a post-social-movement era, one that may be "post" the possibility of freedom. Yet, as events of 2011 such as Arab Spring and the various Occupy movements remind us, social movements and the emancipatory politics they espouse can emerge overnight. Thus, this malaise of postemancipatory politics emanating from the academy may be more indicative of the mental state of Western scholars in ivory towers than that of people on the ground.

In this context, how might social theory speak more effectively to contemporary social phenomena in ways that address the realities of social inequalities, power, and politics? Two contemporary fields of study that seemingly eschew the backward-looking "posting" of contemporary social phenomena in favor of a forward-looking approach speak to this question. As knowledge projects, American pragmatism and intersectionality both aim to use their tools of analysis to grapple with contemporary social issues, and, as such, both might have implications for contemporary social theory.

Despite differences of longevity and contemporary intellectual focus, both discourses constitute works in progress that engage themes of social inequality, power, and politics. American pragmatism, a well-established field within American philosophy, is currently seeing a revitalized scholarly interest whereby "old" ideas from the classical pragmatism of the early twentieth century are made "new again." As part of this process of self-reflexive revitalization, themes legitimated within the canon, such as pragmatism's utility for rethinking democracy, increasingly constitute topics of serious investigation. Yet despite this revitalization, themes of social inequality, power, and politics are not yet central to contemporary investigations, in part because they were not focal points of classical pragmatism. In contrast, social inequality, power, and politics have been primary concerns of intersectionality since its inception. Catalyzed by the social movement politics of the 1960s and 1970s, race/class/gender studies as a knowledge project became visible within US higher education in the 1980s with the arrival of people of color, women, and similarly marginalized groups whose social power had historically limited their ability to legitimate knowledge. Since the 1990s, the term *intersectionality* has emerged as the umbrella term framing this emerging field of study.

Pragmatism and intersectionality potentially complement each other, in that each discourse speaks to gaps in the other. Pragmatism presents a provocative analysis of community that provides a useful framework for understanding the processes by which social structures are constructed, yet its neglect of power relations limits its own arguments. Intersectionality provides a distinctive analysis of social inequality, power, and politics, yet the relative newness of this field in the academy has produced provisional analyses of these themes. In all, in both discourses, using the pragmatist construct of community and infusing it with intersectionality's ideas about social inequality, power, and politics might animate new avenues of investigation.

American Pragmatism: Social Inequality, Power, and Politics

Approaching a field as broad and significant as American pragmatism by emphasizing its omissions may seem counterintuitive. Yet this process of reading the silences, excavating the subtext, and/or reading between the lines suggests that what seems to be absent is actually present. Much as the margins on this page frame the text at its center, the marginalization of themes such as social inequality, power, and politics within pragmatist discourse has enabled *other* themes to occupy center stage. A voluminous literature exists that engages American pragmatism's core thinkers, themes, definitions, and so on, one too broad to summarize in this essay.[1] Instead, my overall approach here is to examine themes that, despite their relative invisibility, have also shaped the pragmatist canon.

One distinguishing feature of classical American pragmatism is that it seemingly paid scant attention to race, gender, class, sexuality, ethnicity, or nationality. Given the Progressive Era, a period of tremendous social unrest and a period during which classical pragmatism emerged, this omission is surprising. Instead, the themes of classical pragmatism, such as attention to democracy, science, enlightenment, fairness, and societal good, seem distanced from the contentious political debates of the day. Pragmatism's arguments rested on its ability to imagine abstract human beings versus particular female or black ones, abstract communities versus particular collectivities such as labor unions or families, abstract citizens

---

[1] Stuhr's view of American pragmatism is especially useful in encapsulating the boundaries of this field: "It may be defined by its exponents' common attitudes, purposes, philosophical problems, procedures, terminology, and beliefs. It is in virtue of such a shared complex of features that we identify, understand, and differentiate philosophical developments, movements, and 'schools of thought.' Such a unity of character, we must recognize, is not a single and simple essence, some necessary and sufficient feature of classical American philosophy, some property present always and only in classical American philosophy. Instead, it is an identifiable configuration, a characteristic shape, a resemblance, an overlapping and interweaving of features (present to differing degrees in the writings of the individual philosophers) that, as a relational whole, pervades and constitutes this philosophy and these philosophers" (2000, 2–3).

versus immigrant and nativist ones, and abstract democracy versus the particularities of US democratic politics. Via this expression of universalism, American pragmatism gained legitimacy primarily as a methodology or set of tools that one might use in studying particular social phenomena. As a result, social inequality, power, and politics were defined out of the *center* of American pragmatism. This does not mean that these entities were not present—they simply were not principle concerns. Social inequality, power, and politics are implicit throughout this discourse but are not core theoretical concerns. Pragmatism could uphold social justice projects, and its practitioners, as individuals, often became important figures within progressive causes. In essence, the discourse lacked a self-reflexivity on its own universalistic assumptions whose understandings of social phenomena were affected by its placement in the social inequalities, power relations, and politics of its inception.

Much issue can be taken with my brief and admittedly critical overview of American pragmatism, but for now, I want to explore the implications of American pragmatism for contemporary understandings of social inequality, power, and politics. Because pragmatism has been very useful to me in conceptualizing social inequality, power, and politics, I find it ironic that these ideas have not been more central to the field itself. In essence, neglecting these themes limits pragmatism's analysis of its core concepts, among them, a social self, the utility of experience, the dynamic nature of social organization, and a theory of action that is inherently political. In the remainder of this section, I examine one important idea within pragmatism, namely, the construct of community, as one that is currently neglected within contemporary social theory. Developing a more robust analysis of community points toward pragmatism's potential contribution to understandings of social inequality, power, and politics as well as how making these ideas more central within pragmatism itself might enrich the field.

Several characteristics of the construct of community, taken together, potentially shed light on social inequalities within the contemporary United States and the intersecting power relations that animate them.[2] First, the construct of community provides a template for describing actual power relations as people live them and conceptualize them. The idea of community as well as lived experiences within actual communities are central to how people understand and organize the social inequalities of

---

[2] For a comprehensive analysis of the construct of community, especially connections with complex social inequalities and systems of power, see Collins 2010.

everyday life. Because people exercise power in their everyday lives as individuals in multiple and crosscutting communities, it stands to reason that ordinary people will use the construct of community to think and do politics. Via its attention to social groups and communities, pragmatism provides a much-needed midlevel of analysis that is in between the individual and broader social structures.

Incorporating analyses of power into pragmatic conceptions of community promises to enrich understandings of social phenomena overall. Social structures such as neighborhoods, schools, jobs, religious institutions, recreational facilities, and physical and cyberspace marketplaces are the institutional expressions of social inequalities of race, class, gender, age, ethnicity, religion, sexuality, and ability. Typically hierarchical, these structures offer unequal opportunities and rewards. Whether intentional or not, people use the construct of community to make sense of and organize all aspects of social structure, including their political responses to their situations. Similarly, social institutions use the symbols and organizational principles of community to organize social inequalities. Communities thus become major vehicles that link individuals to social institutions.

A second dimension of community, directly influenced by the social constructionist bent of pragmatism, concerns the construct's ease of use. Calling attention to discourse analysis well before contemporary concerns, pragmatism introduced the importance of symbolic functions in constructing communities. Community is a symbol that people share in shaping social reality, yet it is a term that is versatile and malleable. These characteristics of versatility and malleability that make community easy to use also make it unexamined, taken for granted, and difficult to define (Cohen 1985). In everyday life and within much academic discourse, the term *community* is used descriptively, with minimal analysis or explanation. As a result, community can be imagined in many ways, from the microlevel of analysis so prominent within social psychology to the macrolevel analysis of nations as imagined communities (Anderson 1983). The versatility and malleability of the construct of community as a symbol also facilitate its effectiveness as a template for power relations. American pragmatism suggests that imaginings of community can be more empirically grounded, drawing upon pragmatic tenets of scientific inquiry that develop definitions by repeatedly reworking them through data. One can imagine community through the simultaneous embrace of the universal of community as a construct that is always understood through an emerging set of particulars that attend to intersecting power relations.

A third significant feature of the construct of community, suggested by pragmatism, concerns the ability of the construct of community to move people to action, often by catalyzing strong, deep feelings. Community is not simply a cognitive construct; it is infused with emotions and value-laden meanings. People may believe and support their political leaders, but their level of emotion and care about their communities is central to their political behavior. Whether an imagined community is a place-based neighborhood, a way of life associated with a group of people, or a shared cultural ethos of an ethnoracial or national group or religious collectivity, people routinely feel the need to celebrate, protect, defend, and replicate their own communities and ignore, disregard, avoid, and, upon occasion, destroy those of others. Here pragmatism's emphasis on rationality seems limited, in that people may be convinced by ideas, but they are moved to action often via emotions. Highlighting emotions as central to community behavior and analyzing template-based systems provide a window into the political behavior of groups who strive to uphold inequality as well as those who aim to change it. Pragmatists quite rightly focused on democracy and on processes of participatory democracy to create democratic communities. Yet they aimed to temper emotions with rationality, not seeing how the two worked together.

Fourth, one outcome of this ubiquity, versatility, and ability of the construct of community to move people to action is that people's imagined communities can hold varied and often contradictory meanings that reflect diverse and conflicting social practices. Contradiction need not be irrational. People can share the same cultural symbols yet understand and deploy them differently, a situation that catalyzes varying meanings and practices. For example, contemporary partisan politics reflect, in part, very different understandings of American citizenship and who legitimately belongs and who should remain an outsider. Democratic politics is the language of community writ large. Thus, the malleable meanings of community simultaneously catalyze contradictions and enable those contradictions to coexist.

Community can never be a finished thing (harkening back to the "post" thinking of contemporary social theory) but is always in the making. A more dynamic, future-oriented understanding of community creates space for imagining something different than the present and a worldview that critically analyzes existing social arrangements. In this sense, participating in building a community is simultaneously political, for negotiating differences of power within a group; dynamic, for negotiating practices that balance individual and collective goals; and aspirational. The challenge, however, of sustaining this dynamic conception of community lies in find-ing ways to negotiate contradictions. In this regard, the symbolism associ-ated with community is key, with the elasticity of the symbol serving as a measure of its effectiveness. Symbols are often most useful when they are imprecise: the specific content of a given political project is less signifi-cant than how the construct of community enables people to imagine new forms of community, even as they retrieve and rework symbols from the past (Cohen 1985).

In the United States, community can be a symbol for egalitarianism, the quest for a place where every individual is recognized as an equal member of the community with entitlements and responsibilities commensurate with his or her ability to serve the greater good. In this sense, ideas about community and participatory democracy remain bundled together—democracy is not a thing that can be achieved but, rather, a relational pro-cess fired in the crucible of lived experience across differences in power. The construct of community may be ideally suited for democratic aspi-rational projects because its effectiveness lies in its ability to wed strong feelings to projects that are designed to advance the greater good. John Dewey, Jane Addams, and Alain Locke, among others, saw this connec-tion between participatory democracy and community, viewing both as never finished but always under construction. These characteristics of the construct of community not only describe the dynamics of actual power relations; they can also serve as a template for aspirational political proj-ects, such as that described by June Jordan.

Because the idea of community is ubiquitous, versatile, multifaceted, and able to marshal emotions that move people to action, it is especially well suited for crafting diverse and often antithetical political projects. Political leaders know that when individuals develop a social self that reflects a sense of belonging to a community, they can be more easily moved to act to defend that community's putative interests. And this social self embedded in community is directly tied to individual expe-rience. The language of community seemingly catalyzes a more robust understanding of *experience* that enables it to be conceptualized as *both* universal (community as a symbolic template) *and* particular (communi-ties as actual social structures). Social justice projects—such as femi-nism's emphasis on consciousness-raising, which enabled women to see their seeming individuality in relation to the collective status of women, the sensibility of which was expressed via the slogan "The personal is po-litical"—demonstrate the effectiveness of recognizing the power of com-munity within politics.

Intersectionality: Social Inequalities, Power, and Politics

Intersectionality is a newly recognized field of study within the academy whose purpose has been to analyze social inequality, power, and politics. Because not only understanding but challenging social inequality has also been central to the mission of intersectionality, the interrelationships among social inequality, power, and politics have assumed distinctive forms within this knowledge project. Because, when compared with American pragmatism, intersectionality is quite new, I approach it using a narrative method (rather than the taxonomic approach, used in the previous section, to the construct of community within American pragmatism).

Contemporary narratives concerning the emergence of intersectionality routinely ignore its links to black feminist politics of the 1960s and 1970s. Toni Cade Bambara's edited volume *The Black Woman* (1970) stands as a groundbreaking volume of work by African American women who were involved in political struggle in the 1950s–1970s. Taking an implicitly intersectional stance toward African American women's emancipation, African American women from diverse political perspectives presented provocative essays concerning how they would never gain their freedom without attending to race and class and gender. Following Bambara, major works by Angela Davis, Audre Lorde, and June Jordan, among others, established the groundwork for what came to be known in the 1980s and 1990s as race/class/gender studies.[3]

By the 1980s, some of the main ideas honed within the context of black women's activism became crystallized within pamphlets, poetry, essays, edited volumes, art, and other creative venues. In 1982, the Combahee River Collective, a small group of African American women in Boston, issued a position paper titled "A Black Feminist Statement" (see Combahee River Collective 1995) that laid out a more comprehensive statement of the framework that had permeated black feminist politics and that subsequently came to be known as intersectionality. This groundbreaking document argued that race-only or gender-only frameworks advanced partial and incomplete analyses of the social injustices that characterize African American women's lives and that race, gender, social class, and sexuality all shaped black women's experiences.

Embracing an identity politics that claimed a collective voice for the group, the statement proposed that what had been treated as separate

---

[3] Several anthologies exist that illustrate the breadth of black women's intellectual production and its connections to race/class/gender studies (see, e.g., Guy-Sheftall 1995).

systems of oppression were interconnected. Because racism, patriarchy, class exploitation, and homophobia collectively shaped black women's experiences, black women's liberation required a comprehensive response to multiple systems of oppression. June Jordan's perception of indivisible freedom permeates the statement. Jordan's discussion of freedom foreshadows important ideas within intersectional knowledge projects, namely, viewing the task of understanding complex social inequalities as inextricably linked to social justice, or the intersections not just of ideas themselves but of ideas and actions. Subsequent expressions of black feminist thought contained an explicit analysis of the interconnectedness of race, class, gender, and sexuality as systems of power that was clearly tied to social justice projects and social movement politics (Collins 2000).

Given the historical derogation of women of African descent, it is tempting to grant African American women a colonial "discovery" of a yet unnamed intersectionality. Yet it is clear that African American women were part of a broader women's movement that incorporated Chicanas and other Latinas, Native women, and Asian American women, a constellation of groups that subsequently became redefined as "women of color." Thus, it would be far more accurate to say that women of color were at the forefront of raising claims about the interconnectedness of race, class, gender, and sexuality in their everyday lived experience and that their intellectual production provides a foundation for race/class/gender studies and intersectionality. For example, Latina feminism also came of age during this same decade of the 1980s, with the work of Gloria Anzaldúa, especially her classic volume *Borderlands / La Frontera* (1987), making an important contribution to framing studies of race, class, gender, and sexuality. Anzaldúa's work in particular sets the stage for examining important contemporary themes such as border space, boundaries, and relationality that have subsequently become so prominent within contemporary intersectionality.

The transitional decade of the 1980s witnessed a shift in the social location of race/class/gender knowledge projects from social movements to the academy, a shift that helped codify the discourse. Women of color arguing for the interconnections of race/class/gender and sexuality not only produced documents within social movement politics; this same decade saw the incorporation of some of these very same women into US higher education. It is important to remember that had social movements not fought for the inclusion of women and people of color inside the academy, ideas about race/class/gender are unlikely to have gained acceptance. Thus, the inseparability of race and class and gender that was drawn from the intellectual production of women of color was increasingly codified in the academy in the 1980s within race/class/gender studies. By this expansion into the academy, the more fluid structural and symbolic boundaries of intersectionality as a knowledge project that were associated with social movement politics morphed into fields of study that fought for space and legitimation within academic politics. Once this change of terrain occurred, the strategies and arguments associated with race, class, gender, and sexuality shifted.

The term *intersectionality* emerged in this border space between social movement and academic politics as a term that seemed to best capture the fluidity of this emerging, influential, yet amorphous knowledge project. Ironically, narratives of the emergence of intersectionality rarely include this period of social movement politics and instead confine themselves to locating a point or origin within prevailing academic politics. It's as if the ideas associated with race, class, and gender did not exist until they were recognized by academic institutional actors, primarily by giving the emerging field of race/class/gender studies a legitimate name.

Prevailing narratives of the emergence of intersectionality routinely claim that Kimberlé Crenshaw "coined" the term *intersectionality* in a much-cited 1991 article, "Mapping the Margins: Intersectionality, Identity Politics, and Violence against Women of Color." Crenshaw's article marks a juncture when the ideas of social movement politics became named and subsequently incorporated into the academy. Her work also serves as a touchstone for evaluating thematic emphases in intersectional scholarship in the academy: for example, the acceptance of the term *intersectionality* and ideas about marginality that had been so central to its development and the increasing criticism and derogation of identity politics that had been so central to launching the field itself. Crenshaw's work is quite valuable for its ability to remind us of how the sensibilities of social movement politics and their commitment to social justice initiatives influenced, and became subsequently shaped by, sophisticated theoretical perspectives, in particular the growing significance of postmodern and poststructuralist analyses within the late twentieth-century American academy.[4]

Since the early 1990s, intersectional scholarship, broadly defined, has gained acceptance in many fields of study in the academy. Issues of social inequality, power, and politics did not disappear, yet they received different emphases as intersectionality became legitimated in the academy. It appears that an initially holistic knowledge project became changed

---

[4] For a close reading of Crenshaw's 1991 article, see Collins 2011.

during its migration into the academy, with an increasing distinction made between intersectionality as a paradigm for studying complex social inequalities and intersectionality as a political project for bringing about social justice: intersectionality as a framework for understanding power relations of race, class, gender, sexuality, and others, on the one hand, and intersectionality as a framework that might catalyze social justice projects, especially those that might empower oppressed groups, on the other hand.

Within the academy, by far the lion's share of attention has gone to using the insights of intersectionality to develop an analysis of complex social inequalities. Here I briefly summarize four themes that operate not only as topics of investigation in the literature but also as framing assumptions for intersectional scholarship.[5] This is a provisional and debatable list of the distinguishing features of intersectional scholarship, yet it does identify some of the themes that currently preoccupy scholars who claim intersectionality as part of their intellectual projects. These themes are not all present in a given work, nor is each theme unique to intersectionality. Rather, the varying combinations of these themes can be seen as distinguishing features of a range of intersectional knowledge projects, all of which are positioned in some direct relation to these themes. Each of these themes provides a provocative glimpse into how intersectionality's initial holistic approach to social inequalities, power, and politics continues to shift as it becomes increasingly incorporated within and legitimated by prevailing academic norms. More importantly, each of these themes presents a potential point of dialogue where intersectionality might be informed by the ideas of pragmatism, specifically its potentially expansive understanding of community.

Intersectionality and Pragmatism in Dialogue

One theme within intersectional scholarship concerns how intersecting power relations of race/class/gender/sexuality shape individual and group-based social locations. This insight has catalyzed considerable attention to questions of individual and group identities. The trajectory of intersectionality has been characterized by increasing attention to individual identities—and less focus on group or collective identities. In essence, the robust understandings of identity politics honed within social movements

---

[5] For a comprehensive analysis of these ideas, including extensive citations, see Collins and Chepp 2013.

have been increasingly challenged within contemporary social theory. Individual identities and the personal politics that accompany them seem acceptable. In contrast, collective identities are less so.

Here American pragmatism's well-developed history of the social self, experience, and the significance of symbols all affecting the construct of community provides a set of tools that potentially might counteract this drift toward decontextualized, individualized identities. Pragmatism's analysis of the social self developed in the context of community provides a provocative argument concerning experience that scholars of intersectionality might find especially useful. Conversely, intersectionality's analysis of complex social inequalities might stimulate pragmatist analyses of communities as infused with power and politics. Stated differently, linking conceptions of identity politics honed within social movements with pragmatism's complex analyses of community discussed above might catalyze an especially fruitful dialogue.

Second, intersectional knowledge projects acknowledge that the distinctive social locations of individuals and groups within intersecting power relations have important epistemological implications. Intersectional scholarship suggests that all knowledge, including its own, cannot be separated from the power relations in which it participates and which shape it. Because intersectional scholarship originated in a stance of critique, its practitioners often initiate intersectional projects by examining patterns of bias, exclusion, and distortion within recognized fields of study. All knowledge is constructed within and helps to construct intersecting power relations; notably, this includes the construct of intersectionality itself. Pragmatism, too, recognizes the situated nature of knowledge in the social, yet its approach to the social underemphasizes the significance of social inequality, politics, and power in what counts as knowledge, including its own.

Despite the absence of overt analyses of power, pragmatism's approach to the social construction of community, with community being conceptualized as a symbolic structure of ideas as well as an actual set of social practices, resembles the epistemological approaches within intersectionality. For example, Stoetzler and Yuval-Davis (2002, 316) discuss the situated imagination as a crucial component of feminist standpoint theory, pointing to the ways in which social positioning shapes knowledge as well as the imagination. This approach yields two unique insights: (1) individuals and groups are differently positioned in a distinctive matrix of domination, which has implications for how we experience society, including *what we know and can imagine*, and the material realities that accompany this experience; (2) individuals and groups can *simultaneously* experience privilege and disadvantage (Stoetzler and Yuval-Davis 2002). I read Stoetzler and Yuval-Davis's analysis of the situated imagination as providing a provocative point of convergence between pragmatic concerns with the social self and the construction of knowledge and intersectionality's emphasis on power.

A third core idea that characterizes intersectional scholarship is attention to relationality and relational processes. This emphasis on relationality highlights the ways in which race, gender, class, and other systems of power are constituted and maintained through relational processes. The analytic importance of relationality in intersectional scholarship demonstrates how various social positions (occupied by actors, systems, and political/economic-structural arrangements) necessarily acquire meaning and power (or a lack there of) in relationship to other social positions. This highlights the intersecting and coconstructing nature of social systems and structures organized around power and inequality. Here, despite the absence of a focus on power, pragmatism provides a robust analysis of relational processes—the construct of community is inherently about relationships across differences. Intersectionality and pragmatism also seem to be in alignment in that both emphasize ideas about relational difference versus oppositional difference. Both fields emphasize the relationship among agents in constructing communities, not the static differences that distinguish individuals from one another.

A fourth and related core idea of intersectional knowledge projects concerns the nature of the connections among the knowledges and social structures of communities. Not only are actual social relations relational (e.g., actual communities), but the worldviews they catalyze (e.g., interpretive communities and standards attached to discourses such as pragmatism and intersectionality themselves) are necessarily relational as well. Intersectionality's ability to draw attention to and account for *inter*social locations—including those on the margins—challenges binary thinking, shifting the analytic focus on the fluidity among, interrelationships between, and coproduction of various categories and systems of power. As a result, epistemologically, intersectionality highlights the various standpoints that "inter" social locations occupy; these alternative standpoints challenge truth claims advanced by historically powerful social actors.

When placed in dialogue, pragmatism and intersectionality both contribute to a potentially more comprehensive understanding of social inequality, power, and politics. Intersectionality contributes the important insight that social inequalities are multiple, complex, and mutually constructing. It sees the theme of complex social inequalities as central to its mission, which draws on a specific, useful, and constantly emerging analysis of complex social inequalities. Because race, gender, class, sexuality, ethnicity, age, nationality, and religion constitute major axes of power in early twenty-first-century global politics, they catalyze multiple forms of social inequality. For intersectionality, pragmatism provides a ready-made set of conceptual tools for advancing arguments about social inequalities. Conversely, intersectionality's more robust analysis of social inequality might push the pragmatist canon further along paths that it is already traveling. All of the major constructs of the pragmatist canon might be strengthened by a sustained engagement with intersectionality's emphasis on power.

Within intersectionality, the emphasis on the social location, multiplicity, and relationality of social locations and worldviews also has enabled the field to develop a deeper understanding of power. In essence, systems of power (such as race, gender, class, sexuality, ability, age, country of origin, citizenship status, etc.) cannot be understood in isolation from one another; instead, systems of power intersect and coproduce one another to result in unequal material realities, the distinctive social experiences that characterize them, and intersecting belief systems that construct and legitimate these social arrangements. Stated differently, racism, sexism, class exploitation, and similar oppressions mutually construct one another, drawing upon similar practices, forms of organization, and ideologies. Pragmatism might benefit from investigating how power operates within communities of pragmatist scholars as well as the knowledges they produce. Placing understandings of power more centrally within pragmatist discourse potentially catalyzes new readings of "old" themes, the case suggested here with my cursory review of the construct of community.

To me, developing dialogues about social inequalities and power constitute fruitful directions for intrafield discourse as well as cross-field communications. Yet both discourses can remain static unless animated by a focus on politics. Intersectionality has much to say about politics, but what are the contemporary politics of intersectionality itself? What are the contemporary politics of pragmatism itself? Pragmatism has said far less about the kind of social justice politics envisioned by June Jordan, yet its focus on ideas of participatory democracy grounded in building communities might provide especially provocative and fruitful avenues of investigation.

Overall, it seems that pragmatism, briefly discussed here via the construct of community, potentially provides a much-needed set of conceptual tools for deepening intersectionality's holistic analysis of social inequalities, power, and politics. Conversely, intersectionality's analyses of social inequalities, power, and politics provide a provocative catalyst for pragmatism to revisit its core tenets.

Works Cited

Anderson, Benedict. 1983. *Imagined Communities: Reflections on the Origin and Spread of Nationalism*. London: Verso.

Anzaldúa, Gloria. 1987. *Borderlands / La Frontera*. San Francisco: Spinsters / Aunt Lute.

Bambara, Toni Cade. 1970. *The Black Woman: An Anthology*. New York: Signet.

Cohen, Anthony P. 1985. *The Symbolic Construction of Community*. London: Tavistock Publications.

Collins, Patricia Hill. 2000. *Black Feminist Thought: Knowledge, Consciousness, and the Politics of Empowerment*. New York: Routledge.

———. 2010. "The New Politics of Community." *American Sociological Review* 75: 7–30.

———. 2011. "Piecing Together a Genealogical Puzzle: Intersectionality and American Pragmatism." *European Journal of Pragmatism and American Philosophy* 3(2): 88–112. http://lnx.journalofpragmatism.eu/wp-content/uploads/2012/01/EJPAP_2011_III_2.pdf.

Collins, Patricia Hill, and Valerie Chepp. 2013. "Intersectionality." In *Oxford Handbook of Gender and Politics*, edited by Georgina Waylen, Karen Celis, Johanna Kantola, and S. Laurel Weldon, 57–87. New York: Oxford University Press.

Combahee River Collective. 1995. "A Black Feminist Statement." In *Words of Fire: An Anthology of African-American Feminist Thought*, edited by Beverly Guy-Sheftall, 232–240. New York: New Press.

Crenshaw, Kimberlé Williams. 1991. "Mapping the Margins: Intersectionality, Identity Politics, and Violence against Women of Color." *Stanford Law Review* 43: 1241–1299.

Guy-Sheftall, Beverly, ed. 1995. *Words of Fire: An Anthology of African-American Feminist Thought*. New York: New Press.

Jordan, June. 1992. *Technical Difficulties: African-American Notes on the State of the Union*. New York: Pantheon.

Stoetzler, Marcel, and Nira Yuval-Davis. 2002. "Standpoint Theory, Situated Knowledge, and the Situated Imagination." *Feminist Theory* 3: 315–333.

Stuhr, John J. 2000. "Introduction: Classical American Philosophy." In *Pragmatism and Classical American Philosophy: Essential Readings and Interpretive Essays*, edited by John J. Stuhr, 1–9. 2nd ed. New York: Oxford University Press.

CHAPTER 9 | Pragmatism and Radical
Social Justice

Dewey, Du Bois, and Davis

V. DENISE JAMES

PRAGMATISM IS RARELY ASSOCIATED with radicalism. In matters of social
change, the classical pragmatists are most often interpreted as piecemeal
meliorists and, in the case of John Dewey, progressive liberals. Radicalism
is a label most often reserved for Marxists and anarchists. It could be
argued that both Dewey and Marx were idealists whose visions for society
suggested a radically different social formation than what existed during
their lifetimes. US black radical thinkers have more often associated themselves in thought and practice with Marx than Dewey.

Placing Dewey's thought in conversation with his contemporary
W. E. B. Du Bois reveals nuances of both thinkers' radicalism. For both,
the best hope for a just social order was a democracy that turned on
ideals of the individual and society that could not be achieved if laissez-
faire capitalism was the organizing factor of everyday life. Du Bois
only became a card-carrying Communist at the end of his life. He was
convinced that racial justice required different means than the active
socialists and Marxists he encountered did, and it is unclear whether,
even in his turn to the Communist Party, Du Bois ever bought in to the
Marxist ideal of the inevitable end of the class struggle. With Dewey,
Du Bois shared a suspicion of the abstract ideology of the Marxists.
Where they diverged is on the attention and importance they placed on
the problem of race in the United States.

Dewey's lack of a racial frame for his social philosophy reveals a lacuna
in his recommendations about freedom and justice. Du Bois's analyses of
oppression and the desperate need for social change offer an important

corrective to Deweyan pragmatism, even as we argue that Dewey's pragmatism is a form of radicalism. What an investigation of Dewey and Du Bois together reveals is that, if we are to think through radical justice, we must reject the common philosophical distinctions made between freedom and justice. The resulting messy, complex attempt to define social justice is thoroughly pragmatic and radical. To those ends, it is fruitful to consider the pragmatic and radical notion of social justice that emerges from the comparison of Dewey and Du Bois on freedom, justice, and social change with the thought of Angela Y. Davis, who is arguably one of the most recognizable radical black thinkers of our times. A sometime Communist revolutionary and all-the-time radical, Davis's historically framed thought serves as an important check for any radical and pragmatist conception of social justice.

Dewey's Radicalism

Dewey was committed to a socially engaged philosophy. As a philosopher of education and a public figure, Dewey risked his reputation on the pragmatist assertion that our lived experience must be the ground for our recommendations. Dewey traveled internationally and risked censure or worse when he attempted to give what he thought was a fair assessment of the Russian Revolution. He is often identified with the American Progressive movement, which, on some views, represented a weakened response to the social perils of the time in comparison to the communist revolutionary zeal.

Dewey was no revolutionary. Two important factors emerge as essential to the label "revolutionary" in Dewey's time. First, Dewey lived during a period of militarized political revolutions. To be a revolutionary was not only about the thoughts one expressed but also the risks to life and limb one was willing to take. Second, to be a revolutionary seemed to require the conviction that the whole of society needed to be made anew, at once; a conviction that Dewey's pragmatism could not bear. It is the last of these two factors that point to Dewey's critique of Marxist revolutionaries.

Jonathan D. Moreno and R. Scott Frey argue that initially Dewey "was a sympathetic observer of the Soviet experiment" (1985, 21). It was only after Stalinism took hold and Dewey participated in Leon Trotsky's Mexico rebuttal of his Soviet trial that he became an anti-Marxist. Dewey was sympathetic to Trotsky's predicament as a social reformer. Trotsky failed to convince Dewey, not that the world was in need of great social change, but of the key principles of Marxism. Trotsky and the Stalinists agreed that a revolution led by the world proletariat was inevitable. Dewey came to see Trotsky and other Marxists as absolutists (LW 13). The unwavering commitments the communists had to their proposed end, and how easily that allegiance led to the oversimplifications of complex problems, concerned Dewey. In that unwavering commitment, Dewey saw the roots of fascism, not the seeds of a robust social democracy. The ends we posit are guideposts; markers that help us frame our current problems. These ends may never come about, and it is unlikely that even if they did we would have solved all of our social problems. There will be social problems that our current formulations cannot anticipate, and our ends should be adjusted accordingly. For Dewey, "All ends and values that are cut off from the ongoing process become arrests, fixations. They strive to fixate what has been gained instead of using it to open the road and point the way to new and better experiences" (LW 14:229).

We can imagine that this is what Dewey is referring to in the introduction to the second edition of his *Ethics*, published in 1932 after World War I and during the Great Depression, where he asserts, "When the whole civilized world is giving its energies to the meaning and value of justice and democracy, it is intolerably academic that those interested in ethics should have to be content with conceptions already worked out, which therefore relate to what is least doubtful in conduct rather than to questions now urgent" (LW 7:6). Dewey is cautious about empty theoretical maneuvers, about concepts with no bearing on reality. The neatness of philosophical ethics is troublesome because it either effaces real-life problems through ignoring them or oversimplifies them when it fixates on some analytically less messy concept or theory. Dewey, however, is guilty of committing the same sins he warned others against.

We only need to look at one of Dewey's most cited essays, "Creative Democracy—The Task Before Us," for both the roots of Dewey's radicalism and his own problems of philosophical tidiness. Dewey praises the pioneer period of US expansion and the democracy of Jefferson as he laments the wasted energies and capacities of the common people. Dewey's democratic ideal turns on his conception of freedom and not, or at least not explicitly, on any conception of justice. The story Dewey tells of American freedom is deficient. It idealizes the freedom experienced by a select few white men during a time of grave injustices wherein the near genocide of Native Americans, the enslavement and subsequent marginalization of African Americans, and the disenfranchisement of white women were the conditions of that freedom. What, then, is radical and worth keeping from Dewey's conception of democracy and freedom for our justice claims?

Dewey recognized that he was operating on a faith in people that others did not share. Dewey claimed for the common person a capacity to help shape and change the social world. While his narrative of the imagined democratic past ought to give us pause, Dewey was explicit that he intended his view of democracy to be inclusive:

Belief in the Common Man is a familiar article in the democratic creed. That belief is without basis and significance save as it means faith in the potentialities of human nature as that nature is exhibited in every human being irrespective of race, color, sex, birth and family, of material or cultural wealth. (LW 14:226)

Dewey's faith in the intelligence and potential of not just white men, but in nonwhite and female others too, is a radical democratic commitment. By separating one's possible contribution to the polity from the person's status in the existing social hierarchy, Dewey was knowingly suggesting a radical social change. Americans had been proud of their democratic experiments long before white woman's suffrage and the end of slavery. Democratic pride in an imagined past that glossed over the slaughter of Native Americans was a common view, one Dewey ostensibly shared in his narrative of American democracy on the one hand, and rejected in his recommendations for inclusive democracy on the other.

Much has been made of Dewey's claim, "Democracy is a way of personal life controlled not merely by faith in human nature in general but faith in the capacity of human beings for intelligent judgment and action if proper conditions are furnished" (LW 14:227). If we look to the "Creative Task" essay for a conception of justice, we do not find one, at least not an explicit one. Dewey does not tell us there what the "proper conditions" are and how they might be "furnished" so much as he is concerned with comparing a democratic way of life for an individual to nondemocratic ways of life. He emphasizes that individuals need to be free to assemble, free to communicate with one another and grow in their talents. He claims, "the task to democracy is forever that of creation of a freer and more humane experience in which all share and to which all contribute" (LW 14:230). Here Dewey is not explicitly talking about justice, but what else could we call the task he outlines? Claims about freedom, humane experience, and inclusive sharing are justice claims. Yet Dewey only nods to talk of justice when he claims that juridical guarantees of freedom are not enough to ensure people are actually free (LW 14:228).

Freedom holds an important pride of place in Dewey's work. In her assessment of Dewey's *Ethics*, Jennifer Welchman characterizes this prioritizing of freedom as an apparent but not explicitly explained feature of his work. Welchman attempts to formulate a Deweyan conception of justice from the *Ethics*. She argues,

> Were he compelled to state what exactly his conception of justice was, Dewey would probably say that it was simply the rational choice of institutions or acts. Societies and their members are more or less just as their institutions and actions more or less contribute to effective freedom. That is, institutions and acts are just to the extent that it is rational for a group collectively to adopt them. If what we most fundamentally want (whatever else we want) is what we are due, then what we are most fundamentally due (whatever else we are due) is freedom. ... If effective freedom is the freedom or liberty to contribute to the general happiness or the common good, might it not seem just or reasonable to enhance individuals' effective freedom through compulsion? (Welchman 1995, 195)

Granting that Welchman's interpretation of Dewey has warrant, it is difficult at first to see how this conception of justice could be radical, relying as it does on what seems to be a sterilized theory of rational choice and an acceptance of a version of liberal freedom. It is unclear why anyone interested in radical forms of social justice might look to Dewey as a resource.

Welchman asserts, "For reasons he does not explain in *Ethics*, Dewey evidently thinks it is freedom, rather than justice, that is the first virtue of social institutions. More specifically, it is 'effective freedom' meaning both freed *from interference* by others as well as freedom *to command* resources essential for the realization of one's desires and aims, that is Dewey's first virtue of social organization" (Welchman 1995, 194). Welchman's reading of Dewey situates Dewey's thought in the language of political philosophy popularized by Isaiah Berlin's "Two Concepts of Liberty." Berlin's assertion that "Everything is what it is: liberty is liberty, not equality or fairness or justice or culture, or human happiness or a quiet conscience" has held sway in much of what counts of political and social philosophy (Berlin 1990, 125).

In his emphasis on freedom as analytically distinct from justice, Dewey subscribes to a notion of freedom that is fraught with historical and experiential problems. It is worth noting that Dewey saw the problem of attempting to pin down definitions when he wrote about the meaning of liberalism in 1940:

> If one thinks the word should be given a precise, sharply marked-off signification on the basis of its most specific historical usage, one may come to believe that this meaning is the only legitimate one. . . . On the other hand, if one neglects all the historical usage one will only be able to tell what he personally thinks liberalism ought to mean, and thus find himself in the position of defining the word on the ground of some personal and perhaps private preference. (LW 14:252)

Dewey understood well the difficulties of definition and the subsequent reification of those concepts even as he often treated effective or negative freedom as a priority without due consideration of his own subject position. Berlin, Dewey, and so many others do not adequately consider that freedom is not so easily distinguished from justice claims. The freedom to grow and have experiences that is so essential to Dewey's position is historically bound to and made possible by unjust social relations and institutions.

The seeds of a conception of radical pragmatist justice are present in Dewey, but they require a black radical corrective. We can look to Du Bois for a corrective that is compatible with Dewey's pragmatism even as it enlarges and enriches it.

Du Bois's Radicalism

In his biography of W. E. B. Du Bois, Manning Marable writes that Du Bois's legacy as a serious, radical thinker was intentionally undermined and undervalued by liberal thinkers who could not forgive Du Bois for his commitments to communism (Marable 2005, viii). Marable acknowledges that Du Bois had a complicated relationship with formal communism, but claims, with Du Bois's friend and Marxist historian Herbert Aptheker, that Du Bois was above all else a Du Boisite (Marable 2005, xix). As a Du Boisite, Du Bois saw the merits of the Marxist critique of capitalism but saw in most instances of communism—both theoretically and in party practices—a failure to take on structural racism. Most known for his philosophical musings and early sociological writings about the race problem in the United States, Du Bois spent his long life deeply engaged in practical political organizing against racial injustice and working for increased social democracy.

During the Red Scare, Du Bois found himself under censure, outcast from the NAACP, an organization he helped found, and increasingly marginalized because he agreed with the communists that a total overhaul of capitalism was needed. Still, Du Bois was willing to participate in an idealism of the American spirit, much like Dewey, writing, "There was a day when the world rightly called Americans honest even if crude; earning their living by hard work; telling the truth no matter whom it hurt; and going to war only in what they believed a just cause after nothing else seemed possible" (Du Bois 1995a, 145). Du Bois also counted poor education as one of the reasons why Americans lacked the ability to think and criticize capitalism and racism. With Dewey, who rejected Marxism on the grounds that it relied on historical inevitability, Du Bois wondered why anyone ought to organize for the revolution when that person was as convinced as those he called the "theoretical" communists were that the revolution was inevitable. Here Du Bois is making a justice claim. Justice requires that we do not believe in inevitability, just as freedom requires that we attend to the practical matters of justice. Communist thinkers and actors, Marx included, who believed that matters of justice would no longer be a concern in a classless society, misunderstood both freedom and justice. However, Du Bois's ultimate rejection of Marxism was found not in his critique of their historical logic but in his suspicions of communism, which came from his lived experience as a black person in the United States. Du Bois was committed to socialism, but found its practices wanting.

Du Bois argued that capitalism in much of the world depended on racist logics of labor and human worth. While Dewey pointed out to Trotsky that the world proletariat was not nearly as international-minded as the Marxist revolution seemed to require, Du Bois criticized the American Marxists for not understanding the racist logic of labor and caste operative in the United States. The revolutionist agitators among the communists in the United States either mistakenly believed that they spoke for white laborers or knew very well that they were using poor, hard-suffering, black laborers as pawns.

Du Bois identified the white laborer in the United States as the class with which black Americans had the most in common and from whom the black person had the most to fear. Du Bois wrote, with no irony, "Throughout the history of the Negro in America, white labor has been the black man's enemy, his oppressor, his red murderer" (Du Bois 1995c, 589). Du Bois had little patience for the idealism of communists who would make believe that racism would somehow disappear if capitalism ended. His cutting assessment of the communist interventions during the infamous Scottsboro case illuminated Du Bois's understanding of the US social context and why claims for revolutionary social change were not attractive to many blacks.

Du Bois argued that the communists went to Scottsboro not to help defend the nine black boys accused of rape and threatened by lynch mobs because their lives were at stake; rather, the revolutionists had come to the aid of the Scottsboro 9 with the hopes of using the local black working population as a symbol of their cause. He wrote, "The ultimate object of the Communists, was naturally not merely nor chiefly to save the boys accused at Scottsboro; it was to make this case a center of agitation to expose the helpless condition of Negroes, and to prove that anything less than the radical Communist program could not emancipate them" (Du Bois 1995c, 586).

Du Bois, like many black radicals, was keenly interested in notions of emancipation and freedom. The specter of slavery and the reign of Jim Crow made freedom not just a theoretical issue but also a practical issue with lives at stake. While Du Bois hoped for a socialist, democratic future of freedom for his fellow blacks, he was quick to point out to the communists at Scottsboro that what justice blacks could count on depended on capitalism. Du Bois contended, "The capitalists are against mob-law and violence and would listen to reason and justice in the long run because industrial peace increases their profits" (Du Bois 1995b, 591). He freely admitted that capitalists sought profit rather than true freedom for the black laborer, but he saw in the communists a similar willingness to sacrifice black lives for their own form of profit. He makes a justice claim against the communists: "Socialists and Communists may sneer and say that the capitalists sought in all this profit cheap labor, strike-breakers and the training of conservative, reactionary leaders. They did. But Negroes sought food, clothes, shelter and knowledge to stave off death and slavery and only damned fools would have refused the gift" (Du Bois 1995b, 592).

Du Bois and Dewey shared suspicions of communism, though it could be argued that they each ultimately asserted radical revisions of capitalism. They both advocated socializing industry, extensive education reform, and the necessity of attending to practical matters such as the health and thriving of citizens over revolutionary social reform. It could be argued that both became more radical in their sentiments as they aged. Through world wars, the Great Depression, and the subsequent triumph of free market capitalism, they each advocated radical claims against prevailing attitudes and practices. Where they differ is that Du Bois tempered his freedom claims with justice claims.

According to Iris Marion Young, "When people say a rule or practice or cultural meaning is wrong and should be changed, they are usually making a claim about social justice" (Young 1990, 9). Young cautions us not to think of justice as only the distribution of goods. Both the Marxist and the champion of Rawlsian distributive justice, on her view, are guilty of reducing the complexity of social relations to economic relations. Rather, she argues, "social justice means the elimination of institutionalized domination and oppression. Any aspect of social organization and practice relevant to domination and oppression is in principle subject to evaluation by ideals of justice" (Young 1990, 15). Dewey and Du Bois understood that while economic distribution was important, cultural shifts toward inclusive democratic ideals were the grounds for action. While Dewey nodded to the wastes of energies and resources of people who were not actively engaged in the democratic polity through work and participation in creating the commons, Du Bois set as his test of any social reform "the Excluded Class." Du Bois argued that in any social movement that argued for some increase of freedom or justice, there was always some class of people whose needs were overlooked, trivialized, or excluded (Du Bois 1995b, 579). In Young's sense, Du Bois's constant critique of the communist program by attending to the oppressed status of black people in the United States and racial logics more straightforwardly attends to social justice than Dewey's.

This straightforward attention is important. As Erin McKenna points out, "While Dewey's theory implicitly recognizes and critiques racism and sexism . . . he does not adequately address how such systems of oppression impact the daily lives of the members of the targeted groups. Racism and sexism are not simply encountered as ideas or attitudes. They are encountered in everyday lived experience" (McKenna 2001, 124). By assuming that what people needed most was to have avenues of freedom, Dewey neglects to attend to the group-based social justice claims necessary to make that freedom possible. As McKenna argues, Dewey does not adequately consider how preexisting racist and sexist attitudes might impede people's ability to participate and lead to the sorts of antidemocratic practices Du Bois claimed characterized white labor's relation to blacks. Acknowledging power and its stagnation in oppression requires us not to idealize creativity and flexibility, but to acknowledge that the needs and desires of others are not simply problems to be meliorated. Rather, they are generated and sustained by what we have done and will do. We have habits of oppression, and perhaps only habits of justice can replace them.

Davis's Habits and Radical Pragmatist Social Justice

There have been various attempts to claim some form of radicalism for Dewey's pragmatism. Michael Sullivan and Daniel J. Solove offer a compelling interpretation of Dewey's radicalism. They explain,

> to the extent that pragmatism is an "attitude," it is one that is radical, for it is skeptical and experimental. The pragmatic temperament is one that is constantly prodding and questioning; it focuses on change and transformation. Although the pragmatist need not be committed to radical ends, she is committed to a radical kind of criticism and experimentation. This doesn't mean that pragmatism must reject the status quo; but it does mean that the pragmatist must be wary of accepting inherited ends uncritically. Far from being mundane and banal, pragmatism takes up the hard work of removing the blinders of existing habits, customs, and conventions by testing accepted beliefs and "truths." The result of this attitude is a critical edge. (Sullivan and Solove 2013, 334)

Under this description, Dewey can be considered a radical but not a revolutionary. It also reveals how Dewey's pragmatism may be improved and extended by black radicalism.

This understanding of the pragmatist's method and attitude are similar to that offered by Charles Mills in his consideration of what makes feminism and socialism radical. According to Mills,

> What is seen as an uncontroversial, largely consensual characterization of sociopolitical reality by mainstream figures is exactly what is contested by the heterodox. The radicalness of their challenge, then, often inheres not in a startling new axiology, but in a startling new picture of the world, which overturns the conventional wisdom and the orthodox consensus about what we know about social reality. (Mills 2003, 197)

Mills argues that the social justice claims that arise from the perspectives of these radicals reveal a crucial flaw in much of the theorizing of justice done by mainstream white philosophers who try to solve juridical problems without interrogating their own "perspective of white privilege" and the history of how the law itself has fostered racism. Mills also helps us understand why any radical pragmatic conception of justice would need to make a distinction between the neat, analytical conversations about the nature of justice and freedom and the messier, more complicated need to think through what Mills calls "corrective justice," which would attend to the legacy of racism and inequality (Mills 2003, 196).

Sources for radical, pragmatic habits of justice are numerous in the history of black radical thought in the United States. As the historian Robin D. G. Kelley points out, while many black radicals have been socialists or communists, such membership has not been a necessary condition for black radicalism. Rather, Kelley posits that black radicalism is characterized by the corrective justice that Mills and Young advocate, but also by what he calls "freedom dreams" and poetic knowledge.

> Progressive social movements do not simply produce statistics and narratives of oppression; rather, the best ones do what great poetry always does: transport us to another place, compel us to relive horrors and, more importantly, enable us to imagine a new society. We must remember that the conditions and the very existence of social movements enable participants to imagine something different, to realize things need not always be this way. (Kelley 2002, 9)

The futurity that Kelley mentions is present in Deweyan pragmatism but receives a fuller expression Du Bois, who attends to oppression more perspicaciously. Among the many black radicals Kelley refers to, Angela Davis offers us a good resource for the habits of justice that might replace the habits of oppression prevalent in our society. Davis's habits of justice turn on a different conception of freedom than found in Dewey and a more nuanced one than found in Du Bois.

Kelley characterizes Davis's idea of freedom in opposition to the liberal view of negative freedom in Berlin's sense:

> Davis's conception of freedom is far more expansive and radical—collective freedom; the freedom to earn a livelihood and live a healthy, fully realized life; freedom from violence; sexual freedom; social justice; abolition of all forms of bondage and incarceration; freedom from exploitation; freedom of movement; freedom as movement, as a collective striving for real democracy. For Davis, freedom is not a thing granted by the state in the form of law or proclamation or policy; freedom is struggled for, it is hard-fought

and transformative, it is a participatory process that demands new ways of thinking and being. (Kelley 2012, 7)

Davis's notion of freedom is tied to a notion of social justice. Freedom is not something that can truly be had by a lone individual; rather, it has social and collective conditions that require us to attend to social justice. In her desires for collective democracy, Davis is not so far removed in her radicalism from Dewey, for whom increased avenues for participation and freedom of self-expression were priorities. They even agree that juridical claims are not enough to guarantee the sort of society where freedom would prevail. Where Davis differs from Dewey, at least in emphasis, is in her insistence that freedom is a collective enterprise that requires we constantly attend to history. We can think of this attention to the historical in the present as a habit of justice: the habit of historical consciousness. Davis also demonstrates a second habit of justice mentioned in Kelley's summation of her work on freedom: the habit of keeping the radically different future in mind.

Davis's habit of historical consciousness is an integral part of her work. Historical consciousness is a disposition to understand present conditions in light of the past. In her theoretical work, Davis models this habit and how to do this as an intellectual interested in social justice at every turn. The *LA Times Book Review* blurb that appears on the cover of her seminal text *Women, Race, and Class* proclaims the book is "as useful an exposition of the current dilemmas of the women's movement as one could hope for" (Davis 1983). The text begins with a chapter on the legacy of slavery, and each subsequent chapter grounds complex theoretical positions about what social justice issues were most important for women at the time of its writing in the past. The text, like most of Davis's speeches and subsequent books, is as much a genealogical, diagnostic effort as it is an exposition of Davis's arguments.

Davis's radical habit of historical consciousness is not merely about looking to the past as the fount of all answers. Challenging the sentiment that the civil rights and social movements of the 1960s and early 1970s demonstrate the way we should address current social problems, Davis asserts, "Sometimes we veteran activists yearn for the good days rather than prepare ourselves to confront courageously a drastically transformed world that presents new, more complicated challenges" (Davis 2012, 17). Having a historical consciousness for Davis is having a practical, present consciousness. Looking to the past helps us understand how we've ended up where we are and gives us lessons on what might happen if we focus our efforts in certain directions. But Davis cautions that "we frequently replace historical consciousness with desperate nostalgia, allowing the past to become a repository for present political desires" (Davis 2012, 18). The second radical habit of justice checks our nostalgia.

In response to a question about defining struggles, Davis answers, "Whatever we are doing, wherever we are, it is imperative that we believe in the possibility of change. We cannot allow ourselves to be ensconced in the present, so the very first step is to actively imagine possible futures— futures beyond the prison and beyond capitalism" (Davis 2005, 83). Davis's concern with the future is compatible with a Deweyan pragmatist orientation, at least insofar as the belief in change is necessary to a Deweyan position. As a habit of justice, this insistence on the possibility of a changed future recurs in Davis's work. In interviews and public speeches, when asked about the persistence of social problems, Davis frequently points out that through human effort, the future need not be like the past.

Davis is an advocate of prison abolition. Abolition differs from reform in that prison reformers concede that prison is a necessary institution. Reformers attempt to restructure prison life to be more humane and often fight for programs like inmate education and recreation. Davis sees those reform efforts as a weak bandage on a deeper social problem. She advocates for revolutionary rethinking and restructuring of criminal law that would abolish prisons in our society.

Dewey posited a Great Community wherein individuals would be free to participate in the social life of the community (LW 2). Du Bois desired a social democracy that attended to the histories of race and class in order to ensure not just individual freedom but also equality and justice. For both of their visions to come to pass, much of what society was like in their time would have to have radically changed. Davis remains committed to a revolutionary view of social change and not just a radical one. Revolutionary theory and work like Davis's require a willingness to abandon the security and stability of existing social forms. Davis has been willing to risk social standing, disrupt business and government proceedings, and suffer punishment for her ideals. For Davis, a total transformation of society is both something to be desired and worked for—a revolution.

Davis's work also reveals that one needn't be a revolutionary to be a radical. One of the most often quoted lines from Davis's speeches is her definition of radical. The quote is often presented as the last of the two sentences cited here, which is a paraphrase of Karl Marx. It is helpful to look at the sentences together. According to Davis, "If we are not afraid to adopt a revolutionary stance—if, indeed, we wish to be radical in our quest for change—then we must get to the root of our oppression. After all, radical simply means grasping things at the root" (Davis 1990, 14). Davis does not seem to distinguish radical from revolutionary as I have done, but the separation is not unreasonable given her definition. If radical means grasping at the root causes and proposing change, then a pragmatist could certainly be a radical. If radical means that one must also be a revolutionary, then it might be difficult for a pragmatist to acquiesce to that demand for reasons previously outlined.

A radical pragmatist can take up an attitude that keeps in mind the robust, messy notions of justice that must include freedom and equality as defended by Du Bois and Davis. This notion of justice is compatible with Dewey's own views, even as it extends his too tidy notion of freedom and emphasizes oppression as a salient factor in our construction of what freedom means. Dewey's social philosophy does not have to be compatible with all forms of radicalism. Rather, in matters of justice, tempering the revolutionary zeal that would take ends as inevitable or absolute with Dewey's critique offers us productive ways to talk about and work for social justice that can meet at least some of the demands of black radicalism.

Works Cited

Berlin, Isaiah. 1990. *Four Essays on Liberty*. Oxford: Oxford University Press.

Davis, Angela Y. 1983. *Women, Race, and Class*. New York: Vintage Books.

———. 1990. *Women, Culture, and Politics*. New York: Vintage Books.

———. 1998. *The Angela Y. Davis Reader*. Edited by Joy James. Malden, MA: Blackwell.

———. 2005. *Abolition Democracy: Beyond Empire, Prisons, and Torture*. New York: Seven Stories Press.

———. 2012. *The Meaning of Freedom and Other Difficult Dialogues*. San Francisco: City Lights Books.

Dewey, John. 1969–1991. *The Collected Words of John Dewey*, edited by Jo Ann Boydston. 37 vols. Carbondale: Southern Illinois University Press. (See List of Abbreviations.)

Du Bois, W. E. B. 1995a. "A Vista of Ninety Fruitful Years." In *W.E.B. Du Bois: A Reader*, edited by David Levering Lewis, 144–147. New York: Henry Holt.

———. 1995b. "Socialism and the Negro Problem." In *W.E.B. Du Bois: A Reader*, edited by David Levering Lewis, 577–582. New York: Henry Holt.

———. 1995c. "The Negro and Communism." In *W.E.B. Du Bois: A Reader*, edited by David Levering Lewis, 583–593. New York: Henry Holt.

Kelley, Robin D. G. 2012. Foreword to *The Meaning of Freedom and Other Difficult Dialogues*, by Angela Y. Davis, 7–16. San Francisco: City Lights Books.

———. 2002. *Freedom Dreams: The Black Radical Imagination*. Boston: Beacon Press.

Marable, Manning. 2005. *W.E.B. Du Bois: Black Radical Democrat*. Boulder, CO: Paradigm.

McKenna, Erin. 2001. *The Task of Utopia: A Pragmatist and Feminist Perspective*. Lanham, MD: Rowman and Littlefield.

Mills, Charles. 2003. *From Race to Class: Essays on White Marxism and Black Radicalism*. Lanham, MD: Rowman and Littlefield.

Moreno, Jonathan, and R. Scott Frey. 1985. "Dewey's Critique of Marxism." *Sociological Quarterly* 26(1): 21–34.

Sullivan, Michael, and Daniel J. Solove. 2013. "Radical Pragmatism." In *The Cambridge Companion to Pragmatism*, edited by Alan Malachowski, 324–344. Cambridge: Cambridge University Press.

Welchman, Jennifer. 1995. *Dewey's Ethical Thought*. Ithaca, NY: Cornell University Press.

Young, Iris Marion. 1990. *Justice and the Politics of Difference*. Princeton, NJ: Princeton University Press.

CHAPTER 10 | Contesting Injustice
Why Pragmatist Political Thought Needs Du Bois

COLIN KOOPMAN

Challenging Pragmatism

Pragmatist philosophy is often characterized in terms of its emphasis on the practicability of getting things done over adherence to ideal principles. But what about situations in which doing anything of import requires the kinds of motivation usually supplied only by shining ideals? Does pragmatism in such situations leave us incapacitated, debilitated, and unable to act? We can sharpen this question by refocusing it in the context of political philosophy. How can pragmatism facilitate action in the face of and against injustice? How can pragmatism be used to motivate critique of entrenched orders of inequality, unfreedom, domination, and oppression?

Recent scholarship in pragmatist political and moral philosophy has raised a version of this question by issuing to pragmatism a *challenge to insurrection*.[1] As formulated by Leonard Harris, the insurrectionist challenge presses pragmatism to show how it can facilitate insurrection and revolt against moral abominations such as slavery. Harris pointedly asks, "is there any reason to suppose that the method of intelligence [developed by John Dewey] would incline anyone to be motivated to seek the abolition of slavery through insurrection or seek the end of servitude?" (2002, 207).

---

[1] A related way of framing the issue is in terms of what might be called the *guerilla challenge*; this would be in light of José Medina's call for a contestational "guerilla pluralism" (2013, 283ff.) that he also brings to bear on pragmatism (2013, 285ff. and 2015, 244).

It is certainly not clear that past pragmatisms can meet the insurrectionist challenge, but nor is it obvious that no future pragmatism could. In the face of such a staggering indeterminacy one way to begin determining how this challenge might be met by future pragmatisms would be to consider related challenges that would press pragmatism in the general direction of insurrectionism. To take one such step, I here pose to pragmatism a *challenge to contestation*.

The contestational challenge presses pragmatism to specify what resources it provides for the crucial task of motivating and sustaining contestation in the face of injustice. It is reasonable to think that a pragmatism that is prepared to meet the challenge to contestation has come at least a little closer to meeting the challenge to insurrection—and this is true even while contestation is clearly more modest in ambition than insurrection. That said, if it were to turn out to be the case that mounting contestation fails to move the needle any closer to insurrection, I believe the contestational challenge is still worth consideration in its own right if there exist political injustices that call for contestation against entrenched orders but which are either not so severe as to call for outright insurrection or are exactly that severe yet unable to be presently unsettled by any possible insurrectionist conduct. Just as the insurrectionist challenge involves the thought that insurrection is a political value in some (certainly not all) situations, the contestational challenge involves the thought that contestation is a unique political value in some (again not all) situations. The more general idea here is that one way to meet the charge of acquiescence frequently meted out against pragmatism is to show with precision how and where pragmatism supplies resources for refusal, instruments for irritation, and catalysts for contestation.

Unfortunately, mainstream pragmatist political theory too often fails to specify these aspects of pragmatism. My hunch is that this is largely due to an overprioritization of John Dewey's political philosophy within the pragmatist pantheon. If this is right, then a related factor is the extent to which contemporary pragmatist political theorists often decline to consider the contributions that other pragmatists of the classical era, such as William James and W. E. B. Du Bois, might offer to political and moral pragmatism. In what follows, I begin by briefly explicating why James's capacious pragmatism might be a preferential starting point over Dewey's narrowly progressivist politics, and I then turn to showing how Du Bois's work furnishes resource for meeting the contestational challenge within the terms of such a capacious pragmatist orientation.

Potentials of Pragmatism in James and Dewey

James's 1891 essay "The Moral Philosopher and the Moral Life" focuses on the flux of morality in a way that admits of an interesting political translation. In the key third section of the essay James is focused on what he calls the "casuistic" analysis of moral realities (WWJ 6:151). Casuistry, for James, is case-based inquiry. The term for James distinguishes the case-based work of the clinician diagnosing a patient's symptoms from more research-based projects that are attempts to furnish etiological theories of disease. James's field of focus is notable: the clinical case is always the context in which action is ongoing.

James argues that what we always meet with in the context of the actual case is "a *pinch* between the ideal and the actual" (WWJ 6:153). Located on the level of the case, this pinch tends toward the transformative. James describes these transformative pinches in differing, even sometimes competing, vocabularies.

In some passages, one gets the impression that James thinks of the pinches being resolved in ever more inclusive and progressive wholes. He writes at one moment that "the course of history is nothing but the story of men's struggles from generation to generation to find the more and more inclusive order" (WWJ 6:155). He even refers to a "series of social discoveries quite analogous to those of science" (156).

Without pretending that this element is not an ingredient in James's political thought, we can also affirm other vocabularies in which his ideas were steeped. For just as James was wont to emphasize the progressive resolution of moral pinches, he was also keen to illuminate the tragic depths of moral conflict they engender. "Some part of the ideal must be butchered," James memorably asserts (WWJ 6:154). In these and other moments we find pragmatism articulated in a key that is about as far from the pitches of utilitarian efficiency and romanticizing idealization as one can get. Though James frequently attuned his pragmatism to this mode of thought and inquiry, it is often overlooked in commentary that would treat James, and all of pragmatism by extension, as tepid or even as forthrightly conservative. This underscores the importance of recent work on James that brings into focus his radicalism, for instance Deborah Coon's (1996) and Alexander Livingston's (2016) arguments that James can today be fruitfully read as embodying an anarchist vision in political theory.

What we find in James is pragmatism in multiple—a double-barreled pragmatism. Shooting through one barrel, James's pragmatism holds that "ethical science is just like physical science" (WWJ 6:157). But shooting just as quickly out of the other, it is a pragmatism that accepts that "victory and defeat there must be" (155) and that asks us to "see everywhere the struggle and the squeeze" (157). Neither is the complete and final word in James's moral and political vision. Both are ingredient in the flux that is political actuality. Both are irreducible aspects of the dynamics of political conduct. That both are there in James's inaugural pragmatism does not mean that both have always been emphasized in subsequent pragmatist political theorizing.

It was the more progressive and scientific wing of James's writings that received the central emphasis in Dewey's political theory. Dewey's vision of democracy was one that was always premised on developing the political valences of his commitment to growth. "Growth itself is the only moral 'end,'" wrote Dewey, in offering a notion of morality as "improvement and progress" (MW 12:181).

This sort of emphasis certainly sounds reasonable, but the problem in short is just that Dewey too often seems eager to get past the moments of conflict that are constitutive of the political. In his most important text on politics Dewey could express the hope that "the divided and troubled publics integrate" (LW 2:315). He could conclude one of his books on morality with the thought that "Even in the midst of conflict, struggle and defeat a consciousness is possible of the enduring and comprehending whole" (MW 14:226). These and other moments in Dewey's political and moral thought are funded by a more general philosophical preference for unity over strife. This is an attitude widely evident in Dewey's writings, for instance in passages such as this: "If life continues and if in continuing it expands, there is an overcoming of factors of opposition and conflict; there is a transformation of them into differentiated aspects of a higher powered and more significant life" (MW 10:20). Where James would regularly push his readers to keep attending to moments of loss, Dewey repeatedly emphasizes a sunny-side Hegelianism in which everything is just about to burst into springtime. As in Hegel, there is in Dewey a risk of totalizing the spring season.

It is thus that Dewey's vision of the political too often, or at least too easily, reads as a tidy administrative conception of politics as an engineering task. Generations of critics have thus accused Dewey, and by extension pragmatism writ large, of collapsing into what Randolph Bourne in a 1917 critique of Dewey called a "philosophy of adjustment" that is captivated by "the allure of the technical" (Bourne 1917, 344, 345). I do not endorse those countless criticisms that would hold Dewey down as a naive instrumentalist. But I also do not think that pragmatists can continue to avoid the painful truth that it is not unreasonable to read Dewey as an instrumentalist in the pejorative sense. So I see little point in trying to rescue Dewey unscathed. Rather than rescuing Dewey, what would make more sense would be to take the criticisms on board so that we might put into motion a pragmatism wielding critical resources that are simply not well furnished in Dewey's work. This is what I now pursue in turning to the work of W. E. B. Du Bois.

Practices of Contestation in Du Bois

If Dewey developed and enriched James's more progressive sensibilities, we should look to other classical pragmatists for a development and enrichment of James's attentiveness to the butchering involved in moral and political contestation. Du Bois's work helps us locate that branch in pragmatism whose course is more uncontainable than its usual comparisons to lukewarm utilitarianism might suggest. For there is real heat in Du Bois when it comes to these matters. His is a practice of critique forged in a hot furnace crackling with conflict and contest. His is a methodology for inquiry swaddled in power, be it in raw forms of noose and lash or more subtle assemblies of a police apparatus. His is a philosophy that is able to countenance the depths of suffering that humans sometimes visit on one another.

The central theme in Du Bois I here seek to retrieve into pragmatism is his emphasis on, and paradigmatic practice of, contestation. The way in which he both manifested and maintained contestation, I argue, is what defines the contribution of Du Bois to the politics of race in the twentieth century. As I develop this reading of Du Bois below I shall also emphasize two corollaries of his contestatory orientation. The first is Du Bois's patient acknowledgment of strife as constitutive of the political. Du Bois understands that conflict is the condition within which the contestatory modality of conduct is most needful. But this does not necessarily make him an agonistic champion of conflict. More likely it makes him a realist who is willing to outflank idealism's disavowals of tragedy, strife, and wintry discontent. This points directly to the second corollary of Du Boisian contestation, namely that he manages to both muster and maintain it without resorting to a moralistic tone. Contestation is easy to foist where one thinks oneself in the presence of a moral truth that can simply be pressed upon others. But where one's moral truths cannot be so pressed, contestation must become cunning, strategic, and politicizing in intent. The moralistic option too easily amounts to a pressing to no avail, with the inevitable endgames of bitter despair. In contrast to this, a politicizing contestation works to mount, and to maintain, an apparatus of hope that can outlast forces of defeat. What Du Bois's manner of contestation offers, I argue, is a way of maintaining itself, and therefore hope too, midst conditions of strife so severe that they would reduce mere moralizers to hopeless despair. Holding these three ideas in mind—contestation, strife, and hopefulness—I thus intend to read Du Bois under the shadow of James Baldwin's paradigmatic practice of critique: "I love America more than any other country in the world, and, exactly for this reason, I insist on the right to criticize her perpetually" (Baldwin 1955, 9).

The critical contestation that runs throughout Du Bois's work is at its most forceful in his 1903 book *The Souls of Black Folk*. The book is composed of fourteen chapters: the first chapter frames the project through his famous notions of double consciousness and the veil, the following nine chapters offer historical-sociological portraits of general conditions within the veil, the book then shifts to three more personal accounts of particularized conditions within the veil (including Du Bois's own lament over the death in infancy of his first child), and then concludes with a final chapter titled "The Sorrow Songs." The penultimate chapter of the historical-sociological portion of the book presents strife at some of its highest pitches in Du Bois's work.

The very title of chapter 9, "Of the Sons of Master and Man," begins by dressing the stage in a fraught tension. Du Bois uses that stage to offer a pragmatist sociological analysis of "a few main lines of action" that constitute the ongoing relations between contemporary descendants of master and slave (Du Bois 1903, 134). The chapter presents a taxonomy of six forms of what Du Bois calls "contact," which is his word for "how the black race in the South meet and mingle with the whites" (135). The forms of contact Du Bois specifies are physical proximity, economic relations, political relations, intellectual contact, social contact, and religious enterprise. In detailing each of these, Du Bois offers language that speaks to the signature theme of "strife" that structures the chapter (134) and indeed the entire book (5). The chapter thus offers what might be advanced as a sociological taxonomy of strife and the sufferings they condition.

Physical contact consists of the strife of "segregation by color" (136). Economic contact involves that of "relentless and sharp competition" (137). Political contact gives rise to "disenfranchisement" with the result that law and justice are experienced as "sources of humiliation and oppression" (142, 143). Du Bois in this section details a penetrating analysis of "the question of Negro crime" as a partial effect of a "police system" that yields "a double system of justice" in that it "was originally designed to keep track of all Negroes, not simply of criminals," under historical conditions of slavery (144, 145). Designed as such, the police system continues to function in Du Bois's day "as a means of reenslaving blacks" (145). Thus political contact continues to be conditioned by the entrenched strife of slavery as constitutive of the form of relation between, returning to the chapter's titular terms, those who cannot but be Sons of Master and Man.

The cumulative effect of Du Bois's discussion of all six domains of conduct is a detailed portrait, composed at the scale of miniatures in collage, of one of the most powerful thrusts running throughout nearly all of his work: a specification of the multiplicitous forms of strife that condition, both historically and sociologically, racial contact in America. In witnessing this collage of miniatures one might miss its point if one insists on reading it as primarily a normative project meant to specify injustices in need of progressive reform. I am not suggesting that Du Bois was in any ways opposed to the rectification of injustices. What I am suggesting, rather, is that the primary function of his work is not so much to fixate attention on principles guiding such a rectification as it is to provide a contestational engagement with his historical-sociological milieu such that the forms of strife that facilitate injustice may find both witness and articulation. My claim is that Du Bois's project is less a treatise in moral theory and more an essay in moral contestation.

That Du Bois's intent in this chapter is more that of witnessing strife than principled rejection of strife can be glimpsed in a moment where, immediately following his discussion of the first three central domains, he pauses in order to reflect on the forms of conduct he has so far recounted. He muses in the manner of a traveler along for a ride and asks if a "casual observer" traveling through the South might perhaps fail at first to notice the strife he has sought to highlight. A traveler might think that "on the question of questions—the Negro problem—he hears so little that there almost seems to be a conspiracy of silence." Perhaps the "astonished visitor" might even find himself inclined to ask "if after all there *is* any problem here." And so Du Bois encourages the observer to wait and linger until "he realizes at last that silently, resistlessly, the world about flows by him in two great streams: they ripple on in the same sunshine, they approach and mingle their waters in seeming carelessness,—then they divide and flow wide apart" (Du Bois 1903, 148). Even in the sunshine there remains division. One might be blind to it at first, indeed for well too long, but it is there, ready for a beholding by those who would linger to look.[2]

Du Bois, here as elsewhere, is an exemplar of the critic who stares hard into the stain of strife. It would be a mistake to infer from this that Du Bois sought to celebrate the conflictual. Rather, Du Bois thereby opened up the possibility for a conception of politics whose very aspirations would be conditioned in the first place by democratic contestation (rather than, say, progressive efficiency). My reading here is indebted to that of Melvin Rogers, who argues that "For Du Bois contestation is at the core of democracy," explicating this as a politics that "ennobles human existence through the iterative process of contestation it makes possible, even as it suggests a darker undercurrent in the recognition that the outcome of contestation can never be known in advance" (Rogers 2012, 191, 202).

To further defend such a view as a reading of Du Bois it is important to explicitly register a point I have only casually flagged above: a reading of Du Bois's political theory in terms of "contestatory pragmatism" entails no small consequences for how we might be tempted to read his relation to what are surely his most famous contributions to American political thought, namely his intertwined notions of the veil and double consciousness. For if the contestatory reading is generative, then it should make us hesitate to read Du Bois as offering moral arguments to the effect that the veil of color ought to be torn down and that doubled consciousness ought to be reunified. Rather, I read Du Bois as patiently acknowledging tragic strife in order to honestly contest injustice. I read him as resonating with George Shulman's reading of Baldwin as "bearing witness to what is dis-remembered and who is counted" in such a manner that "to move from innocence to acknowledgment is not to embrace moral categorization but to turn to what we have evaded in 'life' and inner experience, social practices, political conduct, and national history" (Shulman 2008, 141, 135).

This reading deserves, and needs, development because it feels so easy to want to read Du Bois as offering just such a moral categorization. Consider two textual examples. *Souls* begins its analysis of double consciousness as a peculiar "twoness,—an American, a Negro; two souls, two thoughts, two unreconciled strivings; two warring ideals in one dark body," all of which produces in the doubled "American Negro" a familiar

---

[2] The strategy in Du Bois's chapter bears comparison to that developed by James in his "On a Certain Blindness in Human Beings," where he contrasts the traveler who is unable to see (WWJ 12:133–135) with the loafing spectator who is finally able to look (WWJ 12:141).

"longing to attain self-conscious manhood, to merge his double self into a better and truer self" (Du Bois 1903, 5). This surely sounds like the work of someone who is mounting a moral argument against the maintenance of double consciousness. Consider second that *Souls* ends in its final chapter on a similar note of seeming uplift: "in His good time America shall rend the Veil and the prisoned shall go free" (Du Bois 1903, 215). Again, this surely reads like the conclusion of an argument that would show us that the veil should be lifted.

In contrast to such readings produced along the surface of the text of *Souls*, I want to emphasize that reading Du Bois's writing as working to make these moral arguments involves reading his work as funding an obligation such that we tend to want to read Du Bois as primarily a defender of great moral truths. In contrast, I read Du Bois as attempting to fund not a moral obligation but an ongoing effort of activity. Du Bois's writings do not come to a conclusion so much as they maintain a motion of conduct. Du Bois's work is primarily focused on possibilities for sustaining contestation midst perilous conflict. If this is right, then the vision he offers of rending the veil is not a statement of moral principle so much as it is, as Du Bois explicitly tells his reader, a renewal of "the hope that sang in the songs of my father well sung" (Du Bois 1903, 215). To give focus to the difference between these two modes of writing, or rather reading Du Bois's writing, consider again the two bookends from *Souls* just quoted.

The latter passage in which Du Bois expresses the hope of his inherited songs is followed by four bars of the spiritual hymn "Let Us Cheer the Weary Traveler." Immediately following this, the lines with which Du Bois ends the book are these: "And the traveler girds himself, and sets his face toward the Morning, and goes his way" (Du Bois 1903, 216). Du Bois here suggests that his hope for rending the veil is offered to stay the weary traveler more so than to produce a rational argument concerning our collective moral obligations to abolish the color line. Du Bois would of course not seek to defend the color line, but he also would not moralize on its injustices in service of progressive unification. He is too aware of the entrenchments of history to leave matters at a simple game of "color line, good or bad?" Rather, he seeks a manner of contestation wherein hope can be maintained midst entrenched conflict.

With respect to the earlier passage, it is hard to see why the rest of the book that follows these words would have any point if Du Bois's "longing" for a "merger" was straightforwardly reconciliatory. If reconciliation were quite possible according to Du Bois, then it would seem as if almost the entirety of *Souls* were paradoxically playing against the possibility. But that is not Du Bois's strategy. In the very next sentence after he gives expression to a longing for merger he makes it plain enough that his longing is not for a unifying reconciliation: "In this merging he wishes neither of the older selves to be lost. . . . He simply wishes to make it possible for a man to be both a Negro and an American, without being cursed and spit upon by his fellows, without having the doors of Opportunity closed in his face" (Du Bois 1903, 5). And already before this he had claimed that the African American is "gifted with second-sight," thereby locating something positive in a double consciousness that is itself of course not entirely positive (Du Bois 1903, 5). How can we make sense of this apparent maintenance of double consciousness in light of the strife that Du Bois claims such consciousness produces? As I read him, Du Bois is simply possessed of too much of a historicist sensibility, too much of an awareness that the oppressions of the past are entrenched in the present, to embrace an idealistic optimism about an obligation to shred the shroud that is the veil.[3] In other words, Du Bois is too experienced in the problems of history to play an innocent game of "veil, good or bad?"

I thus read *Souls* as focused on the maintenance of hope midst conditions so desperate that were it not for this hope the conditions would be nothing but those of despair. This is not a normative reconstruction of a problematic situation so much as a set of claims concerning the conditions of possibility of reconstruction where it might seem entirely unimaginable. It is also not an agonistic affirmation of the necessity of conflict for the dialectic of the political so much as a patient practice of contestation that is a condition of possibility for hope itself in the deeply conflictual context to which Du Bois wrote. In contrast to these and other easily available readings, I look to see what follows from understanding Du Bois as developing a mode of political criticism that was later elegantly summarized by Baldwin as "a perpetually cultivated spiritual resilience" (Baldwin 1961, 70).

Pragmatism in Contestation

Why should I insist that contestation as a mode of resilience bears the orientation of pragmatism? I have been insisting that we are with Du Bois very near to the space of pragmatism if not indeed already within it. If this

---

[3] My reading here resonates with philosopher Kirkland's reading of the veil as historically "dyadic" (2013, 142) and biographer Lewis's reading of it in terms of "proud, enduring hyphenation" (1993, 281).

is correct, it is however clearly not Dewey's pragmatism. For Dewey could never write about progress what Du Bois did: "Progress, I understand, is necessarily ugly" (Du Bois 1903, 59). Rather than thereby draining pragmatism of its purpose and promise, Du Bois's attention to contestation can give pragmatism something of what it needs to maintain the motivation to action when progress can seem long off.

In reading Du Bois for a contribution to, and redirection of, pragmatism, I would seem to invite the following question: "But is Du Bois really a pragmatist?" One might be inclined to answer this question by way of reference to Du Bois's education under the partial guidance of William James, about whom he would later write that when he landed in Cambridge it was "squarely in the arms of William James of Harvard, for which God be praised" (Du Bois 1940, 579).[4] But rather than mount an argument from influence, I think it better to resist the very question. For the question itself encourages a response that assumes the unhelpful position of the gatekeeper.

A better question, following Paul Taylor, who is following Cavell on Emerson, would be to ask, "What's the Use of Calling Du Bois a Pragmatist?" (Taylor 2004, 99).[5] Taylor's question is better because it allows this kind of answer: "Declining to see Du Bois as a pragmatist not only obscures important aspects of his work and life but also reinforces our willingness to overlook important aspects of pragmatic thought and practice" (100). Taylor goes on to develop a Du Boisian pragmatist account of a perfectionist ethics of self-realization (103ff.). What I want to emphasize here is not pragmatist perfectionism, an important theme for pragmatist moral and political thought to be sure, but rather pragmatist contestation, for here is where I find Du Bois manifesting what Dewey most lacks.

One way to make this argument is to consider how key pragmatist categories in Du Bois facilitated his appreciation of race as a field of conflict in need of a more robust contestation. I do not deny that Du Bois came to a mode of contestatory protest because of his immersion in racial asymmetries and his experiences with other traditions of thought. Rather, all I seek to affirm is the presence in Du Bois's work of modalities and methodologies that bear an affinity with pragmatism. I would not even wish to declare that because of these moments Du Bois was, in some abstract sense, "a pragmatist." Rather, I would regard them as evidence that Du Bois in

---

[4] See also later reflections by Du Bois (1968, 133).
[5] Taylor's question is prompted in part by others who have documented pragmatism's place in Du Bois's thought, such as Cornel West (1989, 138–150).

certain moments thought, wrote, and acted according to a philosophical perspective which pragmatism is well-positioned to learn from.

This proximity to pragmatism in aspects of Du Bois's work should not be regarded as somehow legitimating his work. It is not my idea that Du Bois stands in need of pragmatism (or some other canonized philosophy) to provide his thought with legitimacy and warrant. Rather, it is my argument that there is enough of a pragmatist spark in Du Bois to motivate my task here of bringing his work to bear on more canonized pragmatisms so as to transform the critical potentialities of that tradition. This argument is not intended to bear on the question of legitimating Du Bois (which I take to already have been settled for other reasons having not much to do with pragmatism). It bears more directly on the matter of how we can transform pragmatism's critical energies in such a way as to learn from, rather than be in the way of, theorists and practitioners of contestation like Du Bois. So if Taylor finds the value of Du Boisian pragmatism in its bringing our attention to undernoticed aspects of that tradition, then I similarly locate the value of such a provocation in its helping to spark underdeveloped aspects of that tradition. If this argument bears on any issue of legitimacy, then, it bears on the fact that American pragmatism needs to more robustly engage African American thought than it has in order to maintain its legitimacy. In fact, perhaps we can go even further and suggest that without such an engagement pragmatism already lacks the legitimacy it has supposed it has.[6]

Consider that few of Du Bois's contemporaries (including many of his contemporary African American intellectuals) were inclined to see race as a doubled twoness. What helped Du Bois to this and other of his conceptual creations? Many things no doubt—and among them are orientations and modalities of critique that bear interesting affinities with pragmatism. What I have particularly in mind is the powerful way in which Du Bois brought his practice of contestation into being through categories of analysis that have also been central for pragmatism, including most notably those of action, historicity and problematicity.[7] Consider each in turn.

With respect to Du Bois's actionistic analytics, the explication of *Souls* above showed how his critical intent is focused on what he there called "a chapter in human action" as seen in "lines of action" (Du Bois 1903, 133,

---

[6] I thank Jacoby Carter for pressing the importance of the concerns that I am attempting to address in this paragraph; see Carter (forthcoming).

[7] It is beyond my scope to here explicate pragmatism's philosophical focus on these three signature categories, but I have done so previously in Koopman 2014 on conduct, Koopman 2009, chap. 2, on historical transitions, and Koopman 2009, chap. 7, on problematicity.

134). The orientation of analysis is thus toward "the thousand and one little actions which go to make up life" (147). This is not an innocent way of framing one's analysis. But it is all too easy to neglect the fact that *Souls* does not operate by way of a critique of ideologies, mentalities, systems, discourses, feelings, or even experiences. Du Bois's focus is conducts, specifically conducts in conflict whose acknowledgment opens up possibilities for counterconducts of contestation. These conducts, furthermore, are analyzed by Du Bois in pragmatistic terms, namely as actions that are historied and problematized.

With respect to historicity, temporality, and transitionality it is surely notable that Du Bois, in contrast to all three of the canonical classical pragmatists, not only theorized the historicity of action but also actually took up the practice of empirical inquiry into historical and sociological transformations. Du Bois presented his 1897 essay "The Conservation of Races" as seeing its subject matter through "the eye of the Historian and Sociologist" (817). Thus does Du Bois there define race in neither conservative nor essentialist terms,[8] but rather by way of what is "historically" entrenched as "the friction between different groups of people" (821). Six years later *Souls* proceeds in similar historicist terms by framing a concept of race through two early chapters on the periods of Emancipation (chap. 2) and Reconstruction (chap. 3). The ensuing chapters comprising the historical-sociological portion of the text explicitly take up this historical framing. Following the "Masters and Man" chapter discussed above, Du Bois concludes this section of the book with chapter 10, titled "Of the Faith of the Fathers." The discussion here condenses the historical sensibility informing his earlier taxonomy of strife. Du Bois masterfully reframes doubleness as the jarring effect of two temporalities out of sync: "The worlds within and without the Veil of Color are changing, and changing rapidly, but not at the same rate, not in the same way" (Du Bois 1903, 164). Du Bois is here recasting his analysis in pragmatist terms of uneven rates of transition and transformation across asynchronous histories. Du Bois specifies these mismatched rhythms as inheritances of both "the current of the nineteenth" and "the eddies of the fifteenth century," that is of Emancipation and Enslavement respectively (Du Bois 1903, 164). The result, Du Bois summarizes in a memorable line, is "the writhing of the age translated into black" (165). What is notable to the pragmatist is

---

[8] For one such misreading see Appiah 1985, the more recent retraction in Appiah 2014, and an interim criticism of Appiah's views by Taylor in favor of a reading of Du Bois's "pragmatic racialism" (2000, 112).

how that writhing is defined by Du Bois as an effect of history in being made possible by "two great and hardly reconcilable streams of thought and ethical strivings" (165).

Du Bois's employment of historical transitions as lenses for analysis throughout his works should not be regarded as innocent. For he was writing in a moment when many, including proponents of hereditarian programs like eugenics, would have refused to define race historically, seeking instead to define it biologically. But for Du Bois it is history specifically that produces the "peculiar sense of doubt and bewilderment" into which he inscribes double consciousness (Du Bois 1903, 165).

This brings me to a second aspect of Du Bois's thought that bears affinities with his pragmatist contemporaries, namely his frequent use of the analytical category of the problematic, which in the preceding quotation he refers to in equally pragmatist terms as doubt. Du Bois offers a vision of racial strife in terms that form a not-innocent alternative to more standard accounts of racial conflicts as dialectical contradictions. This vision shows how to historically dedialecticize the very context for the contestatory mode that is central to his analytics of race.

It is a crucial idea of pragmatism that a problematization is not always a contradiction, even though the latter would be one class of the former. Where is the contradiction in the unsettling conflicts that define the divided world of the sons of master and man who would come into political contact? One would be hard pressed to find a *contradiction* here, but *problems* clearly abound. Du Bois focuses his witness, and also ours, on those problems, thereby refusing the idealist's invitation to moralize against ideological illusion. Thus, for instance, would Du Bois in *Darkwater* maintain a mode of contestation that would not cave into despair over the persistence of forms of political contact that might otherwise be misrepresented as ideological illusions: "The man who cannot frankly acknowledge the 'Jim-Crow' car as a fact and yet live and hope is simply afraid either of himself or of the world . . . [B]oth things are true and both belong to this our world and neither can be denied" (Du Bois 1920, 135). Rather than writing up Jim Crow as an irrational contradiction and leaving it at that, Du Bois here shows himself more interested in acknowledgment of the reality of racial strife such that he might transform this strife through a hopeful contestation.

If I am right that this point, too, is not innocent (that is to say, if pragmatist critique has any force at all as an alternative to dialectical critique), then we should not overlook the presence of the category of the problematic in Du Bois's works. I agree with Cornel West that it is notable that Du

Bois on multiple occasions defines the significance of his own life in terms of his being a problem (West 1989, 142).[9] Du Bois knew existentially the force of the pragmatists' methodological emphasis on problems, hesitations, doubts, and bewilderments. If so, then we should no longer treat as an innocent colloquialism the appearance of this important pragmatist category in what is surely Du Bois's most-quoted line: "the problem of the Twentieth-Century is the problem of the color-line" (Du Bois 1903, 1, 13). Du Bois here imbues the politics of color with a distinctively pragmatist sensibility that promises to sustain us further than would idealist generalities that dialectically wind their way to the inevitable conclusion of despair at the hypocrisies, paradoxes, and contradictions of race. More important than any of these, Du Bois suggests, is the sheer historical weight of race in virtue of which it is the persisting problem that it is. It is the immense weight of that history that canalizes possibilities for action in what Du Bois once called "this narrow Now" (Du Bois 1903, 174).

A Restless Conclusion

All of the pragmatists I have discussed are united by a severe analytical attention to problems, histories, and conducts. But at least one important difference has been identified within that common space: Dewey looks to how we can resolve the problems generated by action in complex historical conditions whereas Du Bois attends to how entrenched histories are always feverishly generating conflicts of conduct. When James inaugurated pragmatism as a methodology he was already inaugurating multiple pragmatisms in a kind of mosaic of pragmatist methodologies. James himself thus emphasized both progressive intelligence and political strife without reducing either to the other. If James's pluralistic approach to pragmatism is the only consistent pragmatism, then we should conclude that we have much to learn from both Dewey and Du Bois (as well as from James). The persisting problem, then, would simply be this: mainstream pragmatist political theory has almost come to be identified with a certain cast of progressivism that too easily risks losing sight of the manners of contestation whereby pragmatic hope might maintain itself in the face of unceasing conflict.[10]

---

[9] West has in mind such passages as those from *Souls* (Du Bois 1903, 4) and *Dusk of Dawn* (Du Bois 1940, 551).

[10] My conclusion here bears comparison to recent work by Alexander Livingston (2016, chap. 5) in which a rereading of Jamesian pragmatism presses the tradition toward a more serious engagement with Du Boisian politics.

Unfortunately, it will be all too easy for those who find pragmatism inviting to accept my conclusion by way of a friendly dismissiveness. Some will avail themselves of the option of acknowledging that Du Bois makes the contribution I have outlined without actually bothering to turn to Du Bois to employ these contributions, and even going so far as quietly declining to employ them when they come into conflict with a Deweyan orientation. So I want to end by attempting to double down on my conclusion. I want to sharpen my claim that Du Bois not only contributes something important to pragmatism, but that pragmatism as it is formulated today actually stands in need of a furtherance of that very contribution. In other words, I want to reiterate my opening challenge that pragmatism needs to show not just *that* but more importantly *how* it can maintain contestation midst democratic progressivism.

To see why my challenge is so pressing for pragmatism today consider that for all the brilliance of Dewey's analysis of how progressive reconstruction works, his pragmatism offers almost nothing concerning how the meliorative impulse would maintain itself precisely when we would need it most. Though Dewey might be used to offer an account of how contestation might remediate a democratic deficit, he could scarcely be used to offer an account of how to muster contestation where democracy is taken to be in a long moment of decline or even defeat. This is not to say that Dewey is wrong, but only that not all political problems can be administered by cleaning up the indirect consequences of our conduct.[11] Sometimes that conduct is itself made possible at the expense of the conduct of others. Sometimes administration is itself a channel of injustice. Sometimes a beautiful and local progress is elsewhere quite ugly. Sometimes, in some way or another, defeat there must be—and when we look only for the victory without keeping our eyes open for the loss therein, we are bound for a certain blindness.[12] Du Bois helps us know this. He thereby helps us see how an unflinching concentration on the strife that pervades the political can foment contestatory conducts that may work to counteract the crush of convention.[13]

---

[11] I here refer to Dewey's definition of the public (LW 2:244); elucidating the strengths of Dewey's political theory in ways that push it closer to Du Bois than has hitherto been recognized see Rogers 2009, chap. 5.

[12] I here refer to one of James's key contributions to moral philosophy (WWJ 12:132).

[13] For comments on an earlier draft I thank Jacoby Carter. For discussion of earlier drafts during presentations I thank Alex Livingston, Brad Stone, Naomi Zack, and other colleagues present at the Making Social Science Pragmatic conference at the University of Oregon, as well as audiences at the Society for the Advancement of American Philosophy, at Royal Holloway University, and at a workshop on Transitionalist Pragmatism at Roehampton University organized by Darren Garside.

Works Cited

Appiah, Kwame Anthony. 1985. "The Uncompleted Argument: Du Bois and the Illusion of Race." *Critical Inquiry* 12(1): 21–37.

———. 2014. *Lines of Descent: W.E.B. Du Bois and the Emergence of Identity.* Cambridge: Harvard University Press.

Baldwin, James. 1955. "Autobiographical Notes." In Baldwin, *Notes of a Native Son.* Boston: Beacon Press.

———. 1961. "East River, Downtown: Postscript to a Letter from Harlem." In Baldwin, *Nobody Knows My Name.* New York: Dell.

Bourne, Randolph. 1917. "Twilight of Idols." In Bourne, *The Radical Will: Selected Writings, 1911–1918.* New York: Urizen Books.

Carter, Jacoby Adeshei. Forthcoming. "Race-ing the Canon: American Icons, from Thomas Jefferson to Alain Locke." In Linda Alcoff, Luvell Anderson, and Paul Taylor (eds.), *Routledge Companion to the Philosophy of Race.* New York: Routledge.

Coon, Deborah. 1996. "'One Moment in the World's Salvation': Anarchism and the Radicalization of William James." *Journal of American History* 83(1): 70–99.

Du Bois, W. E. B. 1897. "The Conservation of Races." In Du Bois, *Writings.* New York: Library of America.

———. 1903. *The Souls of Black Folk.* New York: Penguin.

———. 1920. *Darkwater: Voices from within the Veil.* New York: Dover.

———. 1940. *Dusk of Dawn.* In Du Bois, *Writings.* New York: Library of America.

———. 1968. *The Autobiography of W.E.B. Du Bois: A Soliloquy on Viewing My Life from the Last Decade of Its First Century.* Edited by H. Aptheker. New York: International Publishers.

Harris, Leonard. 2002. "Insurrectionist Ethics: Advocacy, Moral Psychology, and Pragmatism." In *Ethical Issues for a New Millennium,* edited by John Howie, 192–210. Carbondale: Southern Illinois University Press.

Kirkland, Frank. 2013. "Du Bois's Notion of Double Consciousness." *Philosophy Compass* 8(2): 137–148.

Koopman, Colin. 2009. *Pragmatism as Transition: Historicity and Hope in James, Dewey, and Rorty.* New York: Columbia University Press.

———. 2014. "Conduct Pragmatism: Pressing BEYOND Experientialism and Lingualism." *European Journal of Pragmatism and American Philosophy* 6(2): 145–174.

Lewis, David Levering. 1993. *W.E.B. Du Bois: Biography of a Race, 1868–1919.* New York: Henry Holt.

Livingston, Alexander. 2016. *Damn Great Empires! William James and the Politics of Pragmatism.* New York: Oxford University Press.

Medina, José. 2013. *The Epistemology of Resistance.* Oxford: Oxford University Press, 2013.

Medina, José. 2015. "The Will Not to Believe: Pragmatism, Oppression, and Standpoint Theory." In Erin C. Tarver and Shannon Sullivan (eds.), *Feminist Interpretations of William James.* University Park: Penn State University Press.

Rogers, Melvin. 2009. *The Undiscovered Dewey: Religion, Morality, and the Ethos of Democracy.* New York: Columbia University Press.

———. 2012. "The People, Rhetoric, and Affect: On the Political Force of Du Bois's *The Souls of Black Folk*." *American Political Science Review* 106(1): 188–203.

Shulman, George. 2008. *American Prophecy: Race and Redemption in American Political Culture*. Minneapolis: University of Minnesota Press.

Taylor, Paul C. 2000. "Appiah's Uncompleted Argument: W.E.B. Du Bois and the Reality of Race." *Social Theory and Practice* 26(1): 103–128.

———. 2004. "What's the Use of Calling Du Bois a Pragmatist?" *Metaphilosophy* 35(1–2): 99–114.

West, Cornel, 1989. *The American Evasion of Philosophy: A Genealogy of Pragmatism*. Madison: University of Wisconsin Press.

CHAPTER 11 | Pragmatism, Racial Injustice, and Epistemic Insurrection

Toward an Insurrectionist Pragmatism

JOSÉ MEDINA

HOW CAN PHILOSOPHERS ENGAGE in discussions of justice while ignoring the radical injustices in which their own society and their own lives are entangled? And isn't this oversight an even more acute problem for philosophers, such as the American pragmatists, who claim to start their philosophizing from actual and situated experience, from the real problems of real people? American pragmatists have long been charged with ignoring an all-American injustice: the injustice of treating racial minorities as noncitizens or second-class citizens. For centuries, African American philosophers and race theorists have raised deep critiques and challenges to pragmatism in relation to its failure to properly address racial injustices. In recent decades, Cornel West and Leonard Harris have formulated powerful versions of these critiques and challenges. Drawing on West and especially on Harris, I will contend that pragmatism needs to properly address the *tragedy* of racial injustices and the *insurrectionist* challenges these injustices raise. Although many have argued that pragmatism and insurrectionism are incompatible and that pragmatic experimentalism and meliorism exclude radical social change, I will argue that pragmatism can and in fact should allow for insurrection and radical change in response to radical forms of exclusion and subordination such as those we can find in the American racist past and present (slavery, segregation, systematic and institutional violence and exclusion, etc.). An *insurrectionist pragmatism* should understand experimentalism and meliorism as making available not only reforms and gradual changes, but also a broad spectrum of insurrectionist possibilities and radical changes. In other words, I will argue for a *tragic* and *insurrectionist* pragmatism that can look the tragic facts of racial injustices in the face and can offer tools and guidance in resisting these injustices through deeply transformative—*insurrectionist*—thought and action.

In the first section, I turn to contemporary African American critics to identify the challenge that racial injustices pose to pragmatism, to diagnose the historical failures of pragmatism to meet this challenge successfully, and to highlight the resources within pragmatism that can help us with this challenge. In the second section, I argue for the possibility of an insurrectionist pragmatism, offering suggestions for how pragmatism can ground insurrectionary thought and action in order to properly address the racial injustices of our American past and present.

Responding to Racial Injustices: Tragedy and Insurrection

In this section, I will examine the *tragic* challenge to pragmatism raised by Cornel West and the *insurrectionist* challenge raised by Leonard Harris. Both challenges have a key epistemic dimension that has to be brought to light to appreciate their full force. They have to do with the kinds of racial ignorance and insensitivity with which pragmatism is accused of being complicit. The critiques and challenges developed by West and Harris that I will review in this section are addressed mainly against the *melioristic* elements in pragmatism: if pragmatic meliorism is understood as a form of *naive optimism*, it cannot accommodate the tragic aspects of life and the tragic aspects of American democracy (West); if pragmatic meliorism entails a commitment to *reformism* and gradual social change, then it leaves little or no room for radical social contestation and insurrection in American democracy and is ultimately incompatible with insurrectionism (Harris). Although I think that a lot can be learned from these analyses and critiques, the challenges they raise—serious and difficult as they are—can in principle be met by a truly radical pragmatism that is neither naively optimistic nor reducible to a gradualist reformism that rules out insurrection and radical social change.

The *Tragic* Challenge to Pragmatism: Is Pragmatism a Naive *Optimism* That Hides and Disguises Racial Oppression?

At the core of Cornel West's internal critique of American pragmatism is the claim that pragmatism has been inattentive to the "night side" of life generally and to the "night side" of American democracy in particular. West argues that even the most prominent pragmatist political philosopher, John Dewey, failed to see that "the culture of democratic societies requires not only the civic virtues of participation, tolerance, openness, mutual respect, and mobility, but also dramatic struggles . . . that cut off the joys of democratic citizenship" (West 1993, 114). As Eddie Glaude puts it, summarizing West's critique of Dewey: "The history of American democracy in the US is one of the continued exclusion of African Americans from full participation in that process, and that history seriously challenges Dewey's democratic faith" (Glaude 2004, 90).

Although Glaude agrees with West's diagnosis that, for the most part, classic pragmatism has failed to meet the challenge of developing a sensibility that can properly address the tragedy of racism in the United States, Glaude goes on to argue that contemporary pragmatists can meet West's challenge by expanding some of the critical resources within Dewey's pragmatism. According to Glaude, we can find a *tragic sensibility* in Dewey's notion of contingency and we can also enrich this tragic dimension of Deweyan pragmatism with a full appreciation of the history of racial exclusions and racial harms that have been and continue to be a crucial part of American democracy. Dewey's notion of contingency underscores the precariousness, uncontrollability, and dependence of human life and human action. Learning to live with contingency requires a full understanding and appreciation of the tragic and traumatic events in one's life and in one's society—including the historical legacy of radical exclusions and social harms that one sees oneself enmeshed in.

Glaude uses Toni Morrison's novel *Beloved* to illustrate what it would mean to have a pragmatic tragic sensibility as a guide to experimentalism and meliorism. Glaude calls attention to one line in *Beloved* in which one character echoes William James's conclusion in "The Will to Believe" when she says to another character about the tragedy of slavery in their family's past (which included infanticide, rape, torture, etc.): *"Know it, but go on out of the yard"* (2004, 91). One must understand the tragedy and evil that is part of the world of action: know it, but act anyway. Glaude claims that this understanding can be found in Dewey's emphasis on contingency and the precariousness of life, which can be the basis of "a particularly powerful reconstruction of what Dewey called intelligently guided experimentation":

The lesson Morrison's novel holds for Deweyan pragmatism is that the problems of race in the US are best dealt with by confronting our own past and the tragedy therein in order to intelligently invade the future: creative intelligence and an experimental approach enriched by the knowledge of our racial experiences allow us to locate and interpret the more serious conflicts that continue to plague America, and offer up ways for dealing with them. Tragedy remains. We must simply "know" it and act anyway. (2004, 91–92)

Following West, Glaude emphasizes that the problematic of racism "has tragically shaped our national imaginary" (2004, 91). "At the heart of this problematic," he remarks, "is the legacy of slavery and our refusal to come to terms with it"; and "this refusal has resulted in beliefs, practices, and choices that butcher the ideals of this fragile democratic experiment" (92). To this we need to add the refusal to come to terms with the legacy of the genocide and displacement of Native American populations, and with the long history of treating particular groups of immigrants as second-class citizens or even noncitizens.[1] Repairing this refusal and developing an adequate sensibility for American racial injustices requires a long and difficult *process of rethinking values, ideals, institutional arrangements, and practices*, not a mere act of acknowledgment, which would be an empty gesture. And it is crucial to note that the deep acknowledgment and appreciation of the tragedy of racial violence does not concern only laws and policy that have been discontinued, racist subjects and organizations that no longer exist (or are withering away), or racist acts and practices that are no longer pervasive and positively sanctioned (such as lynching, for example). To face up to and properly respond to the tragedy of racism requires a sensibility that is attentive to unconscious, institutional, and structural forms of racial biases. As Dan Flory puts it, "many racial beliefs are embedded in cultural ways of believing and acting typically conveyed through the unconscious learning of social practices rather than chosen by means of an individual's consciously employed decision processes" (2008, 60–61). Many Americans (especially white Americans) "are unprepared to think about race and white supremacy at the level of being embedded in institutions and expressed in our perceptions and actions, rather than as being personal, individually chosen beliefs knowingly embraced and under the control of particular human beings" (Flory 2008, 62).

---

[1] This history is very much ongoing and even in danger of becoming worse with constitutional amendments being proposed to change birth rights to citizenship. For the relationship between racism and xenophobia, and for a discussion of stigmatizing images of the "perpetual foreigner," see Kim and Sundstrom 2014.

Being a racist—acting, thinking, perceiving in racially biased ways—is not a personal choice; it is something one breathes and unconsciously reproduces in one's patterns of action and thought. At least, the subtle, self-effacing, structural, and unconscious racism that is most common today is not an individual matter under the conscious control of particular subjects, even when it is exhibited in the perceptions, thoughts, speech, and actions of particular individuals. The insidiousness of racially biased patterns is precisely that those who reproduce them are unable to see them. Charles Mills has termed this cultivated and self-protecting inability to see racism "the epistemology of ignorance" (1997, 18): "a pattern of globalized and local cognitive dysfunctions" that prevents people from seeing and doing the right thing in relation to racial injustices (93). As I have argued elsewhere, in order to develop an adequate sensibility with respect to racial injustices, pragmatism needs to be attentive to the epistemic side of racism and, in particular, to the epistemology of ignorance that protects it and makes it so insidious (Medina 2012). Racial epistemic injustices need to be unmasked and, as I will argue in the second major section, resisting our complicity with them and actively fighting them requires *epistemic insurrection*, not only at the individual and conscious level, but also and more importantly at the level of subverting institutional designs and social practices so that new and more fair patterns of social perception, social communication, and social relationality can emerge.

The *Insurrectionist* Challenge to Pragmatism: Is Pragmatism a Gradual *Reformism* That Hides and Disguises Racial Oppression?

The rest of this chapter stages a dialogue between two American philosophical traditions: pragmatism and insurrectionism. This is a conversation that African American insurrectionist philosophers such as David Walker and Maria Stewart have been demanding since the early nineteenth century, though their demands fell on deaf ears and classic pragmatists did not answer them. More recently, contemporary African American philosopher Leonard Harris has revived the insurrectionist challenge to pragmatism. Perhaps now pragmatist philosophers will finally begin to respond to this invitation to develop a badly needed dialogue on pressing issues of social justice concerning radical exclusions and subordination. As Jacoby Carter puts it,

It may well be that pragmatism and insurrectionist philosophy constitute two irreconcilable philosophical traditions, or there may be a philosophical position to be articulated and argued for that incorporates consistently important insights from both. ... The choices available to pragmatists are either to incorporate insurrectionist motivations, or its conception of personhood, or to accept its limitations as a philosophy of human liberation. ... pragmatism as a progressive philosophy aimed at social transformation in the interest of justice [cannot continue] to ignore alternative American philosophical traditions that aim at the realization of a more just social order. (2013, 66)

Harris argues that there is a mainstream narrative about American pragmatism and its commitment to the incremental expansion of justice and democracy that sanitizes, downplays, or ignores the complicity with racial injustices of American democracy and American values. There are those classic American pragmatists who did not properly engage with racial injustices (Emerson, Peirce, James, etc.), while there are some dissonant, critical voices who noticed this failure early on (Du Bois, Addams, Locke, etc.). Harris argues for the need to offer counternarratives about American pragmatism and what it has to offer in relation to issues of justice.

One such counternarrative can be developed by highlighting points of convergence between pragmatism and the insurrectionist tradition that springs from activists and philosophers such as David Walker (1785–1830), Lydia Maria Child (1802–1880), Maria W. Stewart (1803–1879), and Henry D. Thoreau (1817–1862). The insurrectionist ethos expressed in the lives and works of these social critics poses a challenge to any American political narrative and self-image. As Lee McBride puts it, the insurrectionist philosophers invite us "to consider the hypocrisy of early claims of democracy in the United States, to consider the brutality that was endured under The Indian Removal Act (1830) or The Fugitive Slave Law (1842)—both federally sanctioned. With such things in mind, we can reassess our commitments to moral suasion, piecemeal social amelioration, and democracy through democratic means" (2013, 30).

Pragmatism is challenged by insurrectionist philosophers to accommodate not only the right but also the duty to disobey, resist, and actively fight against social practices and political institutions that perpetuate oppression. This is how Harris formulates the challenge:

A philosophy that offers moral intuitions, reasoning strategies, motivations, and examples of just moral actions but falls short of requiring that we have a moral duty to support or engage in slave insurrections is defective ... a philosophy that does not make advocacy—that is, representing, defending, or promoting morally just causes—a seminal, meritorious feature of moral agency is defective. (2002, 192)

In a nutshell, the insurrectionist challenge is that for pragmatism to count as a philosophy of progressive social transformation and liberation, it must create *conceptual and motivational space for insurrection.*

Following Carter's insight that "the insurrectionist challenge to pragmatism falls roughly into two broad categories: conceptual and motivational" (2013, 55), in the next two subsections I will explore first, whether pragmatism contains conceptual resources that can be used to ground insurrectionist activity; and, second, whether there are pragmatist commitments that operate as motivational elements for insurrection, either by prompting the recognition of an obligation to resist injustices or, more indirectly, by motivating the pursuit of certain virtues of political actors in a democracy.

The *Conceptual* Side of the *Insurrectionist* Challenge

As Harris points out, it is clear that some pragmatists have engaged in resistance and insurrection against racial injustices, but what is not so clear is that they have done so "as a function of their pragmatism": "Certainly, John Dewey, Alain Locke, and Jane Addams held deep commitments to uplifting the downtrodden. My query is whether there exist features of pragmatism that require, as necessary conditions to be a pragmatist, support for participation in insurrection" (2002, 200–201). Following Carter, I will focus on one of the early insurrectionists, Maria Stewart, and more specifically on a key concept that she uses to ground her insurrectionism, that of *full personhood.* I will argue that if we can find similar conceptual tools in pragmatism that we can use to conceptualize and justify insurrectionary activity, then the possibility of meeting the conceptual challenge and developing an insurrectionist pragmatism stands.

As an advocate of the rights of women of color in the nineteenth century, Stewart's insurrectionism is an important precursor to womanism or black feminism in arguing for the centrality of the lived experience of black women for full human liberation in the United States. As Carter has argued, insurrection is required by (and not simply rendered compatible with) Stewart's account of the normative commitments associated with human subjectivity and human agency and, more specifically, by her notion of *full personhood.* As Carter puts it, Stewart saw that "for a Black woman to be fully human and equal to her white male and female counterparts

and her Black male counterparts required actions whose likely consequences were dispossession, social ostracization, or death" (2013, 56–57).
For Stewart, the assertion of the humanity of people of African descent
against white supremacy, and the affirmation of full and equal personhood
by women against the constraints of patriarchy, required the commitment
to insurrection by any means possible, that is, the duty to discontinue one's
complicity with oppressive practices and institutions and to actively fight
against them. Stewart's concept of "full personhood" can justify radical
acts on behalf of the downtrodden, even if the consequences of such acts
were likely to be destructive of practices and institutions and harmful to
the actors and others.

It is my contention that we can find something analogous to Stewart's
normative concept of "full personhood" in some pragmatist conceptions
of *human flourishing*. Some scholars, such as Pappas (1998 and 2001) and
Medina (2004), have argued that a pluralistic notion of human flourishing
such as the one offered by Dewey has critical and subversive potential
insofar as it calls for resistance when certain identities, cultures, and ways
of living and of community-building are marginalized or subordinated.
If there is a prima facie obligation to facilitate the flourishing of all, in
contexts of racial oppression, citizens have no obligation to cooperate with
the institutions and practices that marginalize and oppress racial groups;
civil disobedience is not only justified, but in some cases demanded, in
order to suspend and uproot complicity with racial oppression. We can find
here a rationale for the self-empowerment of racial groups that have been
excluded or marginalized in and through the institutions, social designs,
and cultural practices of a "democracy" only in name. For the sake of
deepening a democratic culture—a democratic way of life, and not just a
democratic form of government—and guaranteeing the full participation
and the flourishing of all, we can develop pragmatist arguments for the
duty to resist complicity with exclusion and oppression, and for the right
to fight by any means necessary when one's civil status and agency as a
member of society are curtailed. In this way, a radically pluralistic and
egalitarian notion of human flourishing can—just as Stewart's notion of
full personhood could—function as the normative ground for conceptualizing and justifying insurrection.

But a problem on the conceptual side of the insurrectionist challenge
arises in connection with the unpredictability of radical subversion or
insurrection. Even if the further elaboration of conceptual resources in
pragmatism can create conceptual space for insurrection, pragmatism may
contain conceptual ingredients that are *incompatible* with insurrectionist

commitments and strategies, or at least create *obstacles* for them. The following question has been formulated in this debate: Is insurrection compatible with the instrumentalist reasoning strategies employed by pragmatists that require prediction and control of the consequences of our actions?[2] This conceptual issue has far-reaching motivational consequences, and I will discuss it in the next subsection on insurrectionist motivation.

The *Motivational* Side of the *Insurrectionist* Challenge

The motivational challenge of insurrectionism can be formulated in relation to the instrumentalist commitments to predictability and controllability endorsed by many pragmatists. Carter formulates the challenge better than anyone:

> While pragmatism aims at bringing about certain future consequences, the consequences of insurrection are unpredictable and subject to failure. In short, insurrection does not fit the pragmatist problem-solving pattern. Insurrection is an inherently precarious and unstable mode of conduct, one that in many instances is not rendered more controllable by an accurate determination of the facts of the situation, a clear formulation of the problem, a clear hypothesis as to its resolution, or any of the features of instrumental reasoning to which some pragmatists appeal. (2013, 58)

As Carter emphasizes, for insurrectionist thinkers and activists such as Stewart, "the inability to make reliable predictions concerning the consequences of action is not an impediment to action, nor does it absolve one of her obligation" (2013, 60). However, Carter goes on to argue, pragmatists do not seem to leave room for obligations to resist and rebel in situations of crisis: "on Dewey's view, moral crises are situations in which duties strictly speaking do not exist, or at the very least cannot be discerned, and if one is unable to know her duty, she is incapable of acting from duty" (60). For insurrectionists, however, the radical crisis of losing one's humanity and being in danger of never regaining it—of remaining *socially dead*—can only be properly addressed through insurrectionary activities that will lead to survival and self-empowerment, and not by inaction or the suspension

---

[2] Harris writes: "What are the pragmatist sources for justifying insurrection, given that the outcomes of insurrectionist action or support for such actions are not predictable, that the vast majority of insurrectionist actions and movements fail to liberate, and that contributions to liberating a population by insurrection or support for insurrection range from useless to tremendous? Instrumental and functional reasoning can be of limited value for predicting future events" (2002, 202).

of moral or political judgment, which can only result in complicity with *social death*.[3] In a crisis of justice of this kind, in the face of radical forms of exclusion and marginalization, there is more than a *right* to rebel and fight by any means necessary; survival requires a duty to do so. Stewart formulated this strong normative demand forcefully and poignantly in her call to insurrection in her 1832 speech "Why Sit Ye Here and Die?"

The pragmatist obsession with prediction and control creates huge problems for motivating the kind of radical defiance to norms, practices, and institutions that has unpredictable consequences. And even though insurrectionist activities may aim at creating new norms, practices, and institutions, the emerging alternatives have not been established yet and can be envisioned in different ways; in some cases, the alternative norms, practices, and institutions may not even have been envisioned yet. The strong epistemic requirement of knowing the consequences of one's actions becomes a motivational obstacle to insurrection and, therefore, a motivational inducement to inaction and complicity with the status quo. This epistemic requirement has to be substantially relaxed if pragmatism wants to meet the insurrectionist challenge. I contend that *the epistemic requirement of predictability and controllability must be given up in situations of radical exclusion and oppression that call for insurrectionary actions and practices*, for such a requirement functions as an epistemic mechanism of complicity with the institutions, practices, and social designs that perpetuate injustices.

But for pragmatism to meet the motivational challenge of insurrectionism, more is required than merely removing obstacles from the pragmatist framework. What is required are reasons for insurrectionary action within that framework. Motivating reasons for insurrection have to be given at two levels: the personal level of individual action, and the social and political level of collective action. The motivational challenge advanced by insurrectionism operates at two levels: the *subjective and personal* level, where what is called for is a set of resources to motivate individuals to act in insurrectionary ways; and the *collective and institutional* level, where what is called for is a set of social designs, arrangements, and programs that make radical changes possible. In the next section, I will connect these two levels in a brief discussion of *epistemic* insurrection that is meant to illustrate how an *insurrectionist pragmatism* can be conceived

---

[3] As we will see in the next section, Stewart describes racial oppression as "deadening" the black subject in various ways. I see in Stewart's account of "deadening" through racial oppression a precursor of Orlando Patterson's celebrated notion of *social death* (see Patterson 1982).

and developed. In order to begin addressing the motivational challenge of insurrectionism, pragmatism needs to give up the requirement of predictability and controllability and to offer resources to motivate individual and collective resistance even when the outcome of such disruption with the status quo leaves us in the dark.

Toward an Insurrectionist Pragmatism: Epistemic Oppression and Epistemic Insurrection

I want to emphasize that pragmatism's commitment to *embodied, lived experience* as the bedrock of philosophical theory and practice is an important point of contact with the insurrectionist tradition. Grounded in this central focus on embodied, lived experience, we can find an important shared commitment in pragmatism and insurrectionism: the *egalitarian* commitment to facilitate the human flourishing of all subjects and groups. It follows from this egalitarian commitment that under conditions of exclusion and oppression we all have a *duty* to discontinue our complacency with and participation in practices, structures, and institutions that create obstacles to—or simply block—the human flourishing of some. The egalitarian pragmatist notion of human flourishing can be used as the source of motivating reasons for insurrectionary actions both at the individual and at the collective level: this egalitarian notion demands that subjects actively resist practices, structures, and institutions that dehumanize people, both with their individual actions in their personal lives and with their contributions to the collective actions of groups and social movements.

In this way, we find a normative ground within pragmatism that is the source of strong normative demands: it demands that people take responsibility for facilitating each other's flourishing and that they respond to injustices that constrain such flourishing—and the more radical the injustice in question, the more radical the response needed. In order to develop further the possibility of an insurrectionist pragmatism grounded in an egalitarian notion of human flourishing that can address racial injustices satisfactorily, I will focus on a single dimension of racial injustice, its *epistemic* dimension, offering a pragmatic understanding of *epistemic oppression* and *epistemic insurrection*. I will use Stewart's insurrectionist philosophy to explain epistemic oppression and what counts as *epistemic resistance* and as the epistemic self-empowerment of oppressed subjects and groups in defiance of the epistemic side of oppression.

Stewart's descriptions of racial oppression emphasize its epistemic side: "there are no chains so galling as the chains of ignorance—no fetters so binding as those that bind the soul, and exclude it from the vast field of useful and scientific knowledge" (1987, 45). She describes the epistemic oppression that was at the core of antiblack racism in the United States as resulting from being excluded from access to and participation in knowledge practices (education, research, public deliberation, etc.), and from being confined to manual labor under extreme conditions of exploitation. Stewart developed an understanding of epistemic oppression as a form of "deadening" and "numbing" of mental capacities that foreshadows what I have called *epistemic death*.[4] She writes:

> I have learnt, by bitter experience, that continual hard labor deadens the energies of the soul, and benumbs the faculties of the mind; the ideas become confined, the mind barren, and, like the scorching sands of Arabia, produces nothing; or, like the uncultivated soil, brings forth thorns and thistles. (1987, 47)

As argued above, in the egalitarian pragmatist notion of human flourishing we can ground the commitment to promoting the flourishing of all persons and communities, but especially of those who find themselves disempowered and with diminished status and agency. Dewey's notion of *education* can be seen as in line with this egalitarian pragmatist notion of flourishing, and as an heir to Stewart's notion of education as a form of self-empowerment and resistance against epistemic oppression. Stewart saw in education and knowledge practices a venue for activism, for critical interventions and subversion, and for self-empowerment; in short, for fighting the epistemic side of racial oppression with *epistemic insurrection*: "Turn your attention to knowledge and improvement; for knowledge is power" (1987, 41). Stewart insisted that a crucial part of the struggle against racial oppression was the creation of social and civic institutions dedicated to the educational and intellectual empowerment of African Americans. This form of epistemic self-empowerment was insurrectionary at the time. As Carter puts it in his description of Stewart's proposal of epistemic self-empowerment,

> Needless to say this was a rather subversive idea in the United States in the early-19th Century, especially as it pertained to the enslaved population at

---

[4] See Medina, forthcoming.

the time for whom such activity was in many places illegal. In characteristically insurrectionist fashion, Stewart seeks simultaneously to transform the character of individual persons, and to create institutions of the sort that will effect a radical transformation in the existing society. (2013, 66–67)

A great strength of Stewart's view of epistemic insurrection is the way in which her view enables us to link individual acts of resistance in our personal life with collective actions of resistance in our public life. Carter notes, "A salient feature of Stewart's feminist insurrectionist ethics is the understanding that making oneself into the kind of person that the larger society denies that one can be is itself a subversive activity" (2013, 68). Becoming who you are can be a subversive struggle of insurrection when you have not been given "full personhood" and when the kind of person you are defies social scripts and the social norms underlying available institutions and accepted values. In those circumstances, the personal struggle to become who you want to be and to express yourself is simultaneously the insurrectionary struggle for rearranging social relations and social settings in which subjects act and express themselves. This is not at all surprising, but fully explicable in relational views of identity such as those we can find in classic pragmatists such as James and Dewey, for indeed, according to these views, we do not make ourselves in isolation from others and from the practices and institutions that support us and in which our thoughts and actions can be developed. And, just as individual subjectivities don't make themselves in isolation but in communities, subversive subjectivities also need the support of social movements and communities of resistance that cultivate insurrectionary practices.

Another point of convergence between Stewart's insurrectionism and pragmatism can be found in the thoroughgoing pluralism of her view of communities of resistance. She insisted on the unfinished, open, and plural nature of the African American public that needs to be created and maintained through insurrectionary practices. This critical and subversive public needs to be attuned to the diversity and fluidity of African American lives, communities, and cultures. "Though she understood it to be essential to Black liberation that African-Americans in the United States form a nexus of communal solidarity, she also understood that to be a work in progress, something to be created rather than antecedently given" (Carter 2013, 69). Stewart emphasized the important connections between personal and social ways of pursuing self-empowerment, so that the cultivation of virtuous character of black subjects and the creation of black social institutions in public life could reinforce each other and jointly contribute to black liberation:

> Do you ask, what can we do? Unite and build a store of your own, if you cannot procure a license. . . . We have never had an opportunity of displaying our talents; therefore the world thinks we know nothing. And we have been possessed by far too mean and cowardly a disposition, . . . Possess the spirit of independence. The Americans do, and why should not you? Possess the spirit of men, bold and enterprising, fearless and undaunted. Sue for your rights and privileges. Know the reason that you cannot attain them. Weary them with your importunities. You can but die if you make the attempt; and we shall certainly die if you do not. (1987, 38)

But how about *intergroup racial solidarity*? How about recruiting nonoppressed subjects and groups to join the insurrectionary struggle against racial oppression? It is here that contemporary insurrectionists see the biggest (motivational) challenge for American pragmatism. Harris asks, "What resources are available in pragmatism that compels individuals to reject their own community, citizenship, and national allegiance to risk their lives for the well-being of strangers" (2002, 200)? Carter follows Harris in arguing that "there is not a large amount of evidence that suggests that Americans, for example, have a widespread desire—even if somewhat repressed in terms of the outlets of expression and action that are available to them—to radically transform society in the interests of persons outside their immediate sphere of concern" (2013, 62). And, as he forcefully goes on to argue, "insurrection requires more than a methodological concern with some amorphous public and its problems; it requires a deep fundamental commitment to the well-being of, not an idealized 'great community' sought after within the confines of some amorphous public, but a specific and specifiable community" (62). This is particularly pressing for communities whose struggles have been blocked, marginalized, or rendered invisible. Marginalized communities have not been represented in a *generic* American public and their distinctive experiences of oppression have not been properly heard and addressed. What the fight against racial injustices requires is the pluralization of American publics into heterogeneous communities of resistance that can come together to fight against specific forms of racial oppression and to promote the flourishing of particular racially oppressed groups.

As I have argued elsewhere, what racial solidarity and the formation of communities of resistance against racial oppression require is the forging of heterogeneous forms of solidarity through the epistemic friction exerted by multiple publics on one another. What is needed is not so much *collective action*, but *chained* action, the kind of concerted or connected action in which communities of resistance engage in insurrectionary activities of different kinds, discontinuing their complicity with racial injustices and trying to effect change in multiple ways.[5] There is no invisible hand directing connected attempts at resisting injustices, and the trajectories of *chained actions* of resistance are always unpredictable and uncontrollable. But the emerging social movements and networks of solidarity that can develop from connected activism are crucial for the formation of sites of resistance and for the sustainability of insurrectionary acts. There is only so much that isolated individuals and isolated groups can achieve by themselves. Hence the importance of interactive processes of communication being available to social agents, so that they can relate to each other, pool their resources, compensate for each other's blindness, share their (always limited) social lucidity, and collectively exploit possibilities of resistance.

According to the pluralistic view of racial solidarity I have proposed, bonds and shared commitments are established on the basis of (rather than at the expense of) an irreducible diversity of experiential and agential perspectives, and with an eye to fostering and strengthening this diversity.[6] This is a view of racial solidarity in which differences are not overcome, abstracted, unified, or subsumed under a more general viewpoint. This view undermines misconceived restrictions that have been imposed on solidarity, such as Richard Rorty's claim that in order to have solidarity with others, we must recognize them as "one of us" (Rorty 1991). A pluralistic view of racial solidarity unmasks and overcomes the misconception that solidarity requires *assimilation*, which is central to the American multicultural model based on the image of "the melting pot."[7] In recent critical race theory, there has been a movement toward pluralistic views, that is, a movement away from a conception of racial solidarity based on shared properties and toward a conception based on common problems and concerns.[8] *Pace* unitary accounts of solidarity that erode diversity and stifle

---

[5] See Medina 2012.
[6] See Medina 2004, 2012.
[7] See Medina 2004, where I criticize assimilationist models and nonpluralistic views of ethnic and racial solidarity.
[8] Insofar as it does not presuppose unity, identity, or the sharing of common features, my pluralistic conception of solidarity should be understood as in line with recent pluralistic accounts of solidarity in critical race theory and feminist political philosophy, in particular,

dissent and epistemic contestation, my pluralistic view underscores the importance of arranging our practices so as to cultivate diversity, encouraging us to establish sociopolitical structures that promote diversity and empower marginalized publics and perspectives. Both in its epistemic and its political dimension, the radical pluralism I have developed from pragmatist conceptions of community and public life suggests insurrectionary possibilities for resisting racial oppression and for achieving greater degrees of respect and justice for marginalized racial groups.

Insurrectionary publics and vibrant communities of resistance can be understood according to the pluralistic notion of democratic publics and communities available in pragmatist philosophies such as Dewey's. Properly pluralized and contextualized, Dewey's notions of community and public contain the seeds of an insurrectionary pragmatism. But much work lies ahead for the development of such a pragmatism. I hope to have shown that an insurrectionary pragmatism needs an account of *epistemic resistance* that incorporates forms of insurrectionary communication and activism in order to address issues of social apathy, complicity, and social invisibility, which are the epistemic side of racial oppression. I have made some modest contributions to such an account with my recent and ongoing research. But more substantial contributions to an insurrectionary pragmatism that properly addresses racial injustices can be found in the contemporary scene in the works of Harvey Cormier, Eddie Glaude, Bill Lawson, Gregory Pappas, Melvin Rogers, Shannon Sullivan, Paul Taylor, Cornel West, and—I would say—Leonard Harris himself.[9] In this chapter I hope to have shown how epistemic insurrection can, at least in principle, be accommodated in a pragmatist view of subjectivity, community, thought, and action.

Works Cited

Carter, Jacoby. 2013. "The Insurrectionist Challenge to Pragmatism and Maria W. Stewart's Feminist Insurrectionist Ethics." *Transactions of the Charles S. Peirce Society* 49: 54–73.

---

those of Tommie Shelby (2005) and Carol Gould (2007). Shelby (2005) focuses on the intragroup solidarity of African Americans, whereas Gould (2007) focuses on the intergroup solidarity of trans-national movements. Despite their clear differences in focus and orientation, these accounts exhibit some interesting similar features that converge with my own view of racial solidarity.

[9] See especially the essays in *Pragmatism and the Problem of Race* edited by Bill Lawson and Donald Koch (2004).

Flory, Dan. 2008. *Philosophy, Black Film, Film Noir*. University Park: Penn State University Press.

Glaude, Eddie. 2004. "Tragedy and Moral Experience: John Dewey and Toni Morrison's *Beloved*." In *Pragmatism and the Problem of Race*, edited by Bill Lawson and Donald Koch, 89–121. Bloomington: Indiana University Press.

Gould, Carol. 2007. "Transnational Solidarities." *Journal of Social Philosophy* 38(1): 148–164.

Harris, Leonard. 2002. "Insurrectionist Ethics: Advocacy, Moral Psychology, and Pragmatism." In *Ethical Issues for a New Millennium*, edited by John Howie, 192–210. Carbondale: Southern Illinois University Press.

Kim, David, and Ronald Sundstrom. 2014. "Xenophobia and Racism." *Critical Philosophy of Race* 2(1): 20–45.

Lawson, Bill, and Donald Koch. 2004. *Pragmatism and the Problem of Race*. Bloomington: Indiana University Press.

Medina, José. 2004. "Pragmatism and Ethnicity: Critique, Reconstruction, and the New Hispanic." *Metaphilosophy* 35: 115–146.

———. 2012. *The Epistemology of Resistance: Gender and Racial Oppression, Epistemic Injustice, and Resistant Imaginations*. New York: Oxford University Press.

———. Forthcoming. "Epistemic Injustice and Epistemologies of Ignorance." In *The Routledge Companion to the Philosophy of Race*, edited by Linda Alcoff, Luvell Anderson, and Paul C. Taylor. New York: Routledge.

Mills, Charles. 1997. *The Racial Contract*. Ithaca, NY: Cornell University Press.

Pappas, Gregory. 1998. "The Latino Character of American Pragmatism." *Transactions of the Charles S. Peirce Society* 34: 93–112.

———. 2001. "Dewey and Latina Lesbians in the Quest for Purity." *Journal of Speculative Philosophy* 15: 152–161.

Patterson, Orlando. 1982. *Slavery and Social Death: A Comparative Study*. Cambridge: Harvard University Press.

Rorty, Richard. 1991. *Objectivity, Relativism, and Truth: Philosophical Papers*, Vol 1. Cambridge: Cambridge University Press.

Shelby, Tommie. 2005. *We Who Are Dark: The Philosophical Foundations of Black Solidarity*. Cambridge: Harvard University Press.

Stewart, Maria W. 1987. "Why Sit Ye Here and Die?" In *Maria W. Stewart: America's First Black Woman Political Writer*, edited by Marilyn Richardson, 45–49. Bloomington: Indiana University Press.

West, Cornel. 1993. *Keeping Faith: Philosophy and Race in America*. New York: Routledge.

CHAPTER 12 | An Aesthetics of Resistance
Deweyan Experimentalism and
Epistemic Injustice

PAUL C. TAYLOR

IN *The Epistemology of Resistance*, José Medina argues that it is impossible to understand or ameliorate the problems of epistemic injustice while also approaching them as one-dimensional affairs (Medina 2013). Medina argues that these problems are not simply epistemic, any more than they are simply ethical or political; they are all of these at once, and must be approached from that perspective. I propose to push this plea for theoretical breadth one step further and suggest, by appeal to the kinds of considerations that John Dewey enshrined in his experimentalist phenomenology, that these problems are also importantly aesthetic, and that the resources of aesthetic criticism and practice are vital to their amelioration.

Some clarifications and caveats are in order before we get underway. First, I'll not put a great deal of weight on the concept of justice, or on the need to theorize about it. In the place of a theory, and in advance of the work I do plan to do here, I'll just say what one of the thinkers I've sometimes preferred to John Rawls might say: To speak of justice is to pay a compliment to societies (or relationships, or social formations, or whatever) that pass ethical muster. Understood in this way, the concept of justice is of course still valuable, and it might be essential, given the kinds of societies we've built and the frameworks of expectation, meaning, and aspiration that we've built into and around them. But its value comes in the way we argue about it, or, better, in the way we argue with it, or with each other while using (or refusing) it.

That is to say, I have no stake in articulating or defending a particular theory of justice. I am interested in it principally as a gathering notion—as a way of thinking about how we distribute the benefits and burdens of social cooperation. This benefit-burden talk, like other familiar formulas—deciding who owes what to whom, or discerning whether citizens enjoy equal concern and respect—can be helpful. But it is also helpful to realize, as Medina argues, that it is often better to have accounts of specific injustices than to have a theory of justice. That is the orientation I prefer, though I'll do little to push that part of Medina's argument beyond where he leaves it.

Given my interest in Medina's work, I am of course keen to consider the notion of epistemic justice, which treats epistemic and discursive resources as the relevant benefits and burdens. Just as societies have ways of deciding how material goods get distributed, they have ways of deciding whose testimony counts as evidence, and who can aspire to provide authoritative interpretations or creditable explanations. How we decide these things, and whether our methods warrant praise or disapprobation, is key to considerations of epistemic justice and injustice. But—and this is the second caveat—I have no stake in defending a particular way of cashing out the appeal to epistemic justice. One of Medina's aims is to settle accounts between his own work and the work of people like Miranda Fricker. I have no interest in adjudicating those disputes.

Third, I want to give as wide a berth as possible to the thought that pragmatism provides a unique route to the thoughts that I'll work out in what follows. Medina's project draws heavily and clearly on some figures we associate with the pragmatist tradition, and my engagement with Medina will do the same. But I want to credit the possibility that the pragmatist label may not register what is most distinctive or interesting about these figures. In particular, I will be keen to argue that Dewey's contribution to extending Medina's project comes from a move that he explicitly declined to associate with his pragmatism. What was of interest for him, and will be of interest to me, is the radical empiricist move that opens the door to Dewey's pragmatism *and* to his aesthetic theory.

Finally, I will occasionally, for ease of exposition, run together some notions that are worth keeping distinct. Ethics and morality are importantly different, as are race and ethnicity. The first distinction will get blurred as I work to accommodate Dewey's immersion in a philosophical vocabulary from a different era. He uses "moral" typically to refer to the broader domain that I and others would describe as the domain of ethics, but I will follow his usage in order to remain faithful to his language. The second distinction will fall victim to the constraints of space: there just isn't room to say much about what race is and how it differs from ethnicity. I will say what I can here, and refer the reader to the way I develop this distinction elsewhere.

Medina's Project

I'll use Medina's own words to describe his objectives in *The Epistemology of Resistance*. He aims, he says, "to promote critical awareness of [among other things] the crucial interrelations between epistemic injustices and sociopolitical injustices" (Medina 2013, 313). It is important to promote this awareness for the following reason:

> [O]ur obligation to resist and fight oppression has a crucial epistemic dimension, which demands that we critically examine and take responsibility for what we are capable and incapable of communicating, interpreting, and knowing—hence the need to address epistemic injustices concerning active ignorance, silences, [and] expressive harms. (313)

After highlighting the links between social justice and epistemic practice, Medina is careful to indicate the limitations of his approach:

> But there is only so much an epistemology can do. My discussions . . . offer an expanded view of epistemology as essentially normative and social, suggesting that our epistemic lives are inextricably interwoven with our ethical and sociopolitical lives. But my expanded conception . . . also underscores the limitations of epistemological analyses, which remain impotent unless coupled with deep personal changes (new ways of thinking and imagining) and continued with a transformative activism capable of changing social structures and relations. (314)

Why do we need this transformative activism? What is it for? "We need disruptions, provocations, and, in short, resistance from others, so that our interactions with significantly different others can trigger productive self-problematizations" (315). Here we see the dual significance in Medina's clever title. He is giving us an epistemological theory that supports political resistance work. But that theory has at its heart a vision of epistemic and social practices that promote a kind of friction, or epistemic resistance, in virtue of which we can subject ourselves to self-criticism and interrogate our habits of attention, perception, and judgment.

As it happens, the imagination is essential to this brief for "self-problematization" and social transformation:

> Different ways of imagining can sensitize or desensitize people to human experiences; they can make people feel close or distant to others; and they can create or sever social bonds, affective ties, and relations of empathy or antipathy, solidarity or lack of solidarity. Stigmatizing ways of imagining play a crucial role in causing expressive and epistemic harms. . . . But resistant ways of imagining can contest exclusions and stigmatizations, and they can help us become sensitive to the suffering of excluded and stigmatized subjects. (26)

We need "resistant ways of imagining," to combat the "epistemic numbness" that contributes to social injustice. But where do we find these resistant approaches, and how do we cultivate them? "What is needed," Medina explains, "is a way of bringing together the psychological and the socio-historical and structural. . . . [W]e need to explore ways in which subjects can reconstruct their perspectives and learn to inhabit them in new ways" (220). We need, in other words, "to identify the social conditions of counter-performativity" (241).

One way to cultivate counterimagining and counterperformativity, Medina suggests, involves art. He approvingly reports Bourdieu's interest in the prospects for "the cultivation of transgressive attitudes in artistic production" (241). But he passes quickly over this thought, returns to the domain of epistemic practice, and makes no other mention of art or the aesthetic in the book (including in the index).

This glancing encounter with the aesthetic is fraught with intriguing possibilities and silences. Medina declines to notice some natural links between his subject matter and the subjects of aesthetic theory. For example, he draws no connection between his many calls for "interpretative responsiveness" and the work on interpretation that we find in and near aesthetic theory. Even more striking, he takes no notice of the way his dogged insistence on the holistic and multidimensional nature of human experience echoes similar claims in certain approaches to aesthetic experience. He insists that knowing is bound up with emotion, ethics, and politics, and with affect, imagination, and social life, and that being a knower means also being a great many other things. But he devotes no time to the thought that the discourse of aesthetic experience—especially in the wake of Alexander Baumgarten's definition of aesthetics as the science of "sensible cognition"—is a useful resource for considering the convergence of these various dimensions of human striving and capacity (Baumgarten [1750] 2007).

I propose in what follows to pick up where Medina has left off. Aesthetic theory points us to a variety of sites for the formation and training of human judgments, sites that we might productively examine in the manner he suggests. In addition, considering those sites in the spirit of Medina's emphasis on resistance invites us to consider the aesthetic as a domain for the reformation and retraining of our identities and sensibilities. I want to be clear that I mean this to be a friendly amendment to his project, not a critique. Medina has his hands sufficiently full with what he does take on, in his extraordinary and extraordinarily ambitious project, to earn a pass for not doing even more. I mean simply to extend his powerful reflections on epistemic justice by developing his inchoate reflections on the aesthetic dimensions of epistemic justice.

From Epistemology to Aesthetics: Dewey's Phenomenology

Thinking about epistemic justice in a suitably expansive way—in a way that credits the multidimensional nature of our lives as knowers—brings us to the doorstep of an aesthetic of resistance. It will be easier to see what's on the other side of that door once we have a suitable account of the aesthetic in hand. I propose to borrow this account from John Dewey, as developed in the line of thinking that culminates in Dewey's only sustained reflection on art and aesthetics.

Art as Experience is an ambitious book. It joins the other treatises of Dewey's late period in working toward a comprehensive picture of his philosophical system. It does this by bringing the insights of that system to bear on most of the central concerns of interwar philosophy of art: "expression, form, the relation of subject matter to the work of art itself, the relationships of the arts to each other, and so on" (Alexander 1998, 16). These subjects are of less interest for current purposes than the issues Dewey takes up before and after these discussions. The book opens and closes with attempts to locate the aesthetic outside the institutions that govern, promote, and protect the fine arts, thereby connecting aesthetics to ethics, to social history, and to everyday practice.

Early on in the book Dewey explains that aesthetics has to do with "everything that intensifies the sense of immediate living," and with all the things that serve as "enhancements of the processes of everyday life" (LW 10:6). He attempts to drive the point home with examples, mentioning, among other things, the fisherman's "esthetic satisfaction ... in casting and playing" his line (LW 10:26), and Emerson's "exhilaration" at "crossing a bare common, in snow puddles, at twilight, under a clouded sky" (LW 10:28). He might make the point today by appealing to the swoops and curves that distinguish Evian's bottles of water from Dasani's, or to the indifference with which basketball players and fans regard the fact that a stylish dunk is worth the same two points as a simple layup. Or he might rehearse such obvious facts as that we choose ways—styles—of walking, talking, and cooking, we arrange furniture in rooms, and we sing to ourselves while washing dishes or taking a shower. All these behaviors and practices reveal our determination to marry form and function, and thereby to cultivate the aesthetic in everyday life.

We sometimes forget the ubiquity of the aesthetic, Dewey says, because of the stratification of enjoyments wrought by the modern world. On Dewey's reading of his time, nationalism, imperialism, and industrial capitalism, abetted by philosophy, had separated aesthetic experience from community life. While the working classes toiled at jobs that the techniques of mass production had drained of meaning, the wealthy signified and affirmed their higher social standing by purchasing access to works of art. This turned aesthetic objects into rare and therefore expensive commodities, putting the possibility of aesthetic enjoyment further out of the reach of ordinary people and hastening the process whereby artists—the people whose vocation is to create specific occasions for aesthetic experience—worked for the market and became further isolated from any "native and spontaneous culture" (LW 10:9). And where an art institution did cater to the general populace, it did so by presenting aesthetic objects as records of national or imperial triumph, isolated from organic community life like holy relics in a cathedral. Philosophy, for its part, too often expressed these developments and justified them by confining the aesthetic to fine art, and assuming the uselessness of art in everyday life.

Having highlighted the recency and contingency of the modern, compartmental approach to the aesthetic, Dewey has cleared the way for a broader, more egalitarian approach. This alternative conception not only does the socioethical work of liberating art from the exalted preserves of the art world, but also reminds us of the roots of the aesthetic in the phenomenology of ordinary experience. This phenomenological turn is central to the link between aesthetics and epistemology that I mean to forge on Medina's behalf.

Dewey's notion of experience requires some unpacking, given its distance from mainstream approaches in Anglophone philosophy after his heyday. For Dewey, "experience" denotes the temporally extended and object-oriented process of interpreting and using the things that high-modern epistemology thought of as experiences—the "sense impressions" and other "percepts" that we find in the tradition that stretches from David Hume to Bertrand Russell and beyond. At this point it is tempting to echo Richard Rorty's lament that Dewey (like William James) insisted on talking about experience and never learned the analytic habit of talking instead about language. But giving in to this temptation and setting aside the notion of experience would make it needlessly difficult to talk about the aesthetic at all—which, whatever else it is, is about creating and managing experiences. Luckily, a couple of straightforward moves enable us to translate his experience-talk into forms that connect more readily with the work that Medina aims to do.

First, we can say on Dewey's behalf that to talk about experience is to talk about the degree to which our cognitive lives are shaped by contexts. Here we might discuss the theory-ladenness of perception, or the way the aims of inquiry shape its conduct and outcomes, or the way traditions of inquiry inform and constrain the imaginative capacities that inquirers bring to their work, or the framing and shaping powers of cultural discourses. In these and other ways, the move that Dewey aims to make here has become commonplace: contesting the thought that cognition belongs to an isolated faculty, unsullied by contingencies like history, human practice, or other forms of situatedness.

Second, we can say on Dewey's behalf that he uses experience-talk to highlight the roles that affect and immediacy play in our cognitive lives. Here we might discuss the intuitive and associative psychological mechanisms posited by contemporary dual-processes theories of cognition. On these accounts, our consciously managed processes of reflection and deliberation have an unconscious counterpart running in the background, equipping us, once the right cognitive pathways have been formed, simply to perceive, immediately, the states of affairs that we once had to puzzle out. In this way the conclusions of complicated chains of reasoning or reflection achieve the immediacy of perceptual judgments, and we find ourselves inclined toward or away from these perceptions more by feelings of fittingness or unease than by argument.

These two dimensions of experience—its situatedness and its routine recourse to holistic, engaging immediacy—are of course related, and reveal themselves in many domains. For example, we achieve linguistic fluency when we learn to register symbol strings not by consciously assembling the individual components into a broader whole, but by immediately perceiving the words or phrases or formulas they make up, and by literally feeling the appropriateness of these perceptions. Similarly, we demonstrate a kind of cultural competency when we respond instantaneously and reflexively to ritual pageantry in the appropriate ways—with, say, expressions of reverence. In both cases, we cultivate our cognitive-perceptual powers in social contexts, in educative processes both formal and informal. And this education leaves us with a complement of cognitive-discursive resources that in turn shapes the ways we'll conduct our future careers as knowers and as agents.

Dewey would bristle at the way I've restated his view for a number of reasons, only one of which need detain us right now. I've insisted on the cognitive dimensions of his account of experience in a way that he might see as burying the lead. We can get at the thought I have in mind here by considering Dewey's exchange with the Italian idealist Benedetto Croce. After Croce described *Art as Experience* as a work of pragmatist aesthetics (Croce 1948), Dewey testily explained that pragmatism was an intervention in the theory of knowledge, while the point of aesthetic theory is precisely to explore the fact that knowing is not all there is to experience.[1] In Dewey's view, knowledge is what we get when we manage experience in certain ways, while *aesthesis* is what we get when we manage it in different ways. Experience is the primary thing, whether we work mainly to understand it or to enjoy it.

This phenomenological focus brings us very near to the considerations that drive Medina's account of epistemic injustice, but it shifts the ground a bit in ways that will prove valuable. Medina insists on the situated and holistic nature of knowing. But he insists also on using the language of epistemology to do this work, even as he rails against the limits of this language. (Remember his plea for an "expanded" conception of epistemology; and remember, "there's only so much an epistemology can do.") So why not pair these reflections with a turn to the aesthetic domain, where one can safely assume the holism and situatedness that he wants to argue for? Similarly, Medina wants to explore and interrogate the sites of practice where we train our powers of judgment, and cultivate opportunities for retraining. In this spirit, why not examine our aesthetic practices? They are, after all, essential to the reproduction and reinforcement of our habits of judgment and perception, particularly in their vernacular forms. But they also provide fertile ground for

---

[1] See Dewey, "A Comment on the Foregoing Criticisms" (LW 15).

excavating and resisting our cultural habits, as our high-art traditions are often keen to make clear.

Toward an Aesthetic of Resistance

I've suggested so far that the phenomenological turn that informs Dewey's aesthetics can advance Medina's interest in epistemic justice, in at least a couple of ways. It can build on his determination to move beyond narrow conceptions of the epistemic domain, and it can highlight domains of practice—expressive and aesthetic practice—that are bound up with the mechanisms of habituation and counterhabituation that are so central to his project.

The argument so far has been more abstract than I would like, so I would like to concretize it in two ways. First, I'll say a bit more about Dewey's own account of the aesthetic, and about how an aesthetic of resistance begins to come into view once we deepen Medina's brief flirtation with art as a site for counterperformative practice. Then, in the conclusion, I'll offer a more specific example of aesthetics as a site of resistance, drawn from the tradition of black aesthetics.

Dewey's phenomenological aesthetics plays several roles in his overall philosophy. It contests the social compartmentalization that limits aesthetic experience to certain rarefied spaces and reserves it for the elites who have greater access to those spaces. It combats the alienation that comes from thinking of ourselves first and foremost as knowers, and from separating our cognitive powers from our other capacities. It motivates and follows from the genealogical analysis that shows the contingency of our standing practices, and that thereby makes room for cultural and political transformation. And it embodies the democratic impulse that comes from taking ordinary experience, including the experience of ordinary people, seriously.

Two additional consequences of adopting this approach are worth considering. First, this phenomenological turn pushes aesthetics beyond the philosophy of art into the neighborhood of a broader practice of critical inquiry. Arthur Danto starts us toward this point by describing aesthetics as a field that "borders on philosophical psychology in one direction and the theory of knowledge in the other" (Danto 1993, 275). He adopts this view because aesthetic experience "addresses itself to the encoloration of meanings," and "penetrates our experience of the world in such a degree . . . that we cannot seriously address cognition without reference to it" (275).

But as Dewey argues, the aesthetic is itself already saturated with our experience of the world, particularly of the social world. It reproduces and refines and commemorates this experience in ways that we have to take seriously if we want to understand social cognition. Danto's best example of the encoloration of cognition by the aesthetic has to do with the way early modern scientific illustrations embodied rich visions of the world that were not strictly speaking required by the subject matter. These scientific drawings were stylized in ways that reflect and embody—not inappropriately, but ineliminably—a cosmology. We might add in a similar spirit that our perceptions of our fellows in society as threats or dangers, perceptions that we too often act on with lethal effect, closely track—reinforce and are reinforced by—cultural narratives, symbols, and images of threatening human types. Think of the characters—the Terrorists, the Illegals, the Thugs, and so on—that populate our moving picture narratives. And then think of the way these same characters populate and distort our public discourses around politics and policy. In light of these considerations, the broader approach to aesthetics that Danto calls for seems to border not just on philosophical psychology and the theory of knowledge, but also on ideology critique and social-cultural criticism.

A second additional consequence of making a phenomenological turn in aesthetics is that doing so attunes us to the dynamic relationship between aesthesis and social life. This in turn opens us to the potential for social transformation in aesthetic practice. There are three dimensions to this thought, each taken up with care in Dewey's writing.

First, Dewey points out that social life and aesthetic experience are reciprocally constitutive. "[I]ndividuals," he explains, "are what they are in the content of their experience because of the cultures in which they participate" (LW 10:326). At the same time, though, individual choices about how and whether to participate in our cultures actually shape the repositories of meaning that are available to other people across space and time. Individuals pass away, Dewey says, but "[t]he works in which meanings have received objective expression endure. They become part of the environment, and interaction with this phase of the environment is the axis of continuity in the life of civilization" (326). So even as society and culture shape the individual's aesthetic experience, individual aesthetic achievements shape society and culture.

This dialectical relationship leads to the second respect in which the aesthetic-social relation is importantly dynamic. By giving aesthetic form to social meanings and values, expressive cultures not only shape the character of a community's shared life, but also commemorate and preserve that life. We wrap our shared commitments in aesthetic raiment, the better to satisfy the basic human hunger for meaning and to define our shared lives in ways that inspire respect and allegiance. As Dewey says, "If social customs are more than uniform external modes of action, it is because they are saturated with story and transmitted meaning. Every art in some manner is a medium of this transmission" (LW 10:326). The aesthetic is a vehicle for promoting affection and loyalty, for attaching people to their societies. Like most vehicles, it can be misused, as the aestheticopolitical practices of fascism and aggressive nationalism make clear. But it also has the beneficial side effect of enabling a society to live on past its demise. Consider how the expressive practices of some extinct cultures—their ways of organizing ritual spaces, of narrating their origins, or of adorning and disposing of their dead—tell us everything we know about their participants.

The capacity of the aesthetic to bring social formations to life points to a third dimension of the dynamic relationship between society and aesthesis: the centrality of the imagination to social life. A long-dead society's expressive culture can invite us to experience a different world, but we can enter that world only if we use the power of imagination. Benedict Anderson has taught us to speak of nations as imagined communities (Anderson 1991), but all communities result from exercises in imagination. Imagining in this sense is not a matter of conjuring up fanciful mental images with no relationship to reality. It involves thinking beyond what is immediately present: mentally bringing the distant and the absent to bear on the near and the present (Fesmire 2003, 66–67). National duties—all duties—are imagined (but not imaginary) constraints on individual strivings. National communities—all communities—consist of people who imagine distant and absent comrades as they make their choices and chart their life-paths. Similarly, aesthetic conventions—settled ideas about how one should sing, walk, dance, compose, cook, and so on—are imagined but not imaginary constraints on individual expression. And expressive objects encapsulate the meanings of a society only by virtue of an imaginative act of metonymy, whereby a present flag, song, or uniform can stand in for a distant or absent people.

Imagination is central to the dynamism of the aesthetic-social relation because of the relationship between imagination, morality, and aesthesis. For Dewey, the moral life is a necessarily imaginative endeavor, and aesthetic experience may be the best training ground and incubator for moral imagination. He speaks to this point with an uncharacteristic eloquence. "The ideal factors in every moral outlook," he says, "are imaginative. . . . Hence it is that art is more moral than moralities" (LW 10:348). Moral codes too easily become rigid rulebooks, holding out the hope of an algorithm for praise and blame. But moral judgments always have to be made in unique situations, which call less for an algorithm than for creative interventions. Art can remind us of the uniqueness of each experience, and it can hone the imaginative vision that becomes necessary when, as William James put it in "The Moral Philosopher and the Moral Life," we see that our rules have grown too narrow for the case at hand (WWJ 6:158).

For these reasons, Dewey explains, "[t]he moral prophets of humanity have always been poets, even though they spoke in free verse or by parable" (LW 10:348). He uses "poet" here almost the way Richard Rorty does, to indicate someone who throws off old ways of thinking and creates new vocabularies for the human condition. The people we think of as makers of fine art are in some ways ideally positioned to be poets in this sense. But anyone who engages in sufficiently creative ways with his or her culture can act poetically. Developing the theme of poetic prophecy with language from Matthew Arnold, Dewey continues:

> poetry is a criticism of life . . . not directly, but by disclosure through imaginative vision . . . of possibilities that contrast with actual conditions. . . . It is by a sense of possibilities opening before us that we become aware of constrictions that hem us in and of burdens that oppress. (346)

Here, finally, we have all of the resources for an aesthetic that converges with Medina's epistemology of resistance. Dewey's phenomenological turn decenters narrowly epistemological considerations in just the way that Medina's "expanded" epistemology requires. But thinking of this not as an expanded epistemology but as a historicist phenomenology immediately builds in the affective, emotive, and social considerations that Medina takes such pains to highlight. And following these phenomenological considerations out in the direction of the aesthetic points us to a domain that routinely connects "the psychological and the sociohistorical and structural" (Medina 2013, 220), and that routinely insists on the situatedness, immediacy, and multidimensionality of our judgments and perceptions. Finally, allowing this conception of the aesthetic to inflect our orieintation to aesthetic theory leaves us with a mode of inquiry that borders not just on epistemology but also on social criticism, and that takes seriously the role that aesthetic practice can play in reconstructing and transforming social and political practice.

Conclusion: Critical Race Aesthetics

Like Medina's "epistemology of resistance," the locution "aesthetic of resistance" bears multiple interpretations. It might refer to politically resistant aesthetic practices—to forms of art and expression that cultivate the "transgressive attitudes" that Medina uses Bourdieu to discuss. Then again, it might refer to aesthetic practices that promote epistemic friction, or that moment in or aspect of the process of inquiry that brings us up short of our habitual judgments, and that invites us to criticize and resist the selves that unjust societies invite us to be. In still another sense, though, it might refer to a mode of aesthetic *theory* that explores the potential for reaction and for resistance that we find in aesthetic practice. We might think here of those modes of social and cultural criticism that interrogate the way expressive culture reproduces problematic social meanings. But we might also think of those modes of philosophic inquiry that remind us of the liberatory potential of the aesthetic, as when Dewey and Rorty identify poets as moral prophets.

One might regard this vagueness as a problem, but I take it instead as a sign of the fecundity and breadth of the subject in question. There is, as it happens, a great deal to say about the way aesthetics bears on the considerations raised by accounts of epistemic justice. It will help to fix ideas around this subject by briefly considering, in closing, a concrete instance of the sort of work we might use "aesthetic of resistance" to denote.

I have in recent years been concerned to develop an account of black aesthetics. The idea of a black aesthetic comes down to us in its most recognizable form from US liberatory activism and culture work in the 1960s and 1970s. Advocates for a black aesthetic in this context were typically keen to push back against the false universalism of what some would later call "Eurocentric" aesthetic norms, and assert the existence and validity of alternative norms for aesthetic production, criticism, and analysis—norms that were rooted in and responsive to the distinctive conditions of black life. This is one form of the black aesthetic, but does not exhaust the meaning of the expression as I understand it (Taylor 2016).

The need for a broader account of the black aesthetic comes into view once we consider that the sixties-era black arts and black aesthetic movements were in conversation with people who approached black culture very differently, and that all of these people were building on foundations that had been laid by earlier generations. So on the one hand there's Julian Mayfield in 1970, willing to say, "My Black Aesthetic is Bobby Seale, bound and gagged and straining at his leash in a Chicago courtroom"

(Mayfield 1971, 27). But on the other hand there's Bayard Rustin, imploring black artists to leave politics to the politicians, and Albert Murray denying that the idea of a purely black aesthetic is even coherent in an "incontestably mulatto" world (Murray 1970, 22). And before both we had W. E. B. Du Bois and Alain Locke, arguing in the 1920s about the meanings and relative merits of art and propaganda in what would eventually be called the black freedom struggle (Du Bois 1926; Locke 1928).

In light of this intergenerational tradition of reflecting on the aesthetic dimensions of black life, I use the idea of the black aesthetic to name the tradition that includes Mayfield and Rustin, the US Black Arts movement and the Harlem Renaissance, Phyllis Wheatley and Kara Walker. What unites participants in this tradition is not a commitment to a unitary set of norms for black aesthetic practice, or even a commitment to the thought that such norms are available or desirable. What unites them is a willingness to debate about these commitments, and to entertain the other questions and take up the other problems that emerge for anyone who attends with care to the aesthetic dimensions of black life. (Questions like these: What does it mean that black bodies in antiblack contexts are simultaneously demonized and exoticized, despised and desired? When does cultural exchange across racial lines become invidious appropriation—when does borrowing become theft? And can we speak sensibly of cultural authenticity in racialized contexts—that is, in contexts defined by the apparent rootlessness of migration, mobility, and socially constructed identities?)

To speak of black life in this context is to invoke a theory of race. Making that theory explicit will take us the final distance toward concretizing the idea of an aesthetic of resistance. As I understand it, the concept of race is a device for assigning generic meanings to human bodies and bloodlines, typically in the process of making these meanings suitable for various kinds of ethicopolitical and discursive work. Races are the populations that result from these assignments of meaning. We can assign these meanings in various ways, and for various purposes. We might do it to justify a mode of exploitation that relies on observable physical distinctions to segment its labor pools. Or we might do it to account for, track, and ameliorate the social inequalities that result from this exploitation. We might assign these meanings in accord with the facts of human biological diversity. Or we might ignore these facts, transpose racial reasoning from the domain of social theory or social engineering to the domain of natural science, and erroneously read our meanings onto the indifferent physical world (Taylor 2013).

If that's what race is, then the connections to aesthetics and then to justice are easy to see. If race-thinking and racial practices are about the assignment of meaning, then it is clear that the meanings in question are phenomenologically rich and cognitively loaded. This gesture at implicit bias calls to mind the characters of the Terrorist or the Illegal Alien that I mentioned earlier. Or it might call to mind whatever we're supposed to think George Zimmerman thought Trayvon Martin was. These archetypes are laden with immediate significance, which is to say that they work for us like symbols, like flags and uniforms and anthems and ritual objects. And once our environment is saturated with these meanings, they will find their way into the social practices—artistic, political, and otherwise—that we use to express, exemplify, interrogate, and operationalize the meanings that bind us together. Race in this sense will become part of the manifold of social experience—or, to use more contemporary language, it will mark the point at which rationality becomes bounded and defers to heuristics and cues. And all of this will impact the way we distribute the benefits and burdens of social cooperation.

The black aesthetic tradition includes culture workers, expressive objects, and aesthetic practices that clearly exemplify the sort of work that I suggested we might expect from an aesthetic of resistance. There are people like Adrian Piper and Glenn Ligon, who (sometimes) use art—and, for Piper, her philosophical writing—to excavate and interrogate the racial meanings that underwrite social practice in places like the United States (Piper 1996; Ligon 2011). There are people like Toni Morrison, who uses literary production and criticism to insist on the way literature produces, reflects, and reproduces racial ideologies (Morrison 1992). And there are the less well-known culture workers who participate in protests and political actions around the Black Lives Matter movement (Moriah 2015). These are the singers and dancers and poets who are rarely if ever captured in the corporate media depictions of the protests, depictions that routinely prioritize images of destruction and violence. These are the culture workers who use their talents to reinforce the bonds of solidarity, to insist on the beauty of black life in a world that presumes its brutality and viciousness, and to remind each other that, as the slogan from another resistance movement reminds us, another world is possible.

Works Cited

Alexander, Thomas. 1998. "The Art of Life: Dewey's Aesthetics." In *Reading Dewey: Interpretations for a Postmodern Generation*, edited by Larry Hickman, 1–22. Bloomington: Indiana University Press.

Anderson, Benedict. 1991. *Imagined Communities: Reflections on the Origin and Spread of Nationalism*. London: Verso.

Baumgarten, Alexander Gottlieb. [1750] 2007. *Aesthetica/Ästhetik*. Translated by Dagmar Mirbach. Vol. 1. Hamburg: Felix Meiner Verlag.

Croce, Benedetto. 1948. "On the Aesthetics of Dewey." *Journal of Aesthetics and Art Criticism* 6(3): 203–207.

Danto, Arthur. 1993. "A Future for Aesthetics." *Journal of Aesthetics and Art Criticism* 51: 271–277.

Dewey, John. 1969–1991. *The Collected Words of John Dewey*, edited by Jo Ann Boydston. 37 vols. Carbondale: Southern Illinois University Press. (See List of Abbreviations.)

Du Bois, W. E. B. 1926. "Criteria of Negro Art." *Crisis* 32: 290–297.

Fesmire, Steven. 2003. *John Dewey and Moral Imagination: Pragmatism in Ethics*. Bloomington: Indiana University Press.

James, William. 1975–1988. *The Works of William James*, edited by Frederick H. Burkhardt, Fredson Bowers, and Ignas K. Skrupskelis. 19 vols. Cambridge: Harvard University Press. (See List of Abbreviations.)

Ligon, Glenn. 2011. *America*. Edited by Adam D. Weinberg, Franklin Sirmans, and Scott Rothkopf. New York: Whitney Museum of American Art.

Locke, Alain. 1928. "Art or Propaganda?" *Harlem* 1(1): 12–13.

Mayfield, Julian. 1971. "You Touch My Black Aesthetic and I'll Touch Yours." In *The Black Aesthetic*, edited by Addison Gayle, 24–31. New York: Anchor-Doubleday.

Medina, José. 2013. *The Epistemology of Resistance: Gender and Racial Oppression, Epistemic Injustice, and the Social Imagination*. New York: Oxford University Press.

Moriah, Kristin. 2015. "Black Mourning, Black Movement(s)." *Sounding Out!* May 11. Accessed October 1, 2015. http://soundstudiesblog.com/2015/05/11/black-mourning-black-movements-savion-glovers-dance-for-amiri-baraka/.

Morrison, Toni. 1992. *Playing in the Dark: Whiteness and the Literary Imagination*. Cambridge: Harvard University Press.

Murray, Albert. 1970. *The Omni-Americans*. New York: Da Capo.

Piper, Adrian. 1996. *Selected Essays in Meta-art, 1968–1992*. Vol. 1 of *Out of Order, Out of Sight*. Cambridge: MIT Press.

Taylor, Paul C. 2013. *Race: A Philosophical Introduction*. Cambridge: Polity.

———. 2016. *Black Is Beautiful: A Philosophy of Black Aesthetics*. Malden, MA: Blackwell.

CHAPTER 13 | Setting Aside Hope
| *A Pragmatist Approach to Racial Justice*

SHANNON SULLIVAN

Is there a type of work that will, once and for all, alleviate black
suffering? Why would someone continue to do the same thing
repeatedly without any substantial change?

— CALVIN WARREN, "Black Nihilism and the Politics of Hope"

IN THE TWENTY-FIRST CENTURY, significant racial inequalities and antiblack violence continue to be rampant in the United States. Decades, even
centuries, of political and legal struggle have done little to change that fact.
This chapter will argue that black Americans need new tactics and strategies for responding to the white class privilege and white supremacy that
fundamentally structure the country.[1] They need to increase the number
and type of tools in their racial justice toolkit, expanding beyond liberal
faith in civil rights and white people's good intentions to cooperate with
racial change. The political and legal work that black and other people
of color (along with some white people) have done to eliminate antiblack
racism isn't working. Pragmatists in particular need to be able to face up
to that fact given that we value the practical work that ideas, concepts,
and truths can do. Why then, as Calvin Warren pragmatically asks in the
epigraph above, would we expect people fighting racism to keep doing
the same thing? Why would anyone hope that the same failed actions and
strategies would turn out any different in the future? This kind of hope can

---

[1] This probably is true for other racial groups as well, but I focus on black Americans here
because of the virulence and visibility of recent antiblack racism in the United States.

function as a cruel optimism that "works" by keeping black people focused on the very thing that undercuts their flourishing (Warren 2015, 221).

In line with Warren's concerns, I argue that black Americans' hope that political struggle can achieve racial justice tends to be a harmful emotion they should avoid. I make my case in a pragmatist spirit that opposes Cornel West's influential argument for black hope. In contrast to West, I contend that pragmatists and others concerned about racial injustice would do better to draw on Derrick Bell's racial realism and Warren's black nihilism to develop alternative strategies for addressing antiblack racism. In related ways, Bell and Warren urge their readers to reckon with the permanence of racism and to give up hope that additional political struggle will eliminate it. After exploring their complementary accounts, I augment them with concrete evidence from the health sciences that black hope can be physically harmful to black people, weathering their bodies and damaging their psychosomatic health such that they are less able to withstand the inequities of antiblack racism. I conclude by arguing for the advantages of reading Bell's and Warren's claims about the permanence of racism pragmatically, that is, by assessing the truth of their claims via their effects. The result is the working hypothesis that black people will have a much greater chance of developing new practices, habits, and strategies of flourishing in an antiblack world if they no longer hope that political struggle will eliminate racism.

The United States continues to struggle with deeply ingrained racial inequalities and wildly flagrant acts of racialized injustice even after abolishing its Jim Crow laws in the 1960s. From 2014 to 2016, for example, the United States was rocked by news of the violent deaths of unarmed black people at the hands of white police officers: Michael Brown in Ferguson, Missouri; Eric Garner in New York; Tamir Rice in Cleveland, Ohio; Walter Scott in North Charleston, South Carolina; and the list could go on. (For analysis, see Zack 2015.) Their deaths were soon followed by the fatal shooting of nine black people in a church in Charleston, South Carolina, by the alleged white supremacist Dylan Roof; the burning of several prominent black churches in the South as a possible backlash to calls for South Carolina to stop flying the Confederate flag; and the police shooting of Keith Scott in Charlotte, North Carolina, and Terence Crutcher in Tulsa, Oklahoma.

The shocking violence against black Americans has occurred against a backdrop of chronic and growing racial inequality that the elimination of legal segregation has done little to address. Examples include the fact that in 2012, African American women made 64 cents for every dollar that a non-Hispanic white man made (Kerby 2013). Racial disparities in health also exist, for example in disproportionately higher rates of coronary artery disease, diabetes, stroke, HIV/AIDS, and infant mortality for African Americans (Smedley et al., no date). As of 2005, African Americans were incarcerated at nearly six times the rate of white people (Mauer and King 2007). Black families regularly are the targets of child welfare services that shift black children into foster homes, a process that fuels the school-to-prison pipeline since children in foster homes are significantly more likely to go to prison than children who remain with their parents/families (Roberts 2002). A racialized aesthetics continues to benefit white people and penalize people of color: white beauty standards are normative, especially for women, positioning dark-skinned and black women as "the beauty don'ts" in contrast to white women as "the beauty dos" (Bossip 2015). This list could go on.

In the face of this discouraging present-day picture, hope for a better future would seem to be vital. Black hope in particular would appear crucial for enabling black people to carry on in the face of ongoing white domination and racial inequities. On this view, hope for a better world, a world that does not yet exist but that serves as a guiding ideal, is needed to provide the emotional fuel for the hard work that it will take to get closer to that world. To switch metaphors, black hope would seem to emotionally counterbalance the despair that white economic, social, geographical, and other forms of privilege will never end, both the despair of black people who suffer from white racism and that of white people who call for racism's demise. As Patrick Shade has argued, "Hoping can be sustaining, nurturing—indeed, *advantageous.* . . . And so [in a cynical world] we should salvage the good name of hope and actively promote its life at every turn" (2001, 6, 202). While Shade's pragmatist theory makes clear that hope must be grounded in present realities, it also depicts hope as tied inextricably to better possibilities in the future.

Shade's positive view of hope complements that of Cornel West. Fighting what he calls "the specter of despair [that] haunts America," West (2005) has made the most influential case for the importance of hope for African American people and communities. His criticism of black nihilism develops a conception of hope that is as deeply existentialist as it is pragmatist: it responds to the absurdity of a world that is built on the injustices and cruelties of white slavery, white segregation, white supremacy, and white class privilege. Even more important from West's perspective, his conception of hope offers an alternative to the despair that he worries has pervaded African American lives. West appreciates that other emotions such as rage can serve as an antidote to despair, but he instead counsels hope. According to West (1993), the source of the "nihilistic threat" to and "major enemy of black survival in America is neither oppression nor exploitation but rather the loss of hope." For West, hope is the emotion that best describes black Americans' history of struggle and that can keep black people sane in the ongoing struggles of the present. It is communal and inclusive, striving to make the world a more just place for everyone and particularly to "sustain black solidarity in the midst of a hostile society" (West 1999, 437). West's hope is for the end of the "existential alienation, isolation and separation" that is entangled with racist discourses and that plagues many Western cultures (1999, 263).

To its credit, West's particular account of hope is not Pollyannaish. For West, hope is not equivalent to optimism or to any other merely positive feeling. Optimism isn't tough enough to do the job that black people need, as West (2005) charges: "Optimism adopts the role of the spectator who surveys the evidence in order to infer that things are going to get better. Yet we know that the evidence does not look good. The dominant tendencies of our day are unregulated global capitalism, racial balkanization, social breakdown, and individual depression." In contrast, hope is actively participant and grounded, but also not bound by what the evidence tells us. Unlike optimism, West explains, "hope looks at the evidence and says, 'It doesn't look good at all. Doesn't look good at all. Gonna go beyond the evidence to create new possibilities based on visions that become contagious to allow people to engage in heroic actions always against the odds, no guarantee whatsoever.' That's hope" (quoted in A. Smith 2006, 160). Optimism also tends to run out of energy when the going gets difficult. "When you talk about hope, you have to be a long distance runner," West (2008, 209) insists, because it is going to take time and hard work to make racial progress in the United States.

On West's view, however, significant progress *has* been made. He would sharply characterize as "narrow" the view that things are no better for black people today than they were in the days of slavery. He argues that "progressive formations have been the history of black folk" and that additional "progressive possibilities are reemerging" in the twenty-first century (2008, 214). For West, the road toward racial equality might be long, hard, and even difficult to discern, but it can and does lead to a genuinely democratic America that lives up to its constitutional promise of freedom and liberty for all. Black people are crucial to the realization of this possibility according to West, and thus they need to buoy themselves up with hope. In West's opinion, Americans need to acknowledge "the degree to which black people in America provide one of the fundamental keys to the future, if the future is going to be about freedom and equality" (2008, 194). West's ideal of deep democracy in America thus is fueled by black people's "hope linked to combative spirituality," which empowers black people to "go against the grain and muster the love and will to resist" (2008, 209).

For all the absurdity of white domination and West's refusal to be optimistic about its defeat, West's notion of communal hope—like that of most pragmatists, I would surmise—is deeply humanist. I use "humanism" here in the sense that Albert Camus (1991) characterizes it. As Camus would charge, West's humanism refuses to believe in the permanence of white racism and/or that the evil of white racism cannot someday be overcome by human struggle. (I will return to Camus below in the context of Bell's work.) Or perhaps it would be more accurate to call West's progressivism as much religious as it is pragmatist because of the prophetic Christianity that informs it. Human beings alone might not be able to overcome racist evil; they might need religious help to do so. Either way, however, West's existential progressivism/pragmatism is grounded in a conviction that the right thing will happen in the end. However bad things look now, however difficult it is to envision a happy ending, we can go beyond the evidence and engage in heroic actions to create a better future. Racial inequalities might still exist, so the progressive story continues, but think about how our ancestors went against the odds and overcame chattel slavery and Jim Crow. With ongoing political struggle, we also can do that—we can make the leap. We today can improve the world's racial situation even further. Don't give up hope: racial justice can and will be achieved someday.

But what if someday never comes? What if, as Bell has argued, the political, legal, and historical circumstances of the United States have made "racism ... an integral, permanent, and indestructible component of this society" and thus "Black people will never gain full equality in this country" (1992a, ix, 12; see also Bell 1992b)? In that case, ongoing hope that political struggle will end racism is a farce: a joke that mocks black people without their realizing it, hoodwinking them into thinking that better times are on the horizon if they only will suffer and struggle more to reach them. According to Bell, that's a fair assessment of where things stand in the United States at the end of the twentieth century, and by extension at the beginning of the twenty-first. Federal civil rights laws and policies, such as affirmative action, the desegregation of US schools, voting rights acts (which, notably, were eliminated by the US Supreme Court in October 2013), and fair housing acts, have failed to overcome the devastating legacy of chattel slavery in the United States. Bell writes in 1992 that the income gap between the rich and poor—a very racially colored gap—was nearing a crisis point, but the gap he was concerned about is a mere sliver compared to the chasm of racial disparities in wealth that exist today (Bell 1992a, 8–9). The economic recession of 2008 was particularly hard on black households in the United States; by 2010 the median net household worth of white American families was twenty-two times that of black American families (Luhby 2012).

The water fountain signs in the United States that say "colored" and "white" may have disappeared, but post-segregation changes such as these do not mean that racial discrimination has disappeared, or even necessarily been weakened. They might mean merely that the form of racial discrimination has changed and, moreover, changed into something largely unofficial and delivered via race-neutral policies and language that only makes white class privilege more difficult to identify and combat. In that case, as Bell predicts, "even those herculean efforts we hail as successful will produce no more than temporary 'peaks of progress,' short-lived victories that slide into irrelevance as racial patterns adapt in ways that maintain white dominance" (1992b, 373). Black Americans need to accept that white racism is as virulent as ever and that they will always have a "permanent subordinate status" in their country (1992a, 12).

Bell realized very soon after the civil rights era that the idea that the United States is making progress against racism tends merely to inflate the egos and assuage the guilt of good white liberals. "The worship of equality rules benefits whites by preserving a benevolent but fictional self-image, and such worship benefits blacks by preserving hope," Bell observes and then adds, "but I think we've arrived at a place in history where the harms of such worship outweigh its benefits" (1992a, 101). Along with the belief that white people and institutions will ever regard or treat black people as equals, black people need to jettison the hopeful expectation that white racism will ever end. Acknowledging "the permanence of [black people's] subordinate status" in the United States, Bell explains, "allows [black Americans] to avoid despair, and frees [them] to imagine and implement racial strategies that can bring fulfillment and even triumph" (1992b, 373–374).

Most people—especially, but not only white people—have yet to acknowledge how resilient white domination is in the United States. From chattel slavery to Jim Crow to "the new Jim Crow" (Alexander 2012), the more white domination changes, the more it stays the same. "Supposedly, the generation that murdered Trayvon Martin and Renisha McBride is much better than the generation that murdered Emmett Till," Warren dryly remarks, and this so-called improvement is supposed to encourage black people that even more "progress" in black lives—and deaths—can be achieved (2015, 217). As Warren's quip suggests, by participating in hopeful political struggle for a future filled with racial equality that likely never will be present, West's existential pragmatism not only unintentionally benefits white people. It also harms black people by enacting what Warren calls "the politics of hope," which establishes an insidiously false dichotomy between hope and nihilism. On the logic of political hope, if a person or group of people doesn't have a hopeful relationship to the future, then they must be sunk in nihilistic despair. The politics of hope thus "terrifies with the dread of 'no alternative,'" which operates not just via the binary of hope/despair but also by the complementary binaries of "problem/solution" and "action/inaction" (2015, 222). If one hopes and takes action, one can find a future solution to today's problems. According to the politics of hope, hope is necessary for motivating political action to find answers to racial problems. Giving up hope thus raises the specter of inaction, of doing nothing and thus accepting the racist status quo. Hopelessness thus is the equivalent of a failed relationship to the future, which in turn is the equivalent of refusing to fight racial injustice.

The lure of the always-not-yet solution to present-day racial problems is symptomatic of the metaphysical nature of political hope, according to Warren. Political hope's future object of racial justice is "not tethered to real history," which makes it an "object of political fantasy" rather than an achievable goal (Warren 2015, 221). "The objective of the Political is to keep blacks in relation to this political object—in an unending pursuit of it," Warren explains, and this pursuit "strengthens the very anti-black system that would pulverize black being" (2015, 221). Black people's political struggle for this fantastical freedom enables modern societies to pride themselves on their advanced civilization; in this way, black suffering is necessary for modernity's promises of progress. Freedom as modernity knows it was created by means of chattel slavery, and thus "black emancipation is world destructive" for modernity and its ideals (Patterson 1982; see also Warren 2015, 239). Black suffering cannot be ended without the known world coming to an end, and so the world uses black hope to keep black suffering in place (Warren 2015, 242).

While Warren's argument against the politics of hope primarily targets its metaphysical nature, the destruction of black bodies that he analyzes is no mere abstraction. Neither, of course, are the intractable racial inequalities described by Bell. In both cases, antiblackness involves "the literal destruction of black bodies that provide the psychic, economic, and philosophical resources for modernity to objectify, forget, and ultimately obliterate Being (nonmetaphysical Being)" (Warren 2015, 327). This occurred initially through the transatlantic transformation of human beings into things (slaves) and then subsequently through other social, legal, and extralegal ways of annihilating black people and communities, including political tactics such as poll taxes, literacy tests, and the convict leasing system (2015, 216).

Recent developments in the medical health sciences reveal another material way to see how the metaphysical, legal, and economic destruction of black people via hope is both literal and physical. A concrete connection between hope and poor health and death exists for black Americans, and I now turn to that connection to bodily situate Bell's and Warren's accounts. Psychologists and other social scientists in the United States recently have focused on how African Americans cope with so-called mundane racism: not the big-booted racism of chattel slavery, lynching, or even legalized segregation, but rather the more mundane and subtle or "invisible" racial attacks that increasingly are being documented in post–Jim Crow America. Examples include the student who rolls his eyes in class when he realizes that the black woman at the front of the room will be his professor or the black person checking out at the grocery store who gets hassled to show several forms of identification to cash her check when the white person in front of her did not. In many ways, microaggressions such as these are minor in comparison to the major assaults that African Americans historically have experienced and still do experience. At minimum, racial microaggressions are not spectacularly horrific in the way that the overt violence of shootings and chokeholds is. But just because we tend not to notice the destructiveness of racial microaggressions does not mean they are trivial. Racial microaggressions can be deadly, although we (especially white people) often don't recognize or want to acknowledge their violent effects.

De facto white class privilege in the form of racial microaggressions contributes to people of color's "racial battle fatigue," which entails "the constant use or redirection of energy for coping against mundane racism which depletes psychological and physiological resources needed in other important, creative, and productive areas of life" (Smith, Hung, and Franklin 2012, 40). Racial battle fatigue has been linked empirically to depression, tension, and generalized anxiety disorder in African Americans, and the stress associated with all of these psychological problems also contributes to physiological weathering that harms black health, contributing to high rates of hypertension, cardiovascular disease, pre-term birth rates, and infant mortality to name a few (Smith, Hung and Franklin 2012, 37, 40; D. Smith 2012). The effects of white racism literally get inside and help constitute the bodies of black people in harmful ways. They wear down the body's various systems by creating a high allostatic load via stressors that accumulate over time. The results are health problems such as disproportionately high rates of pre-term birth, infant mortality, cardio-vascular disease, diabetes, and accelerated physiological aging (Blitstein 2009). Racism hurts—literally—and it also kills in ways that are subtler but no less deadly than the lyncher's noose or the neighbor's bullet (Drexler 2007). These effects, moreover, can be transgenerational, physiologically passed onto subsequent generations through various epigenetic changes (Sullivan 2013).

So what can black people do to mitigate the harmful effects of de facto white supremacy and racial microaggressions and to ward off racial battle fatigue? As the same study documents, the first answer is simply for them to realize the need for coping strategies that build resilience. Black people living in countries that formally have eliminated racial discrimination and yet that are still informally structured by white class privilege need to ac-tively seek out ways to manage and resist racial battle fatigue. The second answer is that collective methods of coping are much more effective than individual ones. Social support systems that, for example, provide commu-nal spaces for emotional expression and processing of experiences of racial microaggressions were most effective in helping African American people cope with race-related stress, as one recent study demonstrated about African American college students (Smith, Hung, and Franklin 2012, 39).

This advice might seem rather obvious, but it turns out that students in the study with high levels of hope that they could achieve their goals in life, school, and work generally did not use active coping strategies. They tended not to seek out social support or find venues in which they could share their experiences of white racism with others. The explanation for this behavior is that hope on the part of black students was empirically correlated with a sense of personal efficacy: the more that students thought they could individually surmount obstacles in their path, the greater their sense of hope for the future, and vice versa. And the greater their hope and sense of individual efficacy, the less likely a person was to seek out com-munities and networks with other black people. On the flip side, low-hope individuals did actively seek out social support systems. Because they did not have much hope that they could overcome the race-based obstacles in their path, they tended to seek out collective avenues for expressing their anger and frustration and for taking action against racism (Smith, Hung, and Franklin 2012, 39). The upshot here is that black hope not only did not serve as an effective coping strategy for black people, but it actually decreased the likelihood that they would seek out coping strategies that were effective.

This study of a mixed-gender group of African American college students is supported by another study focusing on African American men, which underscores that hope is not always or necessarily a healthy response to an unjust world. African American men with high to moderate levels of hope that racial justice would prevail experienced more stress when confronted with racial microaggressions than did African American men with low to moderate levels of hopefulness (Smith, Hung, and Franklin 2012, 50). It was low-hope African American men who best recognized the pervasiveness of racist discrimination in US society and thus developed racial socialization techniques that allowed them to keep the pernicious effects of racism at bay long enough to develop counterstrategies to it (2012, 50). While some scientific studies that do not consider race have lauded the health benefits of hope, demonstrating how hope can help the body reduce physical pain by triggering the release of natural analgesics such as endorphins and enkephalins (Groopman 2005, 175–179), we should not necessarily universalize these conclusions. "Hope [simply] does not have the same function in the context of African American men dealing with race-related stress and racial microaggressions as it does in previously studied contexts," and thus promoting hope as a way for black Americans to combat the effects of white racism can be counterproductive to racial justice (Smith, Hung, and Franklin 2012, 51). It can tear down, rather than undergird black people by indirectly damaging their health and leading them to neglect effective social strategies for coping with white racism.

These studies provide concrete support for the claim that black hope is not a good alternative to the despair diagnosed by West in black American communities. It does not tend to help African Americans cope well with the insidious effects of white racism, and it even can contribute to a decline in black people's psychological and physiological health. While West likely is right that black communities are crucial for black people to be able to withstand antiblack racism, it is important to note, in accordance with the above studies, that those communities that helped mitigate the harmful physiological effects of antiblack racism were not particularly based on hoping. They instead were based on coping. They were collective outlets for sharing experiences of and venting frustration about stressful racial encounters, for example, which is not the same thing as generating hope that antiblack racism can be eliminated.

What might black communities that cope look like? For starters, "coping" as used here does not mean surrendering, selling out, or merely getting by. Communities that cope would be communities that recognize that "nothing has worked" against antiblack racism and that black people "have exhausted the discourses of humanism and the strategies of equality" (Warren 2015, 228). I want to underscore the pragmatic significance of this recognition. Pragmatically understood, the value of things is found in their effects—including the ultimate effect of whether they enable flourishing (Sullivan 2001)—and the effect of humanism hasn't been the flourishing of black people. Pursuing strategies of racial equality hasn't worked. These realizations are important for the effects they can have: they allow a very different set of strategies in relationship to antiblack racism to emerge. Rather than defeatist, letting go of the goal of racial equality can be liberating and invigorating for black people. It can free them up to envision new goals, to develop new truths about how best to respond to racism, and thus to stop banging their heads against a wall that will not budge. "Casting off the equality ideology," Bell urges, "will lift the sights. . . . From this broadened perspective on events and problems, [black people] can better appreciate and cope with racial subordination" (1992b, 378).

For example, Bell claims that rather than spend energy and time trying to fully integrate American schools—which still has not happened sixty years after *Brown v. Board of Education* and has been reversed in some major cities (see, e.g., Michelson, Smith, and Nelson 2015)—black people should work on raising money for and strengthening all-black schools (1992a, 63). More generally, racial realism would urge that black people devise strategies that acknowledge the "white self-interest principle": white people will never do anything to improve the lives of black people unless it first and foremost benefits themselves as well, particularly economically (Bell 1992a, 54). In many ways, then, successfully fighting white racism is a very crude, nonsophisticated business. It isn't about devising fancy moral arguments or ideal forms of jurisprudence; it instead involves "making a shameless appeal to the predictable self-interest of whites" and their wallets (1992a, 107).

One could add that it also relies on the predictable self-delusion, self-grandeur, and racial ignorance of white people. Bell (1992a, 62) argues that black people—both individuals and communities—need to be like Brer Rabbit of the Uncle Remus stories, who tricks Brer Fox into setting him free by convincing Brer Fox that throwing Brer Rabbit into the briar patch is the worst thing that Brer Fox could ever do to him. Brer Fox acts in what he thinks is his own best interest—an interest in harming Brer

Rabbit by keeping him captive—and in so doing, he does the very thing that enables Brer Rabbit to escape. A masterful tactician at manipulating the canine ignorance and solipsistic focus of Brer Fox, Brer Rabbit doesn't rely on rational argumentation, nor does he depend on the law or any universal rights of animal kind to obtain his freedom. He instead is ruthlessly realistic about the malicious self-interest that motivates Brer Fox, and for that reason he is able to devise an effective strategy for getting out of his clutches. Brer Rabbit doesn't succeed in making any sort of large-scale or structural change in the relationship between foxes and rabbits, nor does he particularly hope to. He instead focuses practically on how to save his life in the midst of a particular struggle with Brer Fox, and through his struggle, he is able to flourish even if the overarching tyranny of foxes has not been eliminated.

Because struggle is central to racial realism, racial realism is neither passive nor apathetic. It is not nihilist in the sense that West uses the term. But neither is it hopeful. Even though they might bear a superficial similarity, the struggle involved in racial realism isn't the same struggle encouraged by West's politics of hope. The struggle of political hope is for the fantastical object of a future without antiblack racism. It insists that "legitimate action takes place in the political" and that "a refusal to 'do politics' is equivalent to 'doing nothing'" (Warren 2015, 223). The struggle of racial realism, in contrast, doesn't involve believing that the right thing will win out. Bell's racial realism invokes a different kind of existentialism than that of West, appealing to Camus (Bell 1992a, x). As Camus's main character from *The Plague* (1991) understands, one resists and must resist the plague—whether in the form of mass death, the Nazi Holocaust, or in this case white class privilege and white supremacy—even though, or perhaps precisely because, one cannot conquer it. There is no ultimate progress or victory to anticipate, no matter whether human struggle is assisted by the divine. The plague might be beaten back for a while, but it always will return. Fighting it is absurd if the goal of the fight is to eliminate it. On Camus's view, one fights the plague for different reasons, ones that have to do with affirming the dignity and value of humanity. Likewise, on Bell's view, black people's "struggle for freedom, is bottom, a manifestation of our humanity that survives and grows stronger through resistance to oppression, even if that oppression is never overcome" (1992b, 378). If this is a kind of humanism, it is absurd rather than progressive.

Bell implicitly develops this point in connection with black personhood when he tells the story of Mrs. MacDonald, an older black woman living in rural Mississippi in 1964 who was fighting white hostility and violent intimidation. When Bell asked her how she found the strength to carry on, she replied, " 'Derrick, I am an old woman. I lives to harass white folks' " (quoted in Bell 1992b, 378). As Bell points out, Mrs. MacDonald didn't claim or even suggest that she thought she could eliminate white oppression with her harassment. Her spirited refusal to be beaten down by white domination was itself the point. It was how she triumphed against white racism, and even though her son lost his job, the bank tried to foreclose on her mortgage, and shots were fired through her living room window, "nothing the all-powerful whites could do would diminish her triumph" (1992b, 379). Bell concludes, "if you remember her story, you will understand my message" (1992b, 379). The message is that Mrs. MacDonald's rebellious spirit was the most important element of her successful fight against white oppression, not whether she hopefully believed that racism could be ended or engaged in recognizable political action against it.

I am not interested in settling the question of whether Bell and Warren are right that racism is permanent in the United States. For starters, I think that the effects of this claim can change significantly when a white person makes it instead of a black one. The different subject positions that Bell and Warren, as black men, and I, a white woman, occupy are relevant, and a white person's declaration that white racism will never end probably isn't likely to help people of color fight it. Aside from that issue, I also am not sure how anyone, of any race, could ever know the Truth about racism or discern what the future holds for white-dominated nations such as the United States. What is more useful than an epistemological claim of certainty is a pragmatic claim about the permanence of racism. Acknowledging that the truth of a claim is found—or rather, made—not in whether it mirrors the way that the world "really" is but in the practical effects that it has in the world, we should ask: what personal and institutional practices, habits, and behaviors would result if black people engaged in the world knowing that racism isn't going away? What strategies for black flourishing might emerge if black people acted on the hypothesis that, beneath a thin veneer of wanting to appear nonracist, most white people do not really want to abolish white class privilege and white domination?

On this score, I would wager that Bell and Warren are right: hoping and struggling politically for the end of racism is less advantageous to black people than approaching racism as permanent. Black people are more likely to develop strategies for surviving and thriving if they give up on political hope. If that pragmatic hypothesis bears fruit—and it needs to be tested in the lives and experiences of black people to know if it does— then black people should relinquish hope for racial equality and instead creatively tap into and devise other strategies to help black people thrive. More so than West's progressive hope, Bell's and Warren's provocative gambles concerning the permanence of antiblack racism could open up practical possibilities for America's future that step outside the civil rights box in which it largely has been contained for the past sixty years.

A related reason Bell's and Warren's positions are pragmatically preferable to that of West is that they are likely to do a better job of protecting black people from the weathering effects of racial microaggressions and other forms of racial discrimination. Low-hope black people do not experience the same psychophysiological effects of stress from white racism as high-hope black people do. This means that they will tend to be more psychosomatically resilient in order to withstand and struggle against white domination, and resilience, which should not be confused with hope, has been empirically linked with low levels of cortisol in response to stressful or negative events (Groopman 2005, 204–205). The physical health of low-hope black people—rates of hypertension and cardiovascular disease, for example—should tend to be better than those whose stress hormone levels spike out of surprised disappointment when their expectations of racial equality are disappointed. And thus their spiritual health—their emotional strength and creative energy—also should be better than that of high hope individuals.

I am not arguing against the importance of black communities or black solidarity (or cross-racial solidarity, which is a story for another time) to deal with racism and white supremacy. I instead am questioning whether hope is a crucial or even a helpful component of black communities that are effective at building up their members' resistance to the harmful effects of racial injustice. Viable alternatives to black hope exist, and thus black Americans perhaps could do without hope. Their physical resilience, their spiritual and emotional fortitude, and their psychosomatic ability to fight white racism might be better off without it.

I also am not suggesting that the United States should return to the days of de jure Jim Crow or that the current political and civil rights gained by black Americans should be rolled back. Instead, I am asking: rather than spend more energy and time hoping that additional legal remedies will solve its postsegregation injustices, could black Americans benefit from Warren's and Bell's analyses, jettison hope for racial equality, and create more racially realistic ways to withstand white class privilege and white supremacy and to promote black well-being? As difficult as this question is, Bell's and Warren's work rightly suggests that it needs to be confronted.

In the wake of the Ferguson shooting and acquittal, some journalists outside the United States have argued "America is but a matchstick away" (Poplack 2014). The country could explode because it has achieved racial "reconciliation without *actually* reconciling ... hugging and making up without addressing the structurally ingrained disparities that keep old legacies alive" (Poplack 2014). While I don't purport to know what the future holds, the possibility of a great conflagration in the United States—literal or figurative—cannot be easily dismissed. In the face of relentless racial inequality and violence, hope and despair need to be recognized as flip sides of the same coin. Both are minted out of a liberal faith in civil rights and white goodwill, and both are highly problematic as a result. Workable alternatives to hope and despair are needed if the United States is to avoid striking the match.

Works Cited

Alexander, Michelle. 2012. *The New Jim Crow: Mass Incarceration in the Age of Colorblindness*. New York: New Press.

Bell, Derrick. 1992a. *Faces at the Bottom of the Well: The Permanence of Racism*. New York: Basic Books.

———. 1992b. "Racial Realism." *Connecticut Law Review* 24(2): 363–379.

Blitstein, Ryan. 2009. "Racism's Hidden Toll." *Miller-McCune*. Accessed October 26, 2016. https://psmag.com/racism-s-hidden-toll-a49b599eef32#.rizq6ixap.

Bossip. 2015. "Mainstream Media Still Pushes the White Beauty Standard, and We're Fed Up." Accessed October 26, 2016. http://bossip.com/1125218/cosmopolitan-magazine-black-models-beauty-donts-racist/.

Camus, Albert. 1991. *The Plague*. Translated by Albert Gilbert. New York: Vintage Books.

Drexler, Madeline. 2007. "How Racism Hurts—Literally." *Boston Globe*. July 15. Accessed October 26, 2016. http://www.boston.com/news/globe/ideas/articles/2007/07/15/how_racism_hurts____literally/?page=full.

Groopman, Jerome. 2005. *The Anatomy of Hope: How People Prevail in the Face of Illness*. New York: Random House.

Kerby, Sophia. 2013. "How Pay Inequity Hurts Women of Color." Center for American Progress. Accessed October 26, 2016. https://www.americanprogress.org/issues/labor/report/2013/04/09/59731/how-pay-inequity-hurts-women-of-color/.

Luhby, Tami. 2012. "Worsening Wealth Inequality by Race." *CNNMoney*. Accessed October 26, 2016. http://money.cnn.com/2012/06/21/news/economy/wealth-gap-race/index.htm.

Mauer, Marc, and Ryan S. King. 2007. "Uneven Justice: State Rates of Incarceration by Race and Ethnicity." Sentencing Project. Accessed October 26, 2016. http://www.sentencingproject.org/doc/publications/rd_stateratesofincbyraceandethnicity.pdf.

Michelson, Roslyn Arlin, Stephen Samuel Smith, and Amy Hawn Nelson, eds. 2015. *Yesterday, Today and Tomorrow: School Desegregation and Resegregation in Charlotte.* Cambridge: Harvard Education Press.

Patterson, Orlando. 1982. *Slavery and Social Death: A Comparative Study.* Cambridge: Harvard University Press.

Poplack, Richard. 2014. "Ferguson Burns, South Africa Simmers: Why America Is but a Matchstick Away." *Daily Maverick.* November 26. Accessed October 26, 2016. http://www.dailymaverick.co.za/article/2014-11-26-ferguson-burns-south-africa-simmers-why-america-is-but-a-matchstick-away/#.VW3mEOt92fQ.

Roberts, Dorothy. 2002. *Shattered Bonds: The Color of Child Welfare.* New York: Basic Books.

Shade, Patrick. 2001. *Habits of Hope: A Pragmatic Theory.* Nashville, TN: Vanderbilt University Press.

Smedley, Brian, Michael Jeffries, Larry Adelman, and Jean Cheng. No date. "Briefing Paper: Race, Racial Inequality, and Health Inequalities: Separating Myth from Fact." Accessed October 26, 2016. http://www.unnaturalcauses.org/assets/uploads/file/Race_Racial_Inequality_Health.pdf.

Smith, Anna Deavere. 2006. *Letters to a Young Artist.* New York: Anchor Books.

Smith, Darron T. 2012. "Dirty Hands and Unclean Practices: How Medical Neglect and the Preponderance of Stress Illustrates How Medicine Harms Rather Than Helps." *Journal of Black Masculinity* 2(1): 11–34.

Smith, William A., Man Hung, and Jeremy D. Franklin. 2012. "Between Hope and Racial Battle Fatigue: African American Men and Race-Related Stress." *Journal of Black Masculinity* 2(1): 35–58.

Sullivan, Shannon. 2001. *Living across and through Skins: Pragmatism, Feminism, and Transactional Bodies.* Bloomington: Indiana University Press.

———. 2013. "Inheriting Racist Disparities in Health: Epigenetics and the Transgenerational Effects of White Racism." *Critical Philosophy of Race* 1(2): 190–218.

Warren, Calvin L. 2015. "Black Nihilism and the Politics of Hope." *CR: The New Centennial Review* 15(1): 215–248.

West, Cornel. 1993. "The Nihilistic Threat to Black America: The Major Enemy of Black Survival in American Is Neither Oppression nor Exploitation but Rather the Loss of Hope and Absence of Meaning." *Philly.com.* May 9. Accessed June 5, 2015. http://articles.philly.com/1993-05-09/news/25966287_1_black-america-black-business-expansion-second-camp.

———. 1999. *The Cornel West Reader.* New York: Basic Civitas Books.

———. 2005. "Prisoners of Hope." Accessed October 26, 2016. http://www.alternet.org/story/20982/prisoners_of_hope.

———. 2008. *Hope on a Tightrope: Words and Wisdom.* Carlsbad, CA: Smiley Books.

Zack, Naomi. 2015. *White Privilege and Black Rights: The Injustice of U.S. Police Racial Profiling and Homicide.* Lanham, MD: Rowman and Littlefield.

PART III | Pragmatism, Liberalism, and Democracy

CHAPTER 14 | Reconsidering Deweyan Democracy

HILARY PUTNAM

Introduction

I want to discuss a philosopher whose work at its best illustrates the way in which American pragmatism (at its best) avoided both the illusions of metaphysics and the pitfalls of skepticism: John Dewey. While Dewey's output was vast, one concern informed all of it; even what seem to be his purely epistemological writings cannot be understood apart from that concern. That concern is with the meaning and future of democracy. I shall discuss a philosophical justification of democracy that I believe one can find in Dewey's work. I shall call it *the epistemological justification of democracy* and although I shall state it in my own words, I shall deliberately select words which come from Dewey's own philosophical vocabulary. The claim, then, is this: Democracy is not just a form of social life among other workable forms of social life; it is the precondition for the full application of *intelligence* to the solution of social problems.

At the beginning of *Ethics and the Limits of Philosophy* (1985), Bernard Williams draws a very useful distinction between two senses in which one might attempt to justify ethical claims. One is a Utopian sense: One might try to find a justification for ethical claims that would actually convince skeptics or amoralists and persuade them to change their ways. (This is like finding a "proof" that Hitler was a bad man that Hitler himself would have had to accept.) Williams rightly concludes that this is an unrealistic objective.

When the philosopher raised the question of what we shall have to say to the skeptic or amoralist, he should rather have asked what we shall have to say about him. The justification he is looking for is in fact designed for the people who are largely within the ethical world, and the aim of the discourse is not to deal with someone who probably will not listen to it, but to reassure, strengthen, and give insight to those who will. . . . If, by contrast, the justification is addressed to a community that is already an ethical one, then the politics of ethical discourse, including moral philosophy, are significantly different. The aim is not to control the enemies of the community or its shirkers but, by giving reason to people already disposed to hear it, to help in continually creating a community held together by that same disposition. (Williams 1985, 26–27)

Here Williams's conception of moral philosophy seems to be exactly Dewey's conception. Yet Williams ignores not only the historical figure John Dewey, but the very possibility of Dewey's particular justification. Instead, Williams considers just two ways in which ethical claims could "objectively" be justified, and associates these two kinds of justification with Aristotle and Kant, respectively (Williams 1985, 29). Even though Williams considers Kantian and Aristotelian strategies of justification to be the only possible ones, he might still have left room for a discussion of Dewey. Some commentators have seen a sense in which Dewey might be an Aristotelian, even though he was much more of an empiricist than Aristotle (Gouinlock 1976, xxiii). But when Williams discusses Aristotelian strategies—strategies of justification based on conceptions of human flourishing—something very strange happens. "Human flourishing" is defined in an entirely individualistic sense. For example, Williams writes, "On Aristotle's account a virtuous life would indeed conduce to the well-being of the man who has had a bad upbringing, even if he cannot see it. The fact that he is incurable, and cannot properly understand the diagnosis, does not mean that he is not ill" (Williams 1985, 40). In short, the only hope for an objective foundation for ethics[1] that Williams considers is what might be called a "medical" justification—an "objective" justification for ethics that would show, in some sense of "ill" that does not beg the question, that the amoral or immoral man is ill. Moreover, the only place that such a justification could originate, according to Williams, is in

---

[1] Although Williams also considers the Kantian strategy, he concludes that it is unworkable, and that if any objective justification could be given—which he doubts—it would have to be along Aristotelian lines.

"some branch of psychology" (Williams 1985, 45). Williams is skeptical about that possibility, although he says that "[i]t would be silly to try to determine a priori and in a few pages whether there could be such a theory" (45). The aim mentioned earlier, "not to control the enemies of the community or its shirkers but, by giving reason to people already disposed to hear it, to help in continually creating a community held together by that same disposition," has been given a radically individualistic interpretation (Williams 1985, 27).

However, when Williams explains why it is unlikely that there will ever be a "branch of psychology" that will provide us with "objective" foundations for ethics, he makes a very interesting remark:

> There is . . . the figure, rarer perhaps than Callicles supposed, but real, who is horrible enough and not miserable at all but, by any ethological standard of the bright eye and the gleaming coat, dangerously flourishing. For people who want to ground the ethical life in psychological health, it is something of a problem that there can be such people at all. (Williams 1985, 45–46)

Note the reference to "any ethological standard of the bright eye and the gleaming coat." Apparently, an "objective" standard of human flourishing would regard us as if we were tigers (or perhaps squirrels)! Williams describes a standard of human flourishing that ignores everything that Aristotle himself would have regarded as typically human. Dewey, on the other hand, thought of us primarily in terms of our capacity to intelligently initiate action, to talk, and to experiment.

Not only is Dewey's justification a social justification—that is, one addressed to the community as a whole rather than to each member of the community—it is also an *epistemological* justification, and this too is a possibility that Williams ignores. The possibility that Williams considers is a "medical" justification; a proof that if you are not moral then you are in some way ill. If we tried to recast Dewey's justification in such terms, then we would have to say that the society which is not democratic is in a certain way ill; but the medical metaphor is, I think, best dropped altogether.

The Noble Savage and the Golden Age

Although John Dewey's arguments are largely ignored in contemporary moral and political philosophy, his enterprise—of justifying democracy— is alive and well. John Rawls's monumental *A Theory of Justice* (1971), for example, attempts both to produce a rationale for democratic institutions and a standpoint from which to criticize the failures of those institutions. This could also serve as a description of Dewey's project. But there are scholars in disciplines other than philosophy, and to some extent even scholars of philosophy, who consider the very enterprise of justifying democracy a wrong-headed one. One objection comes from anthropologists and other social scientists,[2] although it is by no means limited to them.[3] A case I have in mind is an essay by Stephen Marglin and Frederique Marglin, a radical economist and radical anthropologist. These writers reject the idea that we can criticize traditional societies even for such sexist practices as female circumcision. The Marglins defend their point of view in part by defending an extreme relativism, but I think there is something else at work—something which one finds in the arguments of many social scientists who are not nearly as sophisticated as the Marglins. Not to be too nice about it, what I think we are seeing is the revival of the myth of the Noble Savage. Basically, traditional societies are viewed by these thinkers as so superior to our own societies that we have no right to disturb them in any way. To see what is wrong with this view, let us for the moment focus on the case of male chauvinism in traditional societies.

It is important in discussing this to separate two questions: the question of paternalistic intervention and the question of moral judgment, moral argument, and persuasion. It is not part of Dewey's view, for example, that benevolent despots should step in wherever there are social ills and correct them:

> The conception of community of good may be clarified by reference to attempts of those in fixed positions of superiority to confer good upon others. History shows that there have been benevolent despots who wished to bestow blessings on others. They have not succeeded except when their actions have taken the indirect form of changing the conditions under which those lived who were disadvantageously placed. The same principle holds of reformers and philanthropists when they try to do good to others in ways which leave passive those to be benefited. There is a moral tragedy inherent in efforts to further the common good which prevent the result from being either good or common—not good, because it is at the expense of the active growth of those to be helped, and not common because these have

---

[2] See, for example, Marglin 1990.
[3] See, for example, Walzer 1987. In his recent work, Walzer seems to be searching for a middle path between relativistic social scientists and moral philosophers like John Rawls.

no share in bringing the result about. The social welfare can be advanced only by means which enlist the positive interest and active energy of those to be benefited or "improved." The traditional notion of the great man, of the hero, works harm. It encourages the idea that some "leader" is to show the way; others are to follow in imitation. It takes time to arouse minds from apathy and lethargy, to get them to thinking for themselves, to share in making plans, to take part in their execution. But without active cooperation both in forming alms and in carrying them out there is no possibility of a common good. (LW 7:347)

The true paternalists are those who object to *informing* the victims of male chauvinism, or of other forms of oppression, of the injustice of their situation and of the existence of alternatives. Their argument is a thinly disguised utilitarian one. Their conception of the good is basically "satisfaction" in one of the classic utilitarian senses; in effect they are saying that the women (or whoever the oppressed may be) are satisfied, and that the "agitator" who stirs them up is the one who is guilty of creating dissatisfaction.

What the radical social scientists are in fact proposing is what Karl Popper has called an "immunizing strategy," a strategy by which the rationales of oppression in other cultures can be protected from criticism. This is based on the idea that the aspirations to equality and dignity are confined to citizens of Western industrial democracies. The events of Tiananmen Square in the spring of 1989 are a more powerful refutation of that view than any words I could write here.

At the other extreme, at least politically, from the "Noble Savage" argument against attempting to justify democratic institutions is an argument I detect in some of Alasdair MacIntyre's writings.[4] MacIntyre gives a sweeping philosophical resume of the history of Western thought which endorses the idea that one system of ethical beliefs can "rationally defeat" another system and insists that there can be progress in the development of world views. MacIntyre's argument, however, is haunted by the suggestion that such progress fundamentally stopped somewhere between the twelfth and fourteenth centuries, and that we have been retrogressing ever since.

If I am disturbed by the suggestion that I describe as haunting MacIntyre's writing, the suggestion that we have been retrogressing ever since the late Middle Ages (a suggestion that has been put forward in a

---

[4] These arguments are set forth in MacIntyre 1984 and its successor, MacIntyre 1988.

much more blatant way in Allan Bloom's best seller, *The Closing of the American Mind* [1987]), it is because the politics which such views can justify are nothing less than appalling.

What the defenders of the Noble Savage and the defenders of the Golden Age have in common is that their doctrines tend to immunize institutionalized oppression from criticism. The immunizing strategies are different, but they have this in common: they abandon the idea that it would be good for the victims of oppression to know of alternative ways of life, alternative conceptions of their situation, and to be free to see for themselves which conception is better. Both Noble Savagers and Golden Agers block the path of inquiry.

Dewey's Metaphysics (or Lack Thereof)

From what "premises" does Dewey derive the claim that I imputed to him, that is, that democracy is a precondition for the full application of intelligence to solving social problems? As we shall shortly see, the underlying "premises" are some very commonplace assumptions.

Dewey believes (as we all do, when we are not playing the skeptic) that there are better and worse resolutions to human predicaments—to what he calls "problematic situations" (LW 12:278). He believes that of all the methods for finding better resolutions, the "scientific method" has proved itself superior to Peirce's methods of "tenacity," "authority," and "What is Agreeable to Reason." For Dewey, the scientific method is simply the method of experimental inquiry combined with free and full discussion—which means, in the case of social problems, the maximum use of the capacities of citizens for proposing courses of action, for testing them, and for evaluating the results. And, in my view, that is all that Dewey really needs to assume.

Of course, a conventional analytic metaphysician would not hold this view. In analytic philosophy today, one cannot simply assume that intelligent people are able to distinguish better resolutions to problematical situations from worse resolutions even after experimentation, reflection and discussion; one first must show that better and worse resolutions to problematical situations exist. This is, for example, what bothers Bernard Williams. For Bernard Williams there could only be facts about what forms of social life are better and worse if such facts issued from "some branch of psychology" (Williams 1985, 45). Lacking such a "branch of psychology" (and Williams thinks it very unlikely there will ever be one), we have no basis for believing that one form of social life can be better than another except in a relativist sense, that is, unless the judgment of better or worse is explicitly made relative to the principles and practices of "some social world or other" (Williams 1985, 150). For Williams the distinction between facts which are relative in this way and facts which are "absolute" is omnipresent; there cannot be "absolute" facts of the kind Dewey thinks intelligent people are able to discover.[5] Dewey, as I read him, would reply that the whole notion of an "absolute" fact is nonsensical.

However, it is a fact that, while at one time analytic philosophy was an antimetaphysical movement (during the period of logical positivism), it has recently become the most prometaphysical movement. And from a metaphysical realist point of view, one can never begin with an epistemological premise that people are able to tell whether A is better or worse than B; one must first show that, in "the absolute conception of the world," there are such possible facts as "better" and "worse." A metaphysical-reductive account of what "good" is must precede any discussion of what is better than what. In my view, Dewey's great contribution was to insist that we neither have nor require a "theory of everything," and to stress that what we need instead is insight into how human beings resolve problematical situations:

> [Philosophy's] primary concern is to clarify, liberate and extend the goods which inhere in the naturally generated functions of experience. It has no call to create a world of "reality" *de novo*, nor to delve into secrets of Being hidden from common sense and science. It has no stock of information or body of knowledge peculiarly its own; if it does not always become ridiculous when it sets up as a rival of science, it is only because a particular philosopher happens to be also, as a human being, a prophetic man of science. Its business is to accept and to utilize for a purpose the best available knowledge of its own time and place. And this purpose is criticism of beliefs, institutions, customs, policies with respect to their bearing upon good. This does not mean their bearing upon *the* good, as something itself attained and formulated in philosophy. For as philosophy has no private score of knowledge or of methods for attaining truth, so it has no private access to good. As it accepts knowledge of facts and principles from those competent and inquiry and discovery, so it accepts the goods that are diffused in human experience. It has no Mosaic or Pauline authority of revelation

---

[5] For a discussion of Williams's metaphysical views, see Putnam 1993.

entrusted to it. But it has the authority of intelligence, of criticism of these common and natural goods. (LW 1:304)

The need for such fundamental democratic institutions as freedom of thought and speech follows, for Dewey, from requirements of scientific procedure in general: the unimpeded flow of information and the freedom to offer and to criticize hypotheses. Durkheim offered similar arguments up to a point, but came to the conclusion that political opinions should rest on "expert opinion," those without expertise being required to defer to the authority of the experts. While Dewey may not have known of Durkheim's argument, he did consider and reject this view, and he did so for frankly empirical reasons: "A class of experts is inevitably so removed from common interests as to become a class with private interests and private knowledge, which in social matters is not knowledge at all" (LW 2:364). Here Dewey links up with another of his themes, that privilege inevitably produces cognitive distortion:

All special privilege narrows the outlook of those who possess it, as well as limits the development of those not having it. A very considerable portion of what is regarded as the inherent selfishness of mankind is the product of an inequitable distribution of power—inequitable because it shuts out some from the conditions which direct and evoke their capacities, while it produces a one-sided growth in those who have privilege. (LW 7:347)

Thus, if a value as general as the value of democracy is to be rationally defended in the way Dewey advocates, the materials to be used in the defense cannot be circumscribed in advance. There is no one field of experience from which all the considerations relevant to the evaluation of democracy come.

The dilemma facing the classical defenders of democracy arose because all of them presupposed that we already know our nature and our capabilities. In contrast, Dewey's view is that we don't know what our interests and needs are or what we are capable of until we actually engage in politics. A corollary of this view is that there can be no final answer to the question of how we should live, and therefore we should always leave it open to further discussion and experimentation. That is precisely why we need democracy.

Dewey and James

While Dewey's social philosophy seems, as far as it goes, entirely correct, his moral philosophy is less satisfactory when we try to apply it to individual existential choices. To see why, consider the famous example of an existential choice that Sartre employed in *Existentialism and Humanism* (1948). It is World War II, and Pierre has to make an agonizing choice. He has to choose between joining the Resistance, which means leaving his aging mother alone on the farm, or staying and taking care of his mother, but not helping to fight the enemy. Dewey's recommendation to use intelligently guided experimentation in solving ethical problems does not really help in Pierre's case. Pierre is not out to "maximize" the "good," however conceived; he is out to do what is right. Like all consequentialists, Dewey has trouble doing justice to considerations of what is right. This is not to say that Dewey's philosophy never applies to individual existential choices. Some choices are just dumb. But Pierre is not dumb. Neither of the alternatives he is considering is in any way stupid. Yet he cannot just flip a coin.

There are, of course, problems of individual choice which can be handled just as one should handle social problems. If, for example, I cannot decide which school my child should attend, I may decide to experiment. I may send the child to a school with the idea that if it doesn't work out, I can take her out and put her in a different school. But that is not the sort of problem that Pierre faces. Pierre is not free to experiment.

What some philosophers say about such a situation is that the agent should look for a policy such that, if everyone in a similar situation were to act on that policy, the consequences would be for the best. He or she should then act on that policy. Sometimes that is reasonable, but in Pierre's situation it isn't. One of the things that is at stake in Pierre's situation is his need to decide who Pierre is. Individuality is at stake; and individuality in this sense is not just a "bourgeois value" or an Enlightenment idea. In the Jewish tradition one often quotes the saying of Rabbi Susiah, who said that in the hereafter the Lord would not ask him, "Have you been Abraham?," or "Have you been Moses?," or "Have you been Hillel?," but "Have you been Susiah?" Pierre wants to be Pierre; or as Kierkegaard would say, he wants to become who he already is (Kierkegaard 1941, 116). This is not the same thing as wanting to follow the "optimal policy"; or perhaps it is—perhaps the optimal policy in such a case is, in fact, to become who you already are. But doing that is not something that the advice to use "the scientific method" can help you very much with, even if your conception of the scientific method is as generous as Dewey's.

There are various possible future continuations of Pierre's story, no matter what decision he makes. Years afterward, if he survives, Pierre may tell the story of his life (rightly or wrongly) depicting his decision (to join the Resistance or to stay with his mother) as clearly the right decision, with no regrets or doubts, whatever the costs may have turned out to be. Or he may tell his story depicting his decision as the wrong decision, or depicting it as a "moral dilemma" to which there was no correct answer.[6] But part of the problem Pierre faces at the time he makes the decision is that he doesn't even know that he faces a "moral dilemma."

It was precisely this sort of situation that William James was addressing when he wrote the famous essay "The Will to Believe" (WWJ 6) (which James later said should have been titled "The Right to Believe"). Although this essay has received a great deal of hostile criticism, I believe that its logic is, in fact, precise and impeccable, but I will not try to defend that claim here. For James it is crucial for understanding situations like Pierre's that we recognize at least three of their features: that the choice Pierre faces is "forced," that is, these are the only options realistically available to him; that the choice is "vital"—it matters deeply to him; and that it is not possible for Pierre to decide what to do on intellectual grounds. In such a situation—and only in such a situation—James believes that Pierre has the right to believe and to act "running ahead of scientific evidence" (WWJ 6:29). The storm of controversy around "The Will to Believe" was largely occasioned by the fact that James took the decision to believe or not to believe in God to be a decision of this kind. Because religious (and even more antireligious) passions are involved, most of the critics do not even notice that the argument of "The Will to Believe" is applied by James and is meant to apply to all existential decisions.[7] Most critics also have not noticed that it is meant to apply to the individual's choice of a philosophy, including pragmatism itself.

---

[6] See also Putnam 1987. Ruth Anna Putnam uses as an example of a "moral dilemma" the predicament of a pacifist who must decide whether and to what extent he or she is willing to participate in the war effort, for example, by serving in a noncombat capacity. As she says, "sometimes only within the frame of a whole life, and sometimes only within the frame of the life of a whole community, can these decisions be evaluated" (216).

[7] This conclusion is clear not only from the essay itself, but from many other essays in which James offers similar arguments.

James believed, as Wittgenstein did,[8] that religious belief is neither rational nor irrational but *arational*. It may, of course, not be a viable option for those who are committed atheists or committed believers. But those for whom it is a viable option may be in a situation completely analogous to the one Sartre imagines (or so James believed). For James, however, the need to "believe ahead of the evidence" is not confined to religious and existential decisions. It plays an essential role in science itself. Although this is hardly controversial nowadays, it was what caused the most controversy when the lecture, "The Will to Believe," was repeated for the graduate students at Harvard University.[9] James's point—which anticipated an idea that historians of science have documented very well in recent years—was that the great innovators in science (as well as their partisans) very often believe their theories despite having very little evidence, and defend them with enormous passion.

James made a point not just about the history of science, although he was quite right about that. His claim—a claim which the logical positivists paradoxically helped to make part of the conventional philosophy of science with their sharp distinction between context of discovery and context of justification—was that science would not progress if scientists never believe or defend theories except on sufficient evidence. When it comes to the institutional decision, the decision made by academically organized science, to accept a theory or not, then it is important to apply the scientific method; in "the context of justification" (although James did not use that jargon) James was all on the side of scrupulous attention to evidence. Even before logical positivism appeared, however, James recognized that there is another moment in scientific procedure—the discovery moment—during which the same constraints cannot be applied.

The situation with respect to religion is, of course, quite different. Even though the physicist or the molecular biologist who invents a theory, or the advocates who find the theory "*sympatisch*," may believe the theory ahead of the evidence, the eventual acceptance by the scientific community depends on public confirmation. In the case of religious belief however—*pace* Alasdair MacIntyre—there is never public confirmation. Perhaps the only One who can "verify" that God exists is God Himself.[10]

---

[8] Wittgenstein's views can be found in twenty printed pages of notes taken by some of his students on his lectures on religious belief. See Wittgenstein 1966.

[9] Singer describes the reaction of the graduate students (see Singer 1923, 218–220).

[10] This is not to say that religious belief is unwarranted. I believe that it is "warranted," although not by evidence. This stance is intimately connected with a sense of existential decision.

The Pierre case is still a third kind of case.[11] In that case, as I already remarked, Pierre may come to feel afterward that he made the right choice (although he will hardly be able to "verify" that he did), but there is no guarantee that he will "know" later whether he did. James would say that in each of these cases it is valuable, both from the point of view of the individual and of the public, that there should be individuals who make such choices.

James thought that every single human being must make decisions of the kind that Pierre had to make, even if they are not as dramatic (of course, this was Sartre's point as well). Our best energies, James argued, cannot be set free unless we are willing to make the sort of existential commitment that this example illustrates. Someone who only acts when the "estimated utilities" are favorable does not live a meaningful human life. Even if I choose to devote my life to a calling whose ethical and social value is certain, say, to comforting the dying, helping the mentally ill, curing the sick, or relieving poverty, I still have to decide, not whether it is good that someone should do that thing, but whether it is good that I, Hilary Putnam, do that thing. The answer to that question cannot be a matter of well-established scientific fact, no matter how generously "scientific" is defined.

This existentialist note is unmistakable in the quotation from Fitzjames Stephen with which James ends "The Will to Believe":

> What do you think of yourself? What do you think of the world? . . .
> These are questions with which all must deal as it seems good to them.
> They are riddles of the Sphinx, and in some way or other we must deal
> with them. . . . In all important transactions of life we have to take a leap
> in the dark. . . . If we decide to leave the riddles unanswered, that is a
> choice. If we waver in our answer, that too is a choice; but whatever choice
> we make, we make it at our peril. If a man chooses to turn his back alto-
> gether on God and the future, no one can prevent him. No one can show
> beyond reasonable doubt that he is mistaken. If a man thinks otherwise,
> and acts as he thinks, I do not see how any one can prove that he is mis-
> taken. If a man thinks otherwise, and acts as he thinks, I do not see how
> any one can prove that he is mistaken. Each must act as he thinks best,
> and if he is wrong so much the worse for him. We stand on a mountain
> pass in the midst of whirling snow and blinding mist, through which we
> get glimpses now and then of paths which may be deceptive. If we stand
> still, we shall be frozen to death. If we take the wrong road, we shall be

---

[11] See Sartre 1948.

dashed to pieces. We do not certainly know whether there is any right one. What must we do? "Be strong and of a good courage." Act for the best, hope for the best, and take what comes.... If death ends all, we cannot meet death better. (WWJ 6:33)[12]

James's existentialism is all the more remarkable because he had not read a single existentialist writer (except Nietzsche, whom he pitied and read without any sensitivity).[13] At the same time, James never failed to see the need for a *check* on existential commitment. For James, my right to my own existential commitments stops where it infringes upon the similar right of my neighbor. Indeed, James described the principle of tolerance ("our ancient national doctrine of live and let live") as having "a far deeper meaning than our people now seem to imagine it to possess" (WWJ 12:5).[14] If reason (or "intelligence") cannot decide what my ultimate commitment should be, it can certainly decide from long and bitter experience that fanaticism is a terrible and destructive force. James always tempered a sympathetic understanding of the need for commitment with a healthy awareness of the horrors of fanaticism.

If Dewey is less sensitive than James to the limits of intelligence as a guide to life, it is perhaps because of Dewey's dualistic conception of human goods. For Dewey there are fundamentally two, and only two, dominant dimensions to human life: the aesthetic dimension and the social dimension, which for Dewey meant the struggle for a better world, a better society, and for the release of human potential. Dewey was criticized for seeing all of life as social action; he could and did always reply that on the contrary, in the last analysis he saw all "consummatory experience" as aesthetic. The trouble with this answer is that a bifurcation of goods into social goods, which are attained through the use of instrumental rationality, and consummatory experiences, which are ultimately aesthetic, too closely resembles a similar positivist or empiricist division of life into the prediction and control of experiences and the enjoyment of experiences. James, I think, succumbs less than Dewey to the temptation to offer a metaphysics of terminal goods.

---

[12] James is quoting James Fitzjames Stephen from *Liberty, Equality, Fraternity* (see Stephen 1874, 353).

[13] James refers to "poor Nietzsche" (WWJ 15:297).

[14] The entire concluding paragraph of the preface, from which this quotation is taken, is a paean to tolerance and an attack on "the pretension of our nation to inflict its own inner ideals and institutions *vi et armis* upon Orientals" (WWJ 12:4). James was referring to the colonization of the Philippines.

Conclusion

If, in spite of these criticisms, I still take John Dewey as one of my philo-sophical heroes, it is because his reflection on democracy never degener-ates into mere propaganda for the democratic status quo. It is true that Dewey's optimism about human potential is not something which has been proven right beyond all doubt, nor does Dewey claim that it has. As Dewey emphatically reminds us, however, neither has pessimism about human potential been proven to be right. On the contrary, to the extent that previ-ously oppressed groups have been given the opportunity to develop their capacities, those capacities have always been surprising.

I would like to close by saying a little more about this critical dimension of Dewey's thought. When Dewey speaks of using the scientific method to solve social problems, he does not mean relying on experts, who Dewey emphasizes, could not solve social problems. For one thing, experts belong to privileged classes and are affected by the rationalizations of which Dewey spoke. As an elite, they are accustomed to telling others how to solve their social problems. For Dewey, social problems are not resolved by telling other people what to do. Rather, they are resolved by releasing human energies so that people will be able to act for themselves.[15] Dewey's social philosophy is not simply a restatement of classical liberalism; for, as Dewey says,

> The real fallacy [of classical liberalism] lies in the notion that individuals have such a native or original endowment of rights, powers and wants that all that is required on the side of institutions and laws is to eliminate the obstructions they offer to the "free" play of the natural equipment of indi-viduals. The removal of obstructions did not have a liberating effect upon such individuals as were antecedently possessed of the means, intellectual and economic, to take advantage of the changed social conditions. But it left all others at the mercy of the new social conditions brought about by the freed powers of those advantageously situated. The notion that men are equally free to act if only the same legal arrangements apply equally to all—irrespective of differences in education, in command of capital, and that control of the social environment which is furnished by the institution of property—is a pure absurdity, as facts have demonstrated. Since actual, that is, effective, rights and demands are products of interactions, and are not found in the original and isolated constitution of human nature, whether

---

[15] An example that comes to mind is the energies that were released when Polish workers formed Solidarity.

moral or psychological, mere elimination of obstructions is not enough. The latter merely liberates force and ability as that happens to be distributed by past accidents of history. This "free" action operates disastrously as far as the many are concerned. The only possible conclusion, both intellectually and practically, is that the attainment of freedom conceived as power to act in accord with choice depends upon positive and constructive changes in social arrangements. (LW 3:100–101)

We too often forget that Dewey was a radical. But he was a radical democrat, not a radical scoffer at "bourgeois democracy." For Dewey, our democracy is not something to be spurned, nor is it something with which we should be satisfied. Our democracy is an emblem of what could be. What could be is a society that develops the capacities of all its men and women to think for themselves, to participate in the design and testing of social policies, and to judge the results. Perhaps for Dewey education plays the role that revolution plays in the philosophy of Karl Marx. Not that education is enough. Education is a means by which people can acquire capacities, but they have to be empowered to use those capacities. In the above passage, Dewey lists a number of things that stand in the way of that empowerment. Nevertheless, education is a precondition for democracy if democracy is a precondition for the use of intelligence to solve social problems. The kind of education that Dewey advocated did not consist in a Rousseauistic belief in the native goodness of every child, or in an opposition to discipline in public schools, or in a belief that content need not be taught. As Dewey's writings on education show, he was far more hardheaded and realistic than the "progressive educators" in all of these respects. Dewey did insist, however, that education must not be designed to teach people their place, or to defer to experts, or to accept uncritically a set of opinions. Education must be designed to produce men and women who are capable of learning on their own and of thinking critically. The extent to which we take the commitment to democracy seriously is measured by the extent to which we take the commitment to education seriously. In these days, saying these words fills me with shame for the state of democracy at the end of the twentieth century.

Works Cited

Bloom, Alan. 1987. *The Closing of the American Mind*. New York: Simon and Schuster.
Dewey, John. 1969–1991. *The Collected Words of John Dewey*, edited by Jo Ann Boydston. 37 vols. Carbondale: Southern Illinois University Press. (See List of Abbreviations.)

Gouinlock, James. 1976. Introduction to *The Moral Writings of John Dewey*, edited by James Gouinlock, xix–liv. New York: Hafner/Macmillan.

James, William. 1975–1988. *The Works of William James*, edited by Frederick H. Burkhardt, Fredson Bowers, and Ignas K. Skrupskelis. 19 vols. Cambridge: Harvard University Press. (See List of Abbreviations.)

Kierkegaard, Soren. 1941. *Concluding Unscientific Postscript*. Translated by David F. Swenson. Princeton, NJ: Princeton University Press.

MacIntyre, Alistair. 1984. *After Virtue*. Notre Dame, IN: Notre Dame University Press.

———. 1988. *Whose Justice? Which Rationality?* Notre Dame, IN: Notre Dame University Press.

Marglin, Stephen A. 1990. "Towards the Decolonization of the Mind." In *Dominating Knowledge: Development, Culture, and Resistance*, edited by Frédérique Apffel Marglin and Stephen A. Marglin, 1–28. New York: Oxford University Press.

Putnam, Hilary. 1993. "Objectivity and the Science/Ethics Distinction." In *The Quality of Life*, edited by Martha Nussbaum and Amartya Sen, 143–157. New York: Oxford University Press.

Putnam, Ruth Anna. 1987. "Weaving Seamless Webs." *Philosophy* 62(240): 207–220.

Rawls, John. 1971. *A Theory of Justice*. Cambridge: Belknap Press of Harvard University Press.

Sartre, Jean-Paul. 1948. *Existentialism and Humanism*. Translated by P. Mairet. London: Methuen.

Singer, E. A., Jr. 1923. *Modern Thinkers and Present Problems: An Approach to Modern Philosophy through Its History*. New York: Henry Holt.

Stephen, James Fitzjames. 1874. *Liberty, Equality, Fraternity*. London: Smith, Elder.

Walzer, Michael. 1987. *Interpretation and Social Criticism*. Cambridge: Harvard University Press.

Williams, Bernard. 1985. *Ethics and the Limits of Philosophy*. Cambridge: Harvard University Press.

Wittgenstein, Ludwig. 1966. *Lectures and Conversations on Aesthetics, Psychology, and Religious Belief*. Edited by Cyril Barrett. Oxford: Blackwell.

CHAPTER 15 | Dewey and the Problem of Justice

PETER T. MANICAS

THE PROBLEM OF JUSTICE is again a topic of lively debate. The civil rights movement, our anguish over Vietnam, the women's movement, our continuing unease over the economy, skepticism regarding the system of criminal justice, and doubts about our educational institutions identify the main historical forces and problems which underlie the current discussion. The symptoms and issues cover a very wide range: antibusing violence, affirmative action and ERA backlash, proposals for death penalty legislation and attacks on the rights of the accused and the arrested, cutbacks in education and social services, and tax "revolt."

At the level of social theory, John Rawls's *A Theory of Justice* (1971), generated a veritable industry. His difficult and highly praised book seems to have arrived at exactly the right time, perhaps because it offered a powerful statement and defense of what is probably mainstream liberal thinking on justice. Rawls's theory is individualistic, but his recognition of "the least advantaged," coupled with his attention to what he called "pure procedural justice," seemed to confirm our most basic intuitions about justice. To be sure, there were immediate criticisms of some of the more vulnerable arguments, but these received a greater response from the right than from the left. Indeed, Robert Nozick's (1974) critical treatment gave him a recent cover of the popular and liberal *New York Times Magazine*. Not only was the presence there of a philosopher significant and unusual, but he was there heralded as the most articulate of the new spokesmen of conservative, individualistic thinking on justice.

In this context, it may be useful to consider the writings of John Dewey, America's foremost social philosopher. And in this context, if one surveys

the voluminous writings of Dewey, writings which span over seven decades until his death in 1952, the first thing that one notices is the relative
inattention paid by Dewey to the problem of justice. Altogether, there are
perhaps not more than a dozen pages of sustained discussions devoted explicitly to the topic. These discussions are insightful and important, little
gems, and in what follows, it will be a pleasure to appeal to them. But the
first task, really the main task of this presentation, is to try to explain this
apparent imbalance in Dewey's attention.

Dewey's lack of discussion of the theory and problems of justice is not
to be explained by a failure to *see* problems, nor by an unwillingness to
deal with them at the theoretical or practical level. Indeed, the two most
substantial discussions of justice were written during two periods of acute
crisis in our economy, during the 1890s and again, in 1932. Similarly,
Dewey's active involvement in a host of public matters of social and political nature is too well known to recite here. Several of these, e.g., the
trial of Sacco and Vanzetti, raised serious questions of justice (Dykhuizen
1973, 234). There are, I believe, two sets of reasons which do explain this
imbalance. They are important and give us insight into both our problems and Dewey's unique strengths as a social philosopher. One set of
reasons specifically regards this stance. As a social philosopher, Dewey
was a writer who aimed not to write a social philosophy—a *doctrine*—but
who aimed rather to show *how* we must try to seek solution of our social
problems. The other set regards the very *idea* of justice. It seems to me that
Dewey, for various reasons to be detailed, sought to *displace* justice as the
central concept of social philosophy. However, for these same reasons, he
found himself using the term less and less, until ultimately he abandoned
it altogether. These two sets of reasons are definitely related, but it may
nevertheless be desirable to treat them more or less separately, taking the
idea of justice first.

The Concepts of Justice

It is possible to show that there are two dominating conceptions of justice
in Western civilization. The first had its home and only full articulation
in the ancient Greek polis.[1] Plato and Aristotle, of course, develop it with
sophistication and vigor. The other concept of justice was also first formulated in the ancient Greek polis, in Periclean Athens. It is associated with

---

[1] See Manicas 1977.

the names of Democritus and Protagoras. But this idea of justice did not come into its own until the modern period, with Hobbes and Locke, Kant, Hume, and nineteenth-century liberal philosophy. We should call it the liberal concept of justice. It remains the dominating concept in the West, and Rawls and his more conservative critics, despite differences, stand in this tradition.

The liberal concept of justice favors atomistic metaphors and voluntary relations, e.g., the contract; it is conventionalistic, arguing that justice and political society are "artifacts" deliberately and rationally constructed; it is legalistic, emphasizing formal and procedural justice; it employs market notions of distributive justice, presupposes scarcity and finally, it is "harsh and hard." As Hume put it, justice is the "mean virtue."

By contrast, the Platonic-Aristotelian notion of justice favors organic metaphors and conceives of human relations and political society as "natural"; it presupposes natural inequalities, emphasizes morality instead of law, and thinks of justice very widely. As Aristotle said, it is "the whole of virtue."

While this is not the place to develop this radical contrast, an illustration of each concept may be helpful if only to fix our ideas.

Plato's *Republic* aimed to answer the question: What is justice? For him, it will be remembered, justice is a condition of the soul, a "psychic harmony," a prerequisite of just acts and, crucially, of well-being and happiness (*eudaimonia*) itself. Parallel with this analysis, justice is a condition of the polis which is itself constructed as an organic unity. Each element, "class" or person, has a task (*ergon*) which, when performed well, contributes to the well-being of the totality. The four virtues, Wisdom, Courage, Temperance, and Justice, are each defined as functions of the social and psychic unities of society and self.

At the very opposite pole is Thomas Hobbes. Where men are in "the natural condition," for Hobbes, there is neither justice nor injustice. The consensually introduced mechanism of impersonal law which constitutes political society also constitutes the very possibility of justice. Once done, natural equity and justice are replaced by one principle, "performance of the covenant." The whole apparatus of customary rights and privileges is similarly reduced: "To each according to the agreements he has made."

To be sure, Hobbes's theory was too extreme, too tough-minded. And no doubt, subsequent versions of "contract" theory from Locke to Rawls responded with corrections and additions. Nevertheless, there is a clearly identifiable tradition which must be sharply separated from the earlier one.

Where then does Dewey stand as regards these two concepts and traditions of justice? In the last analysis, Dewey could not accept either, even if he did pull strongly toward the Greek.

In his *Syllabus* of 1884, Dewey noted that "in many respects, the discussions of virtue in Plato and Aristotle are still unequaled." Indeed, following them, if in his own novel fashion, he argued that that "courage, temperance and wisdom denote simply phases of every moral act" and that "the name is given according to the phase which, in a given case, happens to be dominant." "Justice, then," argues Dewey,

> is the name for the deed in its entirety.... It is not another virtue, it is the system of virtue, the organized doing: whose organic members are wisdom, the will to know; courage, the impulse to reach; control, the acquired power to do. (EW 4:362, 357)

As this text shows, Dewey is very, very Greek in holding that justice is the virtue of a unity "organically" related, even if at the same time, Dewey rejected the "faculty" psychology which is generally imputed to Greek moral philosophy. He is Greek, too, in couching virtue in terms of self-development and self-realization, even if for him in contrast to the Greeks, the underlying notion of human nature is open, dynamic, and changing; not closed, static, and fixed.[2] Dewey and the Greeks agreed that persons were doers, exerting, developing and enjoying human powers and capacities and that the concern for "realization" of these powers should be at the center of a moral and social philosophy.[3] But if so, then "justice" could not be reduced to "obedience to law" or to "just desert." His text continues:

> the current distinction between justice as penal, and justice as concrete recognition of positive merit by the share awarded an agent ... is far too rigid.
> ... Unconsciously there is smuggled in the assumption that worth is static; that what a man has done is somehow complete in itself, and serves to indicate his merit, and therefore, the way he should be treated. Service is taken as something rendered, not as a function. (EW 4:359)

The idea that "worth" is static and that "deserts" and "entitlements" are like commodities, exchangeable as equivalents for "things," exactly

---

[2] Cf. here, of course, *Human Nature and Conduct.*
[3] C.B. Macpherson (1973) has argued that J. S. Mill tried to incorporate this fundamental feature of Greek idealism into his liberalism, though the result was less than satisfactory.

characterizes the market conception of justice, the dominant mode of modern thinking on the subject. Dewey struggles in this text, as in others, to drive home the limiting and incomplete nature of this framework for justice. He writes:

> When it was said that the ordinary concept of desert concealed a momentous assumption, it was meant that the whole dualism of justice and love is involved. If justice be conceived as mere return to an individual of what he has done, if his deed, in other words, be separated from his vital, developing self, and if, therefore, the "equivalent return" ignore the profound and persistent presence of self-hood in the deed, then it is true that justice is narrow in its sphere, harsh in form, requiring to be supplemented by another virtue of larger outlook and freer play—Grace. But if justice be the returning to a man of the equivalent of his deed, and if, in truth, the sole thing which equates the deed is self, then quite otherwise. Love is justice brought to self-consciousness; justice with a full, instead of a partial standard of value; justice with a dynamic, instead of a static, scale of equivalency. (EW 4:361)

Our "ordinary" sense of justice is narrow, is harsh. Recognizing, though ambivalently and sometimes incoherently, that persons are dynamic selves relating humanly to one another and to the world, we think of justice as requiring supplementation, by mercy, by kindness, by love. But surely *that* misleads as well. It is not either justice or love. It is not justice or charity—from *caritas*, "love." This accepts the dualism and allows us to paste over *injustice* with *gratuities*. But how to overcome this dualism? Dewey had it right: Once we reject the idea that "deeds" are "things" to be exchanged for equivalents, we undermine the dualism, for then it is possible to link the deed with the self. But Dewey remains contaminated by the market theory of justice. Significantly, he puts the matter conditionally: *if* justice be the returning to a person of the equivalent of his deed. And he lets us muse as to whether he would have preferred to deny the hypothesis altogether. But *if* we are to think of justice in these terms, and as moderns, it is hard to see how to do otherwise, then for Dewey, at least at this point, let us try *not* to disconnect the deed from the vital, changing self.

Dewey will return to these themes just twice more, in the *Ethics* written collaboratively with James Tufts, published originally in 1908 and then in substantial revision in 1932. As in the earlier *Syllabus*, Dewey focuses on the notion that justice is "hard" and "harsh" and he develops another dimension of this attitude. Here, he argues that it comes from identifying justice "with the working of some fixed and abstract law ... as if man was made for law, not law for man" (MW 5:373). Although pursuing this idea systematically would take us directly into Dewey's problem-centered and inquiry-oriented style of social philosophy, we should pause here if only briefly to emphasize the pervasiveness of the notion, as it bears on the problem of justice.

Dewey clearly saw that alongside the market conceptualization of justice was another which derived ultimately from Kant. It put heavy emphasis on duty and obligation and its most austere and rigorous form is captured by the Latin *fiat justitia, ruat caelum*, "Let justice be done, though the heavens fall." Dewey took this phrase as the title for a brief, popular essay written for the *New Republic* in 1917. Rejecting the legalism and formalism which so typically characterizes "moral" discussions of justice, whether of war and international relations, as in this case, or of race or sex, Dewey identified such ethics as "resolutely irrelevant to the circumstances of action and the conditions of life" (MW 10:281). In another and earlier 1914 essay, entitled "Nature and Reason in Law," Dewey pregnantly characterized "the chief working difference between moral philosophies in their application to law." It was, he argued, that "some of them seek for an antecedent principle by which to decide; while others recommend the consideration of the specific consequences that flow from treating a specific situation this way or that, using the antecedent materials and rules as guides of intellectual analysis but not as norms of decision" (MW 7:61). This text, we might note here, could well be the point of departure for an extended analysis of the current debate over affirmative action programs as, of course, it compresses an entire potential legal philosophy.

For Dewey, this methodological inversion explained in part the limiting and narrowing conception of justice. And in the 1908 discussion, Dewey again calls, optimistically, for "the transformation of the conception of justice so that it joins hands with love and sympathy" (MW 5:373).

But one can hardly be heartened by these remarks. The problem seems inescapable. The liberal notion of justice was liberating insofar as it made men indiscriminately subject to impersonal law and insofar as it broke the basis of "privilege" based on hereditary status, but Dewey saw early on that the liberal notion was far too narrow, too rigid. So he struggled to enlarge it, to remedy its partiality, to supplement it. And if we grant that love and sympathy are the requisite supplementations, one may legitimately wonder how *good* a merely just society or merely just person would be. For the Greeks, this could not be a question. With their notion of justice, the just man and the just society had to be good. And, of course, if love and sympathy are the requisite supplementations to our "ordinary" sense of justice, then one may legitimately wonder how we are to proceed. Indeed, the deeper Dewey looked into the problems and issues of liberal society, the more disjointed became the effort to transform and widen liberal justice.

Liberal Society and Distributive Justice

Dewey was never sanguine regarding the mechanisms of distribution in liberal society. Still less was he mystified by the rhetoric of the current theories. This may be brought out by considering Tufts's contribution to the collaborative 1908 edition of their *Ethics*. Dewey must surely have endorsed the pertinent pages. Indeed, in the revision of 1932, it seems that Dewey himself wrote the crucial chapter 21 which restated the issues and reaffirmed their earlier stance. We may look first at the earlier version, noting well the early date of the text.

Characteristically, the locus of the critique is "individualism." They begin by arguing that if we take a purely "formal" view and make "formal freedom of contract the only criterion, then any price is fair which both parties agree to" (MW 5:475). This position, characteristic of Hobbes, and of classical and neoclassical political economy, is substantially the position argued for by Nozick in the recent work cited earlier. Although the argument cannot be developed here, Nozick's "entitlement" theory, while very much enriched by detail and the sophistication of modern decision theory, is, I would argue, subject quite precisely to Tufts's criticism. It is this: If the exchange is to be fair, the parties to the bargain must be equal. "*But in a large part of the exchanges of business and services, the two parties are not equal.*"[4] In other terms, where some must accept the conditions of the contract, "formal freedom of contract" is not a sufficient condition. In his 1932 statement of this theory, Dewey characterizes it even more economically. Its motto is to each "what he can get through his ability, his shrewdness, his advantageous economic position due to inherited wealth and every other factor which adds to his bargaining power." Dewey rightly notes that "this is the existing method under capitalism" (LW 7:408), as

---

[4] Dewey gives the same argument against "classical individualism and free enterprise" in his lectures in China. See Dewey 1973, 113.

today, owners of baseball teams, school boards, and the AMA tend to forget.

The "take-advantage-of-your-bargaining-power" theory of justice has another, less rude, version. It is characterized by Dewey by the motto: "To each what he earns." This theory, plausible enough on its face, due perhaps to the multitude of difficulties concealed in the notion of "earn," does not, argues Dewey, characterize capitalist distribution. But it must be rejected in any case, since it cannot be realized. It cannot be realized because production is *social* (LW 7:408). The point is important but often misunderstood.

In "producing"—toasters, services, skills, or knowledge—individuals employ knowledge, skills, and instruments which are the legacy of previous generations of workers. Moreover, and characteristically, "products"—including knowledge—are jointly produced in the more obvious sense that they are products of many hands and minds. Suppose, then, we take the gross national product to represent the combined social product—an entirely artificial measure for the "product" we need to measure, but useful perhaps to fix our ideas. The earning theory of distribution, then (like its sophisticated relative, modern productivity theory), presupposes that it is possible to divide up the GNP and assign to each individual exactly what is hers or his. No part of this is to be shared on grounds that we can't disentangle our contribution; no part is a residue earned by past labor and no part is earned by no one. The problem here is not simply whether this division is *fair*, whether each receives a just share, but whether, indeed, any coherent sense can be given to the idea that respective contributions to the social product can be so disentangled. For Dewey, rightly, it was obvious that they could not.[5]

But this is not the end of the difficulties for the individualistic theories, for as Dewey and Tufts write, they suffer from a serious moral failure. Achievement and failure, what one does "contribute," or "earn," is a function of three things: heredity, social advantage and the socially produced

---

[5] It may be noted here that modern price theory employs the fiction that marginal products are so divisible. This makes for quite a respectable mathematical theory, useful as a praxeology. But it doesn't follow that a theory of justice which assumes the fiction is intelligible. In this regard, Nozick's criticism of Rawls is interesting. Rawls sees, if not clearly, that "social cooperation" does make a difference. By assuming that marginal products can be "disentangled," Nozick argues that Rawls's account of the "problem" created by social cooperation is mistaken. Nozick does show, however, that Rawls's individualism does not square with his view of "social cooperation." See Nozick 1974. This choice of inconsistency or unintelligibility would have been avoided had these contemporary writers understood (or read and understood) Dewey's early critique of individualism.

conditions of knowledge and environment, and, finally, individual effort. It is not a matter of individual effort alone. It is at this juncture that Rawls's influential theory departs from traditional individualisms, for with Tufts and Dewey, Rawls agrees that accidents of birth—the good fortune to be born rich and handsome—are not *in themselves* morally relevant. And indeed, if so, then one can ask, as does Dewey and Tufts, "If all men are accounted equal in the State, why not in wealth?" (MW 5:488).

It is perhaps here that the contrast in the orientation of Dewey and of Rawls is most graphic and where, at the same time, Dewey reveals both his greatest strength as a social philosopher and perhaps, as well, his greatest weakness.

Consider Rawls's response first.[6] For Rawls, the family is the key problem and, short of restructuring it, natural talents and social advantages will inevitably be rewarded. I think that it can easily be shown that Rawls gives up too quickly here. Indeed, as we suggest, Dewey and Tufts have a more encouraging response. But Rawls's originality begins at exactly this point, for his famous "difference principle" is meant precisely to justify inequalities which, however they come about, had best not be removed. His argument is quite straightforward. An egalitarian distribution would be inefficient but an efficient system need not be just. It would be just, however, if social and economic inequalities were arranged so that there was "fair equality of opportunity" and, crucially, so that the "least advantaged" were better off than they otherwise would have been. If Rawls is right, something looking very much like our system is, in his terms, "nearly just." To be sure, we have some way to go in achieving "fair equality of opportunity"—notice that this still rewards natural ability and that, for Rawls, the family remains (and will remain) a crucial limitation even on this. Nevertheless, it is fair to say that, for Rawls, we are doing perhaps as well as can be expected.

Tufts and Dewey take an entirely different tack. After evaluating the extant theories, they offer, instead of their own theory, what they call "a working program." The gist of it is contained in a short paragraph:

A man's power is due (1) to physical heredity; (2) to social heredity . . . (3) to his own efforts. Individualism may properly claim this third factor. It is just to treat men unequally so far as their efforts are unequal. It is socially desirable to give as much incentive as possible to the full development of

---

[6] The following is drawn from Rawls (1971), especially from sections 12, 13, 17, 46, 77.

everyone's powers. *But this very same reason demands that in the first two respects we treat men as equally as possible.* (MW 5:490)

This working program is *radical* since, ultimately, it means that no unequal benefits should accrue to persons exclusively on the basis of their natural talents or on the basis of socially derived advantages. But it is a "working program" in the sense that it leaves entirely open the means by which the ideal is to be achieved. It does not demand radical revolution in order to achieve a radical restructuring of society, even if the realization of the ideal would involve a radical restructuring of society. And it does not insist on any particular ameliorative reforms, even if there are steps which could and should be taken. And it is in this that Dewey's greatest strength and weakness may be revealed. For it is not at all easy to judge whether or not Dewey saw *how* radical the ideal was or how radical would the changes have to be to bring the ideal into existence. In both the 1908 and the 1932 discussions, education characteristically is emphasized as means. But "conditions of food, labor and housing" and "the importance of private property" are also identified. In the later discussion, Dewey responded passionately to the notion that because per capita income had increased greatly—shades of Rawls!—it was "foolish" to raise the question of distribution. Indeed, in direct contrast to Rawls, he argued that wealth, not income is the crucial variable:

The individuals or corporations that have great wealth undertake great enterprises. They control for better or worse the wages and living conditions of great numbers. (LW 7:407)[7]

These same sorts of criticisms are found in many of Dewey's writings and demonstrate that he was keenly aware of the bearing of the system of private property not only on the problem of justice, but on the problem of freedom and democracy as well.[8] Yet, many commentators have found grounds for arguing that Dewey was naive in having unwarranted hopes for the efficacy of education even as an ameliorative factor. This is probably so.[9]

---

[7] Rawls obliterates the distinction between income and wealth by inattention. He persistently refers to "income and wealth" but never addresses the difference. Accordingly, for him it would seem to be unimportant.

[8] See, e.g., *The Public and Its Problems* (LW 2:298f, 301–302); "Philosophies of Freedom" (LW 3:100); *Liberalism and Social Action* (LW 11:45–46).

[9] For example, Bernstein 1971, 228; Mills 1964, 333.

The current backlash on affirmative action and ERA, the decisive, if inevitable failures of poverty programs and efforts to guarantee equal education for all, would indeed have been disheartening to Dewey. And as disheartening, perhaps, is the renewed enthusiasm for what are really quite worn-out individualistic theories of justice. His own theory could be stated in a sentence, first written in 1891: "What is due the self is that it be treated as self" (MW 5:359). In the last analysis, Dewey preferred working programs over theories. Indeed, this takes us to the final part of our account.

Social Knowledge and Social Philosophy

It is another of the commonplaces of commentators on John Dewey's thought that he was preoccupied with method, indeed sometimes to the extent that *content* altogether seemed to dissolve.[10] This is not the place to examine all the difficult questions which attend this criticism, but as regards our particular problem, the problem of justice, I think that it must be said that Dewey's social philosophy does represent a departure from traditional social philosophies and that this shift is perhaps best construed as an orientation which displaced the problem of justice as a substantive theoretical problem and replaced it with an orientation which emphasized problems and ideas that connected more directly to method and to practice.

This alternative point of departure in Dewey's thought may be best expressed in *Reconstruction in Philosophy* (1920) although many texts confirm the idea. Identifying three alternative social philosophies, the individualistic, the socialist, and the organic, Dewey argued that all "suffer from a common defect."

> They are all committed to the logic of general notions under which specific situations are to be brought.... They are general answers supposed to have universal meaning that covers and dominates all particulars. Hence, they do not assist inquiry. They close it. They are not instrumentalities to be employed and tested in clarifying concrete social difficulties.... The social philosopher, dwelling in the region of his concepts, solves problems by showing relationships of ideas, instead of by helping men solve problems in the concrete. (MW 12:188, 189, 192)

This is the touchstone idea of Dewey's emphasis on "inquiry," "experimentalism," and "instrumentalism." Within Dewey's frame, current debate on

---

[10] The most recent discussion and relevant to what follows is Frankel 1977.

justice would suffer from the same defects of abstraction, from the same irrelevance to the *actual* conditions of education, of work, and of association, from the same aristocratic detachment that seems presupposed by the idea that "philosophers" can *solve* human problems.

Dewey's critics on the left are also correct, however, in judging that his experimentalist and method-centered attitude left him vulnerable to two alternative—and at bottom inconsistent—sorts of readings.

On the one hand, Dewey's efforts to shift the focus of social philosophy away from "doctrine" led some to see Dewey as advocating an engineering and scientistic conception of social philosophy and inquiry. This view, inspired by Dewey's repeated assertion that social questions could be treated "scientifically" and "experimentally," meant for those readers something like the sort of practice which presumably goes in "laboratories" manned by persons in white coats and constrained by canons of "efficiency" and "positive" control. On this view—technocratic and still fashionable—a new breed of "social scientists" would provide that "expert" knowledge that would speedily solve concrete social problems.

In the last analysis, this reading cannot be sustained, even if Dewey did give ample room for misconstrual. Perhaps his willingness and openness to incorporate and encourage ideas which seemed congenial to him further confused matters. One might mention here his long association with A. F. Bentley and his attraction in the late 1920s to the "operationist" views of Bridgman.[11]

On the other hand, it led others to see Dewey as committed to a kind of *unprincipled* reformism, to a defense of patchwork suggestions as responses to the outcropping of crisis. Dewey was reformist in his attitude, rejecting consistently the idea that societies could be *intelligently* transformed by radical and revolutionary programs. His approach was "piecemeal," a call to deal amelioratively with concrete and particular problems. Thus, for him, Marxism was "doctrinaire" in offering "sweeping generalizations" and "general solutions" to "general problems." Dewey was surely sensitive to the problem of the "unintended consequences" of radical change and to the ease with which progressive movements become appropriated and distorted. But it must be said as well that while his *ideals* were radical, as we already noted, his appreciation of obstacles preventing their realization was probably naive. Nevertheless, his reformism was hardly unprincipled and his shift in focus was both sound and important. Indeed, I believe that there is much to be learned from him on this score.

---

[11] Although the point can hardly be developed here, there is a "positivist" strain in Dewey. Unfortunately, it is a strain emphasized by his friends and enemies alike.

For Dewey, the problem of justice, as the problems of freedom and democracy, cannot be "solved" by "experts" or by philosophers. They could only be solved—if that is still the right word—by people in the everyday world in their doings and sufferings. Dewey seems to have grasped this and that is why, in the last analysis, the "content" of his social philosophy seems so thin and, finally, so painfully obvious. There are, it seems to me, but two items in it: First, there is the idea that "the level of action fixed by embodied intelligence is always the important thing" (LW 2:366), and second, the idea that "democracy is a way of life, individual and social" (qtd. in Ratner 1939, 400). These crucially related ideas defined the limits of social philosophy. Movement in the direction of their realization was movement toward an ideal in the only sense of ideal which Dewey allowed—"the tendency and movement of something which exists carried to his final limit" (LW 2:328). As with justice, they identified a "working program" and, crucially, a program which could be implemented *only* by people in their individual and collective doings and sufferings.

This did not mean, for Dewey, that philosophy had *nothing* to do. Indeed, there was a great deal to be said about both ideals and about their mode of realization. The whole of Dewey's extensive writings on methods of inquiry and on education, both in and out of the school, issue in the idea of "action fixed by embodied intelligence." As Dewey saw it, the application of "intelligence" to social problems meant not the application of new techniques by "experts," however defined, nor did it reduce to the application of antecedently derived principles to concrete particular situations. Rather, the canons had to be generated in inquiry and realized in practice. And this kind of social knowledge "does not yet exist" (LW 2:366). "The only possible solution," he wrote, to the problems generated by interdependence requires "the perfecting of the means and ways of communication of meanings so that genuine shared interest in the consequences of interdependent activities may inform desire and effort and thereby direct action" (LW 2:332). And as this text suggests, this was both condition and consequence of democracy as a way of life, the other guiding ideal of Dewey's social philosophy. Accordingly, the whole of his writings on democracy, community, freedom, and culture bear on this second theme. Keeping this in mind allows us, finally, to grasp the full force of this wonderful text:

> Philosophy recovers itself when it ceases to be a device for dealing with the problems of philosophers and becomes a method, cultivated by philosophers, for dealing with the problem of men. (MW 10:46)

If it is philosophers who have the task of articulating and "cultivating" these methods, it is people themselves who must employ them. Dewey was insufficiently radical regarding the difficulties standing in the way of transforming "The Great Society" into "The Great Community," but he never fell victim to pat solutions. He saw that we never begin anew, from scratch, from nothing. We either sustain the inherited forms or we transform them, purposefully and intelligently, whimsically and stupidly, coercively or cooperatively. Dewey put his faith in the possibility that action could be conjoint, purposeful, and intelligent. He put the matter crisply in his 1919/20 lectures in China. Responding to the question, "Where should we start in reforming our society?" Dewey answered:

> we must start by reforming the component institutions of the society. Families, schools, local governments, the central government—all these must be reformed, but they must be reformed by the people who constitute them, working as individuals—in collaboration with other individuals, each accepting his own responsibility. . . . Social progress is neither an accident nor a miracle; it is the sum of efforts made by individuals whose actions are guided by intelligence. (Dewey 1973, 62f)

But he also saw, as John J. McDermott has written, that if "the responsibility is ours and ours alone," the transformation of the processes and forms of living is, at the same time, "laced with chance" (McDermott 1973, xxix).

Works Cited

Bernstein, Richard J. 1971. *Praxis and Action*. Philadelphia: University of Pennsylvania Press.

Dewey, John. 1973. *Lectures in China, 1919–1920*, edited and translated by Robert W. Clopton and Tsuin-Chen Ou. Honolulu: University Press of Hawaii.

———. 1969–1991. *The Collected Works of John Dewey*, edited by Jo Ann Boydston. 37 vols. Carbondale: Southern Illinois University Press. (See List of Abbreviations.)

Dykhuizen, George. 1973. *The Life and Mind of John Dewey*. Carbondale: Southern Illinois Press.

Frankel, Charles. 1977. "Dewey's Social Philosophy." In *New Studies in the Philosophy of John Dewey*, edited by S. M. Cahn, 3–44. Hanover, NH: University Press of New England.

Macpherson, C. B. 1973. *Democratic Theory*. Oxford: Clarendon Press.

Manicas, Peter T. 1977. "Two Concepts of Justice." *Journal of Chinese Philosophy* 4: 99–121.

McDermott, John J., ed. 1973. *The Philosophy of John Dewey*. Chicago: University of Chicago Press.

Mills, C. Wright. 1964. *Sociology and Pragmatism*. New York: Oxford University Press.

Nozick, Robert. 1974. *Anarchy, State and Utopia*. New York: Basic Books.

Ratner, Joseph, ed. 1939. *Intelligence in the Modern World*. New York: Modern Library.

Rawls, John. 1971. *A Theory of Justice*. Cambridge: Belknap Press of Harvard University Press.

| Pragmatism, Democracy, and
the Need for a Theory of Justice

ROBERT B. TALISSE

THIS CHAPTER EXPLORES ISSUES emerging from the surprising fact that
pragmatist political philosophers, from John Dewey to the present, have
not attempted to theorize justice. I begin (in the first section) by raising
the puzzle that this omission poses and arguing that the omission poses
a problem for pragmatist democratic theory. Then (in the second section)
I sketch a broad and preliminary view of how pragmatists should begin
thinking about justice. Finally (in the third section), I offer a speculative
diagnosis of why pragmatists have tended to overlook justice.

A Puzzle and a Problem

When looking for pragmatist options in political philosophy, one naturally
turns to the writings of John Dewey. There, one finds a systematic and
highly attractive civic vision rooted in a dynamic conception of human experience that in turn depicts democracy as the social and political embodi-
ment of collective human intelligence. One could say that Dewey's entire
philosophy simply *is* a conception of democracy.

Unsurprisingly, then, Dewey's view of democracy is uncommonly
broad in scope. Dewey's democratic vision drives his analyses of many of
the central concepts of political philosophy that are today commonly regarded as analytically distinct from democracy, including freedom, rights,
authority, individuality, autonomy, community, culture, and civic virtue.
One also finds much more in Dewey; for example, Dewey thought that the
democratic theorist needs to supply a theory of education, a conception

of the relation between science and democracy, a detailed account of the role of art in a democratic society, and a practical model for social action. Consequently, Dewey's writings continue to provide vital resources for contemporary political philosophers. It is no wonder that contemporary pragmatists working in political philosophy are nearly unanimous in taking Dewey as their lodestar and inspiration.[1] And even those contemporary pragmatist political philosophers who do not ally with Dewey nonetheless propose a conception of democracy that is of the same theoretical *kind* as the Deweyan view.[2]

However, one largely unnoticed oddity of Dewey's vast writings in political philosophy is that they contain no sustained discussion of justice. Despite his having devoted sustained attention to neighboring concepts, justice is never brought within his philosophical purview. To be sure, Dewey occasionally uses the word "justice"; however, these sporadic remarks are uncharacteristically platitudinous.[3] Indeed, the concerns that drive familiar disputes about justice seem invisible to Dewey. Yet, given Dewey's own social commitments and much of his social activism, he surely was familiar with such concerns. Prima facie, the absence is puzzling.

One might seek to explain the absence of discussions of justice in Dewey's work as reflecting his judgment that the concept is irretrievably infected with the apparatus of an obsolete mode of philosophizing. To be sure, it is not uncommon for Dewey to simply decline to employ the concepts and problems of traditional philosophy. Yet this explanation only goes so far. When Dewey intends to dispose of a philosophical concept or problem, he typically devotes considerable effort to *exposing* the flaws within it. Consider his extensive critiques of "the industry of epistemology" (EW 5:16; MW 10:23) and its corresponding "spectator theory of knowledge" (LW 4:17ff.), or his trenchant criticism of traditional

---

[1] For a small sample of explicit expressions of allegiance to Dewey among contemporary pragmatist social and political theorists, see Anderson 2006; Rogers 2009; Bernstein 2010; Knight and Johnson 2011; Kitcher 2012; Ansell 2011; McGowan 2012; and Johnson 2014.
[2] I count myself (2007; 2011) and Cheryl Misak (2000; 2004) as the principal non-Deweyan pragmatist democratic theorists. For the present purposes, however, the debates among Deweyan and non-Deweyan pragmatist views of democracy are not relevant; as I'll note below, those involved in those debates are all epistemic participationists.
[3] Remarks like the following are typical. "A good society should aim to secure justice, should keep a right perspective as to the various goods which are desirable, should take account of all the human relations, and should move toward raising all men toward that measure of equality and democracy which has been the ideal and aspiration not only of the finer spirits but of increasing multitudes in the modern world" (LW 7:436). "In a word, a man has not to do Justice . . . he has to do justly. And this means that he has to respond to the actual relations in which he finds himself. . . . to do justly is to give a fit and impartial regard to each" (EW 3:106–107).

liberalism's conception of the state (LW 2:259–303). In these and many other instances, Dewey engages in a kind of *unmasking* of the tacit presuppositions and disguised commitments that are entrenched in traditional philosophical vocabulary, thereby providing *reasons* for discarding them as outmoded artifacts. Moreover, when Dewey dispenses with a concept, he typically proposes a *replacement* for it, as when he introduces "warranted assertion" to play the role of truth (LW 12:16), and "intelligence" to play the role of knowledge (MW 12:108). Had Dewey thought that justice should be discarded in this way, he would have said so, and he would have proposed a successor. Yet one finds in Dewey no reconstructing of justice. One instead finds an atypical silence.

Dewey's inattention to justice is made all the more striking by the positive content of Dewey's view of democracy. In *The Public and Its Problems* (LW 2), Dewey introduces a framework according to which the fundamental unit of political analysis is not the individual, the party, or the voting bloc, but rather the *public*. On Dewey's view, publics emerge out of the recognition of shared problems, and democracy provides the social conditions by which the information distributed across citizens can be harnessed and employed in political decision-making and social action. This image of democracy is undeniably attractive. Yet Dewey takes no account of the ways in which socially and economically entrenched forms of exclusion, marginalization, and homogenization block access to membership in publics; similarly, he provides no analysis of the social mechanisms that would be required in order to assure citizens the kind of equality necessary to make democratic participation effective. And he gives no analysis of the multiple ways in which material disadvantages are causally connected to democratic deficits. Given these omissions, Dewey's culminating celebration of the "face-to-face intercourse" of the "local community," and his corresponding warnings concerning the "invasion" of community by "outside and uncontrolled agencies" (LW 2:367), take on a disquieting resonance.[4]

Notice that the issues that Dewey overlooks all fall within the purview of a conception of justice. Justice is the concept by means of which we examine questions of social inclusion, membership, entitlements to political participation, and the distribution of the material and social benefits and

---

[4] Dewey's further claim that proper community (thus proper democracy) is possible only among those who share "signs and symbols" and a common language (LW 2:371) seems positively irresponsible in light of the fact that he's writing in the wake of the Sacco and Vanzetti trial and its accompanying anti-immigrant sentiments.

burdens of political association. Another way to put this point is to say that when we think of the social failure manifest in familiar practices of institutionalized social marginalization, exclusion, discrimination, and disadvantage, we reach for the concept of justice; we think these ills are not merely *bad*, they are *wrong*. And any society in which they are rampant and entrenched is not merely *in need of improvement*, but also *illegitimate*. Accordingly, without a conception of justice, Dewey has scant resources for drawing the crucial distinction between the kinds of social failures that are merely *regrettable errors* or examples of *ineffective policy* and those that are *delegitimizing*.

The need for the conceptual resources to draw such a distinction is all the more pronounced for a *participatory* and *epistemic* conception of democracy such as Dewey embraces. Recall that on Dewey's view, the *point* of democratic participation is the *sharing of intelligence* among differently positioned citizen-inquirers. Thus, unlike other participatory views, which tend to focus on competition among *interest groups* for political influence (Dahl 1956) or *consensus building* among individuals with antecedently opposed interests (Barber 1984), Deweyan publics are primarily *problem-solving* entities. Therefore they are largely *epistemic* in nature. Dewey's thought, again, is that the aim of democracy is to harness the full potential of human experience, both individual and collective, for addressing and responding to problematic situations.

Any theorist favoring an epistemic participationist view of democracy should quickly come to appreciate the ways in which the distribution of the social and material burdens and benefits of political association can impact the ability of individuals to engage in the activities that the Deweyan view takes to be constitutive of democracy. When democracy is understood to be centrally a matter of shared collective inquiry, then democracy is stunted when key social and material resources are distributed in ways that make access to and participation in those processes significantly more burdensome, costly, and risky for some than for others. Moreover, on the Deweyan view, democracy is *undermined* or *dissolved* when social and material disadvantage serves to block the participation of certain sectors of the citizenry in processes of shared inquiry. Again, where such disadvantage prevails in a purportedly democratic society, we must not simply say that the democracy is erring or malfunctioning; on a broadly Deweyan view, we must say that democracy is *nonexistent* or at best *nominal*.

Allow me to press this point differently. Most pragmatist democratic theorists—Deweyan or otherwise—favor some version of epistemic participationism. And any epistemic participationist needs to distinguish between the policies experimentally enacted as responses to shared problems within a democracy and the commitments which are *constitutive* of a democratic society. That is, according to the epistemic participationist, certain commitments *must* be honored if a society is to count as democratic at all, whereas other policies and rules are democratic just in case they are the products of the collective inquiry of a given democratic community. To use a simplified example, we can say that although different democratic states may enact different laws regarding military conscription, no state can sustain its claim to be democratic while denying the equal citizenship of women. In denying women citizenship, a community *invalidates* its democratic credentials; by contrast, in adopting a policy of compulsory military service, a democratic community does something wise, foolish, or perhaps immoral, but provided that such a policy is enacted according to proper procedures, the community does not thereby render itself a sham democracy. Accordingly, some rules and policies are democratic due to their procedural pedigree, and others are democratic in virtue of their content alone. The latter are *constitutive* of a democratic community, and the former are not.

In neglecting to theorize justice, Dewey loses sight of this central distinction. Yet epistemic participationism depends on it: On Dewey's view, in order for a community's response to a shared political problem to count as *democratic* at all, the social processes which produced it must instantiate certain constitutive norms of collective intelligence: Participants in social inquiry must interact as equals; they must be regarded by one another as autonomous; they must honor practices of nondomination, inclusion, and open-mindedness; they must work together to keep open and fluid the channels by which new information, new experiences, and new voices can be heard; and so on. And it is the role of a theory of justice to examine how the material and social resources of society must be apportioned if democracy, here understood as shared social inquiry, is to commence.

We know, as Dewey knew, that institutionalized material and social disparities can erect practically insurmountable obstacles to democratic participation.[5] Under such conditions, the results of shared social inquiry cannot help but reflect the experiences and commitments of only a segment of the citizenry. And we also know, as Dewey knew, that the task of enacting democracy is not simply that of *removing* formal obstacles to participation; a democratic society must *sustain* the social and political

---

[5] See especially Anderson 2010 and Stanley 2015 for many discouraging details.

conditions requisite for collective inquiry, and this means that it must devise institutions, agencies, policies, and principles by which material and social resources are distributed across its citizenry. The question of how these tasks are to be accomplished is the question of justice.

Hence we see that the absence of theorizing about justice in Dewey's political thought is not simply a puzzle. It poses a *problem* for Deweyan democracy in that without such a conception, the actual mechanics of shared social inquiry are undermined. Hence it will not do to simply rehearse a favorite Deweyan saw that democratic ends require democratic means for their realization (LW 14:367); we are presently concerned not with ills of the kind that afflict democratic communities, but ills that *preclude* or *prohibit* a society from being democratic in the first place. Under conditions of injustice, some citizens are blocked from democratic participation, and thus proper social inquiry cannot commence; consequently, calling for collective social inquiry among the privileged is bound only to encourage, extend, and further entrench the existing unjust conditions.

Preliminary Steps Forward

Thus far, I have been focusing principally on the absence of a conception of justice in John Dewey's writings. Although Dewey's inattention to justice is surprising, I do not mean to criticize him for the oversight. There may be a plausible exculpating explanation of how a major twentieth-century political theorist with Dewey's record of political activism could overlook justice as a topic of philosophical import. However, that Dewey's oversight might be explained does not entail that his conception of democracy can get along without a theory of justice. The arguments presented above have suggested that Deweyan democracy, like any epistemic participationism, needs to implement a conception of justice in order to facilitate democratic processes of shared social inquiry. For Deweyan democracy, justice must be theorized or else the entire enterprise is rendered vacuous. This is why the absence of justice in the work of contemporary pragmatist political philosophers who follow Dewey broadly in advocating an epistemic participationist conception of democracy is far more troubling than Dewey's own neglect of the topic.[6]

---

[6] None of the following works on Deweyan political theory contains a substantial discussion of justice and most ignore justice entirely: Campbell 1992; Festenstein 1997; Eldridge 1998; Hoy 1998; Caspary 2000; MacGilvray 2004; Sullivan 2007; Pappas 2008; Green 2008; Rogers 2009; Koopman 2009; Bernstein 2010; Knight and Johnson 2011; Ansell 2011; McGowan

I won't dwell here on this troubling lacuna in contemporary pragmatist democratic theory. My aim in the current section is constructive. Thanks largely to the almost singular focus on justice among political philosophers since the 1970s, we now know quite a lot about the internal architecture of a theory of justice; and, consequently, the intellectual terrain has been well charted. The question is where pragmatist political philosophers should build camp. The following, then, can be only a sketch of the *kind* of view that pragmatist political philosophers should be working to develop. There's obviously a lot more work to be done.

Given that pragmatist political theorists follow Dewey in taking democracy as their master concept, it is natural for pragmatists to adopt a conception of justice that belongs to the broad family of views known as *democratic egalitarianism*.[7] Democratic egalitarian holds that the *point* or *aim* of justice is to establish and maintain conditions under which citizens are able to interact as democratic equals. The rationale is clear: If democracy is a kind of collective inquiry, then citizens must be enabled to participate in the processes of social intelligence *as equals*. This means not only that citizens must be able to give *equal input* into democratic decision-making processes; they must also be able to interact *as equals*. And this requires that citizens *recognize* one another as equal participants, stakeholders, and contributors to collective inquiry; they must regard each other as fellow sharers in political power and therefore not merely *entitled* to equal political say but *owed* a proper hearing. Unless such norms of social equality are firmly in place, democratic social inquiry cannot be enacted.

This allying of pragmatism with democratic egalitarianism goes a long way toward identifying the *kind* of conception of justice pragmatists should adopt. But it is only a start. Democratic egalitarianism is merely an answer to the question "What is the point of justice?"; it is not by itself

---

2012. A recent special issue of the journal *Contemporary Pragmatism* is devoted to revisiting Dewey's *The Public and Its Problems* (LW2), but none of the papers in that issue (Bohman 2010; MacGilvray 2010; Rogers 2010) mention justice at all. Savage (2002, 128–138) discusses Rawlsian justice, but his discussion is unsophisticated. Weber (2010) explores the comparative merits of Dewey and Rawls, but his focus is not on justice but rather on constructivism and related methodological issues. Westbrook (2005, 165) discusses Rawls favorably, but his aim in doing so is to criticize Rorty. Shapiro (2001) claims to propose a Deweyan democratic view of justice, but he is focused on the democratization of social institutions rather than distributive matters. I add that work in the non-Deweyan pragmatist idiom of democratic theory has also until recently neglected the topic; it is not a central theme in Misak (2000; 2004) or much of my earlier work (2007; 2011).

[7] Canonical articulations of democratic egalitarianism can be found in Anderson 1999 and Scheffler 2003. See also the articles collected in Fourie, Schuppert, and Wallimann-Helmer 2015.

a conception of justice.[8] In order to fill in the further details, pragmatists have to examine at least three other central questions:

1. *Currency*: What is it that must be equalized?
2. *Site*: What is the agent that performs this equalization?
3. *Scope*: Among whom is democratic equality owed?

The currency question has to do with different ways of understanding the *equalisandum* of democratic egalitarianism. Some hold that democratic equality requires equality of certain *resources*; others argue that equality of those resources is insufficient, holding instead that democratic equality calls for equality in *capability* of *functioning*. The former holds that justice calls for an equal distribution of resources such as rights, liberties, protections, and opportunities for wealth and income; the latter holds that justice calls for *equal ability to function* in ways that make for human flourishing (Nussbaum 2004). The "equality of what?" debate has been particularly active over the past several decades, and the disputes between resourcists and capability theorists have been fruitful. It strikes me though that many versions of the capability view tend to overreach; they make the theory of justice a component of an overall theory of the flourishing human life. For reasons I've provided elsewhere (2007; 2011), pragmatists must resist the Deweyan temptation to identify democratic participation with "the one, ultimate, ethical ideal of humanity" (EW 1:248), and much of the current work on capabilities does precisely this. However, the original critical maneuver capability theorists have advanced against resourcism looks decisive. To explain, in launching the capability view, Amartya Sen (1980) argued that the equal distribution of key resources is insufficient for justice because individuals vary greatly in their ability to *transfer* those resources into social and political benefits. It seems, then, that pragmatists should develop a conception of the central *democratic capabilities* and argue that justice requires these to be made equal.[9]

Given this, it looks as if pragmatist should adopt a *basic structuralist* answer to the question of justice's site. If the aim of justice is democratic equality, and if the currency is the political capabilities requisite for democratic engagement, then it seems natural to hold that the basic institutions

---

[8] Moreover, it is only *one* answer to the question of justice's point. Democratic egalitarianism has formidable opponents. See, for example, Tan 2008, 2012. A full pragmatist account of justice would have to defend democratic egalitarianism.

[9] I have attempted this in Talisse 2015, chap. 4, and I've offered a preliminary discussion of democratic capabilities in Talisse 2009, chap. 5.

of society—the central agencies of government, the courts, the system of public education, among others—are the agents tasked with implementing justice. Basic structuralist views of justice's site are to be contrasted with view according to which justice is the task of all social interactions.[10] But, again, that view looks overly demanding; it is true, of course, that democratic citizens owe one another a certain level of goodwill and regard in their day-to-day interactions. But the thought that there's an *injustice* in personal interactions, including those that have no explicit political dimension, where democratic capabilities are not fostered seems misplaced and insufficiently accommodating of the variety of personal associations and pursuits to which citizens may devote themselves.[11]

Thus far, I have suggested that pragmatist political theorists need to theorize justice and should endeavor to develop a conception of justice that embraces (1) a democratic egalitarian view of justice's point; (2) a democratic capabilities view of justice's currency; and (3) a basic structuralist conception of justice's site. There remains the crucial question of the *scope* of justice. And here is where serious difficulties emerge.

There are two leading views about the scope of justice: localism and globalism. The localist holds that justice is an intrinsically *local* phenomenon, and that justice obtains (or fails to obtain) *within* political communities bounded by states. The globalist contends that states are the products of morally arbitrary boundaries, and thus that justice is inherently *global*; on this view, justice obtains (or fails to obtain) in virtue of the moral condition of the world. Now, it seems as if pragmatists would be drawn to localism. After all, pragmatists frequently identify democracy with a kind of *community*, and, as was mentioned previously, Dewey himself held democratic community involves "face-to-face intercourse" (LW 2:367) and the "free gatherings of neighbors" (LW 14:227). However, given the pragmatist's conception of the *epistemic* dimension of democracy, localism is difficult to sustain. If the function of democracy is to gather socially distributed knowledge and apply the full resources of human experience to shared problems, then there is no reason to think that democratic inquiry should be *localized* to the citizenry of any given political state; and if this is the case, then there is no reason to see justice as a local phenomenon. To put the point in a different way, the dual components of epistemic participationism seem to pull apart; the participationism favors a localist conception of justice's scope, whereas the epistemic element must globalize.

---

[10] For this kind of view, see Cohen 2008.
[11] On this point, see Tan 2004.

I cannot here attempt to reconcile this tension within pragmatist democratic theory. My sense is that pragmatism must ultimately side with contemporary theorists of global and cosmopolitan *interactive democracy* (Gould 2014), and eventually abandon the latent communitarian sentimentality found throughout Dewey's work. To be sure, as with every suggestion I've offered in this section, there is a lot more to say. Indeed, I have here only laid out the broadest contours of a conception of justice, and, moreover, I have not ventured any arguments in support of this view. To repeat, my aim has only to have sketched a line of inquiry for further pursuit and development.

Concluding Diagnoses

In the preceding sections, I take myself to have established two central claims. First: Pragmatist political theorists have thus far neglected to theorize justice, but their conception of democracy *requires* such a theory. Second: Given what pragmatist tend to think about democracy, it is not difficult to discern the basic contours of the approach to justice they should develop; specifically, pragmatist should pursue a conception of justice that combines (1) democratic egalitarianism with (2) a democratic capabilities theory and (3) basic structuralism. I have deliberately left the question of justice's scope open, as it remains a pressing difficulty for any pragmatist view.

I want to draw this discussion to a close by *diagnosing* pragmatism's inattention to justice. For it strikes me that there are a number of interrelated traditionally pragmatist commitments that contribute to the tendency to overlook justice, and if the argument of the first section of this chapter is correct, these commitments must be revised.

The Way of Life Thesis

The clarion call of Deweyan democracy is that "democracy is a way of life"; this slogan is frequently accompanied by the claim that democracy is not merely a kind of state (LW 2:325), but a "mode of associated living" (MW 9:93) and "the idea of community life itself" (LW 2:328). To be sure, on any epistemic participationist view, democracy is *not merely* a kind of state. However, this insight has too often been understood to mean that pragmatist democratic theorists need not theorize the democratic state.

The vast contemporary literature on Deweyan democracy contains almost *no* sustained discussion of the state at all.[12] But, after all, democracy *is* a kind of state (among other things), and thus a complete theory of democracy must be in part a theory of the democratic state. As it seems that pragmatists should adopt a basic structuralist view of the site of justice, there is reason to think that the inattention to justice is the product of a broader inattention to the state as a subject of political theorizing. The "way of life" thesis should be retracted at least to the degree necessary to reverse the tendency to overlook the need to develop a pragmatist theory of the state.

Experience and Inquiry as Local Phenomena

A related tendency emerges from the Deweyan emphasis on *experience* as the locus of the problems that prompt inquiry. This emphasis encourages a kind of localism about political problems: The problems to which shared intelligence must be applied are the problems experienced by publics here and now. But the questions of justice are often questions about problems confronting those who currently do not have a sufficient voice and whose experiences are not visible to the broader democratic community, including the young, the disadvantaged, the disabled, the impoverished, the geographically distant, and members of future generations. By tying democratic collective intelligence too tightly to the shared experience of social problems, the pragmatist introduces a kind of bias that cannot adequately capture the significance of the experiences and interests of those who are unable to participate. In order to incorporate a conception of justice into its broader democratic vision, pragmatism must weaken the extent to which its conception of social inquiry relies upon input from those who are already present and able to participate.

Experimentalism and Institutions

The pragmatist vision of democracy is focused on emergent problems affecting a given population of individuals—in Dewey's terminology, a public. The idea is that of applying collective intelligence to common problems in an ongoing process of fine-tuning and experimental tweaking. This model of shared inquiry makes the best sense when thinking of a certain range of collective decisions regarding problems that are close

---

[12] Knight and Johnson 2011 is a notable exception.

at hand. But the experimentalist model does not look especially attractive when considering collective decisions regarding the design and functions of large-scale institutions that are tasked with distributing basic social and material goods. The reason is that institutions of this scale do not merely perform their assigned distributive functions, they also serve as the basis upon which individuals *make plans* and *set expectations* for the future. A society that is constantly reconstructing and experimentally altering its basic political institutions is a society that is fundamentally unstable. In this way, pragmatists have to develop a conception of large-scale social inquiry that can recognize and accommodate the fact that social experiments involving certain kind of institutions must be understood as *temporally extended* beyond a given generation of citizens. To be more specific, the political institutions tasked with establishing and maintaining the conditions required by justice cannot be subjected to continual experimental revision, for not only can even minor adjustments in such institutions wreak havoc in individual lives, but also the time-horizon for discovering how such institutions are performing extends far beyond the immediate.

To conclude: Pragmatists have thus far devoted considerable effort toward devising an attractive epistemic and participatory conception of democracy. But the democratic ideal as they understand it rings hollow unless it is supplemented by an accompanying vision of the fundamental social and material entitlements of democratic citizens. This latter task calls for theorizing justice. I have in the foregoing chapter laid out some principal steps toward filling in pragmatism's political philosophy.

Works Cited

Anderson, Elizabeth. 1999. "What Is the Point of Equality?" *Ethics* 109: 287–337.
———. 2006. "The Epistemology of Democracy." *Episteme* 3(1–2): 8–22.
———. 2010. *The Imperative of Integration*. Princeton, NJ: Princeton University Press.
Ansell, Christopher K. 2011. *Pragmatist Democracy*. New York: Oxford University Press.
Barber, Benjamin. 1984. *Strong Democracy*. Berkeley: University of California Press.
Bernstein, Richard. 2010. "Dewey's Vision of Radical Democracy." In *The Cambridge Companion to Dewey*, edited by Molly Cochran, 288–308. Cambridge: Cambridge University Press.
Bohman, James. 2010. "Participating through Publics: Did Dewey Answer Lippmann?" *Contemporary Pragmatism* 7(1): 49–68.
Campbell, James. 1992. *The Community Reconstructs: The Meaning of Pragmatist Social Thought*. Urbana: University of Illinois Press.
Caspary, William. 2000. *Dewey on Democracy*. Ithaca, NY: Cornell University Press.

Cohen, G. A. 2008. *Rescuing Justice and Equality*. Cambridge: Harvard University Press.

Dahl, Robert. 1956. *A Preface to Democratic Theory*. New Haven: Yale University Press.

Dewey, John. 1969–1991. *The Collected Works of John Dewey: The Early Works, The Middle Works, The Later Works*. 37 vols. Jo Ann Boydston, ed. Carbondale: Southern Illinois University Press.

Eldridge, Michael. 1998. *Transforming Experience: John Dewey's Cultural Instrumentalism*. Nashville, TN: Vanderbilt University Press.

Festenstein, Matthew. 1997. *Pragmatism and Political Theory*. Chicago: University of Chicago Press.

Fourie, Carina, Fabian Schuppert, and Ivo Wallimann-Helmer, eds. 2015. *Social Equality*. New York: Oxford University Press.

Gould, Carol C. 2014. *Interactive Democracy: The Social Roots of Global Justice*. Cambridge: Cambridge University Press.

Green, Judith. 2008. *Pragmatism and Social Hope*. New York: Columbia University Press.

Hoy, Terry. 1998. *The Political Philosophy of John Dewey*. London: Praeger.

Johnson, Mark. 2014. *Morality for Humans*. Chicago: University of Chicago Press.

Kitcher, Philip. 2012. *Preludes to Pragmatism*. New York: Oxford University Press.

Knight, Jack, and James Johnson. 2011. *The Priority of Democracy*. Princeton, NJ: Princeton University Press.

Koopman, Colin. 2009. *Pragmatism as Transition*. New York: Columbia University Press.

MacGilvray, Eric. 2004. *Reconstructing Public Reason*. Cambridge: Harvard University Press.

———. 2010. "Dewey's Public." *Contemporary Pragmatism* 7(1): 31–47.

McGowan, John. 2012. *Pragmatist Politics*. Minneapolis: University of Minnesota Press.

Misak, Cheryl. 2000. *Truth, Politics, Morality*. New York: Routledge.

———. 2004. *Truth and the End of Inquiry*. 2nd ed. New York: Oxford University Press.

Nussbaum, Martha. 2004. "Beyond the Social Contract: Capabilities and Global Justice." *Oxford Development Studies* 32(1): 3–18.

Pappas, Gregory, 2008. *John Dewey's Ethics*. Bloomington: Indiana University Press.

Rogers, Melvin. 2009. *The Undiscovered Dewey*. New York: Columbia University Press.

———. 2010. "Dewey and His Vision of Democracy." *Contemporary Pragmatism* 7(1): 69–91.

Savage, Daniel. 2002. *John Dewey's Liberalism*. Carbondale: Southern Illinois University Press.

Scheffler, Samuel. 2003. "What Is Egalitarianism?" *Philosophy and Public Affairs* 31: 5–39.

Sen, Amartya. 1980. "Equality of What?" In *The Tanner Lectures on Human Values*, vol. 1, edited by Sterling McMurrin, 197–220. Cambridge: Cambridge University Press.

Shapiro, Ian. 2001. *Democratic Justice*. New Haven: Yale University Press.

Stanley, Jason. 2015. *How Propaganda Works*. Princeton, NJ: Princeton University Press.

Sullivan, Michael. 2007. *Legal Pragmatism*. Bloomington: Indiana University Press.

Talisse, Robert B. 2007. *A Pragmatist Philosophy of Democracy*. New York: Routledge.

———. 2009. *Democracy and Moral Conflict*. Cambridge: Cambridge University Press.

———. 2011. "A Farewell to Deweyan Democracy." *Political Studies* 59(3): 509–526.

———. 2015. *Engaging Political Philosophy*. New York: Routledge.

Tan, Kok-Chor. 2004. "Justice and Personal Pursuits." *Journal of Philosophy* 101: 331–362.

———. 2008. "A Defense of Luck Egalitarianism." *Journal of Philosophy* 105: 665–690.

———. 2012. *Justice, Institutions, and Luck.* New York: Oxford University Press.

Weber, Eric Thomas. 2010. *Rawls, Dewey, and Constructivism: On the Epistemology of Justice.* London: Continuum.

Westbrook, Robert. 2005. *Democratic Hope.* Ithaca, NY: Cornell University Press.

CHAPTER 17 | # A Pragmatist Account of Legitimacy and Authority

Holmes, Ramsey, and the Moral Force of Law

CHERYL MISAK

Two Pragmatist Answers to Questions about Legitimacy

The question of legitimacy and authority is one in which the stakes are high.[1] Those subject to a law can ask, "Why is that law authoritative for me?" or "How does this law make a normative demand on me?" The answers go to the heart of a society's political and legal institutions, and to whether they are morally good and practically effective.

The pragmatist tradition has offered us two distinct kinds of answers to questions about the legitimacy and authority of the law, each starting from the fact that there are no certain, infallible foundations given to us by a Great Book or a Great Man or a Great Theory, and that those who seek such an absolute grounding are on a fruitless and dangerous mission. John Dewey captures this insight of pragmatism by calling the formalist or "intellectual" approach to law as hanging on "scraps of paper" and as "voices in the air" (LW 14:118).

We have to start from the ground up; two routes are available, and different pragmatists have gone in each direction. One route is *quietist*. It is most prominently manifested in the work of Richard Rorty, and can be traced back to Wittgenstein. On this version of pragmatism, the absence

[1] Earlier versions of this chapter were given in 2015 at the "Idealism and Pragmatism" conference at the Collège de France, the New England Pragmatism Forum at Green Mountain College, and at the American Political Science Association meetings. Thanks especially to Michael Bacon, Maeve Cook, Steven Fesmire, Bob Talisse, Philip Kitcher, and Danielle Petherbridge for their comments, and to David Dyzenhaus for his truly supererogatory help.

of infallible foundations leads to the idea that we cannot aim at getting things right, but only at agreement with our peers, or within a community or form of life. All we have are the facts on the ground, with no rules or norms or truths that go beyond a description of the facts. I have argued that this brand of pragmatism can only end in the "might is right" view, leaving us with nothing to say to those who disagree with us, and with nothing to say to ourselves as to why, for instance, taking the experience of others into account is better than what one of the promoters of the quietest view, the Nazi-sympathizer Carl Schmitt, advocated—aiming at "substantive homogeneity" in our community. [2] Rorty happened to be a liberal democrat, and he wanted to resist these implications.[3] Nonetheless, he admitted that on his view, one can in principle be a good pragmatist and also a good Nazi.[4] I shall in this chapter only be tangentially concerned with this kind of quietest pragmatism, for it is the other kind of pragmatism that seems to me to be so full of promise.

That other pragmatist answer to the question of legitimacy is *epistemic*. It stresses the value of taking the perspectives and experiences of others seriously, given that we want to reach the right, or warranted, decision. The version of this argument I myself have favored builds on the work of one of the founders of pragmatism, C. S. Peirce. His core idea is that a true belief is one that is indefeasible, or would stand up to all experience and argument. He had a broad account of experience that included experience had in diagrammatic mathematical contexts, and the felt experience of others in figuring out what is valuable. Hence, with respect to questions about what is good or just, if we want to get the right answers—the answers that would *really* be indefeasible—we must take into account as much experience as we can. The epistemic pragmatist answer, that is, takes us to an experience-driven method of decision-making, today sometimes called deliberative democracy, on which legitimacy and authority flow from the fact that we employ a method that takes the experience of all into account, and is thus more likely to give us warranted decisions.

But when it comes to the questions of legitimacy and authority of law, we must turn to Dewey and to Oliver Wendell Holmes for the best epistemic pragmatist argument. Dewey put the epistemic thought as follows. Democracy is the use of the experimental method to solve practical problems; it is an application of "cooperative intelligence" or inquiry

---

[2] See Misak 2000, 2010, and 2013.
[3] See, for instance, Rorty 2010.
[4] Rorty 1990, 636–637; 1999, 15; 2000, 130.

(LW 13:187); it is the space in which we can "convince and be convinced by reason" (MW 10:404). He argued that a broadly democratic method is a precondition of every domain of inquiry, from physics to politics. Inquiry requires the unimpeded flow of information and the freedom to offer and to criticize hypotheses.[5] More recent, if not always explicitly pragmatist, versions of this argument can be found in the work of Hilary Putnam, Bernard Williams,[6] John Rawls, and Ronald Dworkin. They each argue that the best that human beings could do in a reflective, experience-based process is what warrant or truth amounts to with respect to questions about the good, the just, and the right. But before Dewey, and before the contemporary pragmatists, there was Oliver Wendell Holmes, and it will be instructive to look to see how the pragmatist epistemic argument was first carved out.

Holmes: Experience and the Law

It is sometimes forgotten that two lawyers played critical roles in the Metaphysical Club of the 1860s, the reading group in which pragmatism was born. The most prominent of them was Oliver Wendell Holmes Jr. The other was Nicholas St. John Green, whom Peirce credited with urging upon the group Bain's definition of belief as that upon which we are prepared to act. St. John Green is not remembered for much else, but of course Holmes went on to be one of America's most famous Supreme Court judges and respected legal theorists. It is in his view that we can find the most explicit, and I think, one of the best, pragmatist accounts of authority. Anyone familiar with Peirce will hear echoes of Peirce in Holmes's talk of how experience drives inquiry and the settlement of belief. Holmes attended some of Peirce's lectures, on science and inquiry, at the Lowell Institute in 1866.[7] Although Holmes was wary of flying under the pragmatist banner, because of its associations with James's more extreme position, his legal theory was distinctly pragmatist.[8]

Holmes, like all pragmatists, starts from the bottom up. His theory of law is about the common law, which starts with cases "and only after a series of determinations on the same subject matter" does it come "by . . .

---

[5] EW 3:33; LW 11:375.

[6] Bernard Williams has argued that every legitimate state must satisfy "the Basic Legitimation Demand" if it is to show that it wields authority rather than sheer force.

[7] See Howe 1957, 25; and Wiener 1972, 75.

[8] See also Haack 2005 and Kellogg 2007.

induction to state the principle" (Holmes 1995, 213). Law is not something that is set out in advance, and it is not set out in stone or in statute. It is a growing, evolving, ongoing enterprise. It is an enterprise of inquiry, or "successive approximation," that starts from precedent, or our settled body of background belief, and then is driven by experience, conflict, and unanticipated problems. Holmes, that is, was set against taking precedents, legislation, or moral principles as immutable truths. He is the originator of the pragmatist conception of law and authority, on which the concept of law is not abstract, doctrinal, and formal—something set out definitively by the sovereign or by legislators in statute. Law and its legitimacy are not separate from inquiry, politics, and democracy.

In the first few lines of the 1882 book *The Common Law*, Holmes tells us what law is: "The life of the law has not been logic: it has been experience" or "the felt necessities of the time" (Holmes 1882, 1). The law does not consist of a fixed body of doctrines and syllogisms derived from them, but rather, it is an organic structure that has come together in response to experience. He says that all theories that consider the law "only from its formal side" are failures (Holmes 1882, 36–37). Whatever code or set of principles or statutes might be adopted, "[n]ew cases will arise which will elude the most carefully constructed formula" and will have to be reconciled (Holmes 1995, 213). "Truth," he says, is "often suggested by error" and that is why we need always to employ "reason and scrutiny" (Holmes 1882, 37). Law, for Holmes, grows in a fallible way, where doubt, conflict, and disputes about what the law is, are resolved under the force of experience.

This epistemic argument is just as forcefully expressed in his 1897 "The Path of Law":

> Take the fundamental question, What constitutes the law? You will find some text writers telling you that it is something different from what is decided by the courts of Massachusetts or England, that it is a system of reason, that it is a deduction from principles of ethics or admitted axioms or what not, which may or may not coincide with the decisions. . . . The prophecies of what the courts will do in fact, and nothing more pretentious, are what I mean by the law. (Holmes 1952, 172–173)

One (and only one) of the reasons the prophecies of the courts are so important is that people are enabled by them to predict and adjust their behavior accordingly. The Bad Man, for instance, is able to predict what the courts will decide, in order to adjust his behavior and avoid sanction. Holmes says: "a legal duty so called is nothing but a prediction that if a man does or omits certain things he will be made to suffer in this or that way by judgment of the court" (Holmes 1952, 169).

We can hear Bain's dispositional account of belief operating in the background here. Holmes thinks of law in terms of expectancies or predictions. We act on our best predictions of how rules will be interpreted and maintained by the courts. Those rules and interpretations evolve with new experience (which is itself interpretation), so predictions can never be locked in. In 1929, Holmes looked back half a century and remembers how one of the other founders of pragmatism in the Metaphysical Club emphasized the idea of predictions on which we can place bets:

> Chauncey Wright a nearly forgotten philosopher of real merit, taught me when young that I must not say *necessary* about the universe, that we don't know whether anything is necessary or not. So I describe myself as a *bettabilitarian*. I believe that we can *bet* on the behavior of the universe in its contact with us. (Howe 1941, 252)[9]

We must be careful, however, not to take Holmes as a reductionist about the law; we must not take him to hold that all the law amounts to is the behavior of judges and legislators. For Holmes thought that there are standards and grounds enmeshed in the law and at which we aim to get right. "[T]his is how we have always done it" is no reason for continuing to do things that way: "It is revolting to have no better reason for a rule of law than that so it was laid down in the time of Henry IV. It is still more revolting if the grounds on which it was laid down have vanished long since" (Holmes 1952, 187).

Expectations and Legal Inquiry

In the same year Holmes penned his recollection about Chauncey Wright, the young and brilliant Cambridge philosopher, economist, mathematician, and founder of decision theory Frank Ramsey was utilizing that Bainsian thought to great effect. He argued, in a set of papers and a book manuscript, all unfinished when he died in 1930 at the age of twenty-six, that a belief is a habit or disposition to behave, and is to be evaluated in terms of whether those habits are successful. A belief, that is, is a bet or a rule with which we meet the future, and we can evaluate our beliefs in terms of how they work out. He sees that this leads to the pragmatist

---

[9] Indeed, 'bettabilitarian' was a term Holmes used often, for instance, with the young Kingsley Martin and good friend of Frank Ramsey, in 1922. (Martin 1966, 138)

account of truth. This is from "Truth and Probability," perhaps his most famous paper in philosophy:

> We have ... to consider the human mind and what is the most we can ask of it. The human mind works essentially according to rules or habits. . . . We can therefore state the problem of the ideal as "What habits in a general sense would it be best for the human mind to have?" (Ramsey 1990, 90)

This is "a kind of pragmatism: we judge mental habits or beliefs by whether they work" (Ramsey 1990, 93).

This idea, shared by Peirce, Dewey, Holmes, and Ramsey, is a powerful one across the board, but it is especially powerful for questions of law and legitimacy. Legislators, courts, and judges are engaged in the business of inquiry—a fallible search for the best answer we can come to given the time in which we are living and the circumstances in which we find ourselves. Laws are good if they fit with the values of the community, as determined by judges who are looking to experience to decide cases in the *best way* possible. The law must continue to offer reasons, and not rest with "this is the way we have always done things."

The pragmatist needs to guard against two misunderstandings. First, no pragmatist takes legitimacy to be reducible to prediction. Ramsey calls that view an "insane" behaviorism. The law must not merely allow subjects to predict the consequences of their behavior. It must also speak to the subject in that it must offer the subject reasons. It does that by setting up its structures so that they are responsive to reasons. For instance, it requires judges and parliaments to be prepared to give reasons for their decisions. As Lon Fuller puts it, the claim to be presented to a court must be more than a "naked demand." It has to be presented as a "claim of right," that is, as "supported by a principle."

Second, Holmes is, and other pragmatists are, often taken to be skeptics about the law, holding that there is no sense to be made of judgments being better or worse, only a recording of what community ideals are in force here and now. All judges are doing is giving expression to their own views, or perhaps to a societal consensus. But this is a misreading of Holmes and the best of pragmatism—one that has him sliding into that quietist pragmatist camp. One can think (indeed, how could one *not* think?) that custom and motives are part of inquiry. On the pragmatist epistemology, we start from the body of background belief we have, and work from there. But that fact does not give license to judges to import their own values or their whims into their judgments. Nor does it mean that the values that inform law are whatever values happen to be in force in the community. The way that Holmes incorporates background belief and values into his conception of legal inquiry is subtle. He begins with a crucial passage from with Austin and the sovereign account of law:

> Austin said . . . that custom only became law by the tacit consent of the sovereign manifested by its adoption by the courts; and that before its adoption it was only a motive for decision, as a doctrine of political economy, or the political aspirations of the judge, or his gout, or the blandishments of the emperor's wife might have been. (Holmes 1995, 294)

Holmes points out that in many cases such motives do indeed have "as much compulsory power as law could have, in spite of prohibitory statutes." But that is a debasement of the legal process. A statute is the motive that, when offered to judges, "will prevail, and will induce them to decide a certain case in a certain way, and so shape our conduct on the anticipation" (Holmes 1995, 294). And the motives behind a statute are supposed to have a grip not just on the legislator or the judge, but on those who are subject to it.

That is, the pragmatist picture is as follows. We look to the law in part to enable us to predict how our behavior will be received and treated, and that law will embody all sorts of encrusted custom. But when conflicts arise, judges resolve them in an inquiry not unlike other kinds of inquiry. All inquiry is an experience-driven enterprise, with custom and background belief having some real force. But nonetheless, there are external standards. Motives and arguments are offered to judges, for their consideration. Law proceeds via "judgment as to the relative worth and importance of competing legislative grounds" (Holmes 1952, 181). Judges have to use their *judgment* to weigh the competing claims of custom, belief about what is right and wrong, statutes, etc.

While judges are part of an elite, they must take it upon themselves to connect the law to actual, lived experience, as presented by litigants and their lawyers in actual cases. Indeed, in our current age of statutes, one vitally important role for judges might be to make that connection to common experience. They also make statutes concrete by implementing them. One might say that we don't know what the statute requires until it has been interpreted.

"The law," Holmes says, is the "witness and the external deposit of our moral life. Its history is the history of the moral development of the race. The practice of it, in spite of popular jests, tends to make good citizens and good men" (Holmes 1952, 170). The history of law is a history, we hope, of *development*, on which we improve our views about what is good. It is not simply a record of what happened to be thought good at this or that time. Holmes, that is, offers us a progressive account of the law. Judges take the values they find in society and move them forward in light of experience.

Here it is important to take account of what Philip Kitcher calls the distinction between teleological progress, in which we are moving toward some ideal state, and pragmatic progress, in which we are moving from one state of belief to a better state. This particular distinction is Dewey's, but it resides, perhaps less explicitly, in every pragmatist. It is in the "pragmatic progress" sense in which Holmes's view is progressive. A good belief is formed on the basis of all relevant experience, and hence laws should be made in a deliberative process. That deliberative process requires that justificatory reasons have to be offered on a continual basis, when disputes and challenges arise: for instance, when people litigate and judges respond.

The quietist pragmatist camp will understandably press in here, and ask how we can make sense of external standards and improvement if one resists the temptation, as does Holmes, to appeal to God, to Reason, or to some internal logic. That is, does the pragmatist not have to say that we can make sense of only one kind of standard—what the community happens to believe? Are we not returned to the Schmittian, Rortian kind of pragmatism that I warned against at the outset?

Holmes, following Peirce, makes an attempt at articulating this problem and its solution by paying close attention to what makes a belief well settled. In Holmes's words, "a well-settled legal doctrine embodies the work of many minds, and has been tested in form as well as substance by trained critics whose practical interest it is to resist it at every step" (Holmes 1995, 213). A *settled* belief is the belief that fits with the spirit of the times, but a *well-settled* belief is one that will continue to stand up to experience and standards. Those standards will be employed by those many minds, sometimes by very many minds as when public pressure forces an issue (say to change the laws regarding same-sex marriage) and sometimes by trained critics (who will often aid the public groundswell).

Let's take a concrete example of how an external standard might be present in the law: We must consider what a reasonable or prudent person, taking into account the weight of experience, would think. Holmes tells us that when a workman on top of a house tosses a beam into a busy street, he should have foreseen that the beam might hit someone. The standard of a reasonable man applies to his behavior (Holmes 1882, 55–56). This is the kind of thing that looking to objective circumstances amounts to in the legal domain. This is not to say that the law or legitimacy is *constituted* by what the reasonable man would think and do. This standard is one of many evolving standards employed in legal inquiry. It is to say that the reasonable-person standard is part of the set of standards we think our laws and actions must meet. What legitimacy amounts to is that a judgment or the enactment of a statute was put in place by a method that is backed by reasons and experience, and will continue to be responsive to reason and experience. It thus has a call on those to whom it is subject.

In the same vein, we find Holmes gesturing at an aim of our legal inquiries. He says:

> The truth is, that the law is always approaching, and never reaching, consistency. It is forever adopting new principles from life at one end, and it always retains old ones from history at the other.... It will become entirely consistent only when it ceases to grow.... However much we may codify the law into a series of seemingly self-sufficient propositions, those propositions will be but a phase in a continuous growth. (Holmes 1882, 36–37)

The (unattainable) ideal of law would be achieved if we were to find ourselves in a culture of justification in which no disputes no longer arise. It is not that this is what we actually think we'll get. Rather, we aim at something more realistic. We aim at getting things right in law and in morality, and thus we keep striving for that continuous growth.

Dewey said that the law was "a program of action to be tested in action." I have argued that this follows from the pragmatist dispositional account of belief. These tests or evaluations will be complex matters, bringing into play all sorts of reasons, many of which anchor the traditional ethical theories about which states are intrinsically good. But there is no ultimate value, such as freedom or equality. These and other values will be in the mix in democratic decision-making. That kind of decision-making has a normative call on us, for epistemic reasons. We cannot see ourselves as aiming at the right answer unless we accept that the way to deal with the conflict of values is to take in as much argument and perspective as we can and let those conflicts play out in deliberative, democratic structures.

The two pragmatists who focused most on that dispositional nature of belief and its evaluation were Peirce and Ramsey. Here is the latter, echoing the former:

> Logic, Aesthetics, and Ethics have a peculiar position among the sciences: whereas all other sciences are concerned with the description and

explanation of what happens, these three normative studies aim not at description but at criticism. To account for our actual conduct is the duty of the psychologist; the logician, the critic, and the moralist tell us not how we do but how we ought to think, feel, and act. (Ramsey 1991, 3)

The law, too, is a normative science. It tells us what we ought to do—what we *must* do, if we are to avoid sanction. We assume (but we could be wrong in that assumption) that it, like any other science, improves and enriches our concepts. Susan Haack helpfully draws attention here to a thought of Peirce's that is also found in Holmes. Peirce argues that our concepts "grow.... Such words as *force, law, wealth, marriage*, bear for us very different meanings than those they bore to our barbarous ancestors" (CP 2:302). As Haack argues, concepts like *liberty, right*, etc., are also "deepened, thickened, made more specific (and sometimes stripped of old accretions) in the long, ongoing struggle of legal disputes and challenges, interpretations and reinterpretations" (Haack 2005, 90).

It might be thought that on the pragmatist view I have articulated here, one value is, protestations to the contrary, ultimate or foundational—the value of taking seriously the reasons of others, and that backstopping this value is the value of the equality of persons. That is in a sense right, but it is important to understand how thin this value is in the epistemic argument, and hence, how easy it ought to be to accept it. If we aim at getting the answer (or the set of acceptable answers) that best coheres with the experience and reasons of all, then we must take seriously the experience and reasons of all. That leads us directly to deliberative democratic structures of decision-making and to the normative force of those structures. So while in one sense, the pragmatist, naturalist position is monist (there is one value that is fundamental), in another sense it is pluralist (that fundamental value requires that the plurality of values is respected).

Conclusion

My suggestion in this chapter is that the epistemic pragmatist position offers us a compelling account of the legitimacy and authority of law, in which legitimacy and authority lie in the structure of political and legal institutions: in whether or not they are deliberative and democratic, in whether or not they are engaged in *a culture of justification*.[10] If our institutions

---

[10] See Mureinik 1994 and Dyzenhaus 1998 for the use of the concept "culture of justification."

are democratic and offer reasons for the law's being such as it is, reasons that in principle speak to the subject, then that law is legitimate and authoritative for the subject. The claim is not that the subject has to endorse the content of the law, but she has to understand how it makes a plausible claim to authority—she has to be able in principle to understand that reasons stand behind the law, and that those reasons speak to her, whether or not they actually convince her. The pragmatist thus offers a justification of political and legal authority that does not start from a moral theory (about equality, rights, utility, need, and so on), but rather, from thoughts about how reason-giving and the ongoing evaluation of belief are fundamental.

We have seen that the best of these epistemic arguments do not *reduce* all kinds of value to epistemic value. Indeed, part of the pragmatist argument is that there is not a hard and fast distinction between the epistemic and the moral, a distinction that would be required if one concept were to be reduced away into another. It is sometimes thought that questions of justice, legitimacy, and authority, on the one hand, and morality on the other, are fundamentally distinct in that justice is about not merely what is good for people to do, but what they can be made to do. The idea is that a legitimate decision might not be a morally right decision. But, again, the pragmatist sees an artificial barrier erected here. She thinks that a good decision is the product of a democratic and open process. Could such a process give us the morally wrong answer? Only on a view that pulled morality apart from good belief evaluation and good decision-making. The citizen can find herself in the position where she thinks: I object to a law because it goes against my moral code, but I should nonetheless regard it as binding on me or legitimate, because it was made by the best possible process, a process that it also moral. She may feel so strongly about the tension about her own moral code and the law that she decides to engage in civil disobedience. But that is part of the very process that confers legitimacy on our laws and on our democracies, and of course, if a citizen decides to break the law, she understands that she is opening herself up to sanctions.

It is also important to see that there might be all sorts of reasons for wanting to do the good or just thing, and what tend to get called the epistemic reasons will not always seem to us the important ones. When someone is kind to a stranger in need, when someone devotes her life to a cause, rarely does she describe her motivation as being one of aiming at truth or of seeking beliefs that are responsive the evidence. Indeed, on the pragmatist approach that I have traced and advocated, first-order reasons having to do with equality, rights, utility, fairness, or the kind of life one wants to lead, are precisely what the pragmatist says *ought* to drive our decisions. It is only when we ask the second-order questions about what makes those first-order decisions legitimate or authoritative that we get to the epistemic or pragmatist reasons.

When we get to that second-order argument, we get something really worth having: a *justification* of why we should take underrepresented views seriously; of why we should reduce inequalities and coercions that might rob people of their abilities to challenge laws;[11] and, as Dewey emphasized, why our structures of education should be such that peoples are given the wherewithal to participate in democracy and recognize their actual interests. For those are the ways to ensure that we are getting as much of the evidence and perspective we can, and of reducing the number of blind spots we have and mistakes we make. If our aim in belief and assertion is to get judgments that are responsive to all the relevant experiences, we need to include the experience of all, and include it in a robust way.

Everyone recognizes that a feature of authority is that the subject of authority does what he is told because the authority said so, not because he thought the content of the command to be good. As Hobbes explained, that is the difference between command and advice. Hence we get the distinction in political philosophy between authority in fact (de facto) and legitimate authority (de jure). The pragmatist account speaks to the latter—the conditions under which we should regard a de facto authority as legitimate. It explains the idea of authority—of when it is legitimate, and then, *why* it is legitimate. It tells us that there is a fund of inherited social value that is unavoidable, and is itself the product of experience. But what the values are, how they should evolve, or be revised or replaced, and even how to understand them, is open to experience. Hence, authoritative pronouncements are provisional punctuation points in a process of inquiry.

Works Cited

Dewey, John. 1969–1991. *The Collected Words of John Dewey*, edited by Jo Ann Boydston. 37 vols. Carbondale: Southern Illinois University Press. (See List of Abbreviations.)

Dyzenhaus, David. 1998. "Law as Justification: Etienne Mureinik's Conception of Legal Culture." *South African Journal on Human Rights* 14: 11–37.

Haack, Susan. 2005. "On Legal Pragmatism: Where Does 'The Path of the Law' Lead Us?" *American Journal of Jurisprudence* 50: 71–105.

---

[11] I thank Bob Talisse for this point.

Holmes, Oliver Wendell Jr. 1882. *The Common Law*. London: Macmillan.

———. 1952. *Collected Legal Papers*. New York: Harcourt, Brace.

———. 1995. *The Collected Works of Justice Holmes: Complete Public Writings and Selected Judicial Opinions of Oliver Wendell Holmes*. 3 vols. Ed. Sheldon M. Novick. Chicago: University of Chicago Press.

Howe, Mark De Wolfe, ed. 1941. *Holmes-Pollock Letters: The Correspondence of Mr. Justice Holmes and Sir Frederick Pollock, 1874–1932*. Vol. 2. Cambridge: Harvard University Press.

———. 1957. *Justice Oliver Wendell Holmes: The Shaping Years*. Cambridge: Harvard University Press.

Kellogg, Frederic R. 2007. *Oliver Wendell Holmes, Jr.: Legal Theory, and Judicial Restraint*. Cambridge: Cambridge University Press.

Martin, Kingsley. 1966. *Father Figures: A First Volume of Autobiography, 1897–1931*. London: Hutchinson.

Misak, Cheryl. 2000. *Truth, Politics, Morality: Pragmatism and Deliberation*. New York: Routledge.

———. 2010. "Richard Rorty's Place in the Pragmatist Pantheon." In *The Philosophy of Richard Rorty*, edited by Randall E. Auxier and Lewis Edwin Hahn, 27–43. Chicago: Open Court.

———. *The American Pragmatists*. 2013. Oxford: Oxford University Press.

Mureinik, Etienne. 1994. "A Bridge to Where? Introducing the Interim Bill of Rights." *South African Journal of Human Rights* 10: 31–48.

Ramsey, Frank. 1990. "Truth and Probability." In *F.P. Ramsey: Philosophical Papers*, edited by D. H. Mellor, 156–198. Cambridge: Cambridge University Press.

———. 1991. *On Truth*. Edited by Nicholas Rescher and Ulrich Majer. Dordrecht: Kluwer.

Peirce, Charles S. 1931–1958. *Collected Papers of Charles Sanders Peirce*, edited by Charles Hartshorne and Paul Weiss (vols. 1–6), Arthur Burks (vols. 7 and 8). Cambridge, MA: Belknap Press of Harvard University Press. (See List of Abbreviations.)

Rorty, Richard. 1990. "Truth and Freedom: A Reply to Thomas McCarthy." *Critical Inquiry* 16(3): 633–643.

———. 1999. *Philosophy and Social Hope*. New York: Penguin.

———. 2000. "The Overphilosophication of Politics." *Constellations* 7: 128–132.

———. 2010. "Reply to Misak." In *The Philosophy of Richard Rorty*, edited by Randall E. Auxier and Lewis Edwin Hahn, 44–45. Chicago: Open Court.

Wiener, Philip. 1972. *Evolution and the Founders of Pragmatism*. Philadelphia: University of Pennsylvania Press.

CHAPTER 18 | William James on Justice and
the Sacredness of Individuality

DAVID RONDEL

The practical consequence of such a philosophy is the well-known
democratic respect for the sacredness of individuality.

—WILLIAM JAMES, *Talks to Teachers on Psychology and to Students on Some*
of Life's Ideals

IT IS HARD TO imagine anyone more intensely committed than William
James to an "individualist" perspective. In all facets of his thought—
ethical, metaphysical, psychological, epistemological, or religious—James
sought to accentuate the point of view of the singular individual. James
clearly cared a great deal more for subjective inwardness than for scientific
facts, for "private and uncommunicable perceptions" (WWJ 12:4) than for
reasons that can be publicly shared and debated. There are moments at
which James even appears to let individuality dictate to ontology: sometimes insisting that what shows up for us in experience is equivalent to
what there really is, sometimes denying that there exists any "reality" at all
not bound up with the point of view of some discrete individual.

James's celebration of individuality is hardly news. That such an individualist perspective should have anything to contribute to our philosophical
thinking about justice, however, is more contentious. It is widely believed
that "individualism"—sometimes qualified with the adjective "rugged"—
is one of the most serious impediments to a just society. Individuality is
often thought to belong to the private, snobby, idiosyncratic part of our

nature, not the democratic, egalitarian, or participatory part. To the extent that individuality flourishes, the common thought goes, justice wanes. It is surely no *mere* accident that history has produced many "individualists"— think of Nietzsche, Heidegger, or some of the Romantic poets, say—who were, putting it mildly, unenthusiastic about the principles and initiatives many of us see as essential to a just society.

One way to locate the "individualist" wavelength of James's thinking about justice is to reflect on Colin Koopman's question, "Should politics be a matter of institutional crafting? Or should it be a matter of ethical practice, a way of life?" Clearly, this is a false dilemma. But Koopman is right to interpret James as "unequivocally in favor of the latter" (Koopman 2005, 180). Unlike John Rawls, and liberals more generally, who tend to construe justice in broadly institutional terms, as a virtue which applies primarily to what Rawls famously called the "basic structure of society," James focuses decidedly on the level of the discrete individual.[1] I argue in what follows that James provides a paradigmatic example of what George Kateb and others have called "democratic individuality" and that this goes hand in hand with a "personal" conception of justice (where "personal" most naturally contrasts with "institutional").

Democratic Individuality and the Internal Lives of Others

According to George Kateb, the "richest presentation of the doctrine of democratic individuality is found in the work of Emerson and his two great-est 'children,' Thoreau and Whitman, each also, like him, a genius" (Kateb 1992, 78). I want to suggest that yet another American genius—William James, who, as it happens, was also Emerson's godson—justifiably be-longs in this company.

On Kateb's view, "the theory of democratic individuality ... cultivates a sense of individual infinitude; that is, a sense of one's inner ocean, of everybody's inexhaustible internal turbulent richness and unused powers" (Kateb 1992, 34). Jack Turner elaborates on this Katebian theme as follows.

---

[1] Loren Goldman has helpfully described three closely related ways in which James has recently been read in political theory: "as a Liberal concerned with personal freedom, as a democrat concerned with equal participation and access to human flourishing, and as a 'radical pluralist' concerned with fomenting creative human self discovery." What is clear, Goldman rightly concludes, is that James's political concerns are best understood as "matters of ethical life rather than the institutions of government" (Goldman 2012, 38). See Rondel 2012 for reflections on some of the differences between institutions and individuals in respect to justice.

One of the virtues of the democratic individualist is his readiness to reverse perspectives with anyone. His absorption of democracy's ethos of equality leads him to believe that a fundamental similarity unites all human beings—making all *partly* comprehensible. But his awareness of his own inner mystery and depth prevents him from pretending to understand everyone. Just as he insists that others will never be able to fully comprehend him, he realizes that he will never be able to fully comprehend others. (Turner 2012, 8)

It is uncanny how accurately these words apply to William James. Attending to how things look differently when considered from diverse vantage points is a deep and abiding theme in his thought. "To the very last, there are various 'points of view' which the philosopher must distinguish in discussing the world; and what is inwardly clear from one point remains a bare externality and datum to the other" (WWJ 6:6). James is forever laboring to "get inside" other points of view, to understand how things look and seem "from there." He famously reverses perspectives with rugged North Carolina mountaineers after realizing that he had been "blind to the peculiar ideality of their conditions" (WWJ 12:134). He tries to assume the inner point of view of those who end their own lives, recognizing sympathetically that, "In the deepest heart of all of us there is a corner in which the ultimate mystery of things works sadly" (WWJ 6:34). James reflected on many kinds of lives, and virtually always from the first-person perspective of the people who lived them: "the sheltered, refined, and cultured life at Chautauqua; the exposed, daring lives of construction workers on high scaffolds; the dullness of the lives of day laborers that might be redeemed if chosen in the name of some ideal" (Putnam 1997, 286). He even attempts to press upon his readers the inward perspective of dogs, noting "how insensible, each of us, to all that makes life significant to the other!—we to the rapture of bones under hedges, or smells of trees and lamp-posts, they to the delights of literature and art."

As you sit reading the most moving romance you ever fell upon, what sort of a judge is your fox terrier of your behavior? With all his good will toward you, the nature of your conduct is absolutely excluded from his comprehension. To sit there like a senseless statue, when you might be taking him to walk.... What a queer disease is this that comes over you every day, of holding things and staring at them like that for hours together, paralyzed of motion and vacant of all conscious life? (WWJ 12:133)

While James enjoins us to reverse perspectives with as many people and things as possible, he is also adamant that "The inner significance of other lives exceeds all our power of sympathy and insight" (WWJ 11:101). No one's inner ocean is fully navigable. Every private life is partially impermeable. "In every being that is real there is something external to, and sacred from, the grasp of every other" (WWJ 6:111). Just as others will never fully appreciate our own inner depths, so too will we never understand completely in other people "the sort of unuttered inner atmosphere in which . . . consciousness dwells alone" (WWJ 12:119).

Individuality, Tolerance, and Justice

The fact that the inward lives of others are never completely graspable, coupled with the claim that "No one has insight into all the ideals" (WWJ 12:150), generates an imperative of tolerance. It

> absolutely forbids us to be forward in pronouncing on the meaninglessness of forms of existence other than our own; and it commands us to tolerate, respect, and indulge in those whom we see harmlessly interested and happy in their own ways, however unintelligible they may be to us. Hands off: neither the whole truth, nor the whole of good, is revealed to any single observer, although each observer gains a partial superiority of insight from the peculiar position in which he stands. (WWJ 12:149)

James's imperative of tolerance has usually been interpreted in negative terms, as a directive to more or less leave people alone. This interpretation is bolstered by James's oft-quoted words: "The first thing to learn in intercourse with others is non-interference with their own peculiar ways of being happy, provided those ways do not assume to interfere by violence with ours" (WWJ 12:150). While noninterference may be the first thing to learn, it is not the last or only thing. I want to argue that James's ideal of tolerance also implies a *positive* ethical obligation to grapple with the lives and ideals of others, a conclusion hinted at in the preface to *Talks to Teachers* where James vaguely asserts that "Our ancient national doctrine of live and let live may prove to have a far deeper meaning than our people now seem to imagine it to possess" (WWJ 12:5). This involves trying to see where others are coming from; doing our best to put ourselves in their shoes; absorbing the idea that there is something unique and irreplaceable in what it is like to be them; that they, like us, are trying to forge a life for themselves, and that those other lives, just like ours, are animated by a "higher vision of inner significance" (WWJ 12:138). James was well aware that such attempts are never perfect and always susceptible to moral "blindness." Still, that does not absolve us from doing our best.

My argument so far is that James's relentless focus on what Emerson called "the infinitude of the private man" (Emerson 1984, 236) and his imperative of active tolerance culminate in two importantly related questions, the committed consideration of which are at the heart of his "personal" conception of justice. The first question—viz., "What is it like on the inside for those who are not receiving the treatment to which they are justly entitled?"[2]—suggests an obligation to take the inner lives of others seriously, to let their voices be heard, to honor the sacredness of each person's individuality. The second question—viz., "What shall or must I do as someone committed to justice for all individuals?"—suggests an obligation to amend one's habits and behavior in light of insight gleaned from the first question. The first question is perceptual: it addresses the importance of perceiving sympathetically the lived experience of injustice. The second question is an ethical one: it addresses the importance of responding appropriately to injustice by interrogating our own habits, biases, and blindnesses.

But what are the bases for these vague obligations?[3] What has James to say to the person who would rather not accept this onerous ethical assignment? As I read him, James provides two closely related kinds of arguments. One of them is epistemic. The other is metaphysical, and is connected to what I will call James's "cosmic" egalitarianism.

---

[2] Though clearly more interested in social structures than James, W. E. B. Du Bois's work provides an instructive example here. In *The Souls of Black Folk* (1903) Du Bois assigns a certain priority to the inward experience of racism and white supremacy. While they are never *merely* idiosyncratic, Du Bois's analyses in *Souls* depart from the perspective of discrete, subjective lives: precisely the kind of private, inward experience that a word like "souls" is meant to conjure. It is easy to imagine James having been moved, and agreeing enthusiastically, when Du Bois writes that "the longing of black men must have respect: the rich and bitter depth of their experience, the unknown treasures of their inner life, the strange rendings of nature they have seen, may give the world new points of view and make their loving, living, and doing precious to all human hearts" (Du Bois 1994, 66). It is impossible to deny that Du Bois sounds an awful lot like James here.

[3] Let me be clear that in talking about the "obligations" generated by James's idea of tolerance, I am not claiming that James is making a move in what Bernard Williams famously called the "morality system." James would have certainly agreed with Williams that "It is a mistake . . . to try to make everything into obligations (Williams 1985, 180). Ethical life is infinitely richer and more varied than a set of obligations can track. I am using "obligation," then, in the everyday, nonphilosophical sense of that term: the sense in which everyone has obligations not to dump toxic waste in the town lake, to be decent to other people, to provide financially for their children, and so on.

The epistemic argument goes like this. If "There is no point of view absolutely public and universal," and if, as James also insists, "The facts and worths of life need many cognizers to take them in" (WWJ 12:4), it follows that an obligation is generated on epistemic grounds to weigh all ideals and consider all points of view. Simply put, there is "an exuberant mass of goods" and no one has total insight into all of them (WWJ 6:155). "There is no complete generalization, no total point of view, no all-pervasive unity" (WWJ 5:190). Each inner world contains some portion of the truth. "Each, from his peculiar angle of observation," James wrote in *Varieties* (1902), "takes in a certain sphere of fact" (WWJ 15:384). Wrestling with the inward lives of others yields ethical knowledge: reversing perspectives with other people can enlarge and improve ethically our own inner lives, familiarizing us with ideals and inner significances to which we had been "blind" or unaware. This epistemic argument is brought out most clearly in "What Makes a Life Significant."

> Every Jack sees in his own particular Jill charms and perfections to the enchantment of which we stolid onlookers are stone-cold. And which has the superior view of absolute truth, he or we? Which has the more vital insight into the nature of Jill's existence, as a fact? Is he in excess ... ? Or are we in defect, being victims of a pathological anesthesia as regards Jill's magical importance? Surely the latter; surely to Jack are the profounder truths revealed.... *We ought, all of us, to realize each other in this intense, pathetic, and important way....* If you say that ... we cannot be in love with everyone at once, I merely point out to you that, as a matter of fact, certain persons do exist with an enormous capacity for friendship and for taking delight in other people's lives; *and that such persons know more of truth than if their hearts were not so big.* (WWJ 12:150–151; emphasis added)

Jack possesses more knowledge because he "realizes Jill concretely, and we do not." He "struggles toward a union with her inner life, divining her feelings, anticipating her desires, understanding her limits" (WWJ 12:151). In short, insofar as one wants to know more of life's "facts and worths" rather than fewer, one has an obligation to actively entertain as many concrete points of view as possible. For James, this project is interminable: our store of ethical knowledge may grow larger, but so long as new persons and ideals are still to come it will remain incomplete. Until "the last man has had his experience and said his say" (WWJ 6:141), we must keep an open mind and defer final pronouncements.

But even if it culminated in no additional knowledge, an imperative of active tolerance would still be suggested by what I call James's "cosmic" egalitarianism. It is hard to give this a precise formulation but it is bound up with the idea that we are all fundamentally equal *as individuals*, in being possessors of a unique inward view, and we are to be treated as equals—by other people and by political institutions—in light of this fact. It is a deep truth about the world, James thought, that each inner ocean has the same incommensurable value.[4]

A few important theses follow from James's cosmic egalitarianism. First, it endows each individual with an equal power and right to instantiate value. Values are engendered by our practices of valuing (Jackman 2005, 124). Something is valuable if someone values it. "A thing is important if any one *think* it important" (WWJ 9:1267). Because each individual is equal at the cosmic level, and because each individual has the equal power to instantiate value, it also follows that each demand or preference an individual expresses is equally valid, and thus presents an equally strong prima facie claim to be satisfied. "Any desire," James wrote, "*makes* itself valid by the fact that it exists at all" (WWJ 6:149). "Any demand, however slight, which any creature . . . may make . . . ought . . . for its own sole sake, to be satisfied" (WWJ 6:149). Obviously the satisfaction of some desires can be overridden by other considerations, but the mere fact that a desire or preference exists, James seems to have thought, gives us some reason to value its satisfaction. For James, it is just better that preferences be satisfied than frustrated. A universe containing more satisfied preferences is ceteris paribus better than one containing fewer. This helps explain why the guiding principle for an ethical philosophy on James's view is "simply to satisfy at all times as many demands as we can" (WWJ 6:155).

James's "personal" conception of justice is not a theory per se, but something more like an ethos. It is never easy to characterize an ethos but where a theory tends to be definitive and explicit—it "makes it all *Yes* and *No*" (WWJ 1:284)—an ethos is more vague and indeterminate. Since it captures a sensibility, an orientation, a loose cluster of commitments

---

[4] It is possible to believe, with James, that everyone's life matters equally while also affirming, with David Hume, that "The life of a man is of no greater importance to the universe than that of an oyster" (Hume 1998, 319). Everyone's life mattering equally is perfectly compatible with everyone's life mattering very little, or not mattering at all. This is not the view that James takes: he thinks that everyone's individuality matters equally, and that it matters quite a bit. Bernard Williams responds intelligently to this Humean thought when he writes, "No one should make any claims about the importance of human beings to the universe: the point is about the importance of human beings to human beings." After all, "To see the world from a human point of view is not an absurd thing for human beings to do" (Williams 1985, 118).

and inclinations, an ethos usually resists exact formulation. Large swaths of what we care about are not amenable to normative neatness. Many of the valuable things at which we take aim—"wisdom" or "enlightenment," say—are simply not explicable in precise ways. Some ideals can be rendered precise, others cannot. As Appiah points out, *"Thou shalt not kill* is a test you take pass-fail. *Honor thy father and thy mother* admits of gradations" (Appiah 2005, 235). No one denies that being a good father or a good citizen is a valuable achievement, but it would be surprising to find out that the predicate "good" in these examples might be expounded with necessary and sufficient conditions. We may hanker for something more determinate, but James would have almost certainly insisted that a certain vagueness and indeterminacy here is our fate.

James is not giving an argument about when and under what kinds of circumstances it is appropriate to feel bad about the lives people live.[5] Nor would he have denied that even comparatively bad or difficult lives almost certainly have within them a modicum of pleasure and value. Human lives are not disqualified as worthy objects of concern in virtue of their not being *wholly* bad. As if our concern for poor and downtrodden people might be allayed by the knowledge that, difficult though their lives are, these people still lead lives of substance, direction, and some enjoyment. Nor does his argument have any bearing on what many see as the inherent toughness of human beings: the fact that we are magnificently resilient creatures who can learn to cope with all sorts of suffering and disappointment. James's view would not be impinged on if it turned out that human beings were in fact much wimpier than they are. The argument is simply that (*a*) we are cosmically equal as individuals, (*b*) it is important that individual lives be successful rather than unsuccessful, significant rather than insignificant, (*c*) this importance attaches equally to each individual life, and subsequently, (*d*) any consideration with the capacity to bear positively or negatively on human beings having successful and significant lives can, under the appropriate conditions, become germane to a personal ethic of justice.

There are several problems with James's "personal" egalitarianism that are worth briefly reviewing. For one thing, unlike Dewey or Mead, James often overlooked the fact that individuality is formed. He routinely neglected the social, familial, and economic conditions against whose background individuality is shaped in the first place. "Surely," he wrote, "the

---

[5] See G. A. Cohen's "Two Weeks in India" (29–30) in Cohen 2013 for moving ruminations on this question.

individual, the person in the singular number, is the more fundamental phenomenon, and the social institution of whatever grade, is but secondary and ministerial" (WWJ 17:97). James sometimes wrote, moreover, as if all social problems would magically disappear if only we would put ourselves charitably in the shoes of others, to see things from the point of view of *their* inner experience. "If the poor and the rich could look at each other in this way," he mused, "how gentle would grow their disputes? What tolerance and good humor, what willingness to live and let live, would come into the world!" (WWJ 12:167). Someone would be forgiven for thinking that there is a simplistic naiveté in these musings.

It is true that James made occasional remarks about the importance of a more equitable distribution of resources, and the need to create more just institutions, but they were nearly always qualified by the assurance that these sorts of changes would not really—at bottom—make "any genuine vital difference ... to the lives of our descendants" (WWJ 12:166). They might even do harm. As Max Otto perceptively comments, on James's view, "Social institutions endangered the purity of individuality. Even organizations formed to combat economic injustice and to win for deprived men and women a better chance at the basic requisites of a satisfying life were likely ... to be a greater evil than the evil they were intended to remedy" (Otto 1943, 189). This is not to say that James was indifferent to human suffering. He often seemed abnormally sensitive to it. It is rather that "The solid meaning of life is always the same thing—the marriage ... of some unhabitual ideal ... with some fidelity, courage, and endurance," and no "outward changes of condition in life" can add to or subtract from this formula (WWJ 12:166–167). In short, James insisted on a bifurcation of the individual from its social and economic reality. One need only recall James's frequent lionizing of the individual who stoically cultivates a rich inner life while enduring difficult external circumstances to see how radical and rigid this bifurcation could be.[6]

Part of James's clumsiness about institutions and social structures can be explained by his aversion to what he called "bigness." As he wrote in a letter to Sarah Whitman in 1899:

I am against bigness and greatness in all their forms, and with the invisible molecular moral forces that work from individual to individual, stealing

---

[6] Jacques Barzun takes a different view. He thinks, "now that unionization and the welfare state have vastly reduced poverty, the evidence is again on James's side that physical well-being is not equatable with contentment. The source of the 'vital difference' between happy and unhappy

in through the crannies of the world like so many soft rootlets, or like the capillary oozing of water, and yet rending the hardest monuments of man's pride, if you give them time. The bigger the unit you deal with, the hollower, the more brutal, the more mendacious is the life displayed. So I am against all big organizations as such, national ones first and foremost; against all big successes and big results; and in favor of the eternal forces of truth which always work in the individual and immediately unsuccessful way, under-dogs always, till history comes, after they are long dead, and puts them on top. (CWJ 8:546)

Bigness (whether in absolutist philosophical systems or in militaristic foreign policy) is tantamount to arrogance and close-mindedness. Opposing bigness stands for tolerance and open-mindedness. It means sticking up for the "underdogs"—the innocent civilians of the Philippines, for example, or the dabblers in occult and "spooky" ideas. Richard Gale is astute to point out that James "opposed imperialism in every form, be it in its political form, in which one part of our world imposes its will and culture over another, or its metaphysical form, in which the perspective of one world is taken to be dominant over the other world perspectives" (Gale 1999, 197). Individualism and "smaller systems" are on the other side of imperialism and bigness. Yet one would be excused for thinking that there are ways to appreciate the crucial importance of institutions and social structures on the development of individuality without succumbing to "imperialism." There is also plenty of space within which to have opposed US military intervention in the Philippines, for instance, without thereby giving undue credence to strange and silly theses. James tied these types of considerations together it seems in a way that was neither necessary nor particularly plausible. In short, James was guilty of overlooking the importance of institutions and social structures, and it is perfectly legitimate to criticize him on those grounds. Yet such criticism should only go so far. For James's neglect of the importance of institutions and structures seems less troublesome when we realize that the "personal" register of his thinking about justice complements—and does not compete with—more institutionally and culturally focused approaches. We can accept that there is a portion of

---

lives lies elsewhere" (Barzun 1983, 174n). I think Barzun's point misses its mark. For the claim was never that economic and physical well-being should be "equated" with happiness. The criticism against James is rather that these types of considerations are connected (not necessarily, but often and deeply enough), and that, if anything, the rise of the welfare state has corroborated this connection.

truth about justice in James's "individualist" outlook without thinking that it represents the whole truth.

On Strenuous Ideals and Habits of Justice

Morality on James's view is not solely a matter of acting correctly. A large part of it has to do with mood, disposition, and motivation. Moral mood can be easygoing or it can be strenuous. "When in the easy-going mood," James writes, "the shrinking from present ill is our ruling consideration." The strenuous mood is more rare. It requires that we consider not just "present ill" but also the desires and ideals we (and others) may have in the future. It "makes us quite indifferent to present ill if only the greater ideal be attained" (WWJ 6:159–160). As Richard Gale helpfully elaborates, James was interested in the "existential, as opposed to the cognitive, dimension of the ethical life."

> It is one thing to believe or accept an ethical proposition or rule and quite another to get oneself to follow or live up to this proposition or rule. One can know the rules of the ethical language-game but not actively participate in it. In the easygoing mood we do not sufficiently exert ourselves in following the casuistic rule, often because we fail to adopt the required disinterested perspective. A person lazily follows the course of least resistance because she considers only her present desires and not the ones that she and others will have in the future. (Gale 1999, 40)

It is not that the strenuous person has moral beliefs or feelings that the easygoing person lacks. Rather, she is "ready, willing, and able to make the requisite sacrifices to satisfy this more inclusive set of demands" and the easygoing person is not (Gale 1999, 41).

Strenuous morality is thus indissolubly connected to action. It requires not only that an individual hold certain views or have certain feelings but also that she be willing to act upon them when occasion arises. "No matter how full a reservoir of *maxims* one may possess, and no matter how good one's *sentiments* may be, if one has not taken advantage of every concrete opportunity to act, one's character may remain entirely unaffected for the better. With mere good intentions, hell is proverbially paved" (WWJ 12:50). Failing to act on one's principles and feelings results in what James called "the sentimentalist fallacy." The fallacy occurs when one "sheds tears" over abstract ideals of justice and generosity but cannot recognize these qualities when they are encountered in the street (WWJ 1:110). James, like Thoreau, is regularly impatient with people who profess certain ideals but refrain from concretely enacting them.[7]

> Mere ideals are the cheapest things in life.... The more ideals a man has, the more contemptible, on the whole, do you continue to deem him, if the matter ends there for him, and if none of the laboring man's virtues are called into action on his part—no courage shown, no privations undergone, no dirt or scars contracted in the attempt to get them realized. (WWJ 12:163–164)

And similarly,

> There is no more contemptible type of human character than that of the nerveless sentimentalist and dreamer, who spends his life in a weltering sea of sensibility and emotion, but who never does a concrete manly deed. Rousseau, inflaming all the mothers of France, by his eloquence, to follow Nature and nurse their babies themselves, while he sends his own children to the foundling hospital, is the classical example of what I mean.... The habit of excessive novel reading and theatre-going will produce true monsters in this line. The weeping of a Russian lady over the fictitious personages in the play, while her coachman is freezing to death on his seat outside, is the sort of thing that everywhere happens on a less glaring scale.... The remedy would be, never to suffer one's self to have an emotion at a concert, without expressing it afterward in *some* active way. Let the expression be the least thing in the world—speaking genially to one's aunt, or giving up one's seat in a horse-car, if nothing more heroic offers—but let it not fail to take place. (WWJ 8:129–130)

To sum up, while James always accentuated the importance of enlarging "sympathetic insight into fellow-lives" (WWJ 12:161) and while he

---

[7] Consider the indignation expressed in this famous passage from Thoreau's "Civil Disobedience" (1849): "There are thousands who are *in opinion* opposed to slavery and to the war, who yet in effect do nothing to put an end to them; who, esteeming themselves children of Washington and Franklin, sit down with their hands in their pockets, and say they know not what to do, and do nothing. ... They hesitate, and they regret, and sometimes they petition; but they do nothing in earnest and with effect. They will wait, well disposed, for others to remedy the evil.... At most, they give only a cheap vote, and a feeble countenance and Godspeed, to the right, as it goes by them. There are nine hundred and ninety-nine patrons of virtue to one virtuous man" (Thoreau 1977, 115).

routinely stressed the need to overcome moral blindness, it was crucial for him that these private realizations be accompanied by concrete action.

James was the first to admit that all of this is more easily said than done. Becoming morally strenuous requires "sweat and effort," and even then there are no guarantees (WWJ 12:153). Yet he was also troubled by the fact that so many of us seem unwilling even to accept the challenge: people from all walks of life are resigned, underenergized, prone to cynicism and habitually falling short of their best. "The human individual . . . possesses powers of various sorts which he habitually fails to use. He energizes below his maximum, and he behaves below his optimum" (WWJ 11:144). "Compared with what we ought to be," James wrote in 1906, "we are only half-awake. Our fires are damped, our drafts are checked" (WWJ 11:131). Yet he would have also insisted that this is not our destiny. We have the ability as agents to push back against our habitual underachievement, to unleash new energies, and to live better, more "heroic" lives.

Some may find the frequent venerating imagery of "heroism" off-putting, but James was adamant that such possibilities are equally available to all. James Albrecht is correct to argue that "James, in Emersonian fashion, democratizes . . . individuality, insisting that we all can, and should, strive to cultivate the habits of moral and even 'heroic' selfhood" (Albrecht 2012, 144). In short, it is at the heart of James's democratic individualism that becoming a better, bolder, morally strenuous individual is a prospect open to everyone.

My argument has been that James's thought illuminates the "personal" side of a commitment to justice. While he was sometimes amiss about the importance of institutions and social structures, James was constantly challenging his readers to live better lives, to be ever more responsive to others, to recognize the sacredness of all individuality, and to act "strenuously" as their justice-relevant principles and commitments require.

But what can and should individuals committed to justice do? It is impossible to give a neat answer to this question in the abstract, but several things stand out as obvious and uncontroversial. We can become increasingly alert to the ways in which certain individuals or groups are not receiving the treatment to which they are justly entitled. This involves a willingness to listen to others, to learn more about their predicament—in Adorno's memorable phrase, to "let suffering speak." We can, where appropriate, "call out" language, practices, and social behavior that are hurtful or which perpetuate harmful stereotypes. We can found or join movements for justice by marching, mobilizing, petitioning, assembling, lobbying, demonstrating, agitating, organizing—or, more minimally, lending active support to those who do. We can scrutinize ourselves in a spirit of open-minded fallibilism for unseen biases and "blindnesses," and try not to be overly defensive when challenged about behaviors or habits. We can give generously of our time, money, and energy. All of this (and more) is easily within our abilities. One need not endorse a view like Shelly Kagan's (1989), according to which morality obliges us to make the world as good as possible, in order to agree with James that we can do more than we currently do, and be better than we currently are.

Works Cited

Albrecht, James M. 2012. *Reconstructing Individualism: A Pragmatic Tradition from Emerson to Ellison.* New York: Fordham University Press.

Appiah, Anthony Kwame. 2005. *The Ethics of Identity.* Princeton, NJ: Princeton University Press.

Barzun, Jacques. 1983. *A Stroll with William James.* Chicago: University of Chicago Press.

Cohen, G. A. 2013. *Finding Oneself in the Other.* Edited by Michael Otsuka. Princeton, NJ: Princeton University Press.

Du Bois, W. E. B. 1994. *The Souls of Black Folk.* New York: Dover.

Emerson, Ralph Waldo. 1984. *Emerson in His Journals.* Edited by Joel Porte. Cambridge: Harvard University Press.

Gale, Richard. 1999. *The Divided Self of William James.* Cambridge: Cambridge University Press.

Goldman, Loren. 2012. "Another Side of William James: On Radical Approaches to a 'Liberal' Philosopher." *William James Studies* 8: 34–64.

Hume, David. 1998. *Selected Essays.* Edited by Stephen Copley and Andrew Edgar. Oxford: Oxford University Press.

Jackman, Henry. 2005. "Jamesian Pluralism and Moral Conflict." *Transactions of the Charles S. Peirce Society* 41: 123–128.

James, William. 1975–1988. *The Works of William James,* edited by Frederick H. Burkhardt, Fredson Bowers, and Ignas K. Skrupskelis. 19 vols. Cambridge: Harvard University Press. (See List of Abbreviations.)

———. 1992–2004. *The Correspondence of William James.* Edited by Ignas K. Skrupskelis and Elizabeth M. Berkeley with the assistance of Bernice Grohskopf and Wilma Bradbeer. 12 vols. Charlottesville: University Press of Virginia.

Kagan, Shelly. 1989. *The Limits of Morality.* New York: Oxford University Press.

Kateb, George. 1992. *The Inner Ocean: Individualism and Democratic Culture.* Ithaca, NY: Cornell University Press.

Koopman, Colin. 2005. "William James's Politics of Personal Freedom." *Journal of Speculative Philosophy* 19: 175–186.

Otto, Max. 1943. "On a Certain Blindness in William James." *Ethics* 53: 184–191.

Putnam, Ruth Anna. 1997. "Some of Life's Ideals." In *The Cambridge Companion to William James*, edited by Ruth Anna Putnam, 282–299. Cambridge: Cambridge University Press.

Rondel, David. 2012. "G.A. Cohen and the Logic of Egalitarian Congruence." *Socialist Studies* 8: 82–100.

Thoreau, Henry David. 1977. *The Portable Thoreau*. Edited by Carl Bode. New York: Penguin.

Turner, Jack. 2012. *Awakening to Race: Individualism and Social Consciousness in America*. Chicago: University of Chicago Press.

Williams, Bernard. 1985. *Ethics and the Limits of Philosophy*. Cambridge: Harvard University Press.

INDEX

abstraction, 52, 89–90, 276

Addams, Jane, 3, 9–10, 66–67, 71–78, 86, 95

aesthetics, 13; black, 227–29; Deweyan, 219–27, 261; phenomenological, 14, 219–23, pragmatist, 222; racialized, 233; resistance and, 215–29. *See also* art; philosophy

affirmative action, 123, 235, 265, 275. *See also* civil rights

African American men, 240. *See also* African Americans

African American women, 154–57, 203, 232–33. *See also* African Americans; Combahee River Collective

African Americans, 3, 14, 165, 231–45. *See also* African American men; racism

Albrecht, James, 321

Alcoff, Linda Martín, 11, 131–32, 142

analytic fallacy, 92–96

Anderson, Benedict, 225

Anderson, Elizabeth, 10, 65, 73, 76, 81–97; *The Imperative of Integration* of, 81, 86, 91

animal rights, 22

anthropology, 252

antiblackness, 237–38. *See also* injustice; oppression; racism

antirealism, 11, 131–32. *See also* philosophy; realism

anxiety disorder, 238. *See also* microaggressions

Anzaldúa, Gloria, 87, 155

Appiah, Anthony Kwame, 316

a priori theorizing, 4. *See also* philosophy

argument, 242

Aristotle, 23, 250–51, 266, 268

art, 229, 282. *See also* aesthetics; literature

authority, 15, 255–56, 281, 295–306; law and, 298, 304–5. *See also* government; legitimacy; power

autonomy, 281

Baier, Annette, 9, 23; *Moral Prejudices* of, 24

Bambara, Toni Cade, 154

behaviorism, 300

being, 238, 255. *See also* metaphysics; reality

belief, 5, 7, 16, 32–33; complex of, 31; definition of, 297, 299; dispositional nature of, 303; religious, 259; settled, 302; state of, 302; true, 296; web of, 120. *See also* epistemology; fallibilism

Bell, Derrick, 14, 232, 235–38, 241–44

Bentham, Jeremy, 5
Bentley, A. F., 276
Berlin, Isaiah, 167–68, 173; "Two
    Concepts of Liberty" of, 167
Bernstein, Richard, 106
bigness, 317–18
Black Lives Matter movement, 229.
    See also protest; racial justice
Bloom, Allan, 254; *The Closing of the
    American Mind* of, 254
Bourdieu, Pierre, 218, 227
Bourne, Randolph, 182
Bridgman, Percy Williams, 276
Brown, Michael, 232. *See also* police;
    violence
Brown v. Board of Education, 241.
    See also US Supreme Court

Camus, Albert, 235, 242; *The Plague* of,
    242. *See also* existentialism
capability theory, 288. *See also*
    democracy; equality
capital, 22. *See also* capitalism
capitalism, 91, 169, 171, 271; distribution
    in, 272; global, 234; multinational,
    65. *See also* capital; economics
Carter, Jacoby, 201–10, 190n6, 194n13
Christianity, prophetic, 235. *See also*
    religion
citizens, 39, 51, 68, 283, 285–87; of the
    world, 22. *See also* democracy
civil disobedience, 305. *See also* law;
    morality
civil rights, 174, 231, 235–36, 244–45.
    See also protest; racial justice; social
    justice; social movements
Cohen, G. A., 316n5
Collins, Patricia Hill, 12
Combahee River Collective, 154. *See
    also* African American women
common sense, 255. *See also* science
community, 9, 12, 30–32, 34, 86, 151–53,
    225, 252, 277, 281, 300, 283n4;
    black, 240–41, 244; democratic, 72,
    285–86, 289, 291; ethical, 249–51;
    hope for, 233; inquiring, 14; larger,
    22; local, 89, 283; moral, 30, 34, 69,

74; political, 37. *See also* politics;
    social support; society
comparativists, 5–6. *See also* pragmatism
Congdon, Matthew, 133
consequentialism, 257. *See also* moral
    philosophy
constructivism, 29–30, 287n6
contract theory, 267. *See also* justice
Coon, Deborah, 181
coping, 240–41. *See also* community;
    social support
Cormier, Harvey, 134–35
Crenshaw, Kimberlé, 156
Crutcher, Terence, 232. *See also* police;
    violence
culture, 2, 29, 48, 229, 277, 281. *See
    also* media; society

Danto, Arthur, 223–24
Davidson, Donald, 32n9
Davis, Angela, 12–13, 154, 163–76;
    Women, Race, and Class of, 174
deliberative process, 302. *See also*
    experience; law
democracy, 2, 14–15, 71–72, 152–53,
    163–65, 169, 273, 292, 298, 306,
    311; American, 166, 199, 202;
    bourgeois, 263; classical defenders
    of, 256; cosmopolitan, 43; deep,
    235; Deweyan, 249–63, 277, 281–91;
    epistemic dimension of, 289;
    interactive, 290; justification of,
    249, 251–52; as master concept, 287;
    pragmatist views of, 296–97, 282n2;
    sham, 285; value of, 256; Western
    industrial, 253. *See also* democratic
    egalitarianism; liberalism; politics
democratic egalitarianism, 287, 287n7,
    288n8. *See also* democracy
Democritus, 267
Dennett, Daniel, 25
depression, 238. *See also*
    microaggressions
Descartes, René, 33
desegregation of US schools, 235,
    241. See also *Brown v. Board of
    Education*; civil rights

desire, 32–33, 315. *See also* values

despair, 245. *See also* emotion; hope; optimism

Dewey, John, 1–15, 81–98, 116, 122–27, 163–76, 219–26, 249–66, 295–97, 300, 306, 316; absence of theory of justice in, 281–86; *Art as Experience* of, 14; "Creative Democracy—The Task Before Us" of, 165–66; *Ethics* of, 102, 106, 108, 165–67, 269, 271; *Experience and Nature* of, 82, 103; criticism of ideals of, 100–5; Great Community of, 109, 175, 278; James and, 180–83, 257–61; *Logic* of, 83, 102, 104, 108, 110; political ideals of, 105–10; *The Public and Its Problems* of, 98, 105, 109, 283, 287n6; *The Quest for Certainty* of, 100; *Reconstruction in Philosophy* of, 275; social justification of, 251; *Syllabus* of, 268–69. *See also* democracy; education; pragmatism; social philosophy; Tufts, James

Dieleman, Susan, 11

discourse, 9, 37, 74; abnormal, 57, 59–60, 62; democratic, 71; justice, 38, 44, 60, 62; normal, 58–60, 62, 65; revolutionary, 65. *See also* discourse ethics

discourse ethics, 26, 61. *See also* discourse; Habermas, Jürgen

discrimination, 28, 236, 240, 244. *See also* racial inequality; racial injustice

distribution, 288. *See also* equality; justice

domination, 13, 120. *See also* inequality; oppression

Du Bois, W. E. B., 12–13, 163–76, 228, 313n2; practices of contestation in, 183–94; radicalism of, 168–72; *The Souls of Black Folk* of, 184

Durkheim, Émile, 256

Dworkin, Ronald, 297

economic recession of 2008, 236. *See also* economics

economics, 48, 86, 252, 266. *See also* capitalism; global economy; social science

education, 263, 273, 277; equal, 274; philosophy of, 164, 281; public, 289; sentimental, 73; structures of, 306

egalitarianism, 153, 313, 315. *See also* equality

Elshtain, Jean Bethke, 72

Emerson, Ralph Waldo, 220, 310, 312. *See also* transcendentalists

emotion, 152, 233–34; harmful, 232. *See also* hope

Enlightenment, 27, 34, 74, 120

epistemic injustice, 11, 14, 129–42, 201, 207–12, 215–29, 75n14. *See also* epistemic justice; epistemology of ignorance

epistemic justice, 141, 223. *See also* epistemic injustice; justice

epistemic participationism, 15–16, 284–85, 289–90. *See also* democracy; epistemology

epistemology, 14, 74; the industry of, 282; pragmatist, 300; social, 11. *See also* belief; epistemology of ignorance; fallibilism; knowledge; philosophy

epistemology of ignorance, 130–36, 201, 217. *See also* epistemic injustice; epistemology

equality, 235, 283, 315; democratic, 288, 311; social, 287; strategies of, 241. *See also* egalitarianism; inequality; justice

ethics, 3, 270, 313–15; individual, 14; objective justification for, 250. *See also* justice; morality; virtue

eudaimonia, 267. *See also* happiness

existentialism, 242, 261. *See also* philosophy

experience, 5, 13, 66, 83, 86, 153, 291, 296–99, 301–2, 309; aesthetic, 220, 223; democratic, 73–74; historical, 7; human, 255, 284, 296; humane, 166; reason and, 303–4; social, 67, 73–74. *See also* inquiry; pragmatism

experimentalism, 256, 275–76, 292; methodological, 4, 7, 15. *See also* democracy

experimentation, 256–57. *See also* experimentalism; inquiry

individuality, 257, 281, 316; democratic, 16, 310–12; James on the sacredness of, 309–22. *See also* individualism; self

inequality, 12, 173, 245, 273; class, 47; social, 147–61; status, 48. *See also* equality; wealth

information, 256, 283. *See also* knowledge; science

injustice, 2–13, 39, 43–48, 57, 60–61, 65–69, 72, 81–89, 233, 267, 286, 289; contestation of, 179–94; epistemic, 137–40, 75n14; experience of, 16, 84, 110, 313; methodological priority of, 10; political, 49; problems of, 10, 81–96; racial, 91, 197–212; redress of, 67; resistance to, 14; responsiveness to, 10, 78; social, 50. *See also* justice; oppression; racial injustice; racism; subjugation

inquiry, 10, 14, 82, 85–92, 115, 255, 275–76, 297–300; collective, 284–87, 289; cooperative, 94; deliberative, 10; experimental, 254; legal, 301, 303; methods of, 183, 277; pattern of, 116; science and, 85, 297; social, 285–86, 291–92. *See also* knowledge; philosophy; pragmatism

institutions, 4, 27, 318; democratic, 22, 57; just, 317; political and legal, 304. *See also* social structures; society

insurrection, 13, 179–80; epistemic, 197–212. *See also* revolution

intelligence, 14, 124, 166, 179, 277–78, 283–84; authority of, 256; collective, 281, 285. *See also* democracy; knowledge; science

intersectionality, 12, 154–61. *See also* pragmatism

James, V. Denise, 12–13, 88

James, William, 3, 8, 11, 13, 16, 120–22, 181–83, 189, 221, 226, 258–61, 297, 309–22; Dewey and, 257–61; *The Meaning of Truth* of, 120; "The Moral Philosopher and the Moral Life" of, 181; *The Varieties of Religious Experience* of, 314; "What Makes a Life Significant" of, 314. *See also* pragmatism

Jim Crow, 232, 235–36, 244. *See also* oppression; racial injustice

Jordan, June, 147, 154–55

judges, 125–28, 299–302; Supreme Court, 297. *See also* law; legal philosophy

justice, 2, 4–8, 11, 15–16, 305, 321; abnormal, 37–62, 66–70, 72, 75; comparative accounts of, 4–5; concept of, 4, 6, 15, 124–28, 176, 266–71, 290; democratic, 68; distributive, 46, 271–75; freedom and, 164, 171; habits of, 172–76, 319–22; James on, 309–22; as a larger loyalty, 21–35; liberal concept of, 65, 267, 270; market theory of, 269–70; movements for, 321; normal, 39, 58–62, 66; obligations of, 9; perfect, 5–6, 10; Platonic-Aristotelian concept of, 267; pragmatist theories of, 1–2; principles of, 8, 6n4; problem of, 265–78; radical, 12; reflexive, 58–62, 67–70, 77; scope of, 289; social, 10, 68; structuralist views of, 288–89; struggle for, 5, 7; theory of, 1–3, 6–8, 15, 45–46, 281–92; transcendental accounts of, 4–5. *See also* civil rights; epistemic justice; freedom; ideal theory; injustice; racial justice; social justice

Kagan, Shelly, 322

Kant, Immanuel, 1, 4, 9, 23–26, 29–30, 32–33, 75, 106, 120, 250, 267, 270

Kateb, George, 310

Kelley, Robin D. G., 173–74

Kierkegaard, SØren, 257

Kitcher, Philip, 302

knowledge, 77, 255, 272, 283, 315; contingent, 120; ethical, 314; general, 84; intersectional, 158–59; social,

knowledge (*Cont.*)
275–78; sympathetic, 72–78; theory
of, 282. *See also* epistemology;
science; social knowledge
Koopman, Colin, 13, 310
Kuhn, Thomas, 9, 38, 65, 69

law, 15, 25, 242, 267, 270, 295, 304; civil
rights, 235; experience and the,
297–300; history of, 302–3; moral,
26; as a normative science, 304. *See
also* US Supreme Court
legal philosophy, 125–26, 270, 297.
See also philosophy; social
philosophy
legitimacy, 15–16, 295–97, 300, 302, 304.
See also authority; law
Lewis, C. I., 6–7
liberalism, 120, 168, 262, 265, 283.
See also democracy; justice
liberty, 23, 167. *See also* freedom
Ligon, Glenn, 229
literature, 229. *See also* art
Livingston, Alexander, 181
Locke, Alain, 228
Locke, John, 1, 4, 267
logic, 126, 298, 302;
experimental, 126–28
logical positivism, 255, 259. *See also*
philosophy
Lorde, Audre, 154
love, 15, 270–71; justice and, 269
loyalty, 8–9; conflicts in, 21; justice as
a larger, 21–35; parochial, 25; to a
species, 22

MacGilvray, Eric, 3
MacIntyre, Alasdair, 23, 253, 259
MacKinnon, Catharine, 136
Manicas, Peter T., 15
Marable, Manning, 168
Marglin, Frederique, 252
Marglin, Stephen, 252
Martin, Trayvon, 229, 236. *See also*
Zimmerman, George
Marxism, 163–65, 168, 171, 276. *See also*
Marx, Karl; revolution; socialism;
Trotsky, Leon

Marx, Karl, 5, 163, 175, 263. *See also*
Marxism
Mayfield, Julian, 227
McBride, Lee, 202
McBride, Renisha, 236
McDermott, John J., 278
McDowell, John, 133–34
McKenna, Erin, 171
Mead, George Herbert, 87, 316
media, 229. *See also* images
Medina, José, 10, 13–14, 65, 74, 97,
215–19, 223–27
metademocracy, 54–58
Metaphysical Club, 297, 299. *See also*
pragmatism
metaphysics, 249; analytic, 254;
Deweyan, 254–56, 261. *See also*
being; ontology; reality
microaggressions, 238–40, 244;
violent effects of, 238.
See also anxiety disorder;
discrimination; stress
Mill, John Stuart, 5, 268n3
Mills, Charles, 11, 65–66, 73, 130, 134,
172–73, 201
Misak, Cheryl, 15–16, 107
monism, 49, 57; normative, 76;
ontological, 46–47
moral dilemma, 23–26, 258, 258n6. *See
also* morality; moral philosophy
morality, 24, 31, 267; law and, 301–3,
305; strenuous, 319–21. *See also*
ethics; law; moral philosophy
moral obligation, 23–24, 26, 34. *See
also* trust
moral philosophy, 4, 23, 31, 250–51, 257,
268, 270. *See also* ethics; morality;
philosophy
Moreno, Jonathan D., 164
Morrison, Toni, 199, 229
multiculturalism, 47. *See also* pluralism
Murray, Albert, 228

Native Americans, 165–66, 200
National Association for the
Advancement of Colored People
(NAACP), 2, 169
Nietzsche, Friedrich, 261, 310

nihilism, black, 232–33; threat of, 234.
    See also hope
noble savage, 251–54. *See also*
    golden age
nonideal theory, 9–11, 65–78, 81–102,
    107–11. *See also* ideal theory; justice
normativity, 76; abnormal, 76
Nozick, Robert, 1, 265, 271–72, 272n5

ontology, 309. *See also* metaphysics
open-mindedness, 318. *See also* tolerance
oppression, 11–13, 87, 120, 123, 138,
    171–73, 184–85, 242, 253; complex
    experiences of, 88; institutionalized,
    254; racial, 201–7; victims of, 254;
    white, 243. *See also* imperialism;
    injustice; Jim Crow; racial injustice;
    suffering
optimism, 234–35. *See also* hope
Otto, Max, 317

pain, 24, 240. *See also* health
Pappas, Gregory, 10–11, 97, 109–10
paternalism, 252–53
Peirce, Charles Sanders, 15, 121, 254,
    296–97, 300, 302–4. *See also*
    pragmatism
phenomenology, 14, 88, 215, 219–29. *See*
    also philosophy
philosophers, 15, 89–90; empirical, 84.
    See also philosophy
philosophy, 2, 74, 250–52, 257–58;
    analytical, 255; method in, 275–78;
    traditional, 282. *See also* ethics;
    moral philosophy; philosophers;
    pragmatism; social philosophy
Piper, Adrian, 229
Plato, 25, 30, 266, 268; *Republic* of, 267
pluralism, 4, 7, 87, 95. *See also* injustice;
    justice; multiculturalism
political activism, 286. *See also* social
    activism
political economy, 47, 271. *See also*
    political philosophy; politics
political philosophy, 7, 15, 61, 81, 88,
    90, 167, 179, 251, 281–82, 292,
    306; contemporary pragmatist,
    286–87; history of, 4. *See also* moral

philosophy; philosophy; political
    economy; politics
political struggle, 232, 235–37, 242.
    See also protest
politics, 12, 48, 120, 147–61, 228,
    256, 310; black feminist,
    154–55; cultural, 3, 10, 74–75;
    democratic, 77, 152; identity,
    154, 156; transnational, 40. *See*
    also political economy; political
    philosophy; power
Popper, Karl, 253
power, 12, 147–61, 256. *See also*
    authority; politics; privilege
pragmatism, 1–16, 66–67, 82–89,
    93–96, 115–28, 179–83, 258,
    290, 297, 2n1; American, 149–53;
    classical, 14, 66; contemporary, 14;
    contestation in, 188–93; epistemic,
    296–97, 304; insurrectionist, 197–
    212; intersectionality and, 157–61;
    neutrality of, 3–4, 3n2; quietist,
    295–96, 300, 302. *See also* inquiry;
    philosophy
prison abolition, 175
private life, 310–13. *See also* James,
    William; public-private distinction
privilege, 256, 270. *See also*
    authority; power
problems, 5–7, 15, 298; political, 285.
    See also pragmatism
progressivism, 164, 235, 276, 302. *See*
    also reformism; social progress
Protagoras, 267
protest, 3, 41, 189, 229. *See also* civil
    rights; racial justice; social
    justice
psychology, 86–87, 251, 254, 268. *See*
    also social science
public, 283, 291; Deweyan, 284. *See*
    also public opinion; public-private
    distinction
public opinion, 23, 38. *See also*
    public
public-private distinction, 38, 117–18.
    See also private life; public
Putnam, Hilary, 14, 260, 297
Putnam, Ruth Anna, 11, 258n6

race, 228; theory of, 228. *See also* racial injustice; racial justice
racial battle fatigue, 238–39
racial equality, 237, 241, 243–44. *See also* racial justice
racial inequality, 231–37, 245. *See also* discrimination; racial injustice; racism; violence
racial injustice, 14, 237, 244. *See also* injustice; oppression; race; racial justice; racism
racial justice, 14, 231–45. *See also* justice; social justice
racial realism, 232, 241–42. *See also* realism
racism, 14, 93, 169, 173, 239; antiblack, 231–32, 240–42, 231n1; mundane, 238; permanence of, 232, 235, 243; white, 233, 235–40, 243. *See also* race; racial inequality; racial injustice
radicalism, 12–13, 120, 163–76, 181, 60n18; black, 173, 176. *See also* social justice
Radin, Margaret Jane, 120, 123
Ramsey, Frank, 299–300, 303; "Truth and Probability" of, 300
rationalism, 5, 74. *See also* philosophy
rationality, 26, 29–34, 77, 152; Kantian, 33; means-end, 30. *See also* justice; reason
Rawls, John, 1, 4, 25–34, 97, 117, 267, 273, 297, 310, 27n4, 252n3, 272n5; "The Law of Peoples" of, 27, 34; *A Theory of Justice* of, 27, 251–52, 265
realism, 11, 129–37, 142; metaphysical, 255. *See also* antirealism; philosophy
reality, 165, 255, 309; social and economic, 317. *See also* metaphysics; ontology
reason, 23–25, 31; authority of, 30; practical, 30; transcultural, 29. *See also* justice
reconciliation, 245. *See also* racial injustice; racial justice

reformism, 175, 276. *See also* progressivism
relativism, 252. *See also* philosophy
religion, 235, 259, 259n8, 259n10. *See also* Christianity, prophetic
resilience, 244, 316. *See also* resistance
resistance, 14, 136–42, 203–12, 235, 242–44; aesthetics of, 215–29. *See also* resilience
resourcism, 288. *See also* democracy; equality
revolution, 164–65, 172–76, 263. *See also* insurrection; Marxism
rhetoric, 34, 271; rationalistic, 35
Rice, Tamir, 232. *See also* police; violence
Rogers, Melvin, 186
Rondel, David, 16
Roof, Dylan, 232. *See also* violence; white supremacy
Rorty, Richard, 3, 7–8, 10–11, 62–78, 98, 129, 136, 141–42, 221, 226–27, 295–96, 38n2, 60n18
Rousseau, Jean-Jacques, 4
Russell, Bertrand, 221
Rustin, Bayard, 228

Sacco and Vanzetti trial, 266, 283n4
Sartre, Jean-Paul, 257, 259–60; *Existentialism and Humanism* of, 257. *See also* existentialism
Scanlon, Thomas, 31
Schmitt, Carl, 296
science, 9, 38, 94, 122–23, 255–56, 259; democracy and, 282; history of, 259; philosophy of, 259. *See also* criticism; information; knowledge; scientific method
scientific method, 254, 258, 262. *See also* science
Scott, Keith, 232. *See also* police; violence
Scottsboro case, 170. *See also* Du Bois, W. E. B.
Scott, Walter, 232. *See also* police; violence
segregation, 91, 233; legal, 232, 238

CPSIA information can be obtained
at www.ICGtesting.com
Printed in the USA
BVOW03s2051241117
501060BV00003B/10/P